5/1/12

Donald –

Thanks for supporting The
Naked Truth –

[signature]

The Naked Truth
INVESTING IN THE STOCK PLAY OF A LIFETIME

MARK FAULK

2008

Subsidiary of The Owners Group Inc.

www.toginet.com

www.thenakedtruthbook.com

PUBLISHED BY

TogiEntertainment, Inc.   TogiEntertainment, Inc.
56 Expressway Place   602 South Broadway Avenue
5601 NW 72nd   Tyler, TX 75701
Street Suite 342   903-595-4249
Oklahoma City, OK 73132
405-728-5536

Subsidiary of
The Owners Group, Inc.
Tyler, TX

First released by TogiEntertainment, Inc.   9/15/08

ISBN: 978-0-9800085-2-4 (hc)

Printed in the United States of America

This book is printed on acid-free paper.

Although we have made every attempt to locate and credit the correct photographer of every photo
in this book, any errors should be brought to the attention of the publisher, TogiEntertainment,
and corrections will be made in subsequent printings.

All stories from shareholders are in their own words, and, although the author has made every
effort to verify the accuracy of all included stories, we rely on shareholders to honestly recount their
experiences with CMKX.

For updates and additional information about the continuing saga of CMKM Diamonds, Inc.
and our financial markets, go to www.thenakedtruthbook.com

Nevada

NUMBER

47130

CMKM DIAMONDS, INC.

COMMON STOCK • PAR VALUE: $.0001

SHARES

122,000,000

CUSIP NO. 125809 10 3

This Certifies That

JOS CARMANS

Is The Record Holder Of

*** One Hundred Twenty-Two Million ***

Shares of CMKM DIAMONDS, INC. Common Stock.

transferable on the books of the Corporation in person or by duly authorized attorney upon surrender of this Certificate properly endorsed. This Certificate is not valid until countersigned by the Transfer Agent and registered by the Registrar.

Witness the facsimile seal of the Corporation and the facsimile signatures of its duly authorized officers.

Dated: January 12, 2006

Urban Casavant, PRESIDENT

Corey Klassen, SECRETARY

Seal

Countersigned: I' Global Stock Transfer, LLC • (702) 656-4919

By

This reproduced signature is specifically and only for this distribution of CMKM

CARM 27946

CMK 47130

Acknowledgements

Where to begin? First and foremost, I want to thank my family for everything they've given me over the years: hope, love, and a reason to carry on (even when I don't always deserve it). My children Rachel, Justin, Kelsey, and my daughter-in-law Samantha, who mean more to me then anything; Sheralyn, who will always be the love of my life; My father, who inspired me, and my mother, who gave me faith in myself; My stepfather Tommy and stepmother Paula, my brothers and sisters, cousins, nieces and nephews, aunts and uncles, and my extended family that numbers in the hundreds...to all of the Faulks, the Shades, and the Braucht family. I love each and every one of you.

To my yet-to-be-born first grandchild: I wish you the best that life can possibly offer.

A special thanks to my new family at the Owners Group, Inc., TogiEntertainment, and Toginet: John and Jill Martin, Bill Frizzell, Johnny, Ashley, Keri, and Sammy Martin, George Stephenson, Erik Anderson, Goldie Norris, Tom Stephenson, Melody Potter, my super secretary Toni Craig, Leor Zolman, and Anna Anderson.

To my staff of editors: Melody Potter, Toni Craig, Leor Zolman, Rachel Faulk, J. Betty Constantine, and Katie Lauren (who polished this parcel of rough until it shined). This was truly a collaborative effort. Thank you, I would have been lost without you.

To those who have contributed to *The Faulking Truth*, both as writers and supporters. This would not exist without you: Brian Arney, Robin Buckallew, Kenneth Shade, Mike Bohling, Russell Tharp, Cecilia, Darren, Lyza, Leigh, Jen, Anna, CL, Liz, Tiffanie; to Justin Faulk for making it all work using only cyber-baling wire and bits of string, and to Michael Rivero at *Whatreallyhappened.com* for supporting us through the years. To all of my friends, past, present and future; those still with us and those who have passed.

To the advocates, activists and journalists who have expended countless hours in their efforts to bring honesty and integrity back into our financial markets (and to those behind the scenes...you know who you are): Dave Patch, Patrick Byrne, Bud Burrell, Liz Moyer, Bob O'Brien, Darren Saunders, and Rod Young. To Gayle Essary at *financialwire.net*...you will not be forgotten. America will someday recognize the collective efforts of these patriots and see them as true heroes.

And to those who contributed their valuable time and effort into making this project possible:

To the many CMKX shareholders who contributed their efforts, research, and stories to this book. It wouldn't have been possible without you, and there are too many to even name here. A special thanks to BrainDamage, Phxgold, Pedro, Ric, Diamondlil, Sneakerbabe, granny2shoes, Timontoo, chrisl and all of the moderators and contributors of the various CMKX message boards. (I know I'm missing many of you here, but hopefully, you'll see your contributions in the pages of this book). Thanks to Hugo Cancio at Fuego Entertainment, Barry Shipes, Jason Webb and Anthony Pullicino for the photos. Thank you to my friend and colleague Pastor DeWayne Reeves. Thanks to Howie Romans III for his efforts both as an advocate and soldier. Thanks to everyone who graciously agreed to be interviewed for this book.

Thanks to John Martin, the incomparable Bill Frizzell, and Kevin and Angela West for their friendship and relentless efforts on behalf of the shareholders of CMKM Diamonds, Inc.

Thanks to Sabra M. Bellovin, M.D. and Katie Lauren for their contributions in naming this book.

And finally, thanks to God for each and every day that passes. Even with the inevitable trials and tribulations, life is precious. See you on the other side…don't be late.

TABLE OF CONTENTS

PART FIVE

APPENDICES

INDEX

Prologue: The Circle of Greed

On March 19, 2004, I launched a website called *The Faulking Truth*, with modest goals and few expectations. One of the first pieces I wrote was an article about stock counterfeiting, commonly referred to as naked short selling, entitled "Financial Terrorism in America." The response to the article was immediate and overwhelming. After the article worked its way across the self-perpetuating network known as cyberspace, I realized I could help educate the public about what appeared to be a major stock market scandal. I was convinced there were unscrupulous forces at work, targeting mostly small, struggling public companies. The majority of the crooks seemed to be small time con artists taking advantage of a stock market system seemingly engineered to facilitate corruption.

In the course of researching and writing well over a hundred articles on the subject, I interviewed countless high level public officials, experts on stock market fraud, and victimized companies and their shareholders. I meticulously turned over each stone.....only to expose another quarry of deceit, greed, and corruption, filled with hundreds of more stones. I gradually came to the conclusion I was wrong in my assessment of the scope of the stock counterfeiting scandal.

At first, the leads seemed disjointed and unrelated. The stories seemed to be rocks unto themselves, a series of small islands scattered across the world of investing like random dots on a piece of notebook paper. Then, a few details of the scandal began to come together, and a few players, who initially appeared disorganized and scattered across the globe, began to overlap.

I'm not certain there was an exact moment "The Big Picture" emerged, but there were several epiphanies along the way. The first articles led me to the hedge funds, "The Canadian Connection," the offshore lending institutions, the bashers, and the key to the entire scheme, a little-known practice called naked short selling.

Canadian brokers in collusion with hedge funds and offshore lenders were defrauding small companies and their investors. The con artists bet against the company and its shareholders by short selling millions, and in extreme cases, even billions of shares, taking advantage of a trading system that allowed them to sell shares that they didn't own. They simply negated the laws of supply and demand by creating so much negative pressure that the stock eventually collapsed under the weight of the massive selling. The lending practice became known as death spiral financing because often the companies were forced into bankruptcy. But it was the con artists ability to short sell the companies' stock without having to ever borrow the shares to cover their positions that was the key to the scam.

Over the course of the next few months, other pieces of the puzzle began to fall into place:

- "The Berlin Connection," where over a thousand companies were listed on the Berlin-Bremen Stock Exchange without their knowledge or permission.
- The DTCC's share borrow program, where American brokers are allowed to "borrow" stock that doesn't exist to cover their trades.
- The repeatedly postponed and then watered-down *NBC Dateline* exposé of the scandal, which seemed at first to be our moment of truth, but instead became a classic example of the media selling out to special interests and big money.
- The Corporate Media, who for years soundly ignored the issue altogether, and especially the financial press, many of whom seemed to be siding with the criminals themselves.
- The hedge funds, unregulated and growing at an alarming rate, who suddenly appeared as major players in the scandal, and elevated it to new heights of sophistication.
- The Securities and Exchange Commission, who at first seemed to be just pawns in the scandal, but who turned out to be one of the key participants in allowing and even facilitating the massive fraud perpetuated on middle-class Americans.
- The unexpected resignation of embattled SEC Chairman William Donaldson at the height of the scandal, who was replaced by Bush crony Christopher Cox.
- The brokers, who take a cut for every share that changes hands, even if that share doesn't exist except as a notation in an electronic ledger; even if that share is *never physically delivered* to its rightful owner.
- Congress, who we worked with for months to help set up congressional subcommittee hearings, only to have the entire process shot down by "the powers that be."

And all along, the real issue seemed to be naked short selling.

But then, as the details continued to come together, I realized I was still wrong. The seemingly unrelated events began to resemble hundreds of puzzle pieces that fit together to form a disturbing and intricate broader picture.

Somewhere along the line the dots all connected, forming a perfect picture of a scandal that is anything but disjointed, a scheme that is anything but haphazard. The players are interconnected on every level, from those who set up the schemes and perpetuate it in the trenches, to those who allow it to flourish by creating a system that invites corruption. Trillions of dollars have been stolen from the middle-class investor and transferred to the pockets of the ultra-wealthy and their seedy partners in crime. And along the way, at every level, each of the culprits gets a cut of the loot by doing their part to facilitate the crime.

The villain here isn't naked short selling, that is simply the tool used to fleece the victims. When a psychotic killer goes on a shooting rampage, it's not the gun that goes on trial, it's the killer himself. And so it is with naked short selling. The trading system is set up to invite corruption, and undoubtedly, there are loopholes in our securities laws big enough to drive a Brinks truck full of investors' cash through. However, the problem is far bigger than that. This isn't a major scandal perpetuated by small time con artists or a few isolated individuals taking advantage of the system. The real villains here are those who will do anything to line their own pockets with America's wealth, the real culprit here is greed. It's the movie *Wall Street* personified…."Greed is Good," at any cost.

I first began to speak to the broader implications of this systematic draining of our economy in late 2005. In an article on *The Faulking Truth,* entitled "It's Money That Matters," I phrased it this way:

> *"The issue of stock market manipulation and stock counterfeiting through naked short selling is one that affects every American, whether they own stocks or not. By destroying thousands of small businesses and allowing the ultra-rich to defraud investors and then move that money to dozens of offshore tax havens such as Bermuda, the Cayman Islands, and Belize - and out of our economy, the very foundation of our free enterprise system is in jeopardy."*

This is the most elaborate financial scheme the world has ever seen, a modern-day version of an international Ponzi scheme. It's impossible to calculate in dollars and cents how much damage has been done to our country. The real cost must be measured in terms of the thousands of companies destroyed. Untold technological, medical, and environmental advancements will never come to fruition. Our way of life is threatened by the loss of jobs, revenue, and tax dollars, and the accompanying ripple effect on the quality of our schools, roads, libraries, health care system, and even the security of our country.

And so on and on it goes, a seemingly never-ending cycle of escalating wealth transference, money being used to buy influence on Wall Street, in Congress, the media, governmental regulatory agencies, and even in our court systems. That influence is used to further tip the scales of so-called free enterprise in the favor of the already ultra-wealthy, at the expense of the financial health and well-being of our entire country. It's all part of the ever-expanding Circle of Greed.

Introduction: The Naked Truth

When I was initially approached about writing the CMKX story, my instinctive response was a resounding "NO!" I had been covering the issue of naked short selling for two years. I had been looking for a literary vehicle to serve as the subject of my first book about corruption in our financial markets, but the CMKX roller coaster was NOT the vehicle I had in mind. CMKX represented everything that I *didn't* want to write about – a company that on the surface appeared to be nothing more than a classic pump and dump rather than one manipulated by external stock market forces.

In November of 2005, I attended the North American Securities Administrators Association Forum on naked short selling. My initial goal was to work with fellow stock market advocates to awaken America and political leaders in Washington to the massive fraud that persists in our financial markets. This book began with a phone call from Kevin West, a fellow stock market reform advocate and loyal CMKX shareholder. He convinced me to meet with stockholder and shareholders' advocate John Martin and hear his CMKX story.

John and his wife Jill picked me up at the Jefferson Hotel and drove me around Washington D.C. before we stopped for lunch at McDonalds, of all places. John told me about a company whose 50,000 shareholders had bought into a promise and a dream largely created by a former Canadian prison guard named Urban Casavant.

Two hours later I was hooked; the story was as fascinating as it was complex. I decided it was a great tale in and of itself, aside from any social or political agenda I was hoping to promote. Besides, I could always follow up with a book on the broader topic of financial fraud I had been planning to write since 2004, called "The Circle of Greed." Thinking I could research and write the CMKX book in a few months, I came to the conclusion that even though it might not be the ideal poster child for naked short selling, it did embody all the elements of everything wrong with our stock market system.

If I had only known then what I know now…well, I still would have accepted the challenge, but without the self-imposed deadlines, and with regular counseling sessions along the way. As it turned out, two years after that first meeting I *still* hadn't finished the book. In fact, I feel as if I could continue researching this morass of a story for another year, and barely scratch the surface.

There were some things that were obvious from the beginning about CMKX. First and foremost, in this story, nothing is as it seems. For every fact, there are fifteen rumors that only serve to confuse the issue. For every single thing I thought I knew, there were ten more things that I had no clue about. Every path led, and still leads, to another path, or more likely, several more paths, all heading in divergent directions. And as if that wasn't enough, there was real danger along the way. I've been lucky enough to have only received a couple of what I would consider serious veiled threats. I came to realize that some of the players in this saga are exceedingly dangerous men, who were feared by even those who worked with or around them. In the world of stock market fraud, there is no honor among thieves.

The real danger in dealing with CMKX, was, and still is the obsession. There is something about this phenomenon that pulls people in, both emotionally and physically. Once in, it's hard to let it go. I've asked, and been asked a hundred times: "What makes this little company so different from the thousands of other penny stock stories? What is it that has captured so many people's attention, and irreversibly altered so many lives?"

One day I ventured on to one of the message boards, and I began to read. I read rumors so outlandish I couldn't imagine any rational person could possibly believe them, and others so incredibly well thought out and plausible that *I* wanted to believe them. I read stories about the almost mythical CMKX CEO Urban Casavant who was, no pun intended, almost an urban legend, and about the intriguing cast of characters surrounding the company.

One day, I was speaking with John Martin on the phone, asking questions, as I am wont to do. I asked about the message boards, this rumor and that, telling him what I thought about one thing I had read or another, when he stopped me in mid-sentence and said, almost nonchalantly, "It sounds like you're catching the CMKX bug." I laughed him off. After all, I was just writing the story, it had nothing to do with me. I wasn't personally involved with it.

In another conversation, I had mentioned that I hoped to capture the human drama of the CMKX story, and not just the overwhelming mountain of factual information that surrounds the story. I hoped I could somehow come to understand how the shareholders felt about this little company.

I came to realize the main character in this story *is* the shareholders. I say "character" instead of "characters" because they are in some ways a single entity, a living breathing organism that came together as a community. As 50,000 plus members of the same family they discussed, debated, argued, and ultimately bonded together. They became a force that has already done much to bring about the attention that will ultimately be required to change our stock market from one rife with favoritism and fraud to one based on integrity, honesty, and fairness. As in society as a whole, they ultimately fragmented into many smaller communities with opposing opinions, but they still share a common bond.

Now, here I am months later, operating on an average of 3 to 4 hours of sleep a night, obsessing over everything I've learned and how much I don't know, and hoping that I get it right. I'm writing this introduction at 5:30 in the morning, having stayed up all night on little more than caffeine in the form of tea, coffee and chocolate-covered espresso beans, and pure adrenaline. Like thousands of shareholders, I am for all practical purposes addicted to CMKX.

Now I feel as if I'm living the story, as if I've been absorbed into the same living breathing entity that I'm writing about. It has taken over much of my time, energy and focus, and consumed a large part of my life, to the detriment of those I love and cherish, and who depend on me. I have become part of the human drama that is CMKX.

I keep saying that once it's over and the book is sent to the printers, I'll be able to simply let it go and return to living a normal life, with only a passing interest in what happens to CMKX from that point forward. I'll spend more time on the things that should matter – friends, family, love – and generally, live life beyond CMKX.

I'll keep everyone posted on how that goes, but I realize it won't be easy. It hasn't been easy for thousands of shareholders to let it go, to move on with their lives as if none of this ever happened. I know that many of them have been irreversibly changed, for better or worse, and in many cases, for better *and* worse. I have met hundreds of them along the way, bonded with many of them, become close friends with others, and argued with many more. Many have contributed invaluable research and information for this book.

This book is dedicated to every one of them, whether they agree with what I've written about their company or not. It is for those who have found a home and become a part of the CMKX family, those who have moved on with their lives, those who have suffered from the human drama that is CMKX, and especially, those who are no longer with us.

This story is for every single CMKX shareholder. May they ultimately receive the rewards that they so richly deserve.

The Naked Truth

PART ONE

"Profits on the exchange are the treasures of goblins. At one time they may be carbuncle stones, then coals, then diamonds, then flint stones, then morning dew, then tears."

~ **De la Vega**

Chapter 1 – A Million Millionaires

"Say what you want about the sweet miracle of unquestioning faith, I consider a capacity for it terrifying and absolutely vile."
~ Kurt Vonnegut

For the shareholders, it was the party of a lifetime, a fitting celebration for what internet websites had been calling "The Stock Play of a Lifetime." It was the pre-party for a Million Millionaires. After a frenzy of business acquisitions, joint ventures, and mergers, CMKM Diamonds, commonly referred to by its trading symbol CMKX, was finally on its way, and the 50,000 plus shareholders around the world could only do what they had done all along – hang on for the ride of their lives:

> *Fasten your seatbelts. Please keep arms and legs inside of the car while roller coaster is in motion. Do not ride CMKXtreme if you have a heart condition, are pregnant, or are prone to nausea or panic attacks. You might experience some dizziness on the twists, turns, and loops during this ride. That is normal. Above all, just sit back and enjoy the ride.*

In the past two months alone, the company had issued a flurry of press releases. CEO and president Urban Casavant's by now legendary assertion that he wanted to, like Microsoft, create a "Million Millionaires" suddenly seemed somehow possible, even plausible.

In two short months, CMKX:

- Sold five percent of its mineral rights to mining company St. George Metals, Inc. (SGGM) for $10 million plus 200 billion shares of SGGM stock.
- Collected the first $2.5 million as a down payment.
- Collected a second payment of $2.5 million a week later.
- Began test drilling for diamonds on its Canadian property.
- Announced a stock dividend from an alliance with U.S. Canadian Minerals, Inc. (UCAD), a gold mining company.
- Acquired fifty percent interest in mineral rights to 38,350 acres of uranium property in Saskatchewan.
- Purchased 127 million shares of Juina Mining Corp., another diamond company, and distributed them to CMKX shareholders.
- Acquired major ownership in a producing Ecuadorian gold mine already yielding 40 tons of gold ore per day.

So here it was, finally. For many CMKX stockholders, the party was the culmination of two years of eating, breathing, and sleeping CMKX, of riding the dizzying highs and lows of the CMKXtreme thrill ride.

The party had been suggested just two months earlier by Nevada Minerals President Ed Dhonau, who was a shareholder of both CMKX and UCAD, an officer of neither, but who always seemed to be in the middle of everything that happened with either company. CMKX and UCAD agreed to split the cost of throwing what was dubbed a "shareholder appreciation party." Chris Hanneman, head of investor relations for UCAD, was assigned the unenviable task of organizing the party. The next seven weeks were spent in a frenzy of phone calls, reserving the conference rooms and hundreds of hotel rooms at the Las Vegas casino Texas Station, booking the entertainment, ordering the elaborate decorations, food, and a hundred other details. The RSVPs had been pouring in from CMKX shareholders all over the world, over 8,000 had already confirmed, and double or even triple that many could show up.

Wednesday, October 27, 2004

As the countdown for the party began, announcements from both CMKX and UCAD added to the excitement of the coming weekend. First, CMKM Diamonds announced on Wednesday that the first week of gold ore had been mined at the American Mine in Ecuador and had been shipped to CMKX's partner U.S. Canadian Minerals Inc.'s processing facility for "immediate ore extraction." CMKX CEO Urban Casavant even used the "R" and the "I" words – "It's an exciting day for CMKX shareholders. Our diversification plan is well underway and moving toward revenue and income."

Then, U.S. Canadian Minerals announced that the company's 3-for-1 forward split (giving shareholders three new shares of stock for every one that they already owned) had been declared effective, and that their trading symbol would be changed from UCAD to USCA. The announced restructuring of the company was designed to allow UCAD to pursue additional financing and move forward with future acquisitions. Rendal Williams, CEO of UCAD, put it this way: "With the split and new symbol now effective, the company will continue pursuit of its goals as stated by the board of directors. We expect to have some exciting announcements in the next few days."

A few hours later, UCAD announced that it had acquired a controlling interest in a new processing plant in Buza, Ecuador. The first stage of the facility, which would have the capacity to process 70 tons of gold ore a day, was ninety-five percent complete. The already planned second stage of the plant would increase the processing capacity to 400 to 500 tons of gold ore per day, ramping up to stay ahead of gold ore that would be flowing out of the mine in Ecuador.

Thursday, October 28, 2004

Many shareholders were already on their way to Las Vegas when the seemingly never ending stream of good news took a turn for the worse. U.S. Canadian

Minerals, which had declared its forward split only one day earlier, had been temporarily suspended from trading by the Securities and Exchange Commission (SEC), "because of questions regarding the accuracy of publicly disseminated information regarding the company's financing and mining activities and the value of its assets."

However, many CMKX shareholders had an uncanny ability to explain away things they didn't want to hear, and emphasize the positives. And so it was with the UCAD suspension. It didn't take long before savvy shareholders, with the help of an internet stock-picking website called *The Green Baron*, spun the news into something a little easier to handle for the CMKX loyal. They reported that the Saskatchewan Financial Services Commission had just initiated their own special inquiry into CMKX. The Saskatchewan Commission specifically named CEO/president Urban Casavant, Chief Financial Officer (CFO) David DeSormeau, and head of investor relations Melvin O'Neil as the three CMKX officials who had "traded in the securities of CMKI and CMKM while they were not registered."

The news was obviously not good: one company halted from trading, the other being investigated for illegally selling stock. However, *The Green Baron* managed to spin it as a conspiracy against the companies themselves, saying:

> *"We strongly believe we have just witnessed a consorted all out effort to tarnish the images of CMKM Diamonds and US Canadian Minerals. On the day following a statement by CEO Rendal Williams to expect 'some exciting announcements in the next few days,' and only one day before a huge CMKX/ USCA shareholder appreciation event begins in Las Vegas, two separate attacks have been launched with precision.*
>
> *Although a formal statement has not been issued in response at this hour by either company, we expect both CMKM Diamonds and US Canadian Minerals to successfully and quickly resolve any questions that are being raised by the interested parties."*

There was much discussion, both in *The Green Baron* report and amongst CMKX and UCAD shareholders, of sinister "other forces" at work. Forces who for some reason or another, didn't want CMKX to succeed in their quest to create a million millionaires, and who mysteriously chose the exact date leading up to the shareholders' appreciation party to launch their ruthless attack. This was by no means the first mention of a wider conspiracy involving CMKX and its stock, and it would be far from the last.

An article in a paid-subscriber newsletter called *NaabTrade* seemed to bear out the conspiracy theories. They began to short UCAD's stock, betting that the price would drop, just days before trading was halted. Oddly though, they correctly predicted that the SEC would take action against the company days before it was publicly announced. It seemed to the more observant CMKX shareholders that *NaabTrade* had received some kind of advance, and possibly illegal, inside information about the SEC suspension of UCAD's stock:

> *"UCAD currently trades at just over $15, so we are initiating short sales at $15 or above. Many of our Portfolio Managed Program clients will start to see short sales in your accounts over the next few days as we try to find the shares to borrow. Shares may also become more available for shorting after the 3 for 1 stock split goes into effect. UCAD has released no details as to when that will be. Don't ask me why they are doing a stock split either. It may be halted from trading before the split is ever affected."*

Even with the negative news, *The Green Baron* noted that "former SEC attorney Roger Glenn would be involved in responding to both inquiries," and expressed confidence that "Mr. Glenn's vast experience with the SEC would resolve these issues in a timely and professional manner." As always, they closed with their familiar battle cry, saying they would gladly wait for the issues to be resolved, and for "CMKM Diamonds to become what we still believe will be The Stock Play of a Lifetime."

Chapter 2 – The CMKX and UCAD Shareholders' Party

"A company doesn't have a race car called CMKXtreme with diamonds all over it because there are no diamonds"
~abadgoodgirl, *Raging Bull* message board, Oct. 31, 2004

"The CMKX and UCAD Shareholders' Party" splashed across full color banners hanging in the hotel lobby against a vivid backdrop showing the city of Las Vegas at sunset, with crimson skies and of course, purple mountains majesty in the distance. On the banner's right side was the now legendary CMKXtreme Machine, the National Hot Rod Association Funny Car driven by NHRA champion Jeff Arend. Orange and yellow flames licked across the front hood, and a burly Canadian driller, complete with yellow hardhat and jackhammer, drilled into the heart of CMKX land, while polished diamonds leapt out the ground.

While most CMKX shareholders would say they were dedicated and loyal, outsiders invariably described them as obsessed, and every now and then, the word "cult" slipped out. In all reality, the line between dedication and obsession, and even between loyalty and cultism, is a hazy one at best. They believed in the CMKX dream, the almost mythical Five Year Master Plan, and CEO Urban Casavant. If that loyalty happened to border on obsession now and then, so be it. In the end it would be worth it.

Thursday, they began to arrive, first by the hundreds, and then by the thousands, from all corners of America, Canada, and countless points in between and beyond. Even though the disturbing news about UCAD had put an obvious damper on the number of partygoers who made the trip to Vegas, it still had all the markings of a religious pilgrimage. The shareholders gathered together in the lobby of Texas Station, shaking hands, exchanging names, pleasantries, and CMKX stories, while always keeping one eye out for whoever might wander by. The stories and rumors began to circulate almost immediately, and expectations and hopes rose with every whispered word.

Of course, the main thought on every shareholder's mind, as it had been since the party was first announced two months ago, was the burning question of what would be revealed at the party. What exactly were the "exciting announcements of the next few days" that UCAD CEO Rendal Williams had promised to the shareholders? A merger between the two companies? CMKM Diamonds and U.S. Canadian Minerals? CMKX and UCAD? Urban Casavant and Rendal Williams?

Diamonds and Gold...Gold and Diamonds. It was to be the ultimate climax to a dizzying two years, and an even more dizzying weekend.

Chris Hanneman supervised the activity in the hospitality suite, set up long tables to accommodate the shifts of shareholders putting together informational packets on the two companies, planned the weekend's numerous events, and made the table decorations for the banquet room. The centerpieces for the dining tables consisted of CMKX "pirates' treasure chests" overflowing with chocolate gold coins embossed with "CMKX" on one side and "USCA" on the other, Mardi Gras style strings of beads, and diamond shaped Ring Pops. For a company that had yet to unearth much in the way of real treasures, the fake treasure chests seemed almost too appropriate.

Other shareholders were dispatched to Aliante Park, where Friday evening's and Saturday afternoon's entertainment was to take place, to help set up lighting and sound equipment for the shows. If it seemed a little odd that the guests/ shareholders also provided the manual labor and most of the entertainment for the party, no one stopped working long enough to really think about it. It wasn't until long after the weekend was over that more than one shareholder would look back and describe the party as more or less a self-serve event.

Friday, October 29, 2004

The shareholders continued to show up all day Friday, following the CMKX star to Las Vegas and gathering with the early arrivals to be welcomed into the fold. Friday was mostly spent getting to know one another and listening to musicians, comedians, and a host of other performers in the Amphitheater at Aliante Park, with all of the entertainment provided by CMKX shareholders.

Those who couldn't make the pilgrimage gathered in CMKX internet chat rooms and message boards that had sprung up over the past couple of years like so many satellites circling the mother ship. They had become more than just places to exchange information and opinions on the company. They had grown into CMKX cyber-communities, each with its own distinct personality and feel, like real communities, with hierarchies and casts of characters who alternately agreed and argued, and slandered and supported each other. And just like real communities, when one neighborhood got too rough or noisy for some residents, they would pack their bags and move down the road to another CMKX cyber-community. Other times, groups of supporters would band together and stage coups within the existing chat rooms and message boards, banishing some members and mounting insurrections to seize control, imposing their own rules and installing their own leaders. In some extreme cases, they would even splinter into new groups, taking a few other discontented members with them to begin anew in another corner of the internet, like pioneers settling new lands.

But that weekend, they were all focused on the CMKX Shareholder Appreciation Party, gathered by the thousands in CMKX chat rooms with names like *Sterling's Classroom* or Willy Wizard's, and on CMKX message boards on Proboards, Raging Bull and Yahoo. Every board was eager to hear the latest word from Las Vegas, from the CMKX party, to be the first to report on this bit of news or that rumor, to hear what everyone wanted to hear – The Announcement: Diamonds and Gold, Gold and Diamonds.

Rendal Williams posing with gold. Courtesy of Fuego Entertainment, Jason Webb and Anthony Pullicino.

Raw diamonds. Courtesy of Jason Webb and Anthony Pullicino.

CMKX advertising on truck. Jason Webb and Anthony Pullicino.

CMKXtreme sponsored NHRA car. Courtesy of Jason Webb and Anthony Pullicino.

CMKXtreme sponsored car. Courtesy of Jason Webb and Anthony Pullicino.

Chapter 3 – 'Til the Fat Lady Sings

"Any rumor on where this rumor is coming from?"
~Poster from *Paltalk*, October 30, 2004

Saturday, October 30, 2004

It had been a weekend to remember for the CMKX shareholders, and the Main Event was yet to come. Saturday, like the day before, had been a whirlwind of activity. Another afternoon of music and entertainment filled Aliante Park, with sing-a-longs for the kids and an endless supply of food, camaraderie, and conversation. Many of the CMKX faithful spent at least part of their day at the NHRA Races at the Las Vegas Motor Speedway, watching Jeff Arend's CMKXtreme Mining Machine in action as it raced past the CMKX billboard that graced the speedway trackside, highlighting the familiar battle cry of the CMKX faithful with each lap….Got CMKX?...Got CMKX?...Got CMKX?

U.S. Congressman and former Nevada Secretary of State Dean Heller. From government website.

The shareholders who attended the Las Vegas races had another surprise. Nevada Secretary of State Dean Heller (who would later become a U.S. Representative of Nevada) was one of the featured drivers in the *CMKXtreme.com* ASA Speed Truck Challenge, driving a CMKXtreme/Go Fast Sports sponsored truck. An article by *RacingWest.com* spotlighted Heller and his family, citing his background as "an institutional stockbroker and a broker/dealer on the Pacific Stock Exchange" and his oversight of the Securities Fraud Division in Nevada. It was another stamp of approval for CMKX. What better endorsement of their company than having the person in charge of Nevada's stock market driving a CMKXtreme Machine? Heller's involvement at the races sparked rumors that he might be one of the featured speakers at the party.

As much fun as the weekend had been so far, the best was yet to come: The CMKX/UCAD Shareholder Appreciation Party. The rumors, which had flowed from almost the moment that shareholders first arrived in Las Vegas, had continued to grow in both size and scope as the time for the main event neared. Shareholders gathered at the Cadillac Bar in the middle of the casino, making new friends from all over the world, meeting people who they knew only from the CMKX message boards, and sharing stories and rumors about their favorite topics, which incidentally had one common thread, CMKX.

Like so many things that had fueled the entire CMKX juggernaut over the past two years, the rumors materialized out of nowhere, gained credibility as they spread like wildfire throughout the message boards and chat rooms, and eventually became accepted as reality by many of the CMKX faithful. The rumors surrounding Saturday night's party, however unbelievable and farfetched some of them might have seemed in retrospect, appeared not only possible, but in fact, highly plausible.

Most of the rumors centered around the unknown identities of the "many special guests scheduled to speak with shareholders" cited in the party schedule. Along with the obvious cast of CMKX and UCAD related characters, such as Urban Casavant, Rendal Williams, and former SEC attorney Roger Glenn, an interesting list of possible guest speakers began to surface at the party, on message boards, and in internet chat rooms. In one corner, it was decided, since one of the CMKX shareholders was a prime minister of Saudi Arabia (which was true), it only stood to reason that the Prince of Saudi Arabia would speak that evening. Then, the word leaked out that Vice President Dick Cheney was in Las Vegas that weekend....so of course, he was there for the sole purpose of addressing the CMKX faithful.

The day of the party, many shareholders noticed an assortment of out-of-place looking characters walking around the hotel/casino, acting as if they were casing the place and securing the perimeter of the building. There seemed to be Secret Service men everywhere, dressed in dark suits and wearing ear pieces, seemingly communicating with superiors at an undisclosed location. Almost immediately, the rumors intensified (yet again). An ex-president of the United States was going to speak at the party! It was an incredible turn of events, and hopes began to soar even higher, hopes that were fueled by an announcement late Saturday afternoon that all partygoers would be required to wear a security wristband to enter the banquet hall. About ten volunteers (CMKX shareholders) were recruited to man the registration desk, and they furiously tore apart the wristbands as the guests formed a long line to enter the main banquet room.

At first, there was some confusion as to whether the strict security measures would be necessary. Then, suddenly, the word was out! The governor of Nevada, Kenny Guinn, was in the building and on his way to the party. Re-energized, the shareholders/volunteers lined up at the registration table, checking ID's and handing out wristbands. The anticipation rose with every piece of "news" that was whispered around the room.

While many of the shareholders had spent Thursday helping to set up the event, for the majority of the attendees, their entrance into the main banquet room at Texas Station was their first chance to see the elaborate extravaganza. They filed past the balloon arches and lavish "CMKXtreme" ice sculptures adorning the hors d'oeuvre and buffet tables set up in the lobby of the hotel, past the cordoned-off Kia that was to be given away at the party, and past the colorful-to-the-point-of-gaudy banners trumpeting their arrival: "The CMKX and UCAD Shareholders' Party."

And on to The Main Event, where a banquet room suitable for a Roman Bacchanal waited. Everywhere they turned, partygoers were treated to more and more festive excess. Balloon sculptures of all shapes and sizes adorned every corner of the room, and in front of the stage hung hundreds of red, white, and blue balloons suspended by a giant net...the infamous balloon drop, filled with cash, various prizes, and even diamonds, waiting to be cut loose after "The Announcement" (or, as the case may be, "The Announcements"). The main tables were adorned with pyramid displays of what appeared to be gold bars supplied by UCAD.

The food was fit for kings and queens. Pasta, seafood, prime rib, exotic dishes enough to satisfy any taste, and tables filled with desserts lined the entry hall and the banquet room itself. The caterers were busy serving the CMKXers, while a full staff of bartenders feverishly poured drink after drink at the open bar. And since this was Vegas, the obligatory Elvis impersonators mingled with the partygoers, shaking hands, smiling for pictures, and striking the ever-classic Elvis pose.

Finally, the great hall was filled, and electricity filled the air. UCAD president Rendal Williams was already making the rounds, looking dapper and almost overdressed in his black suit and perfectly trimmed goatee, and Nevada Minerals president Ed Dhonau was reveling in his role as emcee, dressed in Texas Station appropriate jeans, western belt buckle, bolo tie, and a half black, half white vest with a sewn-on sheriff's badge.

But then, a buzz began to circulate through the room, and a smattering of applause soon turned into an explosion of excitement and euphoria. An unassuming man, short, a little overweight, wearing glasses, his hair buzzed close to the scalp to cover his receding hairline, had just entered the room. As more than one partygoer later described it, "the King had arrived," and they weren't talking about Elvis either. It was Urban Casavant, so revered by many of the CMKX faithful that one UCAD employee would later comment that "if Urban had told them to drink Kool-Aid, they would have drank the Kool-Aid; I'm serious, they were that obsessive."

Luckily, on this night, there would be no Kool-Aid. Instead, Urban worked his way through the crowd, shaking hands with the men and hugging the women, and posing for pictures with everyone in sight. It was a repeat of the performance of the Elvis impersonators, except that Urban was idolized even more than the King himself.

Ed Dhonau, unknown, Urban and Carolyn Casavant, Rendal Williams at the CMKX/ UCAD Shareholders' Party. Courtesy of Jason Webb and Anthony Pullicino.

The infamous balloon drop. Courtesy of Jason Webb and Andy Pullicino.

CMKX ice and balloon sculptures. Courtesy of Jason Webb and Anthony Pullicino.

While the thousands of partygoers witnessed the spectacle firsthand, every word, every step, every bit of news was sent back to the internet chat rooms via cell phone, text message, and even laptop computer. A woman who went by the screen name of `Audrey Hepburn` on *Proboards66* was typing on her laptop computer and giving the thousands of online followers a blow-by-blow account of the activity, like a news anchor reporting live from the scene:

Topic: Audrey's LIVE Thread

7:20 pm- Ok the doors are open, we are getting food and waiting. No speeches yet will stay live and post as it happens!

7:29 pm- Elvis lives!!!! He is here singing!

8:02 pm- I am at the party and the Love shack is Playing ...no news yet setting the mood for fun. We are jamming and blazing and it is a hot time in the city here!

8:17 pm- The Love Shack is Playing and there are slide shows on the overhead screens from today's races. No speakers up there yet? Also SEC not allowed in!

8:40 pm- Rendal Williams just walked into the room....the time may be near! Stay tuned! The band is on break and we are nearing 9:oo here!

9:06 pm- Urban just arrived! Still waiting hang in there you will know when it happens!

9:20 pm- UC and RW are mingling with the shareholders, the band is playing and we are all waiting...

9:21 pm- Chris, IR from UCAD is here said speakers in about 1/2 hour...

And then, from another poster known as bluediamonds:

9:33 pm - I'm watching this and the Christian Traders updates at the same time. Has anyone else reported that there would be an unnamed guest speaker tonight?

"Just announced that there would be a guest speaker, unnamed. Interesting VP Cheney is in town tonight."

A response from kranker:

9:40 pm- Kind of a coincidence we have a secret service thread bouncing around here also. Maybe that report is correct. Time will tell.

And back to Audrey:

9:46 pm- There is a lot of security here and Rendal Williams has his own security person. FYI Melvin is here...

9:48 pm- Band stopped speakers up here!

9:50 pm- Drawing for door prizes! 15 #'s one will get the KIA

9:55 pm- handing out envelopes 1 has the key!

10:02 pm- KIA winner is...a young lady

10:03 pm- Balloons still up...more drawings

10:05 pm- giving away money now 30 envelopes, prizes are $300-$1000.

A poster from *Paltalk* chimed in:

10:17 pm- Heard on Paltalk that texasredneck was one of the 30 drawn, sucked some helium and said "and the outstanding share count is..." and the mic was taken away.

And still the questions persisted:

10:21 pm- init4me: Again.... IS Roger Glenn there?

10:21 pm- oneluv: some say no he is not there

10:37 pm- GoBoSox: Audrey, have you heard any rumors about Cheney being there as a guest speaker? There are other threads talking about it... Thanks!

10:37 pm- band started no news or speakers yet...sorry folks...I can't make it up

Then, in a matter of just a few minutes, things began to go drastically wrong when a shareholder from Canada, later described as drunk and out of control, took matters into her own hands:

10:42 pm- Audrey: shareholder from Canada grabbed the mic wants info. crowd out of control security took mic

10:45 pm- Jooooeee: Quote from another board.. more detail than audrey's description:

"Lady from Canada got on stage made band stop and is requesting info and is cussing out UC, security is taking her off stage, she is screaming at UC demanding info, is now being escorted off stage."

10:47 pm- Audrey: crowd thinning out...balloons intact... only have tee shirts to take home at this point

10:55 pm- Joooeee: I'm hearing from other boards the band will play for 45 minutes and then possible speech afterwards.

10:55 pm- Audrey: I will be here until or if the FAT LADY sings

10:57 pm- Dr911: Good for you Audrey! Thanks so much for hanging in there!

10:57 pm- bluediamonds: USCA halt may have put a damper on what could take place at the party and remember USCA PR said something about exciting news coming shortly (but that was before the halt).

10:59 pm- crapface: Urban will speak. Told the crazy lady he is gonna speak.

11:02 pm- bluediamonds: Police officer reporting that Urban went out back with the woman. calmed her and told her the party isn't over, that he will still speak.

11:05 pm- darock: The drama unfolds...let see what UC says.

11:06 pm- phingerz: Rumor has it...PRs are ready to go after midnight vegas time

11:08 pm- darock: Any rumor where this rumor is coming from?

11:08 pm- Paltalknews: Hummingbird on paltalk mentioned it came from Dr. D's room. Sounded like it came from Dr. D. but not sure.

11:08 pm- Audrey: it's over peeps are saying... the balloons did not come down cause the KIA winner did not pull the cord..these are reports I am getting people are upset and disappointed with lack of info....

11:11 pm- hickorystick: Audrey, PalTalk and Proboards32 are reporting that UC is still planning to speak in the wake of calming down the hysterical woman. Can you confirm this with anyone?

11:14 pm- Audrey: can't see anyone ready to speak 200 people still here

Finally, at 11:19, Audrey gave up and called it a night:

I heard no one will speak...I am logging off goodnight and sorry we came up w/o news...Thanks for your support.

```
11:25 pm- Golden: What happened to "I'll be here till the
fat lady sings"?
```

```
12:09 pm- LWRFLA 1: And they say what happens in Vegas,
stays in Vegas. Right...........
```

And so ended the Great CMKX/UCAD Shareholder Appreciation Party. Seven weeks of planning derailed in less than thirty minutes, leaving thousands of partygoers stunned and dismayed, and thousands more to continue discussing the "non-event" well into the next morning.

And what about the Canadian woman who set off the near riot that fateful night in October? On the message boards, it was debated whether she was actually a "plant, intended to shut down the event," or just an inebriated shareholder upset about the lack of information from Urban Casavant and Rendal Williams.

Late that night, long after the CMKX and UCAD executives had ducked away into the darkness, a poster on *Proboards35* who went by the name of Driller recounted a phone call from a shareholder named Gina, describing the collapse of seven weeks of intense planning and $100,000 into total chaos:

```
The lady was only 2 tables away Gina said from her husband
and her and they were showing slides and this lady yells
BULLSH-T and she walks up on stage takes the mic away and
starts yelling I need some F'ing answers this is bullsh-
t I didn't come down here from Canada for f'ing nothing!
Everyone in the place all 3500 people started yelling and
say hell yeah and agreeing with her they escorted her off
and UC went to talk to her outside the ballroom and the
place just started emptying out like quickly she said
it was amazing within 5 minutes maybe 200 people were
still left...it was 11:36 when she called me literally
95% of the place walked out pissed off. The mood turned
so bad so fast that even the band was packing up and
getting heck out of there a few minutes ago. Gina and her
husband witnessed a crowd of people starting to surround
Ed Dhonau and it was looking like he was going to get his
ass kicked and there were tons of security there at this
event Gina said all dressed in black and wired up wearing
earpieces looking like pres bodyguards and they pulled
Ed the hell out of there at just at the right moment.
Apparently the 50-60 people that were wound up were taken
into a room where the rest of the shareholders couldn't
see them and were told to calm down and they were yelling
things like we'll call the f'ing SEC Monday we'll get some
f'ing answers...and people inside couldn't see any of this
apparently then the situation eased out from there she
said...pretty crazy stuff.
```

The party ended without a meaningful word spoken onstage by either Rendal Williams or Urban Casavant. No announcement of a merger, no conclusion to the

SEC investigation, no new Board of Directors or Advisory Board members, no "major news after midnight," no speeches from ex-Presidents, no Vice-President Cheney, no Governor Guinn, no Prince of Saudi Arabia, no Secretary of State Heller, no celebrity guest speakers, in fact, no speakers at all unless you count the infamous drunk Canadian shareholder's "f-ing bullsh-t" speech.

The balloons containing their unclaimed prizes never dropped, but instead were given to a lucky couple who happened to be getting married in the banquet room the next day. Audrey Hepburn and thousands of other disappointed CMKX and UCAD shareholders packed up and went home.

And the fat lady never sang.

PART TWO

"Diamonds are nothing more than chunks of coal that stuck to their jobs."
~ **Malcolm Forbes**

Financial Terrorism in America

By Mark Faulk

March 19, 2004

www.faulkingtruth.com

The Sucker

Picture this: You are a small-time investor who stumbles onto a start-up company that has just developed an innovative new product, a cutting edge technology, or maybe a medical breakthrough that could very well be "the next big thing." In the back of your mind, you can't help but think, "This could be the next Microsoft," and you have a chance to get in on the ground floor of a hidden gem that the big investors and analysts haven't even heard of yet. You do your homework, research the outstanding shares, study the recent press releases and filings, and read about the company on the stock message boards. Finally, you take the plunge, and decide to buy 500,000 shares at a nickel a share. That's right, you now own 1% of (there's that thought again) the next Microsoft, for a paltry $25,000. Sure it's a bit of a risk, but you know the saying, "no risk, no reward." You hit the buy button, turn off your computer, and wait for the money to roll in. A couple of weeks later, the company announces that they have secured a major financing deal, and now have the money to take their product to market, and you know you made the right decision. The volume picks up, the message boards are buzzing, and all is right with the world.

But then, something goes terribly wrong. For no apparent reason at all, the stock price begins to tank, and before you even have time to react, your 500,000 shares are down 80%, and you've just lost $20,000 of your hard-earned money. What the hell happened?

The Set-up

This same scenario is being played out time and again in every corner of America. Although there are many reasons for the failure of small, struggling, publicly-traded businesses, including mismanagement and outright corporate fraud, another, more sinister, plot is carried out every day, robbing investors of their money, businesses of their chance to achieve the American Dream of success, and hard working, dedicated employees of their dreams and even their livelihood. And worst of all, up to now, this fraud has been ignored (and in many cases even condoned) by the SEC and our very own government.

This is how it works. Remember that great news that the company just released about securing financing to allow them to take their product to market? It's nothing more than an elaborate scheme perpetuated against the company, its employees, and the shareholders by a network of skilled con artists. It begins with the financial institution (usually an offshore "lending institution" based somewhere like Bermuda or the Cayman Islands), who approaches the company with promises of funding to "help" the company get their product off the drawing board and into the market. The company, who is usually strapped for cash and desperate for some financial support, considers the terms of the offer. The lender promises them say, five million dollars in exchange for company stock at a 20% discount to the market price at the time they are converted into shares (although some deals are much worse, and the lender gets their shares at as much as a half price discount from the current market price). The company does the math: five million dollars converted to shares at 80% of the current price of around a nickel a share, not too bad a deal. Plus, once the news of the financing is released, investors will swoop down in a stock-buying frenzy, the trading volume will go through the roof, and the share price will soar, meaning the company will give up even fewer shares for the money they receive. The lender makes a nice profit, the company gets their product to market, their employees are finally rewarded for their years of dedication, and the loyal shareholders hit the jackpot. Everyone is happy.

Except that none of that actually happens. Before the ink on the contracts has even had time to dry, the lender is on the phone, calling his co-conspirators.

The Con

What happens next is complex, and involves the offshore lender, US Brokerage firms, and Canadian Brokers. The lender calls his broker, who is instructed to short sell the company's stock into the ground. Short selling involves the selling of imaginary shares into the market in the hope that the price will drop, and the short seller can then "buy back" the shares (that they never actually owned in the first place) at a cheaper price, and pocket the difference. Once a stock is sold short, a seller (or their broker) must cover their position by "borrowing" shares from other stockholders (usually those shares that are held in a brokerage house, such as E*Trade, Ameritrade, etc.), and sell them into the market. Sound unethical, and bit confusing as well? Maybe, but it is a legal practice that has flourished unchecked for years. The real problem arises when the short sellers dump so many "imaginary" shares into the market that the selling overwhelms any buying pressure, and artificially causes the stock price to crash. And this is exactly what the lender and their cohorts do.

In order to sell short enough shares to truly cause the stock to tank in price, the broker often has to sell more shares than they can "borrow" from legitimate stockholders. This practice is known as naked short selling (meaning the short sellers never intended to cover their position by borrowing real shares from legitimate stockholders). There is only one problem. Short selling is illegal in over-the-counter stocks (known as OTC, or penny stocks), and naked short selling *any* stock is illegal. However, many short sellers use foreign brokerages to circumvent U.S. regulations, and American brokers take advantage of loopholes in existing regulations to sidestep requirements that all trades be settled in three days or less. If there are buyers for a million shares, they short sell three million into the market, and on and on, until the stock price eventually collapses under the weight of millions and millions (or billions and billions, if necessary) of counterfeit shares flooding the market.

The Payoff

In simple terms, our lender loans the company a small part of the money promised and then immediately calls their co-conspirators in America and Canada, who then flood the market with hundreds of millions of counterfeit shares, causing the share price to collapse. Often, as an insurance policy, bashers are hired to discredit the company on stock message boards such as *Raging Bull*, in effect creating an even darker picture of the company. Then, the lender converts the loaned money into shares of company stock, not at 80% of the nickel stock price that the company envisioned, but at 80% of the market price after they've effectively manipulated the stock price down to almost zero. Instead of the few million shares that the company expected to give the lender, they are forced to give them hundreds of millions (and sometimes even billions) of shares. The lender turns around and dumps those shares into the market, and the price is driven even lower, and they collect their next payment in shares at an even cheaper price. This type of arrangement has become known as "death-spiral financing," because the company is often driven into bankruptcy by the lenders, their American brokers, and their Canadian cohorts.

The Damage

In the end, this practice amounts to financial terrorism against the United States. Legitimate companies are forced out of business, dedicated employees (who often received stock as part of their compensation) lose their jobs and their stock investments, communities lose out on the opportunity to earn substantial revenues and the employee base that a successful growing business can provide, and the stockholders lose their hard-earned money. Even more, they lose their faith in the stock market as a whole, and vow to never take a risk on a small, unproven, start-up company again. Legitimate lenders stop loaning money to small businesses (which appear to be a much higher risk), and eventually, the entire entrepreneurial spirit of America is put at risk. Make no mistake; lives are literally destroyed by this insidious practice.

What Can Be Done About It?

Both the SEC and the NASD have known about this practice for years, yet have stood idly by while foreign brokers, offshore financial institutions, and their American co-conspirators have systematically financially raped and pillaged our small businesses, their employees, and small investors. Dozens of lawsuits have been filed by companies and private investors, who claim to have been the victims of naked short selling, against the federal regulatory agencies and the brokers themselves. Individuals and small independent organizations such as *www.investigatethesec.com* have attempted to draw attention to the problems, and finally, a few small online publications such as *www.faulkingtruth.com* have begun to provide some coverage of the situation.

Proposed NASD and SEC rules don't go far enough to prevent this practice. Until Congress steps in and forces everyone to play by the same rules, and makes those rules tougher in regards to short selling in general (and naked short selling in particular), the OTC market will continue to be a rigged game, and the well being of America will continue to be threatened by unscrupulous foreign (and yes, domestic) interests.

Chapter 4 – The Land of Opportunity

"I've been at this prospecting and claiming land for about 15 years now, so I've been chasing this for a long time, and it's finally all going to come together."
~Urban Casavant

It was November 10, 2003, and even though at 46 years old, Urban Armand Joseph Casavant was rapidly approaching middle-age, he still believed his best days were ahead of him. It seemed that finally, after a series of unlikely events over the past year, his luck was changing. Always the gambler, Urban knew the only way to get ahead in life was to take risks, and continue taking risks, until luck caught up with you. That was the key to Urban's success up to that point; he was the ultimate risk-taker, the gambler who knew that you made your own luck by playing the odds over and over again until you hit the jackpot. To him, life was just that simple. Lose it all? Place another bet, preferably with someone else's money. Lose that money? Not to worry. Find some more and bet that, too. Eventually the odds were going to land in your favor, and then everyone would be happy.

Just two nights earlier, Urban had hit the jackpot...literally. Playing the quarter slots in the Orleans Casino, he had fed coin after coin into the machine, winning a little, then giving it back, then winning a little more only to give that back. Then it happened. With one pull of the lever, he won what seemed like a fortune to Urban, an amazing $59,000. Yup, he thought to himself, his luck had definitely taken a turn for the better.

It was that same mentality, that desire to hit the jackpot, that had led Urban south from Canada, the self-proclaimed country of "peace, order, and good government," to the Orleans Casino in Las Vegas, America. America, the mythical land of opportunity. Urban had his share of success in his hometown of Prince Albert, and it was those early successes in Canada that had led him to this very hotel room where he now sat, looking back over the events of the past few years.

Urban Casavant had spent most of his life working at dead-end jobs in a town where almost every job was in fact a dead-end job. He had been a jailer at the Prince Albert Correctional Center, although his biggest claim of success until the mid-'90s was owning a U-Haul franchise in a town that very few people moved to, and even fewer managed to escape. But then, a chance meeting in a bar changed all that, and Urban suddenly saw an opportunity to make enough money to load up his own belongings and say goodbye to Prince Albert once and for all.

Urban got off work at five o'clock on that day in 1984, just like he did every other day, left his prison guard job and drove straight to his favorite Greek restaurant for a drink, just like he did every other day. In Prince Albert, it seemed as if nothing ever changed, and that *every* day was.....well, just like every other day. But as is almost always the case, the most profound, life-altering events often happen when one least expects them, on days like any other day.

Urban, almost on automatic pilot, sat down in his usual spot, ordered his usual drink, and looked around, just as he usually did. But this time, he spotted someone who wasn't a regular there, off in his own corner, reading a book. But not just any book, this someone who wasn't a regular was reading a book about diamonds. Urban picked up his usual drink and walked over and sat down, and asked the man about the book, about diamonds.

Even though he never saw the stranger again, what he learned that day would change his whole life, and eventually the lives of more than 50,000 other people as well. He learned about the strange cars and trucks driving in, out, and around Prince Albert for the past few months. He learned that those cars and trucks belonged to the De Beers Corporation, the world's largest diamond company, the same company that controlled the flow, availability, and price of diamonds everywhere, and had for over a hundred years. He learned how Harry Oppenheimer, the 29 year old son of the founder of De Beers, had hired an advertising agency way back in 1938 to convince every man in America that when he proposed to the one he loved, he had to seal the deal with a diamond ring, and convince every woman the diamond ring was the only true symbol of undying love. Urban learned how the same advertising agency gave diamonds to movie stars and celebrities, and even to British royalty, and took out ads using the artwork of famous artists like Pablo Picasso and Salvador Dali, just to create the illusion that diamonds reflected success, class, and were in fact, unique works of art. He learned how in 1948 they created the slogan, "A Diamond is Forever," and sold it to America and the rest of the world. They took a shiny, clear stone that was in reality, neither forever or even that rare, and turned it into the most expensive status symbol the world had ever known. And most importantly, Urban Casavant learned how De Beers had used this sleight-of-hand to make a fortune selling that same shiny stone at outrageous prices to every young married couple in America, whether they could afford it or not.

He learned this too: De Beers was in Canada, specifically in Saskatchewan, looking for diamonds, buying up the mineral rights to land in the area, and that they had found something...somewhere (in Canada?)...that convinced them to buy back all their company's stock and regain complete control of their company, just as they controlled the world's diamonds.

Urban saw this as a golden opportunity to finally make his own fortune. He set about learning how to take advantage of the De Beers presence in Saskatchewan, and the numerous small diamond companies springing up in the area, by beating them to the punch and claiming the mineral rights to every piece of land he could get his hands on. When a company came out with positive news, or even before the news came out, he immediately bought up all of the available claims surrounding that company, and then cashed in by selling those same rights to the highest bidder, whether it was a positive test drilling or just a discovery of a particularly rich kimberlite deposit in the area. Sometimes he used his own money for his deals and other times he brought in outside investors in order to buy up larger amounts of claims, and pocket larger amounts of money. In short, while everyone else was busy looking for diamonds in the hope of making their fortune sometime in the distant future, Urban was making his own small fortune without waiting for the distant future, by buying and selling land that so far had yielded nothing more than the promise of the possibility of the potential of diamonds.

This was how it worked: In Canada at that time, mineral rights were assigned by "standing in line," which meant that every time a claim lapsed, the owner of that claim had to literally stand in line and reclaim their mineral rights for each section of property. That practice has now been replaced with a lottery system, where all interested parties buy tickets for a chance at winning the rights to each claim. Urban bought every claim in the areas receiving the most attention, hiring his co-workers at the prison and his employees at the U-Haul to stand in line for him. First, he bought up all of the available claims, and then he picked up other owners' claims by showing up every time anyone missed a deadline. Then, he would sell off sections as they became more valuable due to speculation or hype in the area and use that money to buy even larger claims. Finally, he scored big when a substantial number of De Beers' claims came up for renewal and their representatives were snowed in and unable to stand in line. Urban's hired guards quickly snatched up De Beers' claims, and his dominance in the area continued to grow.

Local news reports told of instances where people standing in line were bullied and intimidated by hired thugs who worked for competing companies. There was even one article about a female employee of one company who was beaten up by employees of a competing company. Later, in retelling the story of his early days in Canada, Urban once said to an almost 300 pound observer, "You are tiny compared to some of the no-necked guys I had standing in line."

And so it went. Urban's land claims, and his bank account, continued to grow. He added even more money to his pocket by trading in and out of companies springing up in the area, always seeming to buy their stock at exactly the right time, and more importantly, to sell it for a handsome profit during the height of the frenzy triggered by whatever report, rumor, or marginally positive news was driving the company's stock. He hedged his bets by using other investors' money through his own companies, until finally, in late 2000, Casavant Mining Co. was created.

By 2002, Urban had accumulated the mining claims to 1.4 million acres of land in the Saskatchewan area, with options on another 500,000 acres. But this time, instead of selling off the land piecemeal, Urban had other plans. Having leased the mineral rights to all of the land adjoining De Beers' claims (a maneuver later known among the shareholders as "Operation Surround"), he was convinced it was time to turn his potential diamond producing land into real gold. He needed money; money to do test drillings on the property, money to expand his holdings, and money to pay himself while he was placing the biggest bet of his life.

Urban decided to take Casavant Mining Company public, to sell shares to finance his ambitious plans, and he went looking for someone who could help him get started, who would help him place the bet of a lifetime. To Urban, what transpired over the next couple of months must have seemed like either pre-destination or the most remarkable set of coincidences ever, or at least in his lifetime. One after another, each piece of the puzzle fell perfectly in place, and every player appeared just as they were needed, almost as if on cue.

And so, in the fall of 2002, the stage was set.

First, enter a group of businessmen representing Ian McIntyre. The details on McIntyre are a bit sketchy, but it is known that McIntyre had connections to Chancery Corporate Services, an offshore financier based in Bermuda, land of "asset protection," where those who are lucky enough, or rich enough, can enjoy anonymous banking, use anonymous credit cards, establish anonymous companies, and, for all practical purposes, become anonymous themselves. Once these millionaires become anonymous in Bermuda, they pay no individual or corporate income taxes, no estate, inheritance or gift taxes, no employment taxes, no death duties, no withholding taxes, no sales taxes, no taxes of any kind. They utilize "private banking" services offered by Chase Manhattan, J.P. Morgan, Merrill Lynch, Morgan Stanley, and Goldman Sachs, as well as Citibank, who alone is said to administer shell corporations and private trusts for over 40,000 clients.

Bermuda, where hedge funds and financial institutions like Chancery Corporate Services operate in secrecy, and anonymously lend money to small American start-up companies. Companies like Casavant Mining.

The four businessmen who approached Urban Casavant fronted a company called BBX Equity Group, a Las Vegas equity financing company that promised to help startup companies "achieve the asset, revenue and profit growth needed to be a top performing OTCBB Stock." Assets, revenue, and profit growth were exactly what Urban needed.

For whatever reason, predestination or coincidence, Gary Walters, Mike King, Richard Taulli, and a seldom seen but always in-the-know man named John Edwards made Urban Casavant an offer too good to refuse: a ready made public company shell, CyberMark International, where Urban could simply move all of the assets of Casavant Mining Company and begin selling stock. Originally incorporated in Delaware, CyberMark had changed its domicile to Nevada, a state whose laws allowed corporations to operate in as much secrecy as possible within the United States and had no restrictions on the number of shares that could be issued and sold to investors.

Over the next few months, so many players would enter and exit the stage that it would take a scorecard to remember who was who, but the four men who originally came to the table would appear again and again, bringing with them a cast of secondary players who seemed to always appear right on cue. Early on, the majority of the action seemed to revolve around one or the other of this quartet of seasoned business professionals.

This is how it happened: On November 25, 2002, CyberMark acquired mining claims held by five companies owned by Urban Casavant and his family in exchange for $2 million in cash and three billion shares of CyberMark stock. On the same day, Ian McIntyre appointed Urban Casavant to take over his positions as sole director, president, and CEO of CyberMark, who in turn appointed his wife, Carolyn Casavant, as vice-president of the company, his 22 year-old son, Wesley, as treasurer, and his daughter, Cindy, as corporate secretary. Overnight, CyberMark International was transformed from an almost defunct online gaming company to a diamond exploration company with 1.4 million acres of mining claims in Canada surrounding De Beers' properties, and Urban had gone from being in debt to having $2 million in the bank, plus a substantial ownership in the new company. It was just that simple, and to Urban Casavant, it must have seemed almost too good to be true.

In November, Mike King was appointed to the company's executive board of directors, and his company, Princeton Research, was hired to handle public relations for Casavant Mining. Less than a week later, David DeSormeau, who was reportedly also introduced to Urban through Gary Walters and Mike King, was hired to "implement over the next 45 days a customized intranet platform connecting the Company's headquarters in Las Vegas with its field operations in Saskatchewan and throughout the world." The purpose of the new accounting system was to "ensure seamless integration with newly enacted Securities and Exchange Commission auditing practices for public companies." The press release announcing DeSormeau's hiring (which oddly misspelled his name "DeSorneau") ended with "The Company welcomes Mr. DeSorneau to its growing team of seasoned experts and advisory consultants." It wasn't long before DeSormeau was named the Chief Financial Officer of the company.

On December 4, Casavant Mining issued a Letter of Intent to acquire Juina Mining Corp., described in the press release as "a diamond mining company with working interests in producing diamond fields in Brazil." The Juina Mining shares, known simply by the trading symbol of GEMM, would be distributed to shareholders of Casavant Mining, and the purchase was heralded as "the first in many targeted acquisitions and roll-ups of existing diamond and other mineral resources companies."

Urban, in the first of what would soon become a tradition, issued an eloquent statement that captured perfectly his vision for the company's future:

"We are a new breed of prospectors and miners. With a quantum leap in technology, both hardware and software, we have the necessary tools to quickly and cost effectively evaluate mineral claims. The bottom line is to find diamonds and other precious metals at minimum cost against the world market price. We can do that, and our fellow junior mining company executives know that, creating for us the perfect opportunity to capitalize on what we know for the benefit of our shareholders."

Two days later, another high-profile board member, Dr. Rupert A. I. Perrin, was brought in by Walters and King. According to the press release, Dr. Perrin, twice nominated for a Nobel Prize in science, had developed the first early pregnancy test, was credited with major advances in HIV-1 and AIDS testing, and was a "recipient of the Wisdom Award, which is given to those persons who display excellence in various fields of study. The first recipients of the Wisdom Award included Albert Einstein, Linus Pauling, Samuel Golding, Dr. Jonas Salk, Dr. Armand Hammer, Harry S. Truman and Dwight D. Eisenhower." And again, the PR ended with a quote from Urban:

> *"We are humbled that Dr. Perrin has agreed to become a member of our Board of Directors. Dr. Perrin has a wealth of inter-disciplinary skills and worldwide contacts. We will endeavor to follow the high mark of excellence and achievements already experienced by Dr. Perrin."*

True to his word, Urban announced another planned acquisition on December 16th, saying "negotiations are underway to acquire 60% of the common shares in Dia Bras Exploration, Inc., a Canadian diamond exploration company with projects in Canada and the Republic of Guinea, West Africa." The Dia Bras projects in Canada were along the Trans Canada Highway in the general area where seven small diamonds had been found while the highway was being built.

After trading as CMKI for the last couple of months of 2002, opening at half a cent per share, climbing to a nickel, and then settling in at around a penny, Casavant Mining began trading under the symbol CMKM on the Over the Counter Bulletin Board exchange in January of 2003, and sold their very first shares of stock under the new symbol at a bargain price of just over a penny a share.

Chapter 5 – Got CMKX?

*"Our mining claims surround the approximate 58,000 acres of Kensington &
De Beers. Recently De Beers purchased themselves back private, for a stock
purchase price of 17+ Billion USD. It is a well known rumor in the area that
De Beers tremendous expense of both time and money to go back private is
a solid indication of the tremendous diamond wealth of the Forte á la Corne
diamondiferous kimberlites.*

*We have not assessed the 'Real Value' of the 1.9 million acres currently under our
control. It is also believed that De Beers may have mines on their smaller parcel
valued as much as $40 Billion USD to $80 Billion USD. Although there are no
guarantees that the company's mineral yields will produce any such amounts-the
likelihood definitely exists.*

*If these projections are even remotely close, which we have reason to believe may
very well be the case, it only makes a whole lot of sense that the mines which may
be discovered on our much larger properties will be a real force to reckon within
the world of Diamonds. The Forte á la Corne area could very well be the most
important diamond discovery of the century. CMKI has strategically planned
more staked acreage than any of its surrounding competitors."*

~Urban Casavant, CEO, Casavant Mining Kimberlite International,
November 27, 2002

In the world of "penny stocks," those stocks priced under a dollar a share, one
million shares was, and still is, the magic number. There was something about
owning a million shares of stock, the way the phrase rolled off of the tongue
during casual conversation, the idea that if the company *did* succeed, and somehow
climbed in value to…say…a measly dollar a share, the shareholder became an
instant millionaire. Goodbye 9-to-5, hello American dream. For shareholders who
bought into the CMKM version of the American dream in January of 2003, even
if they bought at the high of the first week, that shot at a million dollars cost them
a mere $15,000.

If those earliest CMKM shareholders had spent that same fifteen thousand
dollars on shares of Wal-Mart stock, they would have been the proud owners of
somewhere around 270 shares of Wal-Mart, which would have to climb to an
impossible $3,700 *per share* to turn them into millionaires. CMKM, on the other
hand, the little diamond mine company with the big plans, who now controlled the
rights to 1.9 million acres of claims in the diamond-rich Forte á la Corne region
in Saskatchewan, Canada, surrounding the De Beers diamond claims, only had to
go to one single dollar a share to turn every one of those same shareholders into
millionaires. Sure, it was a long shot, but as the saying goes, "no risk, no reward."
And since the average CMKM (soon to be CMKX) shareholder eventually ended

up owning 16 million shares, a little basic math showed that the price would only have to hit just over six cents a share to turn that average CMKM/CMKX shareholder into a millionaire.

They came from all walks of life – and like most things connected with CMKM, they were a microcosm of society as a whole, and as a society, they began to pair off into communities, choosing their neighborhoods according to their politics, their religious beliefs, and most importantly, their belief in the company itself. In this case, the CMKM communities were internet message boards and chat rooms. How diverse was this "microcosm of society," this loose collection of communities of CMKM shareholders? As was usually the case, the message board posters themselves provided the best description of what was going on in the trenches. This is how, years later, a poster who called himself `diggerman`, but posted under the gender-confused name of `diamondlady` on the *cmkx.net* message board, described the wide array of individuals who made up the CMKI turned CMKM turned CMKX shareholders, written in the colorful language that typified internet message boards:

> `Urban's vision of a million millionaires sets in motion if not a million, at least 50-60,000 more visions of charity which beget @ in their own way hundreds of thousands of $charitable acts helping common folk till you have (just as when you pluck a bud and get 2 buds from one) ...."A million millionaires" on the Casavant tree of fortune!!!!!`

> `But not just any million millionaires. We are common folk, rich folk, poor folk, laborers, professionals, all types.. not what the norm is or one might expect....carpenters, mechanics, nurses, police, air force, desk jockeys, navy, teachers, marines, firemen, coast guard, plumbers, army…so many more too numerous to count. All real people who suffer all the same physical and mental sufferings, making up the shareholders of CMKX.`

> `The incredible transformation occurring to all of us is powerful and for the most part hopefully positive... unlike the shielded from reality type of Elite, who have either never known or forgotten what it's like to go without for another's wellbeing, or given up something precious...Many of the CMKX shareholders are the people who will help Mr. Urban Casavant complete his vision of "A million millionaires." Each in their own way will create interesting happenings set in motion by all the CMKXers' new found wealth.`

That's exactly what the CMKM/CMKX shareholders were: common folk, rich folk, poor folk, laborers, professionals, and on and on....and yes, even soldiers. This diverse group of individuals would buy their shares and settle into a comfortable internet neighborhood, where they would make new friends, swap stories, and share dreams. While the discussion often centered on the company itself, many of the shareholders shared a vision of doing something good with the rewards they hoped to reap from CMKX. If they had a tendency to be overly optimistic, it was at least partially fueled by an underlying faith that extended into all areas of their lives. They truly did hope to create, through "hundreds of thousands of charitable acts," a million millionaires, all "set in motion by the CMKXers new found wealth."

In fact, one of the reasons many CMKM/CMKX shareholders bought into the company in the first place was Urban Casavant's promise to promote and deliver what was known as "conflict free diamonds." After the tragic events of September 11, 2001, and with the war in Afghanistan already raging and tensions with Iraq running high, terrorism was suddenly a worldwide concern. In December of 2002, Urban had addressed those concerns in a way that made those earliest CMKM shareholders feel as if they were doing their small part to combat terrorism on a global level.

Casavant Mining announced the opening of an office in Belgium which, according to their press release, "would promote the 'Casavant' diamond brand and assist in the support of 'conflict free' diamonds." The PR stated, "as much as 15% of the $40 billion in diamonds sold in the U.S. annually are 'conflict diamonds.' These diamonds are mined and sold by rebel groups who use the profits to buy arms and to conduct terrorism against legal governments and citizenry." In the press release Urban went on to say:

"Both the European Union and the U.S. governments are actively legislating against the sale of 'conflict diamonds' which are sometimes referred to as 'blood diamonds.' Since the U.S. represents 65% of the world market for gem quality diamonds, the issue of 'conflict diamonds' is something we cannot ignore. Our diamonds come from Canada and other conflict free diamond sources throughout the world. We plan on mining diamonds from our own deposits and buying conflict free diamonds at wholesale. We will merchandise these diamonds under the 'Casavant' brand name. Both retailers and consumers can place their trust that a 'Casavant' diamond is conflict free; mined in an ethical and environmentally friendly manner; and represent the highest in quality and value. We plan on becoming involved in the entire sales chain in diamond merchandising with the view of becoming the largest wholesaler of Canadian diamonds, not just a mining company. This provides our shareholders with a more balanced investment opportunity and gives us income stream while we are developing our Saskatchewan diamondiferous kimberlite claims."

It was just the kind of statement that fostered trust for Urban among the CMKM shareholders. His actions seemed to investors to encompass the perfect balance between an aggressive plan for financial success, and an ethical, moral, and humane approach to business. On December 9, in an article entitled "Firm to

Market 'Non-Conflict' Diamonds" in the *Rapaport News*, Peter C. Mastrosimone discussed the opening of the Belgian office and the aggressive marketing plans for the Casavant brand name:

> *"Casavant Mining Kimberlite International, a Canadian diamond exploration company, is opening an office in Antwerp to market the stones it expects to find in Canada as conflict-free. Until its own claims pan out, Casavant will buy diamonds it can independently certify as conflict-free and sell them to retailers, according to company spokesman John Dolkart. Dolkart said the Casavant brand should start appearing in unique jewelry designs in the first quarter of 2003.*
>
> *The firm holds exploration claims in Canada's Saskatchewan Province and Brazil. It will focus its marketing efforts on Canadian stones. 'It makes sense that you can promote them as not only being Canadian diamonds — with all the attributes of Canadian diamonds — but also conflict-free,' Dolkart said. 'As a consumer, I don't see anybody ensuring diamonds are conflict-free. We'll consider providing an insurance policy that says they're conflict-free.'"*

When they weren't busy pre-spending their fortunes on acts of goodwill, the shareholders were dissecting the frequent press releases the company was putting out...not just reading the news, but reading between the lines of the press releases, and trying to determine the difference between what was fact, what they believed could be "reasonably assumed," and what was just good old-fashioned unsubstantiated rumor.

The game went something like this:

FACT: On January 7, even before CMKI became CMKM, and long before it became CMKX, Urban Casavant initiated a shareholder audit, and advised "every shareholder to hold his shares in certificate form, and if the shares are held in street name to make sure that he registers the shares in his own name." In the same press release, the company went on to say:

> *"CMKI has been informed that majority shareholders plan on holding their shares in certificate form indefinitely if it helps the Company combat 'naked short selling.' Under a naked short sale, short positions are not declared, shares are not borrowed to cover the short sale, and the shares are sold without delivering the stock to the purchaser. Real shareholder ownership is undermined by naked short sales of stock and failed deliveries of real certificates that artificially inflate ownership and devalue the price of the securities."*

REASONABLE ASSUMPTION: It was really just a fancy way of saying that Urban believed there were shares being sold that were never delivered by the brokers, who instead placed "electronic book entries" in their clients accounts, *saying* they owned the shares, but never actually buying the real shares on the open market. Urban was convinced there was a naked short position in the stock, meaning someone was shorting the stock, or selling stock that they didn't own or hadn't borrowed, in essence betting the price of the stock would go down. The endless supply of what were essentially counterfeit shares flooding the market created so much negative selling pressure that eventually the stock would become worthless.

If every shareholder forced their broker to actually deliver their shares in certificate form, the brokers would have to buy back the missing shares from existing shareholders, and the price would inevitably go up, making the CMKM shareholders relatively better off than they already were.

(Good old-fashioned unsubstantiated) RUMOR: The naked short position was so massive that the brokers and bad guys who were responsible for it would be caught in a huge scandal, and the payoff would be so huge that every CMKM shareholder would become an instant millionaire, and the entire financial system might collapse from the sheer scope of the problem.

Would that be the case? At the time, no one really knew for certain, but it didn't matter, because there was an endless supply of good old-fashioned unsubstantiated rumors, ranging wildly in theory and logic, all sharing one thing – every one ended with the prediction that every CMKM shareholder would become an instant millionaire.

Naked short selling was an issue that had just recently began to receive exposure at the grassroots level. Advocates for stock market reform cited the thousands of companies collapsing from the weight of continuous manipulative selling pressure on their stocks. In many cases, more shares were traded in a single day than existed in the entire legal float. Thousands of these small companies were eventually driven to bankruptcy, unable to raise the funds they needed to bring their product, technology, or medical or environmental breakthrough to market. It was obvious something was seriously wrong in the stock market, and even though the mainstream media largely ignored the issue, a handful of internet advocates, along with some of the victimized companies and shareholders themselves, were steadily bringing a greater awareness to the problem.

Even without the inevitable leap from fact to outrageous rumor, the idea that there might be a substantial naked short position in CMKM/CMKX was enough to give shareholders just one more reason to buy. That knowledge, combined with the fact that they held the mineral rights to a huge portion of what some people were calling the largest diamond find in the entire world, was enough to create a buzz that soon spread like wildfire. Fueled by a steady stream of positive press releases magnified a thousand fold by the CMKM internet rumor mill, the company's shareholder base continued to grow.

35

As with most companies that traded on the penny stock markets in the U.S., many shareholders who invested in CMKM first heard about the company on the message boards for other stocks. In late 2002, rumors appeared on the message boards of Pinnacle Business Management, Inc., which traded under the symbol of PCBM, that there was some kind of relationship between PCBM and CMKM. PCBM had been proactively involved in the battle against naked short selling, claiming that unscrupulous characters were selling billions of counterfeit shares to unsuspecting investors, hurting the company's ability to raise additional capital and deflating the stock price. Alan C., one of the PCBM shareholders who also invested in CMKM, recalled how he was first drawn to the company:

"Some posters had posted on the PCBM board that there was a tie between PCBM and CMKM. Reading this several of us began reading the CMKM thread. On December 31, 2002, CMKM announced it had established an 'investor hotline' and listed the number in that PR. The day the PR came out I called the number and explained to the gentleman who answered that while I did not own a single share of CMKM I owned a huge number of PCBM shares, and that it had been rumored that a connection existed. That gentleman then congratulated me and told me I was going to be rich. He went on to say that PCBM was the targeted pink sheet company that CMKM was going to acquire and they would transfer a valuable zinc mine into PCBM. Why were they interested in PCBM? They were interested because of the large, loyal, international shareholder base that PCBM had. He went on to share other information with me that caused me to not buy the stock. Why? Because I felt he had provided me with inside information and the arrest of Martha Stewart for trading on inside information was getting lots of press at this time. While I did not buy I did share this information with some PCBMers via a chat room and another PCBMer called and was told essentially the same information I was. After a few months had passed I felt enough time had passed so I could comfortably begin accumulating the stock, which I did."

Alan C. wasn't the only PCBM shareholder who bought into CMKM. The PCBM/CMKM rumors began around the time CMKM announced they were in negotiations to acquire substantial zinc mining claims in Saskatchewan. They said the zinc claims would then be rolled "into a pink sheet company it has targeted for acquisition based upon its diverse and active shareholder base." Then, shortly afterwards, rumors of an imminent deal seemed to be confirmed by CMKM in a February 14th press release that said the company had "commenced negotiations to reorganize its business, in conjunction with another Bulletin Board publicly trading company." The plan was to transfer all the assets of CMKM into the other company, with CMKM shareholders becoming shareholders in the "new entity." It was another step in Urban's ongoing battle to ferret out and eliminate any counterfeit shares that existed in CMKM. Even though the PR contained the usual "no guarantee" disclaimer and didn't name the company that they were in negotiations with, it seemed obvious it was PCBM. Based on the early rumors and subliminal press releases, thousands of Pinnacle shareholders eventually became

CMKM shareholders as well. After updating progress on the proposed merger in subsequent press releases on February 18th and 24th, the company never mentioned it again.

Unfortunately, while the number of shareholders and the volume of stock traded were rising, the price began to drop. Instead of climbing towards the magic "million dollar" mark, shareholders who paid $15,000 for their one million shares watched helplessly while their investment lost value. Two weeks after those same million shares peaked at $15,000, they were worth only half that amount. By mid-February, the value had dropped to $3,500, and by the end of that month, they were worth $1,500; a loss of ninety percent in less than two months.

Behind the scenes, something seemed to be going on in the company, early hints that things might not be as they seemed on the surface. Shortly after Urban sent out the PR asking shareholders to have their shares delivered to them in "cert" form, a footnote at the bottom of an entirely unrelated press release said simply: "Princeton Research Inc. no longer represents the company. The new exclusive investor relations firm is: Investor Relations, James Kenny/Ginger Gutierrez," with a new phone number and address listed. Mike King was out, a move followed by this cryptic comment: "We believe the recent steps taken by management will enhance the stability of the company stock." With David DeSormeau, Urban, and company attorney Brian Dvorak working together, it appeared to shareholders that CMKM was taking aggressive steps to clean up the company's accounting and share structure problems.

In early January, three Juina Mining (GEMM) executives, Jay McFadden, Richard Bending and BBX Equity's Richard Taulli, were appointed to executive positions and the board of directors of CMKM. Then, on March 31st, CMKM and GEMM abruptly terminated all negotiations pertaining to an earlier proposed merger.

Entering the spring of 2003, many shareholders speculated that Urban was "cleaning house" in order to eliminate whoever was manipulating the company's stock. Urban ousted Taulli and King (both connected with the original shell company that became Casavant Mining Kimberlite International) and announced plans to force a share count by merging *that* company into yet another entity.

What seemed like a mess for CMKM, and what was obviously a negative for those who were losing money on the company's stock, was viewed as an opportunity to buy shares on the .cheap for new shareholders, and as a way to average down their per-share cost for those who already owned stock. Once Urban had cleaned up the company and gotten rid of the criminal element that was illegally depressing the company's stock price, then those who bought low would reap the rewards.

By the end of March 2003, the cost of a CMKM lottery ticket consisting of a million shares of CMKM stock was an incredibly low $400, which unfortunately meant that those who spent $15,000 for a million shares only three months earlier now held stock worth...$400.

Chapter 6 – Viva Las Vegas!

I'm gonna keep on the run
I'm gonna have me some fun
If it costs me my very last dime
If I wind up broke up well
I'll always remember that I had a swingin' time
I'm gonna give it everything I've got
Lady luck please let the dice stay hot
Let me shoot a seven with every shot
Viva Las Vegas, Viva Las Vegas,
Viva, Viva Las Vegas

> "Viva Las Vegas"
> by Doc Pomus and Mort Shuman

John Edward Dhonau, known to everyone simply as Ed Dhonau, was with his wife at the Orleans Hotel and Casino celebrating her birthday on November 10, 2003. Their marriage had been far from perfect, and in fact, she had spent much of the past seven years back in their home state of Ohio while Dhonau was in Las Vegas doing what every entrepreneur did in Vegas…seeking his fortune.

After moving to Vegas in 1996 to help restructure a struggling long distance phone company supplier called Vision Quest, he went on to start his own company, a consulting firm called IB2000. Among his clients was a company called Voyager, where he assisted a Las Vegas attorney named Donald Stoecklein. Stoecklein also represented the legendary Robert Maheu, who had masterminded the attempted assassination of Fidel Castro during the ill-fated Bay of Pigs invasion in 1961, and who later became Howard Hughes' right-hand man.

Another company Dhonau worked for through IB2000 was a publicly traded company called Crystalix; he helped restructure the company after it was discovered the president and vice-president were convicted felons. Dhonau helped insert the new officers at Crystalix; Kevin T. Ryan and John Woodward. Ryan was a partner in a company called Global Intelligence with Bob Maheu and his son Peter Maheu, while Woodward was the attorney for U.S. Canadian Minerals.

But on this night, as Ed Dhonau would later recall, he was sitting in the Orleans Casino, perched on a stool at one of the quarter slot machines that stretched in rows across the noisy room, listening to the man seated next to him talk excitedly about winning $59,000 two nights earlier. After introducing himself, he spent the next thirty minutes listening to stories unlike anything he had ever heard. The man, whose name was Urban Casavant, told Dhonau about Forte á la Corne, about Saskatchewan, about De Beers' presence in the region…but most of all, he talked about diamonds. It was almost a repeat of the life-altering conversation Urban had with the stranger in Prince Albert years before, but this time he was the seasoned expert, and Ed Dhonau was the wide-eyed novice hearing the stories for the very first time.

Like Urban almost twenty years before, Ed was hooked. He spent the next few weeks researching the rush to find diamonds in Canada, and learned about De Beers and other companies' efforts to secure the mineral rights to millions of acres in and surrounding Saskatchewan.

Then, a few weeks later, in another "accidental meeting," he ran into Urban and his wife Carolyn while they were having dinner at the Orleans. This time, it was Ed who was excited, telling Urban, "I researched what you shared with me, and oh my God, there's something up there!" They ended their second conversation by exchanging phone numbers.

By December of 2003, less than two months after Ed Dhonau first heard of diamond mining in Canada, and with no mining experience whatsoever, he started a new corporation called Nevada Minerals. He would later say Urban taught him how to find and file claims in the Saskatchewan area, and he began to acquire a few claims for Nevada Minerals. Suddenly, based on a chance meeting at the quarter slot machines in a Vegas casino, Ed Dhonau was in the diamond mining business.

Almost immediately, both parties mutually benefited from their lucky meeting at the Orleans Casino. Over the prior couple of years, Ed Dhonau had also built a business relationship with a company called Barrington Foods. After his initial meetings with Urban, Ed talked to Rendal Williams, the CEO of the floundering food company, about the mining business. Dhonau had originally met Rendal Williams through Williams' attorney, Brian Dvorak, and as he did later with Urban Casavant, they "exchanged phone numbers." Dhonau and Dvorak had worked together on several other business deals, including Barrington Foods and its prior incarnation as eBait, another failed company. Dhonau eventually became a consultant for Rendal Williams and Barrington Foods, which lost huge amounts of money as a soy protein and whole milk substitute producer. In fact, the only substantial revenue that either company generated was from the sale of stock as publicly traded companies. Dhonau also worked with former SEC attorney D. Roger Glenn in his dealings with U.S. Canadian Minerals.

Was Ed Dhonau's encounter with Urban Casavant entirely by chance, or was it by design? Was that even their first meeting? Dhonau associate Brian Dvorak had already been the attorney for CMKI for almost a year before Dhonau and Urban's encounter at the Orleans casino.

Regardless of when they met and under what circumstances, that single meeting would soon bring together a list of players who would eventually become very familiar names to CMKM/CMKX shareholders. Dvorak was already involved, but in the coming months, Roger Glenn, Rendal Williams, Donald Stoecklein, Kevin Ryan, John Woodward, and even the legendary Robert Maheu would become household names in the CMKX saga. Unknown to CMKM shareholders and the general public at the time, even John Edwards was a major shareholder in both PCBM and Barrington Foods.

Rendal Williams, shortly after meeting with Ed Dhonau in late November, suddenly decided to give up the soy protein business and changed the name of his company from Barrington Foods to U.S. Canadian Minerals. Like Dhonau, Williams, who had absolutely no experience in mining, was now the CEO of a publicly traded mining company. Instead of diamonds, Williams decided he was going into the gold mining business and began selling shares of stock as a gold mining company.

Even before his November 2003 meeting with Ed Dhonau, Urban had been busy creating new alliances and partnerships, while at the same time terminating earlier business relationships. During the Juina Mining negotiations, CMKM had entered into a lease agreement for an ancient Chinese jade collection supposedly valued at $50 million dollars, with the intent of taking it on tour. Then in April, the agreement was cancelled.

In March, CMKM announced plans to spin off a new company called Casavant International Mining Corporation, which would own the zinc mining claims they had acquired earlier that year. The president of the new company was Urban's brother Ron Casavant, and the secretary/treasurer was none other than David DeSormeau. It was a far cry from the original plan to place the zinc claims in a publicly traded company with a "diverse and active shareholder base." Still, CMKM appeared to be moving steadily forward.

On April 1st, CMKM terminated negotiations to acquire a controlling interest in Dia Bras Exploration. The terminations of the jade collection lease agreement, the Juina Mining acquisition, and the Dia Bras deal were all said to be part of an ongoing effort to "streamline operations and continue the company's focus on diamond exploration."

And move forward they did:

- On August 19th, they announced a 2-1 forward split of the company's stock, giving every CMKM shareholder an additional share for every share they owned.

- On August 23rd, they announced plans to go public with Casavant International Mining (CIM), and to give every CMKM shareholder one share of CIM for every share of CMKM that they owned.

- On September 3rd, they purchased 25 additional mining claim leases from North Sask Ventures Limited, two of which were "adjacent to known diamond-bearing property operated by Kensington (KRT), Cameco, and De Beers joint venture in Forte á la Corne."

- On September 18th, they reached an agreement to acquire $900,000 from three publicly traded diamond exploration companies active in the Forte á la Corne area. The following day they revealed the names of the companies: United Carina Resources, Consolidated Pine Channel Gold, and Shane Resources.

As they were busy creating new entities, negotiating with existing ones (and then terminating those negotiations), CMKM seemed to be making steady progress on their quest to find diamonds as well. They hired Fugro Airborne Survey to conduct an "airborne aero magnetic survey" in search of potential diamondiferous kimberlite pipes, and moved forward with plans to commence test drilling. Along the way, they continued to acquire additional mining claim leases, first in the Forte á la Corne area and then expanding into the Green Lake province in Saskatchewan.

CMKM also began an aggressive campaign to buy back their own shares of stock, which was perceived as a sign that not only was the company confident about their future prospects, but that they believed that the stock was undervalued as well. Plus, in the case of CMKM, it was easy to imagine that it was part of Urban's plan to regain control of the majority of his company's stock and expose whoever might be flooding the market with counterfeit shares. Over the course of a three-month period beginning in late September, they announced the repurchase of over twenty billion shares of company stock.

Then, on December 29, 2003, Urban Casavant announced that Casavant Mining Kimberlite International, Inc. was engaged in talks with unidentified mining companies who were interested in purchasing part of CMKM's claims:

"We are negotiating with two public companies who would like to buy sizable portions of our mining claims. Obviously they see substantial value in our claims. We will announce our decision of a buyout and the terms by the end of January 2004. Our goal is to make the best decision which will benefit our shareholders."

Chapter 7 – CMKXtreme

"CMKM management believes the company's future is as bright as diamonds."
~ Urban Casavant

The CMKX billboard looming over Vegas.
Courtesy of Jason Webb and Anthony Pullicino.

Two thousand and four was The Year of CMKX.

Urban Casavant ushered in the New Year by announcing that they would begin drilling in the Green Lake area as soon as they completed the permit process. Four days later they confirmed the buyback and retirement of another 1.8 billion shares of company stock. Seven days after that they announced the board of directors' final approval of the CIM spin-off, with all CMKM shareholders as of January 30th to receive shares in the new zinc mining company. In another CMKM flurry of activity, they issued a total of 22 press releases during the first quarter of 2004, including three in one day. There was so much going on within and around the company that it was almost impossible to keep up, but every new event triggered new excitement, new shareholders, and higher volume.

In January the company announced a pending name change and new trading symbol, and two months later made it official. Casavant Mining Kimberlite International became CMKM Diamonds, Inc., and on March 10, 2004 began trading under the symbol of CMKX. At the same time, the Carolyn Pipe (named after Urban's wife), was found to be diamondiferous when two small diamonds were extracted from a core sample.

Previously announced negotiations to sell part of the company's claims instead became a confusing series of acquisitions, buyouts, stock swaps, cash deals, and mining claim agreements with no fewer than eight companies. Two of the major players in the deals were Ed Dhonau's newly created mining entity Nevada Minerals, and Rendal Williams' soy protein business turned gold mining company, U.S. Canadian Minerals. Three more were companies owned or controlled by Rick Walker: Shane Resources, United Carina Resources and Consolidated Pine Channel Gold.

In March of 2004, CMKXtreme, a spin-off company of CMKM Diamonds, signed a deal to sponsor a National Hot Rod Association funny car. In a March 23rd article on the organization's website, it was announced that Urban Casavant would finance veteran race driver Jeff Arend on the NHRA circuit. The article featured an artist's rendition of the CMKXtreme Machine Funny Car sporting the driller wearing a hard hat with diamonds flying out the ground that would soon grace Arend's car. The rendition also included graphics that didn't make the final design: the words "OTC – CMKX ↑ .001" repeating as a scroll across the side of the car. Representing the company as being listed on more prestigious OTC Stock Market and showing a price that was ten times higher than the current share price was not only misleading, it was optimistic to the point of hyperbole.

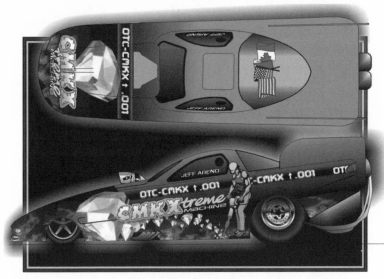

Artist's rendition of CMKXtreme Machine Funny Car.
Courtesy of CMKM Diamonds, Inc.

On April 12th, *DragRaceCanada.com* featured CMKXtreme and Arend in an article written by Bruce Biegler entitled "A New Urban Legend?" In that article, Urban was described as a "highly successful prospector around the world for some 17 years." The article quoted Urban discussing his plans for the company's future and the tie-in to CMKXtreme:

> *"In diamond mining there is never any 100% guarantee. We have a huge site with world class machinery and highly educated people exploring it. The gem quality is at least 2.5 X the world average and we are doing year round*

mining. I saw an opportunity where aligning myself with drag racing would have benefits to all of our thousands of shareholders. Not only does it help get the word out about the exact work we do -- we think it will also help attract additional investors."

Jeff Arend's Nitro Funny Car ran its first race for CMKXtreme on April Fool's Day, 2004. The flashy CMKXtreme logo was there, but the OTC reference and the inflated share price were nowhere to be found. As the season progressed, other additions were made to the car's design. "UCAD" (for business partner U.S. Canadian Minerals) was repeated across the back of the car and a logo for energy drink company Go Fast was added to either side.

The fast-paced excitement combined with the personal interaction with current and prospective shareholders made the races the place to be for CMKXers. When Urban Casavant wasn't there, his brother Ron was. UCAD CEO Rendal Williams was a regular, as was Nevada Minerals' president Ed Dhonau. Shareholders who were enthusiastic enough about the company were given preferential treatment, and often shared information with others on the boards. Sterling from *Sterling's Classroom*, *The Green Baron's* Ed Miller, Topogigio (known as Topo on the boards) and other high-profile shareholders became trusted sources of things to come. Sterling would gather information at the races and then add his own spin by projecting what appeared to be fact into the realm of theory:

"At the races, everyone was there... Urban, Ron Casavant, Rendal Williams, Emerson Koch, Brian Dvorak, Dave DeSormeau, Roger Glenn, Ed Dhonau... from what Ed Dhonau told me, he didn't want to become an official member of CMKX because he was making too much money trading the stock. They all seemed like good guys. They'd be telling you certain things, then they'd go off and tell other shareholders other things, and then those shareholders would be coming back and tell me. Rendal Williams would be walking around showing gold to people, and to me, it looked like the real deal. He would just pull it out of his pocket. There were hundreds of shareholders who saw it.

And Urban would be talking about how much CIM was worth, and all the zinc we had. And when I was researching, I read that wherever there's gold, there's something like a three hundred times better chance that there's uranium too, so I'd go back and post that. They were passing out t-shirts from the back of the painted up Humvee, and they were showing off the gold. It was hard not to believe."

Sterling, like many shareholders, forged friendships with shareholders from the races and met others who he knew from the message boards and chatrooms. He was treated like a celebrity because of *Sterling's Classroom* where he posted his own theories and information from other sources:

"At the races, all the other shareholders acted really happy to see me, like I was part of CMKX or something. And there would be times that I was standing

NHRA driver Jeff Arend's CMKXtreme Machine Funny Car. Courtesy of Jason Webb and Anthony Pullicino.

CMKX diamond driller logo on funny car. Courtesy of Jason Webb and Anthony Pullicino.

CMKX at the races. Courtesy of CMKM Diamonds, Inc.

At the races, Urban courts Sterling, owner of one of the most popular investor boards. Courtesy of Jason Webb and Anthony Pullicino.

Urban and Carolyn Casavant courting the military at the races. Courtesy of Jason Webb and Anthony Pullicino.

*right next to Urban, and people would come up and ask me questions, and I'd be explaining my theories. Urban or Ed Dhonau would be standing next to me, or one of the other company officials, so it coulda looked like it was something that could really be happening, and not just theories. I would be explaining something about what the company **could** do, and Urban could have stopped me and said, 'No that's not going to happen' but he didn't. For instance, I had posted about how the company could issue dividends, and I told Topo about it. He mentioned it to Urban, and Urban said, 'You all are going to be living off of your dividends.'*

Then, at one of the races, Urban came up and said, 'Hey I really appreciate all of you coming out to support the shareholders and the company, put your name on this list. I want to reward all the shareholders here at the race today.' We didn't know what the reward was, but later we found out that he was giving all six hundred or so shareholders who were there three million shares each of restricted stock, and everyone was saying 'Sterling is getting paid to pump CMKX.' I had this idea called 'pay it forward' because the bashers were beating us up about getting the shares, and I was trying to figure how to deflect the criticism. I said that anyone who needed the money, I would give them my 3 million shares; I would 'pay it forward.'"

According to `Willy Wizard`, `Topo` was one of the main sources of information from the races. `Willy Wizard` recalled that `Topo` was telling shareholders at the Denver race that they would be receiving .54 a share for their stock. He claimed that the company would make the announcement in a PR the following week…which never happened. It didn't matter. The story quickly spread, and like most rumors, it became accepted as fact in many circles.

The races spawned story after story, all dutifully reported back to the chatrooms and boards. One report, either fact or legend, was that Ed Dhonau rolled a wheelbarrow full of diamonds into a room of prospective shareholders. No one seemed to know whether the diamonds were real or fake, or even if they belonged to CMKX, but either way, it was a still a memorable story. As time passed, the line between reality and fantasy, and fact and fiction became increasingly blurred. Eric R., a shareholder who attended the races in Chicago, recalled his encounter with `Topo` and Ed Miller:

"We tried to pry information from company representatives there. We were told by some guy going by the name of Topo that a movie deal had been inked with Oliver Stone directing and a 20 million dollar budget. The movie was supposed to tell the story of Urban. While Urban himself was not there, we did have a lengthy conversation with his brother Ron. He was emphatic about their upcoming 'aggressive winter drill program' and the likely appreciation of our investment. We also had a brief conversation with Ed Miller who runs the Green Baron stock promotion web site and he assured us that it was the stock play of a lifetime."

**Shareholders Jason Webb and Topogigio in Ecuador with the CMKX crew.
Courtesy of Jason Webb and Anthony Pullicino.**

Eric's visit was typical of the kind of stories that made their way from the races to the internet. Another shareholder, `chris1`, recalled meeting Urban at the race in Illinois:

> *"Back in May of 2004 I went to the Joliet, Illinois races and I took my daughter. I thought it would really be cool for her to see the cars and 'hey, maybe we will see the car your dad has invested in.'*
>
> *We went to the area where the car was and there he was standing like a God. UC himself, no one around him. He was drinking a Go Fast. Back in those early days you could walk right up to him and have a conversation, no bodyguard.*
>
> *I said 'Hello Mr. Casavant, how are you?' He responded, 'Fine, are you enjoying the races?' I told him I had been a shareholder since day one and was very excited by what was happening.*
>
> *He looked into my eyes and said 'We are driving truckloads of diamonds out of there.' I swear on that phrase.*

49

> *He offered my daughter a Go Fast and put his hand on her head and said, 'Your dad is gonna be very wealthy.'*
>
> *No pump, no bash just a story that is true."*

In July of the same year, an article in *National Dragster Magazine* announced the signing of another driver to the CMKXtreme Team:

> *"Veteran Pro Stock Bike rider Connie Cohen and her husband Marc Cohen of C.C. Rider Racing will have a new sponsor, CMKM Diamonds, a front-runner of diamond exploration in Canada, at the Sears Craftsman NHRA Nationals in Madison. CMKM Diamonds also sponsors the CMKXtreme Machine Funny Car piloted by Canadian driver Jeff Arend.*
>
> *Urban Casavant is the founder and current chairman of the board for CMKM Diamonds. His brother Ron Casavant will be the team manager for the race."*

CMKXtreme motorcycle race driver Connie Cohen.
Courtesy of Jason Webb and Anthony Pullicino.

CMKXtreme soon added one more veteran Nitro Funny Car driver to their growing stable of NHRA teams when they signed Tony Bartone to a contract shortly after the Connie Cohen deal was announced. In addition to the racing teams themselves, CMKXtreme raised their profile by erecting "Got CMKX?" billboards at the Las Vegas Motor Speedway and on the roadsides leading to the racetracks. The billboard at the Vegas track alone was valued at over $800,000, and the sponsorship of the teams ran into the millions. Add the cost of tens of thousands of CMKXtreme logo t-shirts, brochures, handout maps of company claims, and free food and drinks, and it was obvious that CMKX had money to spare. If they were spending that much just to promote the company and its stock, it wasn't difficult to imagine how much they must have been spending on their "year round mining efforts and aggressive winter drill program."

Superstar Sammy Hagar: Got CMKX?
Courtesy of Jason Webb and Anthony Pullicino.

The excitement only escalated as time progressed. At one race, rock musician and celebrity Sammy Hagar was photographed wearing CMKXtreme racing gear, arms outstretched in victory. The pictures quickly made their way onto the internet. Later in the year, Nevada Secretary of State Dean Heller's involvement with the CMKXtreme Team would add even more credibility. FOX Sports showed a car crash directly under the CMKX billboard during a nationally televised race at the Las Vegas Motor Speedway, and the still photograph was circulated across cyberspace.

CMKX even spawned its own lexicon, phrases and words unique to CMKX shareholders. Some were created by the company as part of the hype and others were either coined by the shareholders or the result of typos on the message boards. Other times, phrases pulled from pop culture took on an entirely new meaning when applied to CMKX.

Andy Hill was one of the shareholders rewarded for his loyalty to the company when Urban eventually named him the head of investor relations. Hill went on to spawn several CMKXspeak phrases, including "Trust the Team!" and "SOOn." Hill's version of "SOOn" was actually "CLOSe," implying that once all four letters were capitalized the shareholders would hit the *Wheel of CMKXfortune* jackpot, but for some reason, "SOOn" became the word repeated hundreds of times on the boards.

"To da moon!!" was misspelled "To dsa moon!!" and "The Plan" was accidentally (and then intentionally) spelled "The Plam." Over the next couple of years dozens of words and phrases, including Stock Play of a Lifetime, The Mother Lode, True Believers, Sterling's Perfect Storm, The Sting, stuffium, Operation Surround, and Onward! would become part of the CMKX lexicon.

Jason Webb's truck, painted for CMKX.
Courtesy of Jason Webb and Anthony Pullicino.

While the races provided excitement and gave shareholders the opportunity to bond with company officials and other shareholders, they were also the source of stories of another type. The CMKXtreme teams, many times accompanied by Urban Casavant, would often visit children's hospitals during their stays in NHRA cities. A CMKXtreme press release highlighted one of their hospital visits at the Denver race in July of 2004:

> *"Jeff Arend and CMKX Pro Stock Bike rider Connie Cohen started the weekend with a visit to the pediatric wing of Presbyterian/St. Luke's Medical Center in downtown Denver on Friday morning. The pair went room to room visiting with children, signing autographs, posing for photographs and handing out CMKX souvenirs."*

It was just one of dozens of charitable acts that Urban and others involved with CMKX would become known for. Photo ops, pep speeches, and the distribution of company memorabilia to military troops heading overseas was a common occurrence. As always, the accompanying pictures became part of the visual experience of CMKX.

Other times, the acts were of a more personal nature. A shareholder who posted as `Salty Dog` recalled being at his father's hospital bedside and receiving a phone call from Urban. He told his father that everything would work out with CMKX, and that his family would be well-provided for. It was a reassuring sentiment to a CMKX shareholder who was literally on his deathbed.

At a NHRA race in Seattle, Urban Casavant came to the aid of one of his most loyal followers and company spokesperson, Melvin O'Neil. Uncle Melvi, who considered Urban "not a savvy businessman, but one of the best promoters the world has ever seen," experienced firsthand a side of Urban that most others had only heard about:

> *"Two of my sons died of aplastic anemia, an often fatal bone marrow disease where the bone marrow fails to produce new blood cells. Urban found out that my wife Vickie had the same condition, and he said, 'I'm sending you to a specialist in Seattle, do what I tell you or I'm going to fire you.' When we showed up in Seattle, there were hundreds and hundreds of bunches of flowers for Vickie, and hundreds of emails from shareholders. Urban sent her to a world-renowned doctor for treatment and paid for all of it.*
>
> *We went to the race in Seattle, and the announcer said 'CMKX welcomes Melvin and Vickie O'Neil to Seattle.' He gave a five minute speech, and 40,000 fans stood up and applauded. The doctor put Vickie on drug treatment and Urban paid for it for the first year, four thousand dollars every two months. That's why I say Urban has a heart of gold."*

Shareholder Kevin West recounted a story told to him by a good friend, who was also close friends with the Casavants. This one began 3,000 miles away in Ecuador, where the company had acquired rights to a gold mine in a business venture with Nevada Minerals. Several company officials and a handful of shareholders were flown down to tour the mines:

> *"On the night they arrived in Ecuador, they had a large dinner gathering with a lot of drinking going on. The next morning, they all got into a SUV and traveled for 4 hours into the mountains to get to the mines. On the way, Urban was severely hung over from the previous night's affairs. He was basically sick with his head down and needing to stop every time they came into an area where he could splash water on his face and walk around for a few minutes. With every stop... feeling very sick, Urban walked around and passed out $100 bills to the children on the street. Several thousand dollars worth from what I was told. Ed Dhonau was one of the men in the vehicle and made the comment, 'There goes Urban doing his thing again.' Mind you, no one on that trip was going as an investor and there was no other possible motive for Urban to do what he did, except that it was just his nature. The*

area this happened in is so poor that families live on less than $100 per month. A $100 bill is probably more money then any of these people have ever seen at one time in their entire lives."

CMKX in Ecuador. Clockwise from left front: Jason Webb (shareholder), Topogigio (shareholder), unknown, Rendal Williams, Ed Dhonau, Urban Casavant, Emerson Koch, David DeSormeau, Roger Glenn, and unknown shareholder.
Courtesy of Jason Webb and Anthony Pullicino.

The company-sponsored nationally televised racing teams, "Got CMKX?" billboards, celebrity photo ops, connections with high-ranking state officials, Hollywood movie deals, and stories of diamonds by the truckload kept shareholder excitement at fever-pitch level. The personal attention given to the shareholders and the charitable acts by the company gave them every reason to believe that their company was well on the way to prosperity. And at a hundred dollars per million shares, thousands were becoming charter members of the CMKX family.

Rendal Williams, Roger Glenn, unknown soldier, and Ed Dhonau in Ecuador. Courtesy of Jason Webb and Anthony Pullicino.

Emerson Koch, David Desormeau, and Roger Glenn holding gold from the American mine. Courtesy of Jason Webb and Anthony Pullicino.

Chapter 8 – The Stories Behind the Story

"Money means nothing, people do."

~ From a message posted on *Sterling's Classroom* message board, in remembrance of fellow shareholder Ty Merrick

It was true the shareholders of CMKX were "common folk, rich folk, poor folk, laborers, professionals, all types… not what the norm is or one might expect." With a shareholder base that eventually grew to over 50,000 people worldwide, the stories were indeed as varied as the shareholders themselves. Some invested on a whim, rolling the dice on a bet they knew was a long shot, but feeling this one could be *the one*, that once in a lifetime opportunity that makes millionaires out of nobodies, that could turn lives around in an instant. Unlike many penny stock investors who hoped to catch a quick run in the price and sell for a reasonable profit, the vast majority of CMKX shareholders invested in a dream. They invested with noble intentions and aspirations of helping others as well as themselves.

Dave and Barb Vanguntun first bought into Cybermark International (CMKI) in October of 2000, paying between $.07 to .20 a share. After hearing about the "staggering claims" held by CMKM Diamonds they invested more heavily and accumulated over 80 million CMKX shares. They bought during the peak of the CMKX hype when announcements such as Roger Glenn and Bob Maheu's hiring, the high-tech aerial surveys, and the "Carolyn Pipe" seemed to be a weekly occurrence. Hoping to make their dreams come true, Dave and Barb, "the first shareholders in CMKX," ended up owning 80 million shares of stock.

Bruce Barrett needed special education classes for his nine year-old son, Jake, who had learning disabilities. After making money on several penny stocks, including QBID, Barrett began buying CMKX at over a penny a share, and, attracted by the "sales job by Urban and crew," eventually bought 476 million shares. Bruce planned to establish a trust fund to ensure Jake would always have the care he needed.

Bruce Allen became a believer in the company's potential when Roger Glenn entered the picture, buying 70% of his 30 million shares:

> *"I had read his online 'clean up the markets' manifesto and said, 'WOW! A good guy, a former SEC guy with CMKX. It's legit!' I am 60 years old, and I needed a highly leveraged stock to retire. I had spent 3 years in mining exploration and knew the prospects in the claims. I put $10,000 US into the stock, all I had. Glenn was THE backstop for my confidence."*

Gregory D., one of many military CMKX investors, planned on buying health insurance for himself and his friends who had to rely on an inadequate VA system. He hoped to start a "low cost, donation based funeral program for the impoverished," and to inject capital into his girlfriend's photography business:

> *"It's been an uphill battle with the VA. Veterans are coming home in droves all screwed up, to be redeployed again. I wanted to bring a more even playing field to the funeral home industry, to offer the 'best of the best' for services while donating goods at cost to the family. And afterwards, I believe in calling the widow and asking if she needs groceries.*
>
> *I put myself through school with the GI bill, and took the extra money I got from being in school full time (while doctors had me strung out on morphine) and would buy this crazy stock. I invested about nine grand, and ended up with about 50.2 million shares after all was said and done."*

Forevercmkx, also called rags2riches, had worked on Wall Street in college and then spent fifteen years investing. He bought Cybermark International, 3,000 shares before a 10-1 forward split, giving him 30,000 shares. He researched De Beers, the world's largest diamond producer, but there was no information available. Then he read about Urban Casavant turning CMKI into CMKM Diamonds. Instantly, he held shares in a diamond mining company. He continued to invest after being laid off from a high paying IT job soon after buying a home. Forevercmkx maintained his belief that he would see a return on their investment:

> *"I believe to this day that it was God that put me in the path of this amazing investment story. I was looking to invest in the world's largest diamond company (De Beers) not knowing that I would soon own a piece of the world's largest diamond company...CMKM Diamonds, Inc."*

Most CMKX shareholders wanted to spread the good news to friends, neighbors, and anyone else who would listen. With all the PRs of diamonds, gold, uranium (which became known as "green stuffium" to the shareholders), and other rare metals, there was plenty to go around. Some shareholders brought their entire church congregations into the stock, holding meetings to discuss the company's potential.

The mother and son team of imSINGLEruRICH and Joerockss, moderators on *Proboards29*, spent all their time "sitting at the computer signed on to *Paltalk* or on *PB29*." Wanting to share the wealth, they convinced forty friends to invest in CMKX as well. imSINGLEruRICH realized that her fixation with CMKX extended far beyond a simple interest in tracking her investments:

> *"Never in my wildest dreams did I ever believe I would have an addiction. I prided myself on being an extremely strong individual, after being widowed at the age of 35yrs. My downfall came the day I decided I wanted to learn the basics of the stock market. Penny stocks were all I was able to afford, but hundreds went to thousands as CMKX turned me into an addict. My entire life revolved around CMKX. My social life had become nil as I sometimes*

even feigned illness just to be able to sit at the computer for fear of missing the big PR."

Duke, intrigued by the Million Millionaires promise, sold his house and cashed in his retirement funds as his belief grew with each positive press release. He talked his girlfriend into investing as well. Duke, like countless other CMKX shareholders, invested far more than he could afford. His total investment? Over $190,000. He bought during the huge price spike in June of 2004, and then tried to lower his per share average by buying more while the price was falling.

Scott R. was a senior broker at one of the biggest brokerage houses in the securities industry. Scott R. used his experience in CMKX as both a learning experience and an escape from his job as a broker. He knew from his own background that naked short selling was a very real threat to the financial markets. He and his wife invested after almost a lifetime following the stock market:

> *"The CMKX saga was extremely addictive. For myself, a licensed broker, it had all the mystery of a penny stock with the potential of huge short term gains like QBID. I loved the stock market as a small child when the only part of the newspaper I could not decipher was the stock market pages. It seemed like a beautiful union of the verbal and mathematical worlds a little kid lives in where words and letters melded as one complete sentence. By design I was drawn to the markets. I purchased penny stocks as a child and hit with 'New Coke,' making 20X my paper route money. Later, I used the CMKX saga as a way to escape reality and hear ideas from others. The beautiful dreams of a small mining company hitting the mother load made me think I could help others, setting up a homeless people's kitchen or supporting Christian Children's Fund, Mercy Corps and World Vision."*

Howie Romans III had been serving his country in Afghanistan for several months when he learned about CMKX. Immediately, he recognized all the good he could do with the wealth promised by Urban Casavant and his associates:

> *"With a break in a day's duties, soldiers, airmen, and marines found comfort in the computers that served as a liaison between themselves and their families over half-a-world away. For myself, those computers would be used for routine company message board visits, as well as the occasional purchase and sale of stock. As I invested in CMKX, I encountered many other military personnel who had invested in the company as well.*
>
> *My interaction with the local children highlighted another side of the war in Afghanistan - a side that I felt could be aided by the inflow of cash from the future that many believed CMKX would eventually present. I was always convinced that CMKX may not be able to change the world completely, but the possibility of monetary gain could help make the world a better, and safer, place.*

In May of 2004, my 11-month deployment to Afghanistan ended, yet the CMKX saga remained. While it may have started in Afghanistan, my story would not be the same without documenting the experiences of those fellow shareholders that I had met throughout this journey. While we supported the company, we also supported each other.

Specialist Matthew Edwards, a 2ⁿᵈ Infantry Division soldier, called the barren desert of Korea home for a year. News coverage caught the worst part of the atrocities that continue to this day. Bitter cold enveloped his base that one late, mid-week night. Boredom gave way to an accidental discovery of CMKX - one that would live with him for years. News and rumors, fresh out of Paltalk or accompanying message boards, came with each passing day. Everyone and their brothers, quite literally, wanted to know about CMKX.

Tanks adorned with CMKX stickers, like ornaments hanging on a Christmas tree, were seen rolling through the rubble of Iraq. Courtesy of supportive CMKX shareholders at home, he was able put those stickers on several different military vehicles.

As a lowly private at the time of his entrance into Iraq, Specialist Edwards was solely responsible for opening up over 20 separate brokerage accounts for his battle buddies. With him as a guide, they experienced the dream that he had been convinced would come into fruition, if only they took the first step of faith into a stock market that could eat them alive if they weren't careful.

In early September of 2005, in the aftermath of Hurricane Katrina, my unit and I went down to Louisiana. The same hardened cots that Specialist Edwards knew so well from Iraq were scattered in a collective disorganization as their four metallic legs penetrated into the turf of the New Orleans Saints' practice field in Louisiana. Hurricane Katrina knocked the wind out of America in much the same way that the events of 9/11 did.

Mr. Marshall Peters and I met one October day in 2004 while attending an NHRA racing event in Reading, PA. Like many CMKX shareholders, Mr. Peters' involvement in CMKX demonstrated his awareness of a world in dire need. In his life, any financial windfall from CMKX would be directed towards missionary and humanitarian purposes, including several orphanages that he had dedicated much of his time to in Belize.

To Mrs. Jo Ann Lewis, an Oklahoma native, CMKX revealed an opportunity to pursue the simple things in life. As a widow of 16 years, family meant more to her than the pleasures that any material object could offer. And, just as she supported the soldiers at home and abroad, she also supported fellow CMKX shareholders through their exhaustive letter-writing campaigns concerning the evils of stock manipulation. Whatever she sacrificed for the CMKX cause was worth it to see her children age under the financial security that a trust could offer. That was her hope.

Four states away in a Northeastern direction from Oklahoma, my Grandmother, an author in her own right, lived a life that greatly paralleled that of Mrs. Jo Ann Lewis. Hers was a life of sacrifice and servanthood. Her introduction to CMKX started with my father, her eldest son, who decided to invest into this risky stock after engaging in casual 'water-cooler' conversation at his workplace. Talk of land potential, and a CEO who had seemingly diverged from the norm through his close interaction with shareholders, made my father's decision easy.

From his workplace in Pennsylvania, the hope associated with my father's initial decision to invest in CMKX spread throughout my family. Hope to one day provide a better life for their special needs child made CMKX all that much more attractive to my aunt and uncle in California. Any windfall from CMKX could also have helped her oldest daughter ease the financial burden of an upcoming wedding.

Hope to establish a foundation in loving memory of my sister, Gabrielle, was one of many items on my family's 'to do' list, in the event that CMKX paid off. Two days prior to my leaving for Afghanistan, she had tragically passed away from a rare condition called "Goldenhar Syndrome." This deserving cause was similar to the goals that many CMKX shareholders would pursue in the name of family, friends, and a world in need."

`Hot Lips Houlihan` owned several million shares when she started reading prior CMKX press releases and came across one that talked about naked short selling. After finding the *Investigate the SEC* website, she wrote a letter to Senator Mitch McConnell, her state senator and majority whip at that time.

She received a sincere response from Senator McConnell and posted it on the boards. She then took her concerns to the top and wrote President Bush. A month later, her anonymous letter was published on the *USA Today* website.

She kept writing letters, applying pressure to members of Congress. Other posters followed her lead and CMKXers as a group repeatedly sent thousands of complaints to Congress and the SEC, asking why naked shorting was possible. Gradually some Senators and Representatives began to notice the public outcry and question the SEC about the issue.

On the CMKX message boards the caring nature of the shareholders shined through when someone was in need, or when tragedy struck a fellow shareholder. When someone on the message boards passed away, they banded together and offered condolences and prayers to the families. The message boards and chat rooms became memorials to those lost during the CMKX saga, with talk about diamonds, naked short selling, and kimberlite replaced temporarily with heartfelt prayers and condolences.

In Memory of Ty Merrick, 1966-2004

On October 11, 2004, at 10:22 P.M. EST, two posters named elcamino and
Jumpingjack0 posted a series of somber messages on *Sterling's Classroom*
about one of the most popular and well-respected CMKX shareholders:

> I have just been informed that Ty, a good friend and
> shareholder was involved in a severe car accident today
> in Texas. Ty goes by the screen name Cashflowforme. He is
> being lifeline'd to a hospital in Waco, TX with severe head
> trauma. Many of us met him in Indy and were immediately
> taken by his charm and personality.
>
> Please begin fervent prayer that the Lord will provide
> skill and wisdom to the EMT personnel, Nurses and Doctors
> who are attending him. Pray for his family that they will
> gain unity and strength through this experience and will
> come together in prayer for their loved one.
>
> I will update everyone as soon as I receive additional
> information about his condition and progress.
>
> elcamino

October 12, 2004, 12:26 A.M. EST:

> UPDATE ON TY. He is in critical condition with brain
> swelling and Drs. have said might not make it through the
> night. Pray for my buddy Ty. He has a beautiful wife Karla
> and 2 beautiful kids. Love you Ty.
>
> jumpin-jack0

Later that evening after unsuccessful surgery, Ty Merrick passed away. Immediately,
the message boards began to honor his memory and offer condolences to his
family. Jumpingjack0 added a short tribute to his memory, one of hundreds of
posts about Ty that continued for days:

> Ty Merrick was a man of strong character who possessed a
> love of life and family. When he spoke of his family, his
> words reflected his pride and deep love for them. He was
> a leader in the business world who treated everyone with
> respect and kindness.
>
> Ty was always upbeat and positive and loved the excitement
> and challenge that being a stockholder in CMKX gave him.
>
> The world has lost an honorable, respected and loved
> human being. I know that he is unselfishly looking down on
> everyone from above and wishing prosperity for the CMKX
> shareholders. I thank God for the days that Ty was part of

> my life. Ty and his family will remain in our thoughts and
> prayers as days pass on. May he rest in peace. On behalf
> of Karla and her family, thank you for visiting.

CMKXtreme Racing Team members Connie and Marc Cohen added their
condolences to a shareholder who became a friend through the CMKX
experience:

> My heart dropped to the floor when I was told about what
> happen to Ty, I can't imagine what you are going though. I
> can only give you my deepest sympathy to you Karla & Cole
> and the entire Merrick Family. I had the honor to meet
> with Ty at many of the races, got to really know him at
> the share holder party at the Holiday Inn, he offered to
> give me a ride home (back to the race track to save Ron C.
> the trip because he was tired). He was a true gentleman.
> The energy he had for you and Cole was amazing. Ty was
> always helping some one out, Ty will truly be missed God
> Speed, Connie

At 6:18 P.M. EST, Easternbreezes "membermarked" Ty Merrick, better known
on the boards as Cashflow. A membermark was a way to acknowledge someone
who did something special on the boards, posted a particularly good message, or
exhibited a special character trait. In this case, it honored a fallen friend:

> Your membermark of cash_flow4me was successful. Rest Easy
> Brother.

By the time the night was over, well over a hundred membermarks were added on
Sterling's Classroom, including one that said simply:

> Your membermark forever of cash_flow4me was successful.

Then, a poster named locoforkimberlite came up with the idea of naming
one of the CMKM Diamonds' kimberlite pipes after Ty, and the message board
was filled with a hundred posters who added their name to *"Vote for Cashflow
Pipe."* In all, thousands of messages were posted in honor of Ty Merrick.

LCpl Justin McLeese, USMC, Killed in action, Battle of Fallujah, November
13, 2004

On November 13, 2004, CMKX shareholders lost another friend and fellow
shareholder. Lance Corporal Justin McLeese of the United States Marine Corp.
was killed in action in the Battle of Fallujah. As a soldier fighting in Iraq, LCpl
McLeese was awarded the Bronze Star "V" for Valor in Combat and a Purple
Heart. In the words of his mother Sharon McLeese, "he was an incredible young
man, our pride and joy."

LCpl McLeese was a fallen hero who made the ultimate sacrifice for his
country, was loved by his family and admired by those who knew him. Once
again, CMKX shareholders showed their kindness and compassion by setting up
an online memorial service in *Paltalk:*

> We will hold a one hour Memorial Service for LCpl Justin D. McLeese in Paltalk Saturday, Nov 20th. at 1PM EST.
>
> He was just 19 years old, part of our CMKX extended family, and was an only son. His family is donating his CMKX shares to the Injured Marines' Fund. May God richly bless their generosity.
>
> Please keep this family in your thoughts and prayers. He died fighting for the very freedom's that allow us to gather, share, and love one another. Please visit this site...set up in his memory.

Nearly every CMKX message board paused to pay tribute to a fallen friend, and a website set up in his honor contained scores of messages of condolence from friends, family, and CMKX shareholders alike:

> I return often to Justin's Memorial Page. He is everything American, Young, Handsome, Brave and Patriotic, a man's man. How proud you must be of him. I met him through the stock CMKX shareholders chat room. They held a service for him and I will never forget him. He sacrificed for me and my children and I will be forever grateful. God Bless Justin, He will always be in my prayers and thoughts, All My Respect.
>
> Debbie P.
>
> To the family and friends of a true American Hero... my thoughts and prayers are with you all at this most difficult time. He did not die in vain.
>
> jc
>
> We are so sorry for your loss. May God bless Justin and give him a place in heaven so you all may see him once again. Justin, thank you for defending our nation...thank you for making the ultimate sacrifice so that my children can live in peace. You will never be forgotten.
>
> With love and deepest sympathy,
>
> Jim and Robin F., CMKX shareholders

CMKX shareholders were schoolteachers, soldiers, oilfield workers, software programmers, stockbrokers, nurses, writers, widows, pastors, and even professional athletes. 50,000 strong, they came from every part of the world, as varied in their lives as they were in their locations...all sharing a common bond. Soon, another small group of CMKX shareholders in a small but thriving East Texas community would become central players in the CMKX saga.

CMKX shareholder Ty Merrick. From commemoration website. Family photo

CMKX shareholder and USMC LCpl. Justin McLeese.
From commemoration website. Family photo

PART THREE

"Adversity is the diamond dust Heaven polishes its jewels with."
~ Thomas Carlyle

A Twelve Step Program to Clean up
the OTC Stock Market

By Mark Faulk

Sept. 14, 2005

www.faulkingtruth.com

Let's face the facts: the OTC stock market is in shambles, and if someone doesn't do something about it soon, it will be lucky to survive. It's like a neighborhood that's been allowed to fall into disrepair for decades, if the neighborhood association (the SEC, NASD, and DTC, in this case) doesn't do anything to make the neighborhood safer and more desirable, then all the respectable homeowners will move out, and the only ones left will be drug dealers, gangbangers, and crack whores. And since the stock market's equivalent of a neighborhood association seems content to watch from the sidelines (or, as some critics contend, align themselves with the riffraff that is looting the neighborhood), it's up to the remaining homeowners and neighborhood activists to step in and take back their own neighborhood.

We have to demand that the criminals are arrested, that the laws are enforced (and if the existing laws aren't adequate to address the problems, that new laws are introduced), and that the streets are cleaned up. In other words, it's time to make sweeping changes in OTCLand, and if those in charge aren't up to the task, then it's time for new leadership.

Does anyone here really believe that the SEC gives a damn about the small investor? The truth is, they (and the NASD, the DTC, the market makers, and the brokers themselves) all get a cut every time a neighborhood con artist rips off one of the locals. The only trouble is, once they've fleeced the remaining available victims, the neighborhood will be in such disrepair that no new money will ever get invested into it again. And once that happens, once the money stops flowing, then everyone loses.

So, on the outside chance that someone "up there" really wants to reform the OTC stock market for the betterment of the small investor and the legitimate companies who are struggling to survive in a rigged game, I've taken the liberty of making a few suggestions about how to clean up this neighborhood. You may or may not agree with all of them, but until we begin the process of reform in our markets, our "neighborhood" will continue to deteriorate until it becomes essentially worthless.

1. *Stop naked short selling altogether.* Demand that every broker cover every short sale, and I'm not talking about the electronic shell game that they are allowed to play now. One share, signed, sealed, and delivered, to cover every share that's shorted. That one's a given, if the SEC, the NASD, and the DTC are allowing stocks to be sold short without finding the shares to cover those positions, then they are complicit in the crime. Period.

2. *Publicly report all legitimate short selling information.* It should be as easy as a click of the mouse to find out the number of shares that are short in any given OTC stock at any time. The records are there, why doesn't the DTC release them in order to protect investors? If they can do this on listed stocks, then they can do it on OTC stocks. And while we're at it, why don't we require holders of substantial short positions to publicly disclose those positions? We require those who hold substantial long positions to disclose it, what's the difference? The more information we have, the better our investment decisions will be.

3. *Eliminate all offshore and toxic financing, especially floorless convertible funding.* I realize that this is the only type of loan that a lot of start-up companies can get, but it's the kiss of death in most cases, in my opinion. If a lending company truly has faith in a start-up company's products, ideas, or technologies, then they should be willing to lend them money at a set rate conversion. That might be at, say, a 25% discount to the current stock price, but at least then all parties involved (the company, investors, and the lender) know exactly what they're getting themselves into. Plus, it takes away the incentive for lenders to naked short a stock price into oblivion in order to get their shares for cheaper.

4. *Ban all shorting by company insiders and financiers.* No one should be able to bet against their own company, or the company that they've loaned money to. It's as simple as that, if the owners, insiders, and lenders are betting that the stock will go down, why should anyone else invest in that company?

5. *Require approval from the true owner of shares before those shares can be "borrowed."* This is one that will undoubtedly piss off everyone who makes their living betting that every stock in the world will eventually drop in price, and you will probably never see this rule happen, but it makes sense. It's your stock; shouldn't you have to give permission before someone borrows it? And shouldn't you be somehow compensated for loaning your stock to someone else? That simple rule is true in every other aspect of ownership, why not here? It's just one of the many things that doesn't make sense to the average person, and they're right, it doesn't make sense.

6. *Publicly update outstanding shares and available trading shares on a daily basis.* Why isn't this information readily available already? Why do investors have to venture into the jungle of online message boards (such as *Raging Bull*), just to find out how many shares of stock exist in a company? Why is the information listed in public filings usually months old? I have seen hundreds of cases where investors were led to believe that a company had, say, 50 million shares outstanding (based on the latest officially released information), only to find out that the actual count had ballooned to 500

million shares or more without any current updated information. This is misleading, and should be illegal. If you can call the transfer agent at any time and find out the current number of shares outstanding, why can't it be posted online?

7. *Restrict reverse splits.* This is extremely important. If an individual files for bankruptcy, he or she can't declare bankruptcy again for seven years. Why should a publicly traded company be any different? One reverse split is usually one too many, in my opinion, but multiple reverse splits should be against the law. The most corrupt companies sell hundreds of millions (or even billions) of shares of stock on a regular basis, then declare a reverse split, in effect reducing the number of shares back to near zero, and promptly sell another billion or more shares into the market. In the world of OTC stocks, reverse splits are almost always the kiss of death, especially when they are followed by another round of dilution. I could name a dozen companies off the top of my head that do this for a living (and there are dozens more), but I'm sure every investor has at least one that they've been burned on. Fill in your favorite rip-off company's name here.

8. *When a company does declare a reverse split, reduce the number of authorized shares accordingly.* In other words, if a company has 500 million authorized shares available, and they sell them all to keep the company afloat, they shouldn't be allowed to declare a reverse split and start all over again. If they are truly declaring a reverse split to reduce the float (say, by enacting a 10 to 1 reverse split to reduce the number of shares to 50 million), then the authorized shares should be reduced proportionately. If they only care about freeing up more shares to sell, let them go to the stockholders for approval.

9. *Limit the total number of shares that can be authorized and issued.* There's at least one company, CMKM Diamonds (CMKX: OTCBB), that has issued almost a trillion shares of stock, and there's no end in sight. That's just plain crazy, in my opinion. It reminds me of a passage in the "Hitchhiker's Guide to the Galaxy" trilogy (which, in OTC stock market-style, has four books), where all the dregs of society are launched in a spaceship to a far off planet that happens to look just like Earth. One of their first jobs is to come up with a type of monetary system, and the person in charge decides that tree leaves should be their currency. In his report to the committee, he says something to the effect that "the good news is, since we've made leaves our official currency, everyone is rich beyond their wildest dreams. The bad news is that there are so many leaves, it costs a million leaves just for a loaf of bread." Get it? Massive dilution is bad, and no company should be able to sell their shareholders a trillion leaves, I mean shares of stock. There's a reason so many OTC companies are incorporated in Nevada, and it's not the legalized prostitution.

10. *Allow shareholders to vote on all-important actions affecting their stock.* If a CEO, or his cohorts or financiers, controls over 50% of the stock of a publicly run company, then it's not really publicly run, is it? It happens a lot more than one would like to think: a company declares a reverse split and issues a press release to inform you, but tells you not to bother to vote because they control enough shares to pass it without any stockholder support whatsoever. Instead, limit the amount of voting power any company insiders or financiers have, regardless of how many shares they own. Let the shareholders have a say in how their companies are run (and yes, if they own stock, it is their company).

11. *Require more full disclosure for all OTC and pink sheet stocks, and just as importantly, simplify that information.* As usual, with any government laws or regulations, it takes 50 pages of legal crap to convey one page of information. This is something every faulking branch of the government should have to do, in my opinion (Can you say IRS?). To all lawmakers and attorneys: if you feel it is necessary to write every damn thing so that no normal human being can understand it, then write it twice: once in stupid lawyer/politician speak, and again in plain English, telling us what you really mean. If you're too freaking anal to translate your convoluted legal jargon into normal language, then hire a real person to do it for you. Investors shouldn't have to wade through twenty pages of bullshit just to find the information that is pertinent. What are you trying to hide in the fine print? Give investors a list, in bold print, of pertinent information: How many shares are there? How many shares have been shorted? Has the company ever declared a reverse split? Has the CEO or any of his cohorts been involved in any serious illegal activity, or run any other companies into the ground? Do they ever expect to actually generate any revenues, and if so, when and how much? Do they make a profit, and if not, when do they expect to? See? It's not that hard.

12. *Clean up the message boards.* It's one thing to allow both negative and positive information to be shared, but message boards (*Raging Bull* in particular) have become the Wild West. *Raging Bull*, *Yahoo*, and the various other message boards make big money off of the traffic that posters there generate, and they have a moral obligation to protect those posters, in my opinion. The message boards used to be a great place to find information on OTC companies, now they're just a cesspool and a haven for pumpers and bashers. If the owners of those message boards can't control, at least to a large degree, the obscenities, personal attacks, lies, and on and on and on, then they should be shut down. There are several new message boards that have managed to do just that, and they don't have the resources that the big boys have so there's no question that it can be done. Do it, and quit making excuses. This is not about free speech; it's about honesty and civility.

In the end, the net effect of these rules would be simple. The crooks would pack up and leave town, in search of greener pastures. I'm guessing they would end up as pimps and drug dealers, or possibly politicians or radio talk show hosts. Regardless, once the ability to fleece honest investors is eliminated, these lowlifes would be forced to return to the shadow world where they belong. The crooked CEOs would be forced out of business, the offshore financiers would have to find their suckers elsewhere, the corrupt companies would go under, and the legitimate ones (and their stockholders) would be allowed to flourish under a fair and equitable system.

And that, my fellow neighbors, is the Faulking Truth.

Chapter 9 – Everything CMKX

"God brings men into deep waters, not to drown them, but to cleanse them."
~ John Aughey

Saturday, December 21, 2004

For John Martin, it was a desperate last attempt to salvage something... anything... from a year gone horribly wrong. It was to be THE YEAR for the Martin family; the year they realized all of their dreams, and the year he finally found something he was passionate about, that he could make his fortune at. As he hooked up his trailer and loaded twelve hundred toboggans onto it, ready to head north into Oklahoma in search of snow, he thought back on his own dizzying ride of the past year.

2003 had been a nearly picture perfect year for the Martins, and the coming year promised to be even better. John Martin's business, which he had spent nearly eight years building, was thriving (to the tune of almost $200,000 in net income for the year), and even though he wasn't really passionate about his work, he was good at it. His wholesale customers included almost five thousand stores. John could sell anything....to use an overworked cliché...he could sell ice cubes to Eskimos. Among the various ice cubes he sold to Eskimos were: weight loss products with Ephedra (before they were banned by the government), cell phone antenna boosters, children's clothing, two truck loads of leather Converse athletic shoes, and of course, toboggans.

This wasn't the first time John had sold toboggans. In 1986, he and a friend bought a truckload full after they couldn't find a sled anywhere when it snowed in Tyler, Texas. They were convinced that if it ever snowed in Tyler again, or more optimistically *when* it snowed again, they would be, as John put it, "the sled king-pins of Texas." Incredibly, it did snow again, and not just a few measly flakes, it snowed enough to actually sled! John and his friend, true to their word, sold toboggans to Texans. Years later, this is how John would describe his first foray into sled-selling:

> *"We had a truckload of them. And it was huge! First we had an ice storm. We were standing on the side of the loop 323 in south Tyler, and had a sign "$10 per sled, $15 if snowing." And it was coming down so hard, and it was so icy that people couldn't stop their cars, because we were on a little bit of an incline. So they would come by with money out the window and slide by and we'd hand them their toboggans and they'd give us their money. And we had HUGE quantities of money, stacks of money everywhere from people buying these things. We sold thousands of them. TV crews showed up. We were on TV,*

lines of cars, people coming down that icy road, with money hanging out the window. It was crazy!"

John continued to sell things, often turning the business into a family affair, with his wife Jill and the kids helping to sort shoes or package whatever it was John had added to his inventory that week. He sometimes recruited the kids to help sell items at flea markets or on the side of the road, holding up signs to lure passersby to stop and purchase his latest version of toboggans to Texans. His business grew, his family prospered, and life was good. But there was always a nagging feeling of dissatisfaction lingering inside John Martin's head, that feeling that there had to be something more to life than just selling whatever he could find to sell. Then one day he got a tip from a friend that would ultimately change his life. It was a penny stock company called GamezNFlix, and John invested a few thousand dollars in the company. Lo and behold, he made twelve thousand dollars in a matter of two days, and felt an adrenaline rush like never before. Twelve thousand dollars in two days!

It didn't matter that John was one of the lucky ones who made money on GamezNFlix, or that the stock soon became virtually worthless; John Martin had found his passion. He began researching stocks on the message boards and in the stock chatrooms, and it wasn't long before he was hooked. He studied charts, watched the volume in stocks as they went up, and spent more and more time online, looking for the "Next Big Thing." Then he heard about a company called Casavant Mining Kimberlite International, a diamond mining company trading literally hundreds of millions of shares a day. Trading at the time under the symbol CMKM, posters on other stock message boards were constantly talking about it, and the shares were cheap, like one one-hundredth of a penny cheap. A quarter found between the cushions of a couch was good for 2,500 shares of CMKM.

The volume was incredible. After trading a few million shares a day when it first went public, activity gradually increased over the next few months, breaking a hundred million shares sold in one day (or bought, depending on ones viewpoint) in August of 2003. CMKM surpassed the unbelievable level of one billion shares traded on September 18, and then topped *three billion shares* traded in a single day on September 30th. Granted, the price by then had dropped over 95% from its high, but that just meant the upside was that much greater, the potential for return that much higher.

While the volume was constantly going up (a sure sign of demand), the company was busy buying back shares of stock and "retiring" them to the treasury, which meant less supply to go around. The laws of supply and demand told John, as it did everyone who was feeding the buying frenzy, that it was just a matter of time until the stock price took off.

On September 30, 2003, the same day trading hit the magic three billion share level (higher demand), CMKM announced the retirement of six billion shares (less supply).

On October 10, they retired another 9,020,371,427 shares (even less supply).

Ten days later, they retired another 4.4 billion shares (less supply). Oddly, on that date, they listed the total shares bought back as 13,420,371,427, but no one seemed to notice the minor 6 billion share math error.

But they weren't finished yet. On November 6, they bought back and retired another 6.7 billion shares, listing the total at "over 20 billion" shares retired.

Then, another slight discrepancy appeared in their math calculations. A month later, on December 7, they announced "that the company had officially retired 16,520,477,200 shares of CMKM stock back to the Treasury." A few pessimists on the message boards pointed out that adding up all of the announced buybacks actually came to 26,120,371,427 shares that should have been retired, and not the just over 16.5 billion the latest PR touted, but to most shareholders it didn't seem to matter. This was Economics 101, not Introductory Math. And it looked like this:

HIGHER VOLUME = HIGHER DEMAND

LESS SHARES = LESS SUPPLY

HIGHER DEMAND + LESS SUPPLY = HIGHER SHARE PRICE

HIGHER SHARE PRICE = ONE MILLION MILLIONAIRES

And so, in January of 2004, John Martin bought his first million shares of CMKM for one hundred dollars. That weekend, John and his wife Jill sat on the back porch at their friends' house, chatting and sipping coffee, and John casually told them, "Yeah, I just bought a million shares of a diamond mine."

John Martin was hooked on trading, and like tens of thousands of other shareholders, he was hooked on CMKM as well. There was *something* about it – the allure of investing in diamonds, the psychological boost of buying shares not by the hundreds but by the millions. He bought another million, and then another, and then another. With every million shares, he spent just that much more time on the message boards, in the chat rooms, and watching the trades go through – million upon million upon million….upon million.

For John, watching the stock trade and talking to the thousands of shareholders who practically lived on the message boards was even more exciting than buying the shares. Trading rumors, information, tips, and more rumors was the biggest thrill of all. For those who believed in the company, and in Urban Casavant, it was all about common ground, about finding others who shared their excitement, their enthusiasm…their passion…and their growing belief that CMKM was their ticket to prosperity, to massive wealth, to the realization of the American dream. Like most of the others on message boards, John began to spend more and more time online, especially during trading hours.

Even when John wasn't on the message boards discussing CMKM, he was talking to friends – about CMKM. He was a true believer in the company, and just as it was with thousands of other shareholders, his enthusiasm was contagious. He talked about it to friends, to family, and eventually many of them became CMKM shareholders as well. One of the friends John convinced to buy into CMKM was Bill Frizzell, an attorney in Tyler, Texas, who had made a little money off John's GamezNFlix recommendation. Bill made his first purchase of CMKM stock in May of 2004, and even he began to think this one might really take off. As more and more news came out, and more and more shares traded, it became obvious to everyone involved that it was simply a matter of time until CMKM hit…and hit big.

Like so many other CMKM shareholders, John Martin's passion soon turned into obsession, and obsession grew into full-blown addiction. At first, Jill was somewhat caught up in John's enthusiasm, but she soon began to see the downside of his passion-turned-obsession-turned-addiction to anything CMKM. The more time he spent on the message boards, the less time he devoted to his business, and the less time he devoted to his business, the more debt the Martin family accumulated. Still, it didn't matter to John, he just knew that when CMKM hit, and make no mistake, CMKM *would* hit, all their problems would be solved.

On March 10, 2004, CMKM Diamonds officially began trading as CMKX, and John Martin, and thousands of other shareholders, bought more and more stock. By the time John Martin would become a household name to CMKX shareholders around the world a year later, the "word on the boards" was that he had invested over a million dollars in CMKX. The reality (as was often the case) was much more modest – in fact, it was so much more modest that anyone who knew the truth would have been more than a bit surprised. John had invested what to him was a lot of money, especially considering the fact that his obsession with everything CMKX had become so all consuming that his income had dropped to practically nothing.

So what was John Martin's total investment in CMKX? A million dollars? Half a million? $250,000? $100,000? The correct answer was none of the above. After everything was said and done, the Martin family had invested around $10,000 total in John's dream company, a mere fraction of what many shareholders had bet on this little diamond company waiting to happen. Looking back, John would comment that he was very thankful he didn't have a million dollars in the bank, or half a million, or even a hundred thousand, because he would have sunk every penny into CMKX.

For the Martin family, for John and Jill and their four children, the bigger burden wasn't what they spent on CMKX stock, it was what John *didn't* earn while he was busy being obsessed with everything CMKX. After his stellar $200,000 year in 2003, he earned a paltry $23,000 in 2004 – "The Year of CMKX."

And so there he was, four days before Christmas, loading up twelve hundred toboggans onto a trailer, getting ready to kiss his wife and kids goodbye and drive north into Oklahoma, in search of snow.

Chapter 10 – The Calm Before the Storm

"I then asked Melvin about the initial reaction to the kimberlite samples. He said 'Let me put it to you this way, we're not waiting on the samples to come back, we're waiting to start counting the diamonds!' I asked him to elaborate. He continued: 'When the samples first came out of the earth, the eyes of the geologist lit up like a Christmas Tree.' He told me to be patient and wait on a PR, it won't be long. That was the entire conversation. Take it however you like; I'm just the messenger of the messenger."

~An Unidentified Message Board Poster

John Martin wasn't the only one obsessing over CMKX in 2004. In fact, the shareholder base grew exponentially with the level of excitement generated by the company, the race car sponsorship, and of course, the shareholders themselves, who were the best salespeople of all when it came to CMKX. The company would release news, and the message boards would spin it in a way that made it look even brighter.

At the heart of it all was Urban himself. While the involvement of several shadowy characters had been detected by observant posters on the boards, the belief in Urban and his dream, and his family approach to business, was enough to give shareholders faith that he would eventually turn this little diamond company into a huge success. It made the shareholders feel like they were a part of the company, as opposed to so many anonymous faces in the crowd, and gave them a sense of belonging that other companies couldn't offer. And while distinguishing fact from rumor became more difficult with every passing day, there were a few basic rumor/truths accepted as gospel.

Most shareholders believed there was a huge naked short position, with estimates ranging anywhere from a couple of hundred billion to several trillion shares of counterfeit stock flooding the market, holding the stock price down.

And finally, there was the valuation of the company itself. This was another point of contention, and while almost all shareholders agreed the company's claims were valuable, the debate raged on about whether they were valuable enough to send the stock price "to da moon," as one poster put it. Would the shareholders become incredibly rich, or merely rich?

Either way, the good news flowed, and even when it didn't, the shareholders on the message boards could find something positive to grasp. While the rumors spread that Urban was busy buying up shares and retiring them to the company vault, the plans to discover and begin drilling for diamonds marched steadily forward.

In December of 2003, the company announced in a press release they had targeted five test drilling sites, one in the Green Lake area in Saskatchewan, and four in the Forte á la Corne area:

> *"Urban Casavant, President of CMKM stated, 'These targets for drilling have been selected after analyzing all of the data and we feel that they have the highest potential for finding Kimberlite bodies. We know that many Kimberlite bodies found in Forte á la Corne have turned out to be diamondiferous, and this is our goal for CMKM.'"*

A week later, the company announced that zinc deposits owned by CMKM subsidiary Casavant International Mining Inc. would be spun off into another company, with CMKM shareholders owning shares in that company as well. A week later, they began negotiating with two other companies to sell a small portion of their claims to bring in more cash. And like clockwork, almost every press release came out at precisely midnight, and usually on Friday. It kept the boards buzzing all weekend, and invariably generated a buying frenzy on Monday morning.

In January of 2004, they announced the name change from CMKM to CMKX, and requested that all shareholders request their paper stock certificates in order to receive shares under the new trading symbol. It seemed a sure sign that Urban was hot on the trail of the naked short sellers, and was trying to flush them out by forcing brokers to physically deliver the shares.

In February, CMKX announced a joint venture with four other publicly held Canadian companies, U.S. Canadian Minerals (UCAD), Shane Resources (SEI. H), Consolidated Pine Channel (KPG), and United Carina Resources (UCA), to "share the cost on this major airborne survey." It was a joint venture described by UCAD CEO and President Rendal Williams as "mutually beneficial to all the companies involved." Afterwards, UCAD and CMKX signed one agreement after another, each one bringing the two companies into closer alignment with each other.

While the official press releases showed a company moving forward at a rapid pace, the first of an increasing number of not-so-positive articles appeared. Carol Remond of Dow Jones wrote the first of several unflattering pieces about CMKX in March of 2004, entitled "CMKM Diamonds' Stock Not a Girl's Best Friend." While Remond couldn't find much about the company to complain about (other than, like all Pink Sheets Exchange companies, it didn't file financial records with regulators), she did make a big deal of the number of shares traded, saying that the company "apparently has a mine full of shares." She pointed out that on February 17, it traded 3.82 billion shares, saying there were "more shares traded in this one stock than ALL of the shares traded that day on the New York Stock Exchange, NASDAQ and the American Stock Exchange – combined." Remond continued her mining motif in her closing comment: "Good luck to shareholders drilling for information that most would consider routine. Hopefully, holders don't keep striking a dry well."

As good as the news was in the company press releases, the message board gurus, pundits, and experts took the excitement, and the speculation, to a whole new level in early and mid-2004. Theory after theory and rumor upon rumor appeared on the boards, and each one seemed intent on outdoing the one before it.

Among the rumor mill highlights in May was this message on *marketmillionaires.com*, posted by Bigrod40, reposting a post from Alvin from another unspecified message board, who read it on a post by swwstn on Raging Bull, who read it on yet another message board by "someone who just got off the phone" with CMKM head of investor relations Melvin O'Neil:

CMKX and MELVIN ?????

I had to post this one, I found it rather unusual, whether to believe it or not, but it sure got my attention.

This is from the RB board someone's supposed conversation with Melvin today...this is not mine.

From: "Alvin"

Date: Thu, 13 May 2004

Subject: [CMKXtreme] MELVIN SAYS WE HAVE DIAMONDS

By: swwstn

13 May 2004, 01:21 PM EDT

Melvin's latest phone call from another board:

This just in: I hung up from Melvin 5 minutes ago. He returned my call from about an hour ago. I called to ask him why CMKX was no longer sponsoring the Chicago race. He ask me where did I get my information stating that they were sponsoring the race in the first place since CMKX had not issued a PR stating such. I told him that I picked up the info from a message board. He said, "Well there's your answer." "Unless you hear it from us, it's still just speculation."

I then ask Melvin about the initial reaction to the kimberlite samples. He said, "Let me put it to you this way, were not waiting on the samples to come back, were waiting to start counting the diamonds!" I ask him to elaborate. He continued: "When the samples first came out of the earth, the eyes of the geologist lit up like a Christmas Tree." He told me to be patient and wait on a PR, it won't be long.

That was the entire conversation. Take it however you like, I'm just the messenger of the messenger.

Then another poster "confirmed" the reported conversation with O'Neil:

yabba: It's true. Melvin finally responded to this and confirmed the conversation took place and that was what he said.

But that post, however convoluted the thread seemed, was topped by a couple of posts from Sterling of the popular *Raging Bull* message board, *Sterling's Classroom*. First, he relayed secondhand information from a "very reliable source" identified only as Frank:

May 21, 2004

CMKX-Great News-Must Read...

I just talked with, Frank, a very reliable source that many of you know from the CMKX board. We just got info directly from Urban himself to one of our sources whose name is Topogigio on the RB board. Here is a quick rundown of info:

** We have diamonds! Many of them!!!

** We have the largest diamond find ever!

** We have Platinum!

** We have Gold!

** We have other resources!

** We have a naked short position of 1 Trillion shares!

** We don't have 1.4 million acres, we have millions of acres!

** Urban said that CMKX will be at .50 to .60 cents even without the covering of the naked short position!

** There is much more that I will get with you all later!

** My apologies if this sounds like hype!!!

If the information that Sterling got from Frank, who heard it from Topogigio, who spoke directly to Urban, who placed a (pre-naked short) value of $.50 to $.60 cents seemed a little far-fetched, then Sterling's next theory topped them all. He utilized the "trillion share" naked short position theory and a complicated mathematical formula that valued the CIM shares at 50 times their CMKX investment. It was a long, complex, and carefully thought out piece that combined logic with some major leaps of faith, the highlight of which was that a $10,000 investment in CMKX would soon be worth over $10 million dollars. In extremely edited form, this is what he posted:

*CMKX & Urban Casavant*The Perfect Storm*

I chose this title because I think this is the name that fits the upcoming success story with CMKX. I think I heard either Peter or Frank mention it too and I liked it. Urban Casavant has the same goal as I which is to create a million millionaires for those who have read my initial posts on my board. What a coincidence.

Please consider these thoughts that you are about to read as "theory" until proven as "facts" from Urban and CMKX.

Urban believes that the naked short position on CMKX could very well be 1 trillion shares. To force the shorts to cover, an accountability process must take place. The changing of the CUSIP# (the stock trading number) was done earlier for them to first gather internal accountability of all CMKX shares. Also to kind of serve as a warning for the market makers, MMs, to consider covering any naked shorted positions.

You can do a lot when you own billions of dollars in gold, platinum, uranium, kimberlite, and diamonds to say the least. Buying us out to go private at $1.00 per share still might be too low, but I'm sure many would appreciate such yet still.

Sterling then explained that because CIM was worth $5.00 a share, and based on his estimate of 40 billion total CMKX shares, each CMKX shareholder would receive one share of CIM for every thousand shares of CMKX they owned. Since CMKX was selling for $.0001 a share, one thousand shares, which cost a dime, were worth one share of CIM valued at $5.00. By utilizing a complex and somewhat confusing 12-step mathematical formula, he eventually summarized it all into one simple equation anyone could understand: "10 cents = $5.00."

Sterling then assigned a separate value to the CMKX shares by calculating the value of De Beers mineral claims now thought to be held by CMKX. Of course, he utilized the same 40 billion outstanding shares estimate from his earlier calculations, arriving at a "minimum valuation of $1.30 a share."

Sterling still wasn't finished. He listed a whole series of speculations, an item by item list that contained 28 "what if" scenarios in all, highlighted by:

** Now what if we really do have a huge abundance silver, zinc, gold, uranium, platinum, and diamonds to say the least?

** Now what if CMKX is 1 trillion shares naked shorted as anticipated?

** Now what if we do have miles and miles of kimberlite that was discovered from the aerial survey?

** Now what if one of the newly found kimberlite pipes is miles and miles long?

** Now what if there really are lots of corporate investors that are about to join the party?

** Now what if there were huge zinc deposits found to be issued under the CIM shares?

** Now what if our claims are now up to nearly 3 million acres in the FALC region?

** Now what if all of this is the big plan Urban has to get the shorts?

** Now what if we have all the money and support we need to make all of this happen?

** Now what if Urban really love the shareholders as many of us thinks?

** Now what if all above is true?

As I stated earlier in this post, please consider these thoughts that you have read as "theory" until proven as "facts" from Urban and CMKX. The above will only become official only when Urban and CMKX make such official. Until then, these are only my thoughts. It is my opinion that CMKX will make many of us prosperous!

And so began Sterling's Perfect Storm, a theory waiting to be turned into fact by Urban Casavant, an opinion hoping to become a reality for a million potential millionaires.

Chapter 11 – The Perfect Storm

"Ever get this feeling when your toes start tingling? That you may be standing on something very valuable? Not only are my toes tingling, but my whole damn leg is tingling. Uncle Melvi don't lie. Just telling how it is."
~ Melvin O'Neil, CMKX Investor Relations, June 4, 2004, IBC Radio

The Martins had pinned all of their hopes on CMKX, and, somewhere along the line, John had decided he could make a living buying and selling stocks, except for one problem – after his early success with GamezNFlix, and discovering the world of CMKX, it wasn't long before it was his only interest. CMKX became an addiction worse than gambling, because this casino was always open. Even after the stock market closed, there was "research" to be done, discussions between the message board devotees about what the latest press release meant, who was spreading what rumor, and of course, there was always the "what if" factor. What if news came out after the market closed? What if someone said something profound? What if a new theory or rumor surfaced?

After buying his first million shares for one hundred dollars, John fed his addiction every chance he got, adding shares a million or two at a time. He spent almost all of 2004 on the message boards, living off of money they had (thank God) accumulated from selling their house when they moved to the suburbs. But it wasn't long before that money was gone too, John constantly lobbying Jill to buy another million shares before it hit.

Jill had her doubts about the whole thing from the very beginning, but she knew there was nothing she could say or do to change John's mind. She saw the excitement in his eyes, heard it in his voice, and felt it in his actions. When the stock went up in June of 2004, he would call her into his home office, where he spent most of his waking hours, eyes glued intently to a computer screen, watching numbers flash by in real time, every number representing millions upon millions, and, eventually, billions upon billions of shares of CMKX passing from one hand to the next. He would refresh the screen continually, always looking for the next post, checking the size of the last trade, anticipating the next press release, pausing only long enough to calculate how much money they would make when it hit.

As always, John wasn't alone. Sure, he *appeared* to be alone, sitting and staring fixedly at the computer, hands moving wildly across the keyboard - clickclickclick... refresh... clickclickclick... refresh... but his actions and his mannerisms were as animated as if he was entertaining a room full of guests. Across the country, in fact, around the world, thousands of CMKXers were doing the exact same thing John was doing, mimicking his every action as the excitement rose and fell with each new development, hearts pounding and expectations rising.

At the end of May, things suddenly began to heat up. The company completed phase one of their test drilling on the Carolyn Pipe, intersecting potentially diamond-rich kimberlite on four out of five holes, and sent the core samples to an independent lab for testing.

Frequent appearances by Melvin O'Neil, affectionately known as Uncle Melvi, on IBC Radio pumped up the excitement of the shareholders, and even some of the so-called message board gurus began to get into the act. Sterling appeared on IBC Radio on May 28, taking his "Perfect Storm" theory to a wider audience, explaining his complex formula that led him to believe Urban would swoop in and buy the entire company for a dollar a share and expose the criminals who were shorting the stock into the ground.

June was *the* month for CMKX. Even when John told the story years later, it was impossible not to get swept away in the moment, hearing the excitement in his voice and watching his gestures become more animated with every twist and turn of the month that made believers out of even the most cynical shareholders.

"And at this point, we had two or three million shares, four million shares, and I'm thinking...if something comes out and it hits, I want to watch it. And there's something about being on the boards when news comes out in a stock, and watching it run. It's exciting and everybody's electrified on those boards. It's very addictive. Time would go by and the information that would come out would be bigger and bigger and bigger, and then the stock in June started to run and the news was big with Roger Glenn and we would be filing and I started buying as it was going up, a million shares here, a million shares there..."

Tuesday, June 1, 2004

Fourteen billion shares traded, over seven times the volume of an average day... and once again, many times over more shares than were traded on the entire rest of the stock market combined! On one stock! Something had to be up! John excitedly called his wife from the other room:

"Jill! Come in here and look at this! Look at the trades flying by! They're going by so fast you can't even see 'em. We're already over ten billion shares today, do you have idea what that means?"

"Not a clue."

"It means it's getting ready to run! It means someone is buying up the entire float, someone knows something!"

Indeed, someone did know something. Uncle Melvi was interviewed on IBC radio that same day, and his cryptic words only served to trigger even more buying, and worked the shareholders into an emotional frenzy. It was, as John put it, "electric."

> *Melvin: "I've got a real quick question for you and your listeners. Remember what happened back in 1981 with a certain mountain in the United States called Mount St. Helens? Remember what they did back then when they knew this thing was gonna erupt, they put up seismic crews and everything else and they maintained it and they watched it and watched it and watched it, and then finally, what did happen?"*

> *Announcer: "It exploded."*

> *Melvin: "There you go, there you go buddy, there you go folks – you heard it from old Uncle Melvi."*

And John Martin, and thousands of other CMKX shareholders, bought more stock, snapping up the 14 billion shares that flashed by in real time as little more than a blur on a computer screen.

Wednesday, June 2

Only 1.3 billion shares traded that day, meaning the supply was drying up, and sure enough, the price broke through the .0002 barrier and ended the day at .0003, and just like that, everyone who had bought at .0001 tripled their money. John hollered at Jill again:

> *"Jill! Come in here!" (calculator in hand, account now up to 8 million shares.) "We just tripled our money! Look how much we made!"*

> *"Really? Where is it?"*

> *"Well, I'd have to sell it to get the money...but it's gonna go higher. It was a penny and a half last year, even if it only goes back to that level, that's...(fingers flying over calculator)...that's a hundred and twenty thousand dollars! Just like that! What if we had more shares? What if we had twenty million shares? That would be...(fingers flying again)...three hundred thousand dollars!"*

Thursday, June 3

Another seven and half billion shares traded, and the price peaked out at .0004 before settling back to close the day at .0003 again. But that was okay, just one more chance to get it while it was still cheap. John bought another couple of million shares, and across the country and around the world, 50,000 plus shareholders kept buying more, too. 7,458,114,424 shares more, to be exact.

Friday, June 4

On Friday, Urban announced that CMKX had "entered into discussions with a large New York securities law firm to represent the company and has paid a retainer to that firm to begin the process of bringing the company into full compliance in order to be fully reporting," and just like that, the volume began to take off again, only this time, the price jumped to .0004 and stayed there. Anyone who bought at the low had just *quadrupled* their money. John bought a couple of more million shares at a higher price, but it didn't matter. CMKX was going "to da moon"!

"Jill! Come in here!"

And the day wasn't over yet. Uncle Melvi made another appearance on IBC radio, calling in from Forte a' la Corne in Saskatchewan, Canada, site of the by now famous Carolyn Pipe, "Ground Zero" for CMKX's diamond claims.

"Ever get this feeling when your toes start tingling? That you may be standing on something very valuable? Not only are my toes tingling, but my whole damn leg is tingling.

Uncle Melvi don't lie. Just telling how it is."

By now, the excitement was at a fever pitch, and the boards were buzzing with every rumor and every scrap of news. Every word from anyone even remotely connected to the company was deciphered, analyzed, and interpreted by the thousands of shareholders who were by now collectively living, breathing, and eating as one, afraid to sleep for fear of missing something important on the message boards or from the company, or, worse, afraid of missing "The Run." By the end of trading on Friday, just under 15 billion shares had changed hands, and Monday promised to be even bigger.

Late Friday night, after midnight in most of America, CMKX announced the hiring of D. Roger Glenn, an event that rocketed the shareholders' excitement level to a new high. Roger Glenn, a nationally respected attorney with the prestigious New York law firm of Edwards and Angell, LLP and over 20 years experience in securities law. Roger Glenn, who had personally masterminded several huge buyouts of other public companies and began his career as an enforcement officer at the SEC, was the new attorney for CMKX.

Suddenly, Sterling's Perfect Storm made perfect sense – Glenn, the ex-SEC attorney was being brought in to combat the evil forces, to bury the criminals, and to help get the company reporting again. And if Sterling was right about the one trillion share naked short position, maybe he was right about everything else too.

A dollar a share.

No one needed a calculator to do the math on that scenario. A dollar a share meant every CMKX stockholder would become an instant millionaire, all 50,000+ of them. John Martin, and thousands of other nearly rabid shareholders, kept buying.

Like almost every other CMKX shareholder in the world, John knew this was the stock that would make his family rich, and the fact that he was still completely neglecting his business, and that they were rapidly draining their savings accounts with every passing week, suddenly didn't seem to matter at all. Not only would they catch up, they would do it all at once, and even make enough money to live comfortably for the rest of their lives. All from this one little diamond mine company. John felt invincible, as if nothing could stop him from finally realizing his dreams.

Glenn gives shareholders the thumbs up.
Courtesy of Jason Webb and Anthony Pullicino.

Monday, June 7, 2004

That was the day. After a weekend of around-the-clock postings on the message boards and continuous anticipation on *Paltalk* and the other chat rooms, after Uncle Melvi's "my whole damn leg is tingling" interview, after a weekend that seemed as if it would never end, the stock opened strong on Monday morning and never looked back. It traded a stunning 18 billion shares, but more importantly, it closed at .0008 a share, a gain of eight hundred percent for the lucky ones who were smart enough to buy at the lows. On CMKX message boards all over the world, in every chat room, in dozens of different languages, the feeling was the same – this stock was never coming back down. Mount St. Helens had officially exploded.

> belgamees 7 Juni 2004, 21:02– "CMKX, ziet er naar uit dat we nog een trap hoger zullen gaan, Nite en Scwab on bid at 0.0007, ask at 0.0008 is al behoorlijk uitgedund. A close of 0.001 is possible !!!!"

> Anoniem, 7 Juni 2004 - 23:43- "Belgamees, ik denk dat we
> hiermee goed zitten. - Ze zeggen hier "zot zijn doet niet
> zeer" -Maar wij gaan het spreekwoord veranderen, en dat
> is dat van" 't zijn zotten die werken " -want dit is " the
> sky is the limit"

John Martin bought another million shares.

Over the remainder of the week, the stock continued to trade tens of billions of shares, and except for stopping and catching its breath a couple of times, the price never really wavered. Then, just as it had the week before, CMKX came out with news Friday night at midnight. It was short and to the point:

"LAS VEGAS, Jun 10, 2004 (BUSINESS WIRE) -- CMKM Diamonds Inc. (Pink Sheets: CMKX) is very excited to announce that the 'Carolyn Pipe' is confirmed to be diamondiferous. Saskatchewan Research Council (SRC), an independent lab located in Saskatoon, Saskatchewan reported to the company today that the core samples from the 'Carolyn Pipe' has come back positive for diamond content."

Along with the report of diamond content in the core samples, *The Faulking Truth* reported that weekend that *Dateline* had a huge exposé in the works on the naked short selling scandal, that had been dubbed Stockgate, involving over a hundred hours of interviews and thousands of hours of research. Rescheduled from earlier in the year to August, it could only help Urban's master plan to trap the short sellers, and with the help of Roger Glenn, set off the mother of all short squeezes.

The weekend was essentially a repeat of the one before, with the seconds ticking by like hours, marking time before the stock market opened again on Monday morning. John Martin began to despise weekends and holidays, and spent the majority of what should have been his time away from the world of CMKX, doing research on the message boards. Weekends that would have been better spent with his family, visiting friends, or rebuilding his sorely neglected business were whiled away with the thousands of other shareholders, counting the minutes until they could again experience the adrenaline rush of watching the CMKX ticker reel off trades faster than any stock in the entire history of the stock market.

Monday, June 14, 2004

Once again, the anticipation from the weekend triggered even more buying, and of course the single magic word "diamondiferous" just added fuel to the CMKX rocket ship. The price continued its climb, breaking a tenth of a penny for the first time since March 14, 2003 – fifteen months ago to the day. No news came out that day, but it didn't seem to matter. Another 17.5 billion shares traded, and it closed the day at .001. If an investor was smart to invest a hundred thousand dollars at the low of only two weeks earlier, he or she was now officially a millionaire, just like that. But still, CMKX felt like a rocket ship hurtling into the stratosphere, like an exploding volcano, like Mount St. Helens. Most shareholders not only didn't cash in their fortunes at that price, they were still accumulating more shares for the next leg up.

Bill Frizzell, at the urging of John Martin, made a couple of phone calls and did a preliminary background check on Roger Glenn after his hiring was announced by the company. Everything looked good, and as far as Bill could tell, Glenn was legit. Bill Frizzell bought another 2,895,000 shares of CMKM stock at a tenth of a penny, and John Martin bought another million shares at the high of the day, at .0011, at a total cost of eleven hundred dollars. It didn't matter that he had only paid a fraction of that amount for his first million shares, the stock was running. After languishing between .0001 and .0002 for almost a year, it couldn't be stopped. John Martin, and 50,000 thousand other shareholders, some of whom had invested, incredibly, upwards of a million dollars in this improbable long shot of a dream, could scarcely wait to see where the CMKX roller coaster ride would take them next. CMKX finally became The Perfect Storm.

Chapter 12 – From the Perfect Storm to the Mother Lode

"It WILL pay off for these people. I can't emphasize this enough. This thing WILL pay off. Just trust us, believe in us. I've seen it with my own eyes, guys. I know what's here. The potential is astronomical. It is unreal."

~ Melvin O'Neil, CMKX Investor Relations, June 16, 2004, IBC Radio

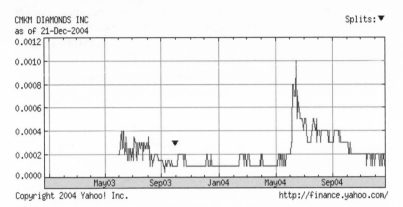

The spike in CMKX price when Roger Glenn came on board.

Tuesday, June 15, 2004

In a single day, CMKX's stock lost half its value. Just like that, the CMKX roller coaster ride crested at the top of the hill, paused for a single breathtaking moment, and began a nauseating plummet into the void. People who had become paper millionaires on Monday were only half as rich on Tuesday. Another 21 billions shares traded, but this time it felt like shareholders unloading their shares instead of accumulating, or at least it was clear that someone was selling. The selling seemed to be triggered by a press release from two of CMKX's venture partners revealing that the diamonds found in the Carolyn Pipe core samples were actually just two microdiamonds, later described by *StockWatch.com* as "two tiny stones with a combined weight of 0.000005 carats."

Even so, for the true believers on the message boards, the drop in price just didn't make sense. The company still owned the rights to 1.4 million acres of land surrounding De Beers property in prime potential diamond territory, and they had just hired a high-powered attorney who would presumably deal with the naked short problem, get the company reporting again, and maybe even take it to a more prestigious stock exchange. Veteran penny stock traders, who had seen this happen countless times before with other bulletin board stocks, were taken by surprise as well. Very few people claimed to be sellers, yet somehow, tens of billions of shares were still being unloaded into the market.

93

Talk of a massive naked short resurfaced, of counterfeit shares being dumped off on unsuspecting buyers. On a market wide level, internet advocates of stock market reform called for an investigation into the SEC, who had admitted themselves that the overall stock market abuse had resulted, in some instances, "with settlement failures exceeding the entire float of some companies."

It wasn't long before Sterling's Perfect Storm guesstimate of one trillion counterfeit shares had somehow been upwardly revised on the message boards to three trillion shares, shares that would eventually have to be purchased from existing shareholders, and they weren't selling. Somehow, CMKX traded over 130 billion shares in the span of eleven short days, by far the largest number of shares ever bought by one group of shareholders in the history of the stock market. It was a mind-boggling, heart pounding, adrenaline-fueled rush unlike anything most of these investors had ever experienced before.

The same people who were the most vocal advocates of the company seemed to back away from some of their earlier hyperbole, but for the masses who had invested their hearts, souls, and millions and millions of dollars in Urban Casavant's dream. It was a heart-wrenching turn of events, to say the least.

Even Uncle Melvi seemed to momentarily lose his enthusiasm as the price dropped and phone calls from irate shareholders increased by the day.

"A press release came out today; they found a couple of micro diamonds. I want the shareholders of CMKX to realize something... that it's better than not finding anything, correct? They have to realize that Rome was not built in a day. We've got a lot of work ahead of us. We have a lot of holes to drill.

Like I said, I am a straight shooter, I don't BS nobody. The results we got today back from this other company, yeah I'll admit it, they're not that great. Is this the tip of the iceberg? Well, certainly it is.

Is Mt. St. Helens ready to blow up? No. I never said it would. I'm just saying that she's a rumbling, and uhh....just be patient folks, is all I ask, from Uncle Melvi, just be patient. You gotta walk before you run.

I've gotten calls the past two weeks, you wouldn't believe the calls I've gotten in the last two weeks, and everyone seems to ask the same thing, where do you see this thing going? How high can we go? Hell guys, I don't know, I'm not a stock market guru, my crystal ball is in the shop getting fixed.

It's not like we can't pick up a rig and move it someplace else and try somewhere else. What do you think Kensington and De Beers have been doing for the last 20 years? If you walk up to Kensington's site right now, they've punched over 80 holes in the last five years.

I never said we had the biggest find ever. I never said CMKX is the largest diamond find in the world. When I said the largest diamond find in the world, I meant the ENTIRE area.

CMKX, as we all know, is a small junior diamond mining company. What do we do for a living? We drill for diamonds. That's what we do. The fact is we have over a million acres that we can drill. I believe in this company.

All I'm saying is people, for God's sake, give us a chance. Hang in there with us. That is all Uncle Melvi asks."

When a caller to the IBC show asked about CMKX releasing information about the number of shares in the company, O'Neil responded in classic Uncle Melvi style:

"I can sum that up in one word: We want to become a reporting company. Okay, that's more than one word. He (Mr. Casavant) WILL bring out the share structure of this company come hell or high water, because when you become a fully-reporting company you have to do that."

Wednesday, June 16, 2004

Uncle Melvi regained his composure a bit the next day, beginning his IBC radio interview that day with "I'm not going to pump it up, but..." and then closing with:

"It WILL pay off for these people. I can't emphasize this enough. This thing WILL pay off. Just trust us, believe in us. I've seen it with my own eyes, guys. I know what's here. The potential is astronomical. It is unreal."

That same day, a CMKM shareholder called in to IBC Radio, and he seemed to put things into perspective for all of the CMKX shareholders. Not only was he was articulate and well-spoken, he was rational as well. None of the far-fetched pie-in-the-sky predictions for this shareholder, just a well thought out analysis of the situation. It was exactly what the shareholders needed, a calming voice amidst the ups and downs of the stormy sea that CMKX had suddenly become:

Announcer: *"Hello, you're on the air."*

Caller: *"Yeah, I just wanted to call, this is Joel from Florida."*

Announcer: *"Joel from Florida."*

Joel from Florida: *"I haven't called in awhile, and I am a big CMKM shareholder, and I was wondering how many people have actually taken the time to look at the press release that came out. If you look at the PR itself, it clearly identifies that CMKM is the operator, but what people don't realize is that all four companies have to share in the cost of the samples being tested and so forth, and it says that after the testing of the first samples that all four companies had decided to do further testing on the other samples. Now those four companies would not have done that if there wasn't something there.*

When you look at the maps that everybody pays attention to, what De Beers did when they did the first aerial surveys, there was a massive cluster of magnetic kimberlites that were identified, and they bought the lease rights to that property. This new anomaly that CMKM and these four partners have found is a non-magnetic kimberlite in that same cluster. Now those kimberlite bodies that belong to De Beers are already known to have the diamond content that is sufficient for mining. This is what I think Melvin and some of the others have been excited about, is that this other site is right next to the major seventy kimberlite clusters that belong to De Beers.

Everything in this PR is actually very positive if somebody will take the time to read it and realize that this is something that progresses over time. We've got day-traders that are falling out because you didn't have five-carat rough stones in a sample that's two-inches in diameter drilled down through the ground.

What people need to understand is, out of this million point four acres, all they need is one. One good kimberlite find would take the price of that stock and shoot it from where it is now to what we would consider "to the moon."

So if you're going public, you're going to release your share structure, you're going to a major exchange, you've hired a major law firm, and you've targeted a new drilling site right next to the De Beers cluster, you're re-sampling those samples that you have…"

Announcer: *"Well, I wouldn't call the OTCBB a 'major exchange.'"*

Joel from Florida: *"Well, I agree with that, but I think, and rightfully so, that maybe this is a stepping stone. I think until the price per share gets up to around a dollar, why try to go to NASDAQ or the American Stock Exchange or something? You have to establish legitimacy, we all understand that, but this is mining, and mining is prospecting, and if you hit gold, you hit gold, if you hit dirt, you hit dirt, you know?*

There are some companies that are day-trades, and there are other companies that are long-term plays, and I think that CMKX is a company that is at least trying to find that value and get this company off the ground. It only takes one of substantial size to make the value of the company just skyrocket. I would suggest that everybody pull out the PR and read through it, and you won't find anything negative in it. Somebody got on one of the boards and wrote 'BAD

NEWS' and buddy, people clicked on that, and that's all that they saw, and buddy, the selling went wild."

Wednesday, June 17, 2004

The next day, "Joel from Florida" called again, and by this time, his comments from the day before had already been spread throughout the message boards as if they were gospel. Listeners hung on his every word as he seemed to be both the voice of reason and a beacon of hope:

Announcer: *"Hello, you're on the air."*

Caller: *"Yeah, this is Joel from Florida."*

Announcer: *"Hey Joel, how you doing?"*

Joel from Florida: *"Good. Listen, I just wanted to share something with the investors out there that are in CMKM, just to kind of put something in perspective for some of them that I don't think really understand what's going on.*

Just like when there was a gold rush in California, why did everybody go to the same spot, why did the mining towns grow in the same areas? Because everybody wanted to go where somebody had already found gold, and what has happened in Forte á la Corne is the same identical thing. De Beers found what at the time they thought was the mother lode. As soon as that became known publicly, people started rushing there just like in the gold rush. The only thing that people don't realize is that while everyone was kind of debating on what to do, Urban was doing the right thing. He was going around and securing all of that land, and when you think about that, he has one point four million acres to look in right now – that is an unbelievable thing. He went in and literally did a clean sweep throughout Forte á la Corne to make sure that he could secure as much land adjacent to those kimberlites as possible.

One of the things that I guess is important to kind of dispel is the myth that Melvin and Urban are sitting up there in Forte á la Corne like Laurel and Hardy, sitting around the campfire just saturating the market with shares, and then they're gonna pack their bags and go home, that's simply not the case. If I was gonna bet my money on a company that was doing what we consider treasure hunting for all practical purposes, I would want to invest my money with a company that has basically staked a claim right next to somebody who has already found the mother lode, and that's what he has done."

Announcer: *"We've got some listeners that want to know your credentials."*

Joel from Florida: *"My credentials? I'll just say this. I have an intimate knowledge of the wholesale diamond industry, and we'll leave it at that. Actually, not so much on the mining scale, but definitely on the cutting and the distribution, and that type of thing. In fact I've been all over New York, and I actually am a diamond cutter, and I've cut diamonds in the past, so I have a little bit of experience in that.*

A week later, the company released results of an "airborne magnetic survey" of their claims, which were apparently positive enough that Uncle Melvi said on IBC that "when I spoke to Mr. Casavant yesterday on the phone, I had to peel him off the wall. He knows what we have. We all know what we have."

What CMKX had, according to the press release, was "hundreds of magnetic anomalies" that indicated potential diamond content.

Casavant said, "the company is very pleased with the results of the survey. For the first time in the history of diamond exploration in the Forte á la Corne area, a complete and comprehensive magnetic picture of the whole area is available to the company."

The magnetic surveys were enough give hope to the shareholders, and just as Roger Glenn being brought in to combat the naked short sellers seemed to give credence to Sterling's Perfect Storm analogy, and Uncle Melvi's and Urban's latest comments seemed to add instant credibility to Joel from Florida's "Mother Lode" scenario.

On June 29th, the company fired 1st Global Transfer and hired a new transfer agent, Pacific Stock Transfer, reportedly to help Roger Glenn clean up the naked short selling problem and get rid of the trillion plus shares of counterfeit stock that the message boards were certain existed. The stock price went up one one-hundredth of a cent.

Then, the following day, Joel from Florida called IBC Radio again, and one could almost see every listener lean forward in anticipation waiting for Joel to speak, except this time the news wasn't what shareholders wanted to hear:

Announcer: *"Hello you're on the air."*

Caller: *"Hey, this is Joel from Florida."*

Announcer: *"Hi Joel how are ya"*

Joel from Florida: *"Pretty good. Listen, I know there's a lot of buzz going around about the outstanding shares for CMKM coming out this week, and I was just told what the actual outstanding shares are. There was 500 billion authorized, and there have been 400 billion issued. 400 billion."*

Announcer: *"What? Is that right? That's the buzz you've heard, huh?"*

Joel from Florida: *"Well, no I just got that directly from the transfer agent. I just got off the phone with them."*

Announcer: *"Wow! Okay hold on – say that again. 400 billion?!"*

Joel from Florida: *"400 billion shares have been issued for CMKM according to the new transfer agent."*

Announcer: *"Okay...okay."*

Joel from Florida: *"We were hoping obviously it would be much lower than that."*

Announcer: *"That's breaking news, the company itself hasn't even released that."*

Almost immediately, Melvin called IBC to refute Joel's claims:

"Okay, here we go, let's put a cap on this sucker right now. That is not true. Okay? I'm gonna say to each and every one out there again, and read my lips folks, if you don't hear it from an official press release from this company, if you do not hear it from Melvin, not Uncle Melvi, but Melvin, then disregard it. I'm tired of this BS going around. If you want to speculate about things like this, then that's totally fine with me, but until you hear it in a one hundred and ten percent official press release, please disregard it. End of conversation."

But then, a few minutes later, Audrey Hepburn called in to IBC Radio and confirmed Joel's information that, according to the transfer agent, CMKX had indeed issued a staggering 400 billion shares of company stock, ten times the number of shares Sterling had used in his Perfect Storm analogy. If the anticipation could be sensed from the listeners before, the collective shock they felt now was even greater. Joel once again called in and commented that shareholders would now have "to make an intelligent decision about whether they want to wait this thing out knowing there's 400 billion shares."

Over the next few days, the "intelligent decision" that many shareholders made was to dump their stock. By the following week, the price had dropped another forty percent, and the company promptly fired Pacific Stock Transfer, who had told Joel and Audrey Hepburn about the 400 billion shares of stock the company had issued. They rehired 1st Global, in a press release that read in its entirety: "CMKM Diamonds Inc. (Pink Sheets:CMKX) announces 1st Global Stock Transfer, LLC. has been re-engaged as the company's transfer agent." Not a single word was mentioned about the 400 billion shares that had been issued and confirmed by Pacific Stock Transfer.

Even after Uncle Melvi's "I can sum that up in one word: We want to become a reporting company" comment, even after his "come hell or high water" promise that Urban would bring out the share structure, even after his "until you hear it in a one hundred and ten percent official press release" assertion, the company never said a word about the 400 billion shares of stock that had been issued, and presumably sold to unsuspecting shareholders.

Chapter 13 – The Stock Play of a Lifetime

"The company's accountants are working to complete the audit of the company's financial statements. When that has been accomplished, the company will be well on its way to becoming a reporting company again."

~D. Roger Glenn, Sept. 24, 2004

400 billion shares.

It was a staggering number; one so large it was difficult to appreciate how many shares that actually represented, and even more difficult to explain it. However, the message boards, as always, found a way to spin the latest setback for CMKX shareholders. The plan was as simple as it was brilliant: Urban had raised the authorized shares to 500 billion, and let the news leak out there were 400 billion shares on the market, but in reality, those shares had never been sold into the market.

In fact, many message board posters believed the company was secretly buying back billions of the shares already out there. They theorized that hundreds of billions of shares were being bought and sold by the bad guys, explaining both the massive volume and the low share price, but only a hundred billion *real* shares existed. Then, when the brokers and naked short sellers had flooded the market with hundreds of billions of counterfeit shares, Urban and Roger Glenn would force them to buy back the shares at a huge premium.

After the run of mid-June 2004, the company continued to issue press release after press release, but once the 400 billion share count was revealed, the stock settled back into the three one-hundredths of a cent range, and for the time being, stayed there. The daily volume remained in the billions, but it was difficult to tell if the same shares were being bought and sold between the shareholders themselves, if the brokers and naked short sellers were still flooding the market with counterfeit shares, or if the company itself was dumping shares by the billions. There were no more twenty billion share days, in fact, over the next three months, trading only broke ten billion shares once.

In June of the same year, Hartley Bernstein began writing about CMKX. He was a former attorney who had been convicted of stock fraud before reportedly turning over a new leaf when he started a website called *StockPatrol.com* to expose penny stock scams. While many federal regulators touted Bernstein's website as a valuable tool in exposing fraud, it was also well-known that similar websites had been utilized by hedge funds to bash companies in stock manipulation schemes. *Stock Patrol* wrote several articles about CMKX, and in many cases, raised valid questions about the company.

Bernstein's earliest articles, like those of *Dow Jones* writer Carol Remond, dealt mostly with the massive volume of CMKX shares that were traded on a regular basis, and about the lack of public information the company released. He did, however, make note of information he had received about "almost 7 billion shares or 85.8% of the outstanding stock, purportedly held by individuals, corporations and trusts" who were owed money by the company, implying this might be the source of some of the stock that seemed to be flooding the market. He also pointed out that another one billion shares had been issued to two unnamed consultants on May 2, 2003.

In July of '04, *The Green Baron* ran the first of many positive profiles on the company, beginning by calling it a "stock to watch," then, after interviewing Urban Casavant in mid-July, became CMKX shareholders themselves. *The Green Baron*, run by CEO Ed Miller, became more and more positive on CMKX, and by August, were ending their articles by saying that CMKX could be "The Stock Play of a Lifetime."

The following month, yet another internet website, *Stockwatch.com*, began coverage of CMKX as well, siding with Bernstein and *Stock Patrol* and writing several unflattering articles about CMKX over the next few months. It became obvious there were two sides to the story, and that those two sides were miles apart.

But still, the press releases kept coming, and for all practical purposes, the company's prospects still looked good, their future as bright as diamonds. In mid-July, they signed a deal with US Canadian Minerals (UCAD) to sell part of their mineral rights in exchange for shares of UCAD and $15 million in cash. The stock price went up one one-hundredth of a cent, but the next day dropped back down a hundredth of a cent. On July 19, CMKX bought ten percent of the mineral claims of another Casavant company for one million dollars. The stock price went back up two one-hundredths of a cent.

Then, in a four day period between July 22 and July 26, the company bought sixty percent of the mineral rights of a half-million acres of potential kimberlite mineral property from Nevada Minerals, collected a $3 million down payment on the UCAD deal, and bought twenty-five percent of the shares of Juina Mining (GEMM) for $500,000. The stock price went up one one-hundredth of a cent, dropped two hundredths of a cent, then went back up one one-hundredth of a cent – and ended up exactly where it had begun, at .0004.

In August, the company distributed the GEMM shares to their shareholders as a dividend. They began test drilling for diamonds on CMKX land near where Shore Gold had found an almost 20 carat diamond and 33 other diamonds larger than one carat. They then offered a "VISA Pre-Paid Stored Value" credit card to their shareholders and CMKXtreme racing fans. The stock opened the month at .0004, and ended the month at .0003.

In September, the company sold five percent of their mineral rights for $10 million dollars and 200 million shares to St. George Metals (SGGM) and collected a $2,500,000 check as down payment, picked up another $2,500,000 check eleven days later, cashed a third check for $2,500,000 on September 22, and collected the last $2,500,000 check on the 28th. They also drilled two test holes looking for diamonds. The stock opened the month at .0003....and once again ended the month right where it started, at .0003.

In September, *The Green Baron's* Ed Miller agreed to debate *Stock Patrol's* Hartley Bernstein on a national internet radio show on *Christian Financial Radio Network* called "Prosperity for God's People," hosted by Pastor DeWayne Reeves, also a CMKX shareholder. Billed as "The Great Debate," the interview was hyped for weeks, but fizzled out when, as *The Green Baron* later put it:

> *"Stock Patrol's Hartley Bernstein had an accident the day before our scheduled debate, and wound up on an ill-timed airplane trip with spotty telephone service during the radio show. We had been anticipating a healthy debate, but instead Mr. Miller was left alone to support our feelings about CMKX.*
>
> *The Green Baron Report still has a lot of unanswered questions for CMKM Diamonds, many of which may be the same questions that Mr. Bernstein may have. However, Mr. Bernstein fails to recognize that CMKM Diamonds has received $13 million in cash over the past two months and has struck deals with U.S. Canadian Minerals (UCAD), Juina Mining (GEMM), and Casavant International Mining (CIM – private) in stock transactions that we estimate are currently worth about $70 million to CMKX."*

After citing the numerous developments that the company had released, and predicting that "September will be the month that we will begin to see the price per share move higher in CMKX," *The Green Baron* closed with their by now familiar mantra:

> *"If CMKM Diamonds begins to announce significant diamond content in samples on its vast mineral right claims CMKX may well become The Stock Play of a Lifetime!"*

A message board poster who called himself Oaks, who in reality was Andy Hill, phrased it in more colorful terms, claiming that the *Green Baron's* Ed Miller "scored a STUNNING first round technical knockout win against Hartley Bernstein of *Stock Patrol*." He continued by comparing it to a prize fight, an analogy that seemed to be appropriate considering the battle lines that were clearly forming between the believers and the bashers.

> In a no contest, Ed Miller came fully prepared to debate the Green Baron's pro position on CMKX. In utter amazement Mr. Hartley announced he was on a plane and might be unable to keep his connection alive to participate in the debate. Several minutes later Mr. Hartley did confirm he was UNABLE TO CONTINUE and left the RING.
>
> The judges unanimously applauded Mr. Miller for coming to the debate fully prepared to defend Green Baron's integrity.

> In looking back at history, Mr. Hartley's failure to
> continue reminds us of Roberto Duran's 'NO MAS' boxing
> defeat when he refused to continue in his fight against
> Sugar Ray Leonard.
>
> Will there be a rematch after today's pitiful performance
> by Mr. Hartley? It looks highly improbable that Hartley
> will enter the ring again against Miller.

The same month, *Stockwatch*'s Lee Webb wrote a lengthy article about the aborted debate, on the one hand discussing Bernstein's stock fraud conviction, and on the other hand, repeatedly referring to *The Green Baron's* Miller as a stock tout. In the same article Webb dropped another bombshell: he released information showing CMKX's authorized shares had been raised yet again, this time to 800 billion shares, and estimated an actual share count in excess of 700 billion.

All in all, over the three and a half month period immediately following the run of early June, the stock lost over seventy-five percent of its value, with a closing price of .0003 at the end of September. The one million shares John Martin bought for eleven hundred dollars were now worth $300. Shareholders who owned stock worth a million dollars at the peak, now held $272,000 worth of stock. They lost $828,000 in three weeks. The stock did not, as *The Green Baron*, John Martin, and tens of thousands of other shareholders hoped, "begin to move higher in September."

However, during that same time period, a total of 265 billion shares were bought and sold, bringing the total number of shares traded from June to September to a staggering 400 billion shares. Ironically, that matched the total number of shares CMKX had issued...before *Stockwatch* revealed the increase to 800 billion. Tens of thousands of shareholders were turned from average citizens into potential millionaires, and back into average citizens again. And still, after all of that, even after the price ran up over 1000 percent...and right back down again...most shareholders never lost faith in CMKX, in Urban Casavant, and in the Stock Play of a Lifetime.

Chapter 14 – All That Glitters

Sitting here staring at the snow on the mountains
Dreaming of my house with gold covered fountains
Some of my friends slingin' gold in ounces
That was never really just how my ball bounces
Some day I'm gonna drive a nice car
CMKX gonna make me a star
You never really know how close you are
Every day I pray that it's not very far

~"Wild West Desperado"
By Aaron Rose
From the CD "CMKXtreme Music"

December 21, 2004

Northeast of Tulsa.

That's where the snow was supposed to be. John was driving north from Tyler, twelve hundred sleds in tow, and still, the events of the past year were rolling around in his head. The past couple of months had been incredibly hard for John and the entire Martin family, just as it had for most of the other 50,000+ CMKX shareholders. Luckily, John and Jill had sold their house and bought another one, and the money they put aside from the move kept them more or less afloat for the first half of 2004.

Then came the second half of the year, and their savings were pretty much shot, and the bills began to pile up. To save money, they cut corners - lights were turned off when they left every room, showers were limited to no more than five-minutes. When asked about it later, John described it as "six months of steadily..." and his voice broke just a little and trailed off.

Jill finished his thought, "...sinking."

"...Sinking the rest of our money into it," John added.

Six months of barely staying afloat and six months of steadily sinking.

It was not the year John or Jill had envisioned, but it didn't dampen John's optimism heading into Fall. He was still spending almost all his time on the message boards, mostly *Sterling's Classroom* on *Raging Bull*, or *Proboards66*, reading every post and analyzing every word, every theory, and every rumor. He could always go onto the message boards and find things to be optimistic about; every interview, every event, every press release was quickly spun in the most positive light possible, and it helped John justify the hard times they were going through.

And still, with almost no income coming in, John looked for ways to feed his habit, for money to buy more shares. He described it later as being "like a drug addict going through withdrawal." In retrospect, it was easy for John to see how addicted he was to the stock, to the excitement of the message boards and to the company itself, but at the time it was a different story altogether:

"You want to be on those boards with the people that are in the same boat with you. They understand...they have the same motivation. When the days were down, everybody fed off of each other. When the days were up, everybody fed off of each other. And it's an irrational mentality to some degree, but unfortunately, that's the way people are sometimes.

And the one little thing that goes out on those boards can change the entire face or outlook of the entire group. One little thing! Based off of what one person says! And I think that's what happens when certain people, people who have earned some degree of credibility for one reason or another, get out on the boards.

In this particular case...I remember distinctly, we would get odd number trades that would go through. Well, that was a signal from one market maker to the other. So, we figured out, every time one of the market makers would do something, what was going to happen next based on the trade. So, we're analyzing everything. We're analyzing the trade size...why would one hundred shares of a .0001 stock go through? Must have been a signal! So, now I look back at that and I think...why can't you call a market maker with a cell phone? You don't need to run a hundred share trade through! What's wrong with an email or an instant message?

'By the way, we're going to run the stock' - click, click, click. And in this particular case they had code! And we had the whole code written out! And it was ironic, but every time the hundred share trade would go through, the same thing would happen! There might be a computer glitch, who knows, but we had this thing...a hundred meant this; a hundred and fifty meant that, two hundred mean that, it was like Morse code!

I look back now on the things that some people on the boards tend to believe, things that look so silly. But when I was there in that boat, those same things made perfect sense to me."

Secret codes or no secret codes, one thing was very real. The planning for the CMKX/UCAD Shareholders' Party was in full swing and the Martins' "temporary" money woes would surely be nothing but a bad memory by Christmas. John was confident that the shareholders' patience would be richly rewarded by August, and certainly no later than the party at the end of October. And as he told Jill time and time again, "even if it only goes to a nickel, we're set for life!"

Maybe that was true, but hope didn't pay the bills. Jill did whatever she could to keep a little money coming in, charting out his routes and making lists of the clients he needed to see in an effort to coax him away from the computer and his obsession with CMKX. Even on those rare occasions when Jill persuaded him to leave the house for a couple of hours and make the rounds to his rapidly diminishing list of clients to bring home enough money to at least keep the utilities on, it was only because she took over his post at the computer. Jill became John's unwilling accomplice just so a little money would trickle in, and even then, he would call in between every stop, anxious to hear what he missed while he was away from the action:

"So what is everyone saying? Any news out, any new rumors going around? What's the volume? What're the headlines on the boards?"

It was a struggle to keep from drowning in the sea of debt piling up from every direction – they were months behind on their house and car payments, their credit cards were useless - maxed out and long overdue. Even checking the mail and answering the telephone became a depressing ritual. They finally resorted to having their phone number changed, but that backfired when bill collectors began calling their neighbors and asking them to "go next door and deliver a message to the Martins." After that, it became an embarrassment to leave the house and walk out to the mailbox to get the mail, which came in rubber-banded bundles of delinquent bills that would barely fit into their mail box.

Just months earlier, they had been upwardly mobile, moving into a gorgeous home in a nice neighborhood in the suburbs. Now they were reduced to taking five-minute showers, eating beans and rice, and selling the pecans that fell from the trees in their backyard…and their neighbors' backyards as well.

But the big shareholders party was just around the corner, and CMKX was certain to hit by then. John, like thousands of other shareholders, was one hundred percent certain there would be huge announcements at the party – a merger between CMKX and UCAD, a release of the information Roger Glenn had been putting together to place a real valuation on the company's considerable assets, an announcement that the naked short sellers, the corrupt brokers, and the market makers had all been trapped by Urban's brilliant plan of issuing shares but never selling them into the market. It would still be the best Christmas ever at the Martin household.

John and Jill Martin, like thousands of other shareholders, weren't interested in simply lining their own pockets, or padding their personal bank accounts. They hoped to share their soon-to-be good fortune with those who needed it the most after paying off their debts and catching up on their house payments. John and Jill had one more secret hope – to use part of the money they made from CMKX to build a church for the Reverend John Martin III.

Then, just a few days before the big party, shareholders were hit with a double whammy. The SEC temporarily halted the trading of UCAD stock, and at almost exactly the same time, Canadian regulators placed a halt on CMKX trading as well, charging Urban Casavant, David DeSormeau, and Melvin O'Neil with selling unregistered shares of CMKI and CMKM in Saskatchewan.

The shareholders were convinced it was nothing more than a desperate act on the part of the SEC to slow down the CMKX juggernaut, a last-ditch effort to bury the avalanche of stock counterfeiting Urban and Roger Glenn were getting ready to expose to the entire world. The common belief was that the ensuing "short squeeze," where the bad guys and corrupt brokers would have to buy back stock that had never been delivered in the first place, could potentially crater the entire stock market. They were equally convinced it was just another speed bump on their road to riches, another twist in the CMKXtreme roller coaster ride to prosperity.

Although the vast majority of shareholders were unaware that anything was amiss until the SEC halted trading in UCAD, and Canadian authorities did the same to CMKX, a few message board posters were feeling uneasy about apparent connections between people associated with the two companies.

One poster on the *Allstocks.com* message board, who called himself tic_ toc, posted a complicated and disturbing message just two weeks before the big party, questioning connections between BBX Equity and both CMKX and UCAD. He pointed out that before UCAD became U.S. Canadian Minerals it had been a company called Barrington Foods, and that BBX Equity funded Barrington Foods. Mike King, who was director of BBX Equity and also ran Princeton Research, was on the board of directors of CMKX, appointed at the same time as Richard Taulli...who was listed as the treasurer of UCAD, and was connected to Juina Mining...who had ties to CMKX as well. A man by the name of John Woodward was the president of UCAD, and had also recently resigned as the president of Crystalix, another publicly traded company that had received $2 million in funding from CMKXtreme. If that wasn't confusing enough, Mike King and Princeton Research handled public relations for Crystalix, and King was a director for another company called CCO, Inc., along with an attorney named John Dolkart, who had been disbarred for misconduct in 1997. King had also been charged with securities violations concerning CCO, Inc., and was represented by Dolkart. Finally, Dolkart was the spokesperson for CMKX in late 2002, when it was still CMKI.

In summary, Mike King had ties to UCAD, Crystalix and CCO. Richard Taulli was connected to UCAD and Juina Mining. John Woodward was linked to UCAD and Crystalix. Disbarred attorney John Dolkart was connected to CCO... and all four of them were connected to CMKX. Not quite certain what it all meant, but bothered by the apparent shady dealings of some of the players and their ties to CMKX, tic_toc ended his comment with "It gets more complicated the deeper I dig, and I'm not liking some of the things I'm finding."

Like most shareholders, John Martin chose to ignore the occasional disconcerting post on the message boards, and upheld complete faith in Urban Casavant and CMKX. In fact, up until UCAD was shut down from trading in the US and CMKX was halted in Canada, John and Jill were making plans to go to the shareholders' party in Las Vegas, even though they had no idea how they were going to pay for the trip. Once the news broke, they decided to stay home, knowing that the SEC action against UCAD would probably prevent the two companies from making their scheduled major announcements.

John was one of thousands of shareholders who attended the party vicariously, monitoring the message boards, reading Audrey Hepburn and the other attendees' blow-by-blow accounts of the infamous nonevent turned near brawl. He was glued to the message boards while the Elvis impersonators performed for those lucky enough to make the pilgrimage to Vegas, belting out the lyrics to the unofficial theme song for the city that never sleeps, *Viva Las Vegas*. He read along while the Canadian shareholder, who was ridiculed on the message boards for speaking out, gave her impromptu speech while the members of *Love Shack* looked nervously on. Had he been there, John would have seen that the infamous "drunk and crazy" Canadian shareholder was neither drunk nor crazy, she was merely voicing the frustration of most of the shareholders who had traveled all the way to Vegas to hear "The Announcements."

In between songs from the band, she climbed onstage and grabbed the microphone, angry but clearly in control of her faculties. While the B-52's dressed lead singer and her Devo look-alike band mate looked nervously on, the shareholder gave the only real speech that anyone would hear that night:

"I came here tonight trusting that CMKX would be honest with us, and that they would give us some information."

An anonymous voice from the crowd shouted "It ain't over yet!" but the Canadian woman was undeterred, continuing on with her comments, interrupted only by the sound of applause and cheering.

"It ain't over yet? I know it's not over yet. But you know what? I'd sure like some information tonight. Didn't all of you come looking for some information tonight?"

The crowd applauded.

"Everyone came looking for some information tonight. I'm from Canada, I'm from Canada, Alberta...Calgary. And I'd sure like some goddamn information. I really would."

Another round of applause erupted from the crowd. She continued:

"All of you deserve that. I know all of you are dissatisfied here tonight. Sure, it was a great party, we all danced and drank, whatever...but we don't know

any more than what we started with. I'm not satisfied with the information I got tonight."

And with those final words, she walked offstage. As *Love Shack* launched into *99 Red Balloons,* Urban Casavant, Ed Dhonau, and Rendal Williams were quickly ushered out of the room by their hired bodyguards. The party ended, leaving John Martin and thousands of others wondering what was going on in Las Vegas *and* with CMKX and UCAD.

While he tried to believe the halt was only temporary and that Roger Glenn, ex-SEC attorney extraordinaire (and who was known to be in Las Vegas at that very moment), would swoop in and save the day, a small nagging voice of doubt crept into his head after the party. At that moment, even though he still tried to consciously deny it, he knew there was a real chance that CMKX wasn't going to pay off, at least not before Christmas.

By November, the considerably less colorful Andrew Hill had replaced Uncle Melvi as head of investor relations and even the *Green Baron* had begun to temper their predictions:

"The Green Baron Report would love to predict that CMKM Diamonds will begin its move higher in December. We originally thought that the 'Christmas in July' rumors were hogwash, and the 'Santa is arriving in August' was a little premature. The Green Baron Report itself even thought September would ring in the Holidays early based on the idea that CMKX naked shorts (its existence now appears widely accepted) would need to cover prior to the US Canadian Minerals (UCAD/USCA) dividend payout. Instead, we all saw what happened to the price of UCAD when these shorts decided not to cover CMKX and try to pay out the UCAD dividend.

So now Thanksgiving is just about upon us, and Christmas truly is right around the corner. We would love to tell our members that CMKM Diamonds stock will provide you with the best Christmas ever, but the only thing we can predict with certainty is that Christmas will indeed be in December. However, if we all just try to take a moment this time of the year and do something kind for another in need, perhaps by the time we hit the New Year we might discover that CMKM Diamonds is The Stock Play of a Lifetime (that is, unless you are short)."

Christmas. After John had promised Jill and the kids the "best Christmas ever," it looked as if Christmas wasn't going to come at all in the Martin household. John did what he had always done when things got tough, he looked for something to sell, some way to make a few dollars to get the family through the end of the year. He borrowed $10,000 from his father, Rev. John Martin, bought a trailer load of toboggans, and got on the internet and tracked the snow across northeastern Oklahoma, clicking over to check on CMKX every few minutes…just in case something happened.

But by the end of the year, the price was a paltry two one-hundredths of a cent. The stock still traded like crazy and on December 9, 44.4 *billion* shares changed hands. That was enough shares to give every man, woman and child in the entire world eight shares of CMKX stock, valued at somewhere between one and two hundredths of a cent. It was, and still is, by far the most shares ever traded in one day by a single stock in the entire history of the stock market.

John snapped out of his daydream and back to reality. Heading north on the Indian Turnpike in eastern Oklahoma, he called Jill again to ask about the snow. She was back at home, trying her best to maintain some semblance of normalcy with her entire family staying at their home, twenty-one houseguests in all. John's mom and dad had loaned them enough money to feed their guests, because John and Jill were too embarrassed to tell everyone how bad things had gotten.

Jill went into John's office and checked the weather on the internet. She found out it was in fact, snowing, and heavily too, as much as ten inches in some spots… in Galveston, Texas, on the Gulf of Mexico, over 500 miles south of where John was driving with his trailer load of toboggans. It was the first time in recorded history that Galveston had a white Christmas, an event so rare it was dubbed "The Great Christmas Eve Snow Storm." And John Martin and his load of toboggans were nowhere near it.

On his radio, John heard that another potential snowstorm was headed for northern Arkansas, so he set his sights even further northeast, hoping to sell enough sleds to buy a few presents for the kids, to salvage Christmas. This is how John and Jill told the story later:

John: *"I'm sitting up in Arkansas. It's two days before Christmas. And I have leftover miles from my Quality Inn stays, so I have a free night. So I go up there on one last ditch effort to get Christmas bought. I go out to set up, and it's still dark. And it's still not snowing. But it's coming, I could hear it on the radio, and they're saying that it's at this certain location, and it's on its way there.*

So it's almost daybreak and it starts to snow…and I'm really thrilled about that. So I'm out there right at the break of dawn with a sign on the side of the road and nobody will stop! And I'm thinking that it's really strange, because any time I've set up before to sell sleds down in Texas, they stop all of the time. So I sit there for an hour with the sign, and nobody will stop, and it's snowing pretty heavily. Then the snow stops! So I get on the radio, and they say that that was just a little strand of it, but there's more on the way. So I stay there for another hour, and still nobody stops. Well, I finally get ticked off and put the sleds back in the truck and drive down the road, and one block down the road is a hardware store with about 3000 toboggans sitting outside. And I had no idea.

But, it never does snow again. I'm driving around town, and I decide that at least I could stop by at a few locations and see if I could wholesale them to a retailer. Well I sell about 200 or 300 sleds and you know, I made a little bit of money, barely enough to pay for the trip.

And this is Christmas Eve now, so I'm going to go due west because the snow is developing in Tulsa. So I go due west and it's like three hours! And I finally get down close to where Tulsa is and I realize that this is Christmas Eve and if I turn right to Tulsa, I'm not going to get home in time for Christmas. And so I take a left and start heading south on a state highway, and I'm going through the mountains.

So I'm driving along, and it starts to snow. And I turn on the radio, and they say, 'Well it's going to snow in eastern Oklahoma, and we expect there to be a half inch, and so it's not any big deal.' Well, it starts snowing...big time...and I'm out in the middle of nowhere! And so I'm going towards the next town, and by the time I get there it's snowing so hard they've shut down the highway. And I'm in that four-wheel drive out there with these sleds. So I take the detour, and stop in this little town, but by this time it's getting dark, and I might get stuck. I'm thinking 'Alright, well I'm probably three or four hours from the house, and it is more like seven...IF it wasn't snowing. So I make a beeline for the Indian Nation Turnpike, by the time I get there there's eight inches of snow on the Turnpike. And I'm doing 65-70 mph, in that four-wheel drive trying to get home in the storm. And people are in the ditches, and people are on the sides of the roads. It's blinding snow, and I've got my head lights on and I can't tell what's the road and what's not the road. The only thing that's keeping me going is when there's somebody out there doing the same thing that I'm doing, trucking down through there – watching their tail lights. I don't know how many wrecks I almost got in to, but I get home at about 11:00 at night."

Jill: *"...and I'm TRYING my best to be supportive of my husband to my whole family, because he's always been a maverick, and here he is out selling sleds on Christmas Eve. And no one knows about our money problems. I'm fearful that the electricity or the cable will be turned off and I have the phone off the hook so the bill collectors can't call. I'm trying to entertain, to be positive for the kids. We don't have any gifts. And I come out and visit and talk with the family, and smile and laugh and act like everything is fine, and then...I lock myself in the bedroom for a while and just cry. And then I try to regain my composure, come back out and do it all again.*

Finally, John's Dad calls just before John gets home, and he's the only one who knows how bad things are. And he tells us that he'll lend us the money to make our house payment so we won't lose our house, and says to buy presents for the kids with the money John made selling sleds, so we go to Wal-Mart at midnight on Christmas Eve and buy a few things for the kids. And so John's dad saves Christmas for us, John barely makes it home in time...and alive, and we put what we can under the tree, and we count our blessings."

The kids, who were only marginally aware of just how bad things had really become, awoke on Christmas morning to presents under the tree. But it was not the car that John and Jill had planned on giving to Ashley, not the "best Christmas ever" John had promised the family, not the extravagant gifts they had hoped to buy for Keri, Johnny, and Sammy, but somehow it didn't matter. Instead of a new car parked out front, there was a car brochure under the Christmas tree. Instead of some of the more expensive gifts they had planned, there were pictures of the gifts they wanted to give their kids...cut out of catalogues, "redeemable for one real gift"...after CMKX hit it big.

Jill put the year, and the moment, in perfect perspective, a moment that John recalled as "rock bottom, the moment when I realized that I had to turn my life around":

"It was a very humbling experience, an extremely humbling thing. And amazingly enough, by the grace of God, it brought our marriage even closer, if it could even be closer. We clung together and said you know, the two of us, whatever we have to do, we will work, and we will fight, and we will crawl, and we will do everything we can to make it through this situation."

John nodded silently. Nothing else needed to be said.

Chapter 15 – Money, Guns and Lawyers

"Yes, club members my resolve is still intact and I am not selling my position. I will hold until Urban Casavant makes his move bringing us forward into our next step to become millionaires. Yes, I still believe shareholders are the New Age Miners of the Twenty First Century. I still believe I will leave a legacy for my family for generations to come about how their great grandpa hit the glory hole via the stock market. Does that sound crazy? Lets all see how this turns out over the next year or longer."

~Hal Engel a.k.a. Willy Wizard

2005 brought a new year, and hopes of a new beginning for the Martin household, and for thousands of other CMKX shareholders as well. The Canadian order that temporarily banned CMKX from trading north of the border was extended when Urban Casavant, David Desormeau, and Melvin O'Neil failed to respond to charges of unauthorized insider selling of unregistered stock. The Saskatchewan Financial Services Commission claimed the three had illegally traded shares of CMKM Diamonds and its predecessor Casavant Mining Kimberlite International.

Although the company never responded to the charges, they did continue to make new moves that seemed to always give the shareholders a reason to cling to hope…and a reason to buy more stock. In an odd and somewhat suspect coincidence, the company announced they were repurchasing 75 billion restricted shares of CMKX stock from Nevada Minerals for $2.2 million one week after the day that a record 44 billion shares were traded. Over the seven day period preceding the 75 billion share repurchase announcement, almost exactly 75 billion shares of CMKX were sold on the open market. By then CMKX was back down to the .0001 - .0002 trading range, and it seemed that no amount of good news could move the stock price up.

On January 31st, Casavant made a move shareholders heralded as nothing less than brilliant. The company brought on board a legendary figure to presumably clean up the company's problems once and for all, a person so revered he soon became known on the message boards by only his nickname, "Iron Bob."

LAS VEGAS, Jan 31, 2005 (BUSINESS WIRE) -- CMKM Diamonds Inc. (Pink Sheets: CMKX) is pleased to announce that Robert A. Maheu has joined the board of directors of the company. Maheu will serve as the co-chairman of the board of directors and will assist Mr. Casavant in the immediate and long-term objectives of the company.

In the company's agenda for 2005, it has become paramount to bring in individuals and companies that can make significant contributions to the company. As the company begins to accomplish short-term goals, we decided to bring in an individual who can manifest an atmosphere for success. Mr. Maheu is that man," stated Casavant, chairman of CMKM Diamonds Inc.

Maheu is probably most famous for his role with Howard R. Hughes. Maheu served as the alter ego to Hughes. Maheu negotiated for the purchase of many Nevada properties on behalf of Hughes and the Hughes Tool Co. As a consequence, seven hotel/casinos, one airport and millions of dollars of raw land were acquired. In each case, Maheu became the chief operating officer. Additionally, he was responsible for the acquisition of an airline. He also represented the Hughes' interests before local, county, state and national regulatory bodies for many years. At an earlier time in his life, Maheu served as supervisor of the administrative section of the New York City Federal Bureau of Investigation Office and special assistant to Assistant Director E.J. Connelly, who was in charge of major cases for the entire Federal Bureau of Investigation.

Throughout his life, Maheu and Robert A. Maheu & Associates served as an advisor(s) to many great men and companies throughout the history of America. To list all of Maheu's accomplishments would turn this brief announcement into a novel.

Casavant and Maheu will together be looking into the company and setting forth exactly what CMKM Diamonds needs to do in order to be successful in its current endeavors. The two look to bring in a president to the company that has successful history in geology and mining of natural resources.

Immediately the message boards went into action, spinning news that really didn't even require spin to make it sound positive. Although he was 87 years old, Maheu's credentials were legendary and his entrance onto the scene seemed to fit perfectly into the Urban Casavant master plan. Roger Glenn would deal with the feds and bring the company into compliance, legendary CIA/FBI-connected Iron Bob Maheu would take down the crooks, and Urban Casavant would find the diamonds. A Million Millionaires suddenly seemed possible again. The CMKX rocket ship was back on the launching pad.

Maheu's presence brought a sense of credibility the company never had before. Here was the man known as Howard Hughes' alter ego, a former FBI agent, and CIA operative who had been entrusted by the CIA in 1960 with planning and carrying out the failed plot to kill Fidel Castro. He seemed connected and powerful enough to get the job done for CMKX and just ruthless enough to handle the criminal element that was trying to keep CMKX, and its shareholders from achieving their dreams.

In the 1960 plot to assassinate Castro orchestrated during the Eisenhower and Kennedy administrations, Maheu had acted as the go-between for the CIA and the Mafia. They had plans to invade Cuba, but thought that putting out a gangland-style hit on Castro would make the job that much easier. Besides, it was common knowledge the Mafia still held a grudge against Castro for forcing them out of the casinos in Havana. What sounded like murder to Maheu was described as an act of war by the CIA, who also wanted to take out Fidel's brother Raul and revolutionary Che Guevara. They recruited Maheu, who convinced mobster Johnny Roselli to set up the hit on Fidel Castro, who in turn introduced Maheu to Chicago Mafia boss Sam Giancana and former Havana syndicate chief, Santos Trafficante. The CIA agreed to pay the Mafia bosses, both on the FBI's Ten Most Wanted List, $150,000 to arrange Castro's untimely death.

The assassination was to take place just before or during a US government-backed invasion of Cuba in March of 1961, and in fact, years later Maheu was quoted as saying that "taking out Castro was part of the invasion plan." The plot fell apart when Castro's private secretary Juan Orta, who was supposed to slip a poisoned pill into Castro's drink, chickened out and took refuge in the Venezuelan Embassy just before the invasion. As a result, Cuban refugees dropped off on the shores of Cuba were left to fend for themselves in the infamous Bay of Pigs fiasco after it was discovered that Castro was still alive.

If Maheu's escapades with the FBI and CIA were legendary, even more so was his stint with the famously reclusive billionaire Howard Hughes. Reportedly hired to intimidate would-be blackmailers and spy on several Hollywood starlets whom Hughes was involved with, Maheu then took over Hughes' Las Vegas operations, helping him secure control of the Strip. According to Maheu, Hughes "wanted to tie up all the property on the Strip to develop it properly. He didn't want it to be honky-tonk or like Coney Island. Hughes was a catalyst in the city cleaning up its act."

After Maheu parted ways with Hughes in 1970, he established his own investigative agency in Las Vegas. Robert A. Maheu and Associates acted as an advisor for dozens of well-known companies, including Westinghouse, Del E. Webb Corp., United Steel Workers of America, Pacific Investments, Greyhound Exposition Services, Central Intelligence Agency, Global Intelligence Network, Las Vegas Investment Advisors Inc., Paradigm Gaming Systems, Sunbelt Communications and Castle Rock Pictures Inc. In 1993, he published a book about his exploits called *Next to Hughes*.

A poster on *Raging Bull* named `particleswaves` summed up the general sentiment of most of the CMKX true believers:

> CMKX is faced with formidable foes, all brandishing money, guns and lawyers. The only way to fight money, guns and lawyers is with (you guessed it) your own money, guns and lawyers. We've got the lawyer in Roger Glenn, the money in Urban Casavant and now the guns in Robert Maheu. We may now respond in kind, i.e., go for the throat of the crooks who set out to destroy us. Hard not to chuckle. I hope Carmine and Vito get a lot of work.

If adding Iron Bob Maheu to the mix wasn't enough, CMKX shareholders quickly found a connection between Maheu's son Peter and the well-known hedge fund sting operation dubbed Operation Bermuda Short. From there, it was easy to come to the logical conclusion that Peter and Bob Maheu were brought on as a sting operation designed to trap the criminals who were holding back CMKX by illegally flooding the market with hundreds of billions of shares of counterfeit stock. Unfortunately, Peter Maheu had no known involvement in Operation Bermuda Short in any way, shape, or form. The closest connection he had to Operation Bermuda Short was this somewhat confusing Google search result for "Peter Maheu Bermuda Short":

Conference Highlights – OffshoreAlert Due Diligence Conference...

Among our speakers this year are Peter Maheu, a Las Vegas - based private ... who was instrumental in initiating Operation ' Bermuda Short ' , a joint FBI ...

www.offshorebusiness.com/Conferences/highlights.asp - 10k - Supplemental

For CMKX enthusiasts that was enough evidence to connect Maheu and CMKX to a covert sting operation of epic proportions. However, following the link to the *offshorebusiness.com* website revealed that in reality, the person who was "instrumental in initiating Operation 'Bermuda Short'" was Boca Raton Police Chief Andrew Scott, *not* Maheu. This was the complete quote that had been condensed to fit the Google search:

"Among our speakers this year are Peter Maheu, a Las Vegas-based private investigator who previously helped manage the extensive Nevada gaming, real estate and mining investments of Howard Hughes; Chris Mathers, who has gone undercover for investigations by the FBI, DEA, Interpol, Scotland Yard and RCMP; and Andrew Scott, the Chief of Police in Boca Raton, who was instrumental in initiating Operation 'Bermuda Short', a joint FBI/RCMP investigation that led to 58 stock promoters, fund managers, bankers and accountants being criminally indicted in 2002 for money laundering and securities fraud."

Peter Maheu was at the conference to discuss "internet casinos, and its relationship to organized crime," while Police Chief Andrew Scott was there to discuss sting operations. It didn't matter. Once posted on the CMKX message boards, Peter Maheu's connection to Operation Bermuda Short was accepted as irrefutable fact.

The stock price jumped briefly to $.0003, including one 200 million-share purchase for $60,000, and traded over 30 billion shares in a five day period, but once again dropped back down to $.0002. Whoever made the $60,000 purchase lost $20,000, at least on paper, before the day was over.

Still, with Bob Maheu joining forces with Urban Casavant and Roger Glenn, the company finally had an unstoppable combination of money, guns, and lawyers. It was just a matter of time before, as one message board poster so aptly put it, Iron Bob would take CMKX:

"To da Maheuoooooooooooooooooooooon!!!"

Chapter 16 – The Beginning of the End?

"Solving problems has been my occupation for many years. Tough assignments are not solved by wishful thinking, but rather by tough action."
~Robert A. Maheu, February 11, 2005

CMKX shareholders were re-energized by the addition of Iron Bob Maheu to the company's board of directors and once again pinned all their hopes on The Stock Play of a Lifetime. With the help of his family and closest friends, John Martin was working towards pulling himself and his family out of their financial abyss. The year began even worse than the one before it. The "pictures of Christmas" were still nothing more than pictures, and the bills that had been piling up for months now threatened to bury John altogether. He realized that CMKX wasn't going to pay the thousands of dollars in late house, car, credit card and utility payments, at least not for the time being.

Rev. Martin knew his son was teetering on the brink of financial and, even more significantly, emotional collapse. He had watched the events of the past year unfold and seen the changes in John's actions and attitude, but his admonishments had gone largely unheeded.

The phone call Rev. Martin made to his son right after Christmas wasn't an easy one, but someone had to force him to face his problems head on. It's possible he could have intervened sooner, but then, John probably wouldn't have listened to his father's advice or accepted his offer before the ill-fated Christmas trip to Oklahoma.

But when Rev. Martin offered his help John reluctantly accepted, feeling ashamed and broken. He began the long slow process of healing, both financially and emotionally, the one day at a time journey back to normalcy. Kept afloat by what he would call "an enormous amount of help" from his father, John went to the bank in an effort to keep his house and cars from being repossessed, armed with far less cash than what he owed. His banker, a CMKX shareholder himself, helped him restructure his debts, a compassionate gesture that bought him the time he needed to dig himself out of the dark hole he had been living in for the past year.

He spoke to Jill about his future and when the new year began, he finally mustered the nerve to tell her what he wanted to do. "Honey, what if I got involved in the stock market full time?" At the time, CMKX was worth a mere fraction of their initial investment and going nowhere, and other than his one winner with GamezNFlix (which eventually dropped from John's selling price of twelve cents a share back down to $.001), every penny stock in his portfolio was essentially worthless. Jill, who had yet to see anything positive come from his trading, was less than thrilled. But still, she couldn't bring herself to kill his dreams, to take away the first thing he had felt passionate about in years.

John decided to take a job with Edwards Jones Securities to become a broker. Although they fell in love with him from the beginning, he had apprehensions about the low starting salary and the travel required during his training period:

"You only make two thousand a month with them for the first month or so when you're in training, and there wasn't any way I could do that. And I was going to have to travel, and of course in my mind I was thinking, I can't watch the boards if I travel. So I got the different computer technology so I could travel with my laptop in the truck, online at the same time, so I can sit there, drive and watch the boards. And watch the CMKX ticker. So I had it set up with AT&T and it was so slow. I hit refresh and I'm driving down the road and I can't see because the sun's so bright that my screen...so I have to pull off the side of the road. So I pull off the side of the road regularly, and it's like a dial up connection, really slow. So I'm like...refresh...might as well eat a sandwich here...refresh...that way I can watch it with two or three more refreshes...you know. I got tired of that really quick. So I turned Edward Jones down and decided to get my real estate license. That way, I could study for real estate on the computer while I was watching the stocks, watching CMKX."

Rev. Martin was a successful real estate agent, which gave John the incentive to go into real estate himself. Once again, he was moving into a profession he wasn't passionate about, but the potential was there to pull his family out of debt. As he began his online studies for his real estate license, he continued to monitor the message boards and the trading for CMKX, secretly hoping that some major announcement or event would send his stock, and the stock of 50,000 other shareholders, "to da moon!!!"

In February of 2005, CMKX announced the addition of Michael Williams to their board of directors. While he wasn't the household name that Iron Bob Maheu was, his credentials were in many ways equally impressive. Williams was chairman of another publicly traded company, Broadband Wireless International Corp., and was a co-founder of EDTV. Prior to his involvement with EDTV, Williams was the Chief Operating Officer of O2 Entertainment, a company that traded on the American Stock Exchange. According to the press release:

His experience has included the administration and career management of Snoop Doggy Dog, the Dove Shack, professional athletes and many others. Williams has consulted for and advised people like Wesley Snipes and J Prince on particular matters. He began his executive career at A&M Records under John McClain, Herb Alpert and Jerry Moss, and then moved on to Island Records, signing a $2 million contract as an artist, songwriter and producer under Kevin Fleming and Chris Blackwell. As a hobby, Williams is a co-owner of a prominent record label under WEA (Warner Electric Atlantic)

Original Man Entertainment, which currently has artists like Tony Lucca and Ballentine in stores now. He holds a Bachelor of Science in management.

"As we continue our agenda for 2005, it was obvious that Mr. Williams could bring a great deal of opportunity, organization and expertise to the company. He is a friend of Mr. Maheu and family members, has already made significant contributions to the company and I welcome him to the board," stated Urban Casavant, chairman.

While his appointment was welcomed on the message boards as another name to add to the credibility quotient of the company, the stock price didn't respond one way or another. Nor did it move up in value when the company appeared on ROBTV two days later, or even the following day when CMKX finally released a detailed updated corporate strategy:

LAS VEGAS (Business Wire) 02/11/2005-- CMKM Diamonds Inc. (Pink Sheets: CMKX) today announced a corporate strategy plan designed to dramatically and comprehensively transform CMKX's internal corporate governance. The aggressive plan is being spearheaded by Robert A. Maheu, the recently appointed co-chairman of CMKX.

"Solving problems has been my occupation for many years," said Maheu. He continued, "Tough assignments are not solved by wishful thinking, but rather by tough action." A new team of securities attorneys has been instructed that their prime assignment is to correct any deficiencies of the past and to cooperate fully with regulatory bodies both in Canada and the United States to minimize the possibility of such deficiencies in the future.

Maheu has also instructed management that regular reports to stockholders and the financial community are imperative.

"Today, CMKX is embarking on an aggressive, strategic plan that is intended to transform the entire corporation into a tightly focused mining and development company," said Urban Casavant, president and chief executive officer of CMKX. "It is our intent to use all available resources to generate consistent, long-term growth and profitability for our stockholders."

Additionally, Casavant said, "We shall be recruiting a team of experienced advisors, professionals and management executives. We intend to structure the company for a move to the Over-the-Counter Bulletin Board or an exchange."

Another major announcement was released just six days later. Iron Bob Maheu, now known on the boards simply by his acronym, "IBM," was obviously running the show, and things were moving forward at a rapid pace:

LAS VEGAS-- (BUSINESS WIRE)--Feb. 17, 2005--CMKM Diamonds Inc. (Pink Sheets: CMKX) today announced the reinstatement of its reporting status under the Securities Exchange Act of 1934 through the filing of an amended Form 15.

On Feb. 9, 2005, CMKX engaged Stoecklein Law Group, a firm specializing in securities matters, as new securities counsel to assist with the correction of past deficiencies and guide CMKX through its regulatory compliance requirements. "When I joined the board one of my prime assignments was to improve corporate compliance. A prime component was to reinstate reporting status, which was efficiently and expeditiously handled by the Stoecklein Law Group," stated Robert A. Maheu, co-chairman of CMKX.

"On behalf of the company and its stockholders, we would like to sincerely thank Roger Glenn and his firm for all of their past efforts," stated Urban Casavant, CEO/president of CMKX.

"We are extremely appreciative of Stoecklein Law Group's immediate attention to our needs. I have worked with them in the past and they have always exceeded my expectations," said Maheu.

CMKX is currently working toward completing an audit of its financial statements and the preparation of the necessary SEC filings. All corporate updates will be made in press releases and filed in current reports on Form 8-K as they become available.

At long last, CMKX would become fully reporting. The message board fairly buzzed with excitement and many shareholders once again, began to pre-spend their money. A few posters questioned Roger Glenn's contributions to the company, and why he was being replaced:

rah47: What did Roger Glenn do for 6 months?

cadiddlehopper4: Regarding R. Glenn: Just my opinion but I have to believe that RG has been paving the way for this to happen and to make it happen as smoothly as possible with the SEC. I also believe after all the paperwork is cleared up then we will see RG's behind the scenes work as we begin merging all the JV partners together with CMKX to become the largest mining empire in the business; CIM !!! Go Long...Go Strong...Go CMKX.

Tradernut: On behalf of the company and its stockholders, we would like to sincerely thank Roger Glen and his firm for all of their past efforts" I think that pretty much sums it up for us. He came and kicked AZZ and now we are at a fully reporting status. AMEN hxpe: Look at who IBM gives credit for "expeditiously" restoring reporting status. It wasn't Roger Glenn but instead was Stoecklein. IBM doesn't even mention RG. The perfunctory "thanks for past services" comes from Urban. I firmly believe that RG is not only not with us but he was unceremoniously handed his hat and shown the door.

Whether Glenn was for or against CMKX didn't really matter now. The shareholders knew that CMKX, under the guidance of Iron Bob Maheu and Urban Casavant, was taking the necessary steps to create a Million Millionaires:

Faithandlogic: Basically, Maheu is doing what he does best... reorganizing and restructuring. Doing for U.C. what he did for Howard Hughes and others. Some people were worried about his age, but I think that his age is a bonus for he will want to finish what he started before he dies...

xxdiamondchildxx: CMKM Diamonds, Inc. is moving forward whether a percentage of the investing world wants to admit it or not. You are either going to be on this freight train or be watching it from the distance.

faithandlogic: We're all about to become so freakin' rich!

And of course, there was fatlittleyana, with the ever-popular:

We are ready for lift-off and to da MOON!!!!

Then, three weeks later, at exactly 11:23 EST, on March 3, 2005, the SEC dropped a bombshell on the CMKX rocket ship:

SEC Temporarily Halts Trading In CMKM Diamonds

NEW YORK (Dow Jones)--The U.S. Securities and Exchange Commission temporarily halted trading in the shares of CMKM Diamonds Inc. (CMKX) Thursday.

The SEC said it is suspended trading in the stock because of questions about the "adequacy of publicly available information concerning, among other things, CMKM Diamonds' assets and liabilities, mining and other business activities, share structure and stock issuances, and corporate management."

PART FOUR

"The primary mission of the U.S. Securities and Exchange Commission (SEC) is to protect investors and maintain the integrity of the securities market."
~SEC Mission Statement, 2005

Stockgate Goes to Congress

By Mark Faulk

March 10, 2005

www.faulkingtruth.com

Congress finally took the first steps towards addressing the naked short selling issue known as "Stockgate" yesterday. A whirlwind week began with a major court ruling in a lawsuit pertaining to naked short selling, gained momentum when a Michigan man provided Congress with a clear "smoking gun," and culminated with Senator Robert Bennett telling SEC Chairman William Donaldson in a Senate hearing that "Rule SHO is not working."

Letting the Courts Decide

In what attorney Wes Christian described as "a significant victory in our ongoing battle to bring restitution to our clients for the brazen manipulations that were perpetrated against them," a New York court last week ordered the Depository Trust and Clearing Corporation (DTCC) to produce trading records for shares of Eagletech Communications (OTCBB: EATC). Eagletech is a plaintiff in a stock manipulation action pending in the state of Florida. It commenced a special proceeding in the Supreme Court of the State of New York to obtain certain trading reports from the Depository Trust and Clearing Corporation.

It was the first major ruling against the DTCC in the naked short selling scandal. The decision could open the door for other similar rulings in the dozens of cases filed by Christian, famed attorney John O'Quinn and others on behalf of companies and investors who claim that they have been victimized by naked short selling.

The Smoking Gun

In what was the most significant development this week, a Michigan man, Robert C. Simpson, claimed to have acquired 100% of the shares of Global Links Corp (OTCBB: GLKCE). He filed his purchase with the SEC, and according to Financial Wire, had the certificates delivered to him, and then watched as over 50 million shares traded over the next two days. In fact, GLKCE traded another 447,000 shares just yesterday. How did major brokers buy and sell tens of millions of shares of stock in a company that had zero shares available? It's a question that the SEC, the DTCC, and the brokers themselves will have to answer in the coming weeks.

And, if that wasn't enough, another investor, Paul J. Floto of Dallas, Oregon, bought another 15% of Global Links' stock just his week, and filed his shares with the SEC as well, even though Simpson had filed his claim to 100% of the shares of the same company a month earlier. This is how Floto described his purchase in his SEC filing:

"On February 3, 2005 a single investor reportedly purchased all the common shares issued by the company, plus 145 additional unissued shares.

Subsequent to that date, over 95 million shares (or over 82 times the total shares issued) were reportedly traded, none of which were reportedly sold by the 100% owner of the common stock.

On March 4 and 7, I purchased a total of 180,000 shares, resulting in my obtaining 15.54% ownership of a stock reportedly already 100% owned by another investor. I assume that there may be additional investors who may also claim ownership of common shares of this company.

I have requested that certificates be issued to me representing my full 15.54% ownership interest, to protect my right to vote and enforce any other claims that may accrue to an actual documented owner.

I understand that Reg. SHO was supposed to detect and prevent the fabrication of millions of nonexistent shares. It would appear that my securities purchases prove that Reg. SHO has been systematically violated by market-making brokers and securities-clearing firms."

Major Media Coverage

While this has been largely a grassroots effort in the past, with only a handful of publications covering the story, including *www.faulkingtruth.com*, *www.financialwire.net* and *www.investigatethesec.com*, there has been an upsurge in media coverage lately as the major media has finally begun to recognize the significance of the story. But while media outlets such as the San Antonio Express-News and WNBC in New York have done recent stories on Stockgate, NBC's Dateline continues to sit on a segment that has been in the works for well over a year. Their segment, which was originally scheduled to air in early 2004, has been postponed numerous times and according to our sources, is now scheduled to air "sometime before April 15th." I'll believe it when I see it.

Congress to SEC: "Regulation SHO is Not Working"

While thousands of investors have joined advocates for stock market reform in speaking out publicly, others have been quietly working behind the scenes to convince Congress to launch an investigation into the naked short selling scandal. We have been working with a number of people who have been busy lobbying members of Congress to take steps to end the rampant corruption that has plagued the market for years, and yesterday those efforts finally began to pay off.

In a hearing in the US Senate Committee on Banking, Housing and Urban Affairs, Senator Robert Bennett grilled SEC Chairman William Donaldson about the naked short selling scandal, citing the Global Links story and opening his statement by telling Donaldson, "You put out a new rule in January to deal with naked short selling, and as nearly as I can tell from my constituents, who feel victimized by this - it's not working." He then went on to read from the Global Links article and said that "this article just last Friday in a national publication indicates that people are still selling short shares that they don't have and clearly are never gonna acquire."

When Donaldson tried to argue that "short selling is not illegal," Bennett interrupted him by saying "I approve of short selling, it's the naked short selling we're going after." Donaldson then tried to describe how the recently enacted Regulation SHO was dealing with the naked short selling problem and was again interrupted by Senator Bennett, whose final comment was "My main message here is that the evidence is Rule SHO is not working, so that's what we need to get into in detail." He concluded by directing Donaldson to present an "in depth briefing" to the committee.

What Now?

This is a major victory for those of us who have often felt as if we have been beating our heads against the wall in this crusade. Mark this day down on your calendars as the day that our voices were finally heard in the halls of Congress, but be aware that this is only the beginning. There is much work yet to be done. Now is the time to step up efforts to spread the word like never before. Contact Senator Bennett and all the members of the US Senate Committee on Banking, Housing and Urban Affairs, the Senate Finance Committee, as well as your own Congressmen and Senators. Tell them that we demand justice. Remind them that President Bush wants to invest our Social Security money into a stock market where corruption is rampant. Tell them that a full Congressional investigation is the only solution to this national scandal and continue to spread the word to the media and through the internet. Then, and only then, will our markets once again be safe for investors.

Chapter 17 – Revocation or Redemption?

"Like the SEC, protecting our investors is a primary concern. We have been aggressively gathering the essential information needed to comply with our public disclosure obligations and anticipate working with the SEC to ensure our compliance with all federal regulations. We are not letting these regulatory matters impede our primary focus of creating stockholder value through the mining and development of our mineral assets."

~ Robert A. Maheu, CMKX co-Chairman, March 7, 2005

"The SEC did not provide us with any notice of the temporary trading halt. This was an unwelcome surprise, especially since our counsel has had ongoing dialogue with the SEC."

~Urban Casavant, CMKX CEO, March 7, 2005

The shock was instantaneous and widespread. After the financial beating the shareholders had taken over the past two years, it didn't seem possible that CMKX could come to such an untimely end. Every event up to that time had been transformed on the message boards into a positive. The worse the news appeared on the surface, the more elaborate and imaginative the posters became.

The facts in this particular case seemed clear-cut and straightforward: CMKX hadn't filed any financial reports with the SEC since July of 2003. The company claimed they were exempt because they had less than the 500 shareholders that would require periodical filings. When Donald Stoecklein was hired, he filed an amended report stating the earlier filing had been in error, since CMKX actually had 698 shareholders at the time. In other words, the company should have been submitting financial records to the SEC all along. The SEC also claimed that CMKX had issued unrestricted securities, meaning the company had issued shares that should have been held for an extended time, but instead were sold immediately into the market.

The day after the SEC announced its action against CMKX, the company released its own statement, reiterating their desire to cooperate with SEC officials and promising aggressive efforts to bring their financial records up to date. Then, in order to "quell any inaccurate rumors," they dropped their own bombshell on the shareholders by announcing the total number of shares issued and outstanding:

> *Of the 800 billion authorized shares of common stock, CMKX currently has 703,518,875,000 shares of common stock issued and outstanding to approximately 2,032 stockholders of record (excluding shares held in "street name").*

Again, the shock was instantaneous. How could their company, or any company for that matter, go from 350 *million* shares outstanding to over 703 *billion* shares in less than two years? As usual, it wasn't long before the message board gurus began to spin the news. Because Bob Maheu was involved, it was immediately rumored that a cash settlement had been negotiated and that a payout to CMKX shareholders would happen before the trading halt was lifted. As always, the dollar figure of the impending settlement was a huge question mark, with estimates ranging from a penny to $.54 a share. Since Congress was finally acknowledging the existence of naked short selling, and with Bob Maheu's close ties to the U.S. government, it didn't take much of a leap to believe he was sent in to clean up the stock market using CMKX as a vehicle to trap the criminals.

Typical of the rumors that were posted and reposted, until they found their way onto every CMKX message board in the world, was this one originally posted by mikecmkx:

New Rumor - Monetary Payout

I'm sure those of you who visit Willy Wizard's Room know who Allen Treffrey is, aka (very_tired). This guy showed up a couple months ago slandering Urban and the company, and also making some major allegations about what UC has been up to with OUR hard earned money.

So tonight he comes in and changes his tune, does a complete 180 and states his source who is very close to the 'inner circle' of the company, says a monetary payout is coming to the shareholders. He didn't know if it was .01 or .54, but this guy was pumped and now has a very positive outlook for CMKX. He says he will have more info in the next day or so.

Take this info for what's it worth. I did personally hear the guy with 200 hundred others in the room. I'm sure they will confirm....Best to ALL!

Within a day, the rumor from Treffrey, aka very_tired, was "confirmed" on the *WillyWizard.com* chatroom by a poster citing Accadacca, who had been claiming for months that a buyout by Citigroup, through its subsidiary Smith Barney, was imminent:

"It appears that the rumor of a buyout by Citigroup has some new allies. Both WillyWizard and Very_Tired have seen evidence that the buyout will happen. What that evidence is, they will not say but let's just say that they are preparing for the news to break anytime within the next 5 days. Of course, it could be longer but that is very doubtful. This rumor appears to be REAL.

This is not a joke. Before the hearing, this should all be over and we should be wealthy."

Of course, then the same poster added this footnote to his enthusiastic "appears to be REAL" and "this is not a joke" comments:

"Again, take it for what it's worth, it is just a RUMOR."

The following day, Citibank and its subsidiary Smith Barney issued a denial statement concerning the buyout rumors:

"It has come to our attention that various website chat room postings have suggested a relationship between Citigroup and/or Smith Barney and CMKM Diamonds (Symbol: CMKX) and CMKXtreme Racing. Please be advised that there is no relationship or connection whatsoever between Citigroup or Smith Barney and CMKM Diamonds or CMKXtreme Racing, and any statements to the contrary are false."

Citibank also issued a letter to *cmkxpics.com* that made their position on CMKX clear:

It has come to the attention of Citigroup/Smith Barney that your website contains photographs--specifically in the section reflecting photos from the "Phoenix Race"--depicting a "Citigroup/Smith Barney" logo on a CMKX racecar, with a legend identifying the individuals in the photo as a "Citigroup Rep and UC."

Please be advised that any reference to Citigroup and/or Smith Barney in connection with CMKX, in any capacity, was, and is, unauthorized. "Citigroup" "Smith Barney" and the "Citigroup Umbrella Logo" are registered trademarks owned by Citigroup Inc., and those marks were used without the permission or approval of Citigroup. The person identified in the photographs as a "Citigroup Rep" was not, and is not, authorized to represent Citigroup in connection with use of Citigroup's registered marks. Citigroup has never sponsored, does not sponsor, and has no intention of sponsoring CMKX or CMKXtreme Racing.

Citigroup hereby demands that CMKXpics.com cause those photographs referencing Citigroup and/or Smith Barney and/or any of its affiliates, agents or employees to be immediately removed from its website. In addition, Citigroup demands that CMKXpics.com cease and desist from making any statement which states or implies that there is any relationship or connection between CMKM Diamonds and/or CMKXtreme Racing or any of their affiliates, agents, employees, officers or directors and Citigroup, Smith Barney or any of their affiliates, agents, or employees.

In the event that CMKXpics.com does not immediately comply with this demand, Citigroup will take all necessary and appropriate legal action to ensure that these demands are met.

James S. Goddard
Director
Associate General Counsel

Amazingly, even that didn't deter Accadacca and Willy Wizard, who continued to spread rumors of a payout after Citibank and Smith Barney publicly denied any connection whatsoever with CMKX. Willy Wizard, whose real name was Hal Engel, had been charged several times with SEC violations for selling unregistered shares of stock in companies his website was promoting.

Another website accused Engel of staging pump sessions for CMKX in his *Paltalk* chat room, called *Willy Wizard's Underground*:

> *"Recently he has been hosting a session with a user named 'accadacca.' While in the room, accadacca talks about a supposed buyout rumor of CMKM Diamonds from Citigroup. Accadacca states some vague rumor from his brother in law who he states is employed by Citigroup at their office in Chicago. When queried about Citigroup's supposed buyout of CMKM Diamonds, he states it will happen and soon. He states he is not sure of the price per share of the buyout offer but thinks it is around 20 cents. Not bad for a stock currently trading at .0001. Engel systematically allows the booting and banning of users of the room who seem to have a different opinion than Engel or his administrators.*
>
> *It's odd that Engel still supports this rumor even though Citigroup itself refuted it through a press release posted on their website. It is sad that a large corporation should have to waste time refuting such a rumor based on such a source."*

Up until the temporary halt on the company, most shareholders had managed to remain more-or-less unified in their common belief that CMKX would eventually make them all wealthy. But the series of disappointments, beginning with the SEC actions against UCAD and the fiasco of the shareholders party and escalating with the CMKX trading halt, had left shareholders feeling frustrated, emotionally shaken and betrayed. With no one person or group to direct their frustration and anger at, members of the various message boards and chats rooms began to turn on each other. They argued about how many shares were on the market and whether or not to believe the cash payout rumors. They debated whether or not Urban was one of the bad guys or the good guys, what value the company's assets had (if any), and on and on and on.

This much was fact: On March 17, 2005, after a two-week suspension, CMKM Diamonds Inc. began trading again. The day before, on March 16, the SEC began administrative proceedings to determine whether the company's registration "should be suspended for a period not exceeding 12 months"…or permanently revoked.

Chapter 18 – 50,000 Davids and Goliath

"Unfortunately management and others involved in CMKX's previous operations were not blessed with the trait of being perfectionists. Past professional guidance has left a void which prevented the Company's ability to prepare complete and accurate periodic reports under Section 12(g) of the Exchange Act."

~ Robert Maheu, co-chairman, CMKX, March 24, 2005

While the message boards spun the temporary trading halt in a hundred different directions, a decidedly different mood was taking hold in the Martin household. John and Jill were both stunned by the news, and all the rumors and positive spin in the world couldn't lighten the mood. John had become painfully aware of the mistakes he had made over the past year and knew he had only himself to blame. It wasn't that he had lost faith in his family or in God; he had lost faith in himself. While his Dad had helped to bail him out financially, pulling himself together emotionally was a more difficult task, one he couldn't face alone:

> *"That was one of the only times in my life where I thought that I was not capable of actually doing it. I didn't think I could get out of it on my own. I was so bitter. I didn't think that I deserved, in any form or fashion, to be pulled out of it...because I put myself there."*

Even though Jill hadn't shared entirely in John's enthusiasm for the stock market or CMKX, it was impossible for her not to feel the shock of losing something that had been the basis of their hopes and dreams for well over a year:

> *"Here we had spent months and months and months of desperation, and addiction, supporting it, feeding it, and feeding it and feeding it. And then, just like that the company was halted. All of the sudden that 'dream' looks like it's not going to work out, and it's like...panic attack!! What do we do? All of our eggs are literally in one basket!"*

She knew there was nothing she could say that would change his mind. She just had to just be there for him when he needed her. It was up to him to realize his own mistakes:

> *"He went through two or three months of basically whipping himself on the back, of telling himself, 'We don't deserve to get out! Look at the stupid decisions...I sat back and I sat behind that computer...I didn't do anything.' He was sitting there realizing and seeing everything fall away. Denying it at the time...but knowing that he was responsible.*

He did start getting bitter. God truly broke his heart. At some point I think he forgot repentance and God's forgiveness, and he wasn't going to allow himself out of it.

But I know John, and he knows that he's responsible before God for his actions. It was something that I had to deal with...One day you're going to let me say, 'I told you so.' There's nothing I can tell you now. Later on when I can say 'I told you so,' I'm not going to, and you are going to do everything within your God-given ability to get us out of the hole that you got us in, and I know that you're going to make it right! So, I'm willing to go the ride with you. It's going to be awful. It's a big mistake but I'll be there for you.'"

Finally, John did begin to regain control of his life, to slowly pull himself and his family out of the morass that had taken them to the brink of financial ruin. There were times when they seemed to survive on little more than faith, but ultimately that faith was enough to get them by. John realized that he would have to rely on his family, his friends and perhaps most importantly his faith in God, to lift himself back up.

John was beginning to think clearly again. After the initial shock of hearing about the SEC charges filed against the company a remarkable thing happened. His addiction to CMKX slowly began to turn into concern for the shareholders, and from there into a desire to do something to help. He began to see the potential power in the tens of thousands of CMKX shareholders who were just as shaken as he was. He wasn't sure what he could do or how he could help, but he knew *some* action had to be taken. So he did what he had done so many times before when he needed advice; he went to see his good friend and fellow CMKX shareholder Bill Frizzell. In a meeting that John would later describe as an intervention, they came up with a plan.

Bill Frizzell found a rarely used rule that allowed for third party participation in SEC hearings. They then decided to organize a grassroots CMKX shareholder group and file a motion to intervene in the May 10, 2005 SEC administrative hearing. Many people on the message boards still believed that the company, with Iron Bob Maheu leading the way, had the situation firmly under control. John Martin and Bill Frizzell knew there would be opposition to their plan. John struggled with some feelings of guilt for questioning the company's actions, but in his heart he knew they were doing the right thing.

John and Bill went to the message boards looking for allies; voices of reason that could help them sway the other shareholders to their way of thinking. They immediately settled on CMKX shareholder Kevin West as the perfect person to act as a liaison between them and the message board gurus. Kevin had originally invested in CMKX as a purely short-term play, hoping to turn a quick profit on the bounces that penny stocks make, known as "swing trading." He bought his first shares in February of 2004, but instead of selling them short term, he found himself buying more shares, lured by the same potential of a home run play that attracted nearly every CMKX investor. He soon held millions of shares, and impressed by Sterling's reputation as a seasoned trader in penny stocks, began to frequent *Sterling's Classroom* message board on *Raging Bull*.

It was Kevin's reputation on the message boards as a kind, caring person and a professed Christian, and the respect he earned with his calm demeanor that led John and Bill to choose him as their go-to man to get the word out to other shareholders. Plus, Kevin was an outspoken critic of the naked short selling problem he believed plagued the entire stock market in general and CMKX in particular, which made him the perfect ally in their campaign.

Kevin recalled his early efforts as an advocate against naked short selling, and his first introduction to Bill Frizzell and John Martin:

"I started a nonprofit website called AmericaNeedsToKnow.com to help make others aware of the problem. With the daily support of people from Sterling's Classroom and from Sterling's Paltalk room, I began to pick out a newspaper or other news media on a daily basis and promote the writing of letters to various editors and others to start carrying stories about naked short selling in an effort to bring national attention to this crime being committed upon the American public every single trading day. Our very first success was in getting the San Antonio Express News to do an article on naked shorting.

After this had been going on for some time, one day I got a phone call from an attorney by the name of Bill Frizzell. On the call with him was a gentleman by the name of John Martin. Their initial call to me was to be able to have a 'warm' introduction to Sterling as John shared with me at a later date. However, our relationship grew from that point and I helped to bring in the chat room moderators that would actually help bring attention to and start Phase 1 of the CMKX Owners Group led by Bill Frizzell and John Martin."

With Kevin and Sterling's help, John and Bill enlisted the aid of several message board moderators and gurus to encourage other shareholders to join the aptly named CMKX Owners Group. It was a clear allusion to the belief that ultimately it was the shareholders of a company who owned the company and that (contrary to historical precedence and popular belief) those shareholders had rights.

John and Bill knew it was entirely possible only a handful of shareholders would join the CMKX Owners Group, but it was a venture they felt compelled to undertake. For a cost of only $25 per shareholder, they hoped to put together evidence proving that far more shares had been sold by brokers than could possibly exist.

Bill had little over a month to file his motion to intervene in the SEC hearing, so he had to quickly devise a method for shareholders to sign up, pay their $25 fee, and submit personal information. John's son, seventeen year old Johnny Martin, was recruited to set up the PayPal accounts, the sign-up sheets, and the computer system to back it all up. Most importantly, he had to do it for almost no money in less than two days. His instructions from his dad were simple, and not very informative, "Just do it!!!"

Johnny: *"This was the initial Owners Group Agreement, for Bill, and I'd never done that before, and we had to figure out how take an agreement and take a PayPal payment. PayPal at the time didn't have the same thing that they have now, where I can go in there and program something, and it will automatically tell PayPal, and PayPal actually will tell me back and let me know if it goes through or not. But that wasn't available at this time. With this I had to just kinda slap something together to make it work. And it worked...I think."*

The rest of the Martin children followed suit. It was truly a group effort, all volunteer and no questions asked. Ashley Martin came in after her regular job at Drug Emporium to help with data entry, while Keri and Sammy spent long hours addressing, stamping, and mailing letters of thanks to the shareholders.

The small trickle of shareholders signing up turned into a steady stream. The cramped offices began to swelter from the numerous people working, crowded equipment, and record breaking heat. Unfortunately, the computer system was not adequate to handle the volume thrust upon it. The system crashed on just the third day of use, deleting 350 accounts.

John: *"Johnny called me and I asked him what was wrong and he said, 'I don't know!!' He hung up the phone, and then all of the sudden he comes running around the corner, just white as a sheet, and he looks at me and says, 'I've done something really, really bad!!' And I said 'Don't tell me that you've lost everything!'*

Fortunately, most of the ones we lost had paid through PayPal. So that saved our butts. Otherwise we would have had no history of any of these people.

When they would email, or when they would call and complain that they didn't get the update that everybody else did, we'd be like, 'Hmmm. There must have been a glitch in the system!!' So we restructured everything and we got the system back together. And I told Johnny, 'Back everything up! Back everything up!'"

On April 5, 2005, Bill Frizzell filed a Notice of Appearance and Motion for Third Party Participation on a Limited Basis to Chief Administrative Law Judge Brenda P. Murray. He was to represent John Martin and 400 other shareholders who collectively owned over 50 billion shares of CMKM Diamonds stock. Three days later, CMKM Diamonds attorney Donald J. Stoecklein gave notice to Judge Murray the company wouldn't object to the motion from the shareholders. The SEC had different ideas. On April 11th, SEC attorney Leslie Hakala filed a response urging denial of the intervention motion from the CMKX Owners Group.

Judge Murray, however, saw things differently than the SEC, and issued her ruling the very next day:

"To provide as much transparency as possible to the Commission's actions given the high level of investor concern, I GRANT, pursuant to Rule 210(f), the Owners Group limited participation on the following terms. Bill Frizzell, Frizzell Law Office, Tyler, TX, 75702, shall be placed on the service list as attorney for the Owners Group and shall receive copies of all filings. The Owners Group will not be allowed to present witnesses or exhibits or to object to any stipulations or offers of settlement agreed to by the parties. As a limited participant, the Owners Group will be allowed to: participate in prehearing conferences; request leave to cross-examine witnesses at any public hearing; and file prehearing and posthearing pleadings, if those are ordered."

With the simple phrase, "I GRANT," the CMKX Owners Group became the first shareholders group in history allowed to participate in an SEC enforcement hearing. Described in a press release by the Owners Group as "a classic David and Goliath battle," the four hundred shareholders represented soon swelled to well over a thousand strong. Only a few weeks earlier, the shareholders had resigned themselves to sitting on the sidelines while the fate of their company was decided. Under the leadership of Bill Frizzell and John Martin, they now had a front row seat at the May 10th hearing.

Chapter 19 – The Fax-in Campaign

"The charter of the SEC is to protect the investor. What the SEC has done is they have protected the pockets of Wall Street. The SEC does not want guaranteed delivery buy-ins of any of these stocks. They don't appreciate the small business stocks, they don't appreciate the penny stocks, they want them all to go away. That's why they have the last four reform packages against small businesses... against penny stock companies; they're trying to shut every one of them down. The SEC is in my mind cowering to Wall Street, and as usual, the SEC is not out to protect the small investor."

~Stock Market reform advocate Dave Patch on *Paltalk*, November 3, 2004

CMKX Shareholders Retain Attorney Bill Frizzell for Representation During SEC Hearings

Phoenix, AZ (PRWEB) May 6, 2005 -- Christian Traders, the internet's fastest growing faith-based online investment community, in partnership with CFRN - the world's first Christian Financial Radio Network, is conducting an exclusive in-depth interview with Mr. Frizzell today. The interview will be broadcast at 10:45AM PST online at http://cfrn.net.

A grass roots movement, spearheaded by Mr. John Martin, will address the issue of "Naked Shorting" next Tuesday during the SEC administrative hearing in Los Angeles. Mr. John Martin has assembled a team that will be working around the clock until Monday evening to assemble the information necessary to prove once and for all that "Naked Shorting" really does exist. With numerous data entry clerks, multiple fax machines, and computers back to back, this is a true grass roots effort. The assistance of every CMKX shareholder is being requested. This is the American people taking back America.

On Thursday, May 5, 2005, Bill, his assistant Goldie, George Stephenson (an old friend and business associate of John's), and John and Jill Martin along with their four children assembled in Bill Frizzell's law office. The various offices of the suite were transformed into war rooms. One was set up for filing, another was filled with fax machines and a dinosaur of an industrial printer, and one was lined with a bank of computers to be manned by the six temporary secretaries. The computers, the fax machines, the printer, the modems, and every single function they performed hinged on the expertise of 17-year old home schooled John Martin V. When Johnny first began working for Bill Frizzell a year earlier, John gave his son advice on how to survive in the business world. "If Bill asks you if you can do something, you say, 'Yes, I can.' Never admit that you can't do it."

Johnny had learned a lot from the Owners Group signup campaign, but that couldn't possibly prepare him for what transpired over the next few days. Like everyone in the office, he was sleep deprived, overworked, and overstressed, but he had the added pressure of knowing that if the system crashed then the hopes of 50,000 shareholders would most likely crash with it. After the near disaster of the Owners Group sign-up campaign, they had to be prepared, and the equipment they saw before them seemed more than adequate to handle the job.

John and Bill worked with Kevin West to contact message board administrators and coordinate the release time of the announcement. John and Bill relied heavily on the message board moderators to advise them on how to get the word out to as many shareholders as possible in the shortest amount of time. It wasn't the last time the shareholders would pull together to help the Owners Group with their seemingly quixotic plan.

The boards were filled with impassioned posts from shareholders energized by the enthusiasm and seeming dedication of John Martin and Bill Frizzell. Canuck, the founder of *Proboards66,* posted a stirring call to arms that recalled one of the most inspirational photographs ever taken:

Whenever I think of the power of the human spirit I am reminded of the image of the lone protester standing in front of a tank minutes before the Tiananmen Square massacre.

"A citizen, armed only with his battered briefcase staring down a column of tanks. A makeshift lady liberty, flimsy and idealized, warning Communist Party bosses that there were alternatives to their rule."

Now, we are that lone protester, facing a battle that seems un-winnable. We have watched nothing happen for months and for some of us years. We surf the net, check the stock price, cruise the boards, waiting, just waiting for something to change; and nothing does; and there is nothing we can do about it.

Naked short selling is theft. Not only is it theft of our money, it is the theft of something much bigger. It strips us of trust in the establishments that are supposed to protect us. Is the SEC protecting us? Who are they protecting?

In all of history, the most extraordinary events have always been started by ordinary people, ordinary people just like us. The greatest moments in history grow from a lone voice in the crowd, a single person that has had enough, someone who shouts from the roof tops, someone who will not give up.

John Martin is that lone person who had enough and stood up with his fists clenched in a in a fit of rage. He is the one who took it upon himself to start a movement to try and bring an end to the corruption and injustice, to show the SEC that we are not going to roll over and die. That we are here, we are strong and we will fight for what is right.

Friends, this could very well be the genesis of a huge movement to bring down the SEC, to show those in power that "we" are in control, that we will not be punched, kicked, spit on and dragged through the mud. Stand up and be counted. Be a part of the solution. Show that we are united, we are mighty, and we are fighting back. This is the America I know.

And so the stage was set. The temps were brought in that afternoon, and while George was elected to train the workers, it was definitely trial by fire every step of the way. On that day, John's advice to Johnny, "never admit that you can't do it," applied to every single person in that building.

On Thursday evening at six o'clock, less than five minutes after the message board moderators posted the Owners Group request for CMKX shareholders' brokerage statements, the first fax came in. And then, almost immediately afterwards, a second one, and then a third, and then they began to pour in as fast as the machines could spit them out, one after another. Almost instantly, the mood went from one of quiet anticipation to frenzied activity. As John later described it, "it went from zero to sixty miles an hour in two or three minutes." All four fax machines were running constantly, and the phones were ringing with shareholders complaining that the fax lines were busy and they couldn't get their statements sent through. The industrial printer, capable of printing 32 pages per minute, almost 2,000 pages an hour, was printing out page after page of statements nonstop.

Retelling the story, Johnny said that while his father was confident in his ability to get it done, Johnny himself wasn't quite as sure:

> "I had noooooo idea how to do it. We ended up with eight computers in that office. And we had 12 people in the suite. We had to have everything in order to verify all our data to the SEC; we have to compile a big huge list with ALL of the information. Very imperfect!!! And I'm in control of the whole entire, stinking thing. Which is really, really scary! But the thing is, it never really occurred to me until after it was over. I mean, if I knew that that much weight was on my shoulders earlier... I... I don't think I could have done it."

The following day, *CFRN.net* aired the Frizzell interview with DeWayne Reeves to motivate the shareholders to send in their brokerage statements, an effort that probably wasn't necessary considering the fact that the fax machines, printers, computers, and every person in the building was working non-stop. As always, the message boards and chat rooms duly reported every minute of the interview and in fact, counted down the minutes leading up to Reeves' call to Frizzell's office. Frizzell was rarely referred to by his real name, instead earning the status of "one of the guys" by being anointed as either "Frizzle," "Frizzie," or simply "Frizz."

A poster named nathaniel kept a detailed running commentary for those who weren't able to access the show live, ticking off the minutes in anticipation and giving a summary of Frizzell's comments throughout the interview:

Frizz SAYING...EMAIL AND FAX MACHINE RUNNING EVERY SEC!

Frizzle...extrapolating numbers....NSS could (COULD) be in the trillions.....no firm number.....will not speculate.

Frizzle: No enforcement by SEC of SHO. Answer may be forced covering and that is why SEC is doing nothing.

Only 4 days left. Did you send your statement? If not please do so ASAP. Every share counts.

Frizzle: if you don't want to be an official member.... that's ok....still figure out how to send last statement... needs the numbers to prove this NSS as he thinks we can.

Over the next four days, the offices were busy sorting, counting, and documenting thousands of faxed brokerage statements. While John, Bill, and George worked around the clock, the temps worked in shifts, learning on the fly. George would tell them one thing, Bill would explain it another way, and John would tell them something entirely different. Then, Jill would sum it all up and translate it into more-or-less easy to understand directions.

Just as they had in the original signup campaign, every member of the Martin household became involved in the fax-in campaign. Ashley and Keri spent long hours inputting data into the computer system. Sammy became the office gofer, keeping paper and supplies at hand for the printers and bringing food for the dozen or more workers who barely had time to eat as they worked around the clock.

If the pandemonium among those in charge wasn't enough to keep the project teetering on the brink of disaster, the confusion caused by the different types of brokerage statements made the task almost impossible. Some shareholders would fax in their entire statement, many as long as six or eight pages and the workers would spend ten minutes looking for the information they needed. On top of that, some people would send in their information three or four times...just to make sure it went through. Some pages were totally blank and others were faxed backwards or upside down.

Then there were those people who, for whatever reason, tried to skew the information by sending in false statements. According to Bill Frizzell, "We had people sending in statements with names like Michael Milken and Ivan Boesky (two prominent Wall Street figures who went to prison for fraud), and others who said they had 100 billion shares, and we had to sort out which ones were real and which ones were trying to screw up our totals." There seemed to be a concerted effort to screw up the process, with posters on *Raging Bull* and some other message boards telling others to "take your cert, scan it to the computer, change ten million shares into one hundred million, and fax it to the lawyer."

There was also considerable confusion from entering the astronomical numbers themselves. While some brokerage statements had decimal points on the share totals, adding extra zeros to the numbers, other listed theirs as whole numbers only...whole numbers with as many as six, seven or eight zeros on the end of them with no commas. It was easy for the temporary workers to add an extra zero, inadvertently turning ten million shares into a hundred million, or worse yet, a hundred million shares into a billion. Every number had to be checked and double checked, and they were still pouring in as the days went by.

And throughout it all, Johnny Martin was expected to keep everything running more or less smoothly. John recalled Jill's frustration at the amount of pressure her son was under, mostly exerted by his father:

"I know that one of the things that was so tough for Jill was knowing that Johnny was working with me. I know Johnny's capabilities, far more than he's able to see his capabilities. And when he has a problem, he looks at me and says, 'I've got a problem.'

'So... figure it out.'

'What do you mean figure it out?'

'Son! Make it happen! You can make it happen. Just do it.'

And he got it done."

Jill saw things from a slightly different viewpoint, playing her role as mother not just to her son, but to everyone in general:

"While he was going through all of that, he was coming to me... 'Mom, I don't know what to do!'

And I'm a mother. I'm a feeler. He's only 17!!! How can Dad put all this pressure on my son, and expect him to do it, with no one to help him, and not having slept in forever? And he says that Dad will just tell me to fix it. 'He's not listening to me, Mom.'

And so I'm trying to play mediator and explain emotions between the two males, who won't communicate. And so now that he knows that Dad is really not upset with him and that takes a load off of him. So now he can sit behind his computer and say, 'Okay, Dad's not upset; now I can work.'"

To complicate matters even more, John and Bill were becoming nervous about their crusade and were convinced they could easily be making enemies of the still shadowy and potentially dangerous figures they knew were manipulating CMKX's stock. They received death threats on their fax machines, mostly directed against Urban Casavant. It was obvious there were a lot of people out there who would rather not have them complete their fax-in campaign.

They hired a security guard to police the parking lot and walk everyone back and forth to their cars, especially during the night. They would radio out to him and he would meet whoever was coming or going and escort them safely to their cars. On the second night, the guard suddenly quit answering his radio and John and Bill, fearing the worst, went out to the parking lot to investigate. As they approached the car, there he was…slumped over the steering wheel, completely motionless. They moved closer, scanning the parking lot for signs of foul play when suddenly he stirred, shifted positions, then settled back against the wheel…fast asleep. He was still there the next morning when the nine o'clock shift arrived.

The fax-in campaign continued day and night, with a deadline etched in stone. Late Friday, a FedEx truck pulled up at Frizzell's office…filled with over 15,000 pages of documents from the SEC, conveniently sent just three days before the hearing. Bill and John went through the boxes as best they could, pulling the most pertinent files to take to Los Angeles the following Monday: the auditor's records from Neil Levine, records from the transfer agent Helen Bagley, deposition transcripts from the U.S. Canadian Minerals (UCAD) investigation and assorted stock, bank accounts, and trading records.

By late Sunday, May 8, after four days of around the clock work and little or no sleep, Bill Frizzell, John Martin, and their thrown-together team of volunteers and temps had amassed and recorded an amazing 7,600 brokerage statements and had 5,400 shareholders signed on as Owners Group members. They made five copies of the records on CD-ROM and hid them in five different locations so, as John put it, "if they take one of us out we'll still have the evidence."

On Monday, May 9, 2005, Bill Frizzell and John Martin carried as many files as they could check into baggage with their luggage. They had copies of every statement from the fax-in campaign and one of the precious CD-ROMs. They climbed aboard a flight from Tyler, Texas to Los Angeles, California, a three-hour trip that gave them their first real sleep in four days. Arriving in Los Angeles the day before the hearing, they checked into their hotel room. As John later put it, "it was elbows to heels from the time we got off the plane until we came back home."

John settled into his room and got himself ready to meet with Bob Maheu and CMKX attorney Don Stoecklein, looking through the clothes he had shoved into his suitcase, to find something wearable for the evening. Some trusted shareholders knew where John and Bill were staying, and as John was haphazardly ironing a shirt, a knock came at the door. He answered it wearing only his boxer shorts and an undershirt:

"I was ironing a shirt because we were going to dinner with Bob Maheu that night. So, a CMKX shareholder comes in and you can tell that everything that he was wearing was perfectly pressed, perfectly matched and I was just a little bit concerned...you know? He's fifty years old; he's not married and perfectly matched and ironed! I'm sitting over there and while we're talking I'm on one side of my room and he's on the other side of my room and we're talking and he says, 'Evidently you don't know how to iron, let me do that for you.'

And...well...he insisted, okay? So he comes over and starts showing me, and I said, 'Don't show me, if you want to do it, just do it, I'm going to go over there!'

So, I'm over there and the phone rings and its Bill. 'JOHN! What're you doing?'

'Um...Gregory's ironing my shirt...'

And you can hear Gregory in the background, 'Tell Bill I'll be down to iron his in a minute' and Bill's like 'You tell him he's not doing any such thing!!'

And I'm thinking to myself...oh gosh, I hope another shareholder doesn't show up. And then 'Knock, knock, knock'...It was ANOTHER SHAREHOLDER!

And he walks in and he says 'Oh I hope I'm not messing anything up...am I?'

I said 'NO! Thank you for being here!'"

They met with Stoecklein and Maheu for lunch and again for dinner, talking to some degree about the next day's hearing but mostly regaled by stories of Maheu's years with Howard Hughes and as an operative for the U.S. government. For John, meeting Maheu was like meeting a living legend:

"The majority of the conversation at dinner was listening to Bob tell stories about his past. Whenever we're together and we're talking with other people, especially in this type of situation, if Bill doesn't like a direction I'm going he kicks me under the table.

So I was calling Bob by his last name, Mr. Maheu, and he said 'John, I'm not Mr. Maheu to you, I'm Bob. Don't call me that again. I'm open for questions of any kind, I'm an open book, and you ask me any question you want to ask me.'

I had already had a couple of glasses a wine so I said 'Did you really put a hit on Fidel Castro?' I think I still have a bruise on my leg from the kick I got from Bill. Bob just laughed. Then he started talking about Castro a little bit."

That evening, Bill stayed up late yet again going through what evidence he could absorb from the files they brought with them from Tyler. He paid particular attention to the UCAD investigation depositions, knowing how little time he had before the hearing:

"When you do a lot of litigation, I think your effectiveness in the courtroom is directly contingent and dependant on the preparation you do before you get there. You can be the greatest courtroom lawyer in the world but if you're not prepared when you're in there, you will not be effective. And that was really, really bothering me because I had all of this information and Rendal Williams was going to be on the stand, Urban was going to take the stand, and Bob Maheu! We had all these people connected with the company; the transfer agent Helen Bagley was going to be on the stand as a witness. I needed to be fully prepared to represent these shareholders, I didn't want to miss something in case the company was trying to hide something, and the SEC didn't want naked shorting to be part of the hearing. And I had not had a chance to go through these fifteen thousand pages of documents.

I spent most of my time reading the depositions. There were just volumes of depositions that were taken in the UCAD investigations. Rendal Williams, Urban...They tried to take John Edwards' deposition, he never answered any questions but I wanted to see what they were asking him! So I had spent my days reading the depositions that the SEC had taken. That was the best way I felt I could prepare. I didn't have time to go through all those boxes!"

Finally, well after midnight and for the first time in five days (other than the occasional nap and their three-hour respite on the flight out), Bill Frizzell and John Martin collapsed into bed. Exhausted and spent, they hoped to catch five or six hours of sleep before awakening on the day they would walk into a federal courtroom carrying the hopes and dreams of 50,000 CMKX shareholders on their shoulders.

Chapter 20 – The SEC Hearing

"There are 60,000 shareholders in this company. And what this Court does, of course, is going to affect those shareholders in that company. The SEC counsel has said there are 700 billion shares that have been issued by this company. I'm going to suggest to the Court that there are trillions of these shares that are in shareholders' hands."

~CMKX Owners Group attorney Bill Frizzell, SEC Hearing, May 10, 2005

Bill Frizzell and John Martin arrived at the Los Angeles Federal Courthouse on the morning of May 10, 2005, barely off the plane and seriously sleep deprived after four days of compiling CMKX shares and pouring over mountains of documents from the SEC. They knew that they were stepping into the middle of something far bigger than either of them had bargained for. Something…they weren't sure exactly what yet…but *something* was terribly wrong with this picture. Maybe it was the fact that every person who was subpoenaed to testify had their own attorneys and several of them had more than one. In all, well over a dozen attorneys walked into Judge Brenda P. Murray's courtroom that day, prepared to argue either for or against the revocation of CMKM Diamonds as a publicly traded company, or to protect one of the nine witnesses who had been subpoenaed to testify.

It wasn't just protecting their legal rights that some of the witnesses were concerned about. UCAD's Rendal Williams, later described as "terrified and looking white as a sheet," was accompanied by three attorneys *and* two personal bodyguards. Williams hid out in a building across the street until he was called to testify because he didn't want to wait in the hall outside of the courthouse.

And Rendal Williams made it a point to let everyone know that he was wearing a bullet-proof vest.

The courthouse itself looked like a scene out of a John Grisham novel. There were armed government agents everywhere. Outside the courthouse, company supporters were handing out "Urban's Warriors" and "Got CMKX?" t-shirts and other paraphernalia. Shareholders who didn't make it into the hearing were gathered in groups out front, some on their cell phones reporting back to the thousands of shareholders who were glued to the message boards. Filmmaker Hugo Cancio and his camera crews were interviewing and recording the general mayhem for his documentary about Urban Casavant, tentatively entitled *A Million Millionaires*. He asked to film John and Bill on the way in to the courthouse, and John promised him he'd return later for an interview.

The near circus atmosphere was magnified by the hundreds of shareholders cheering and applauding as Bob Maheu, dressed in clothes befitting his status as a legend, and CMKX attorney Don Stoecklein walked up the steps to the courthouse. Maheu stopped to do a short interview with Hugo Cancio, and every moment was relayed to posters on the various the message boards, who gave blow-by-blow accounts of the action:

> Drymouth: Hugo is interviewing Maheu right now, before the hearing. Everyone else is still busy hauling in boxes of documents.

> Dr.D: Info from Hugo Cancio, Frizzell and Urban already entered into the Hearing room, very upbeat and ready to go. Smiles and very encouraging.

> Mr. Maheu just entered the Hearing. Brief interview with Hugo Cancio and Mr. Maheu smiled and said: "They're in for a BIG FIGHT"

> 5 attorneys accompanied Mr. Maheu and many CMKX shareholders outside the room cheered Mr. Maheu, Urban and others as they approached. Mr. Maheu smiled and took a bow.

> Very exciting.

Urban Casavant arrived accompanied by two high-profile attorneys, David Z. Chesnoff and Gerald W. Griffin and wearing an ill-fitting green polyester-looking suit. His white shirt was longer than the coat, and the sleeves folded back over the coat sleeves. He had almost no hair, his flat top haircut cropped close to his head. None of that mattered to the loyal CMKX shareholders, who cheered and applauded for Urban as if he were a major celebrity. If anything, his persona as a blue-collar millionaire made him seem even more down-to-earth and accessible.

That was the scene that shareholders' advocate John Martin and attorney Bill Frizzell walked into that morning, only one day removed from the quiet town of Tyler, Texas.

The courthouse itself was filled beyond capacity. Extra chairs were brought in to accommodate the over 250 shareholders who showed up for the hearing. There would have been far more spectators, but the SEC convinced the judge to deny Frizzell's request to broadcast a video of the hearing into a rented ballroom.

Instead, John told DeWayne Reeves, who went by the on-air moniker of CT, that he would do live phone reports with *CFRN.net* during every recess. Because *CFRN* was still in its infancy, the primitive studio system made it impossible for John to hear CT. As DeWayne Reeves later put it "John would dash into the hallway and dial my cell phone. That was the signal to go live. I would dial John's cell phone back from our single studio line and that was his cue to answer the phone and start reporting." John made his first connection with CFRN on the front steps of the courthouse, thanking the shareholders for coming out and supporting the company, and went inside.

The administrative hearing for CMKM Diamonds began at 9:34 AM, with Judge Murray announcing the case: "We're going on the record. This is the first day of public hearings in the Securities and Exchange Commission Administrative Proceeding in the matter of CMKM Diamonds, Inc."

And so it began. Judge Murray introduced the attorneys: Leslie A. Hakala and Gregory C. Glynn representing the SEC, Donald J. Stoecklein, Esq. and Anthony N. DeMint representing the company, and Bill Frizzell, Esq. representing the Owners Group. Then a list of the witnesses and their respective attorneys was presented: Neil Levine, Christopher Wall, Helen Bagley, Suzanne Herring, Rendal Williams, Urban Casavant, John Dhonau, Robert Maheu, and Kristen Buck.

While after every other attorney had addressed her by the customary "Your Honor," Bill Frizzell, no more than fifteen words into his opening comments, responded in that distinctive and decidedly misplaced East Texas drawl:

> *"Judge...you may recall the Court has allowed me to participate just in a limited fashion on behalf of the shareholders. And, Judge, it might be - at this point, just so we could clarify for the record, I think the Court's order that was entered says that at the time of the hearing that I could participate in cross-examination with leave of the Court."*

Then Judge Murray laid out the ground rules for the hearing, a lengthy process in which she described the proceedings, defined burden of proof, and explained how she would eventually render her decision based on the facts of the case.

Mountains of documents were introduced into evidence by the SEC, many of which were the same ones received by both Frizzell and Stoecklein only three days earlier. Each attorney addressed Judge Murray with their comments about the various documents: Leslie Hakala: "Your Honor." Gregory Glynn: "Your Honor." Anthony DeMint: "Your Honor." Donald Stoecklein: "Your Honor."

And finally, Bill Frizzell:

> *Judge, here's what I think. Juuudge, I think that we agree to stipulate that this is admissible evidence. What we might suggest is, at the conclusion of the hearing, instead of closing off the hearing, if the Court might adjourn the hearing for two weeks or three weeks to allow for some documentation that might be necessary.*

> Judge Murray: *At any time in the case, until I issue a decision in the case, which I believe is due by the 15th of July, at any time you can file a late filed exhibit.*

> Bill Frizzell: *Wonderful.*

> Judge Murray: *Let's move on to something else now. This is a little bit unusual, but I received -- I think it's twenty letters in this case from concerned people about the outcome of the case. In the old days, the Commission had a special portion of the docket that they called a "Correspondence" section of the docket, and this type of material went in that correspondence section*

of the docket. You could read them and consider what the people said, but you couldn't use what the people said in their letters to decide the case because those people weren't here and weren't subject to cross-examination by the opposing side. The SEC, as I understand it, has done away with that "Correspondence" section of the docket.

These letters are written by people who are concerned about the outcome of the case. It's my opinion that these letters should be part of this official record. So the only way I can figure out on how to treat them so they're in here some way is to say -- is to treat them as exhibits that were proffered but not allowed in evidence. All those letters are going to accompany the record to Washington as exhibits that were not admitted in evidence, but they will be in the docket, and I'm handing them now to the court reporter.

The next few minutes of the hearing dealt with the topic of what John Martin and Bill Frizzell had been working on for the past weeks, the issues of naked short selling, of whether excessive shares had been sold into the stock market that were in essence, counterfeit. They knew that if they could somehow introduce evidence that the company's stock was manipulated, that illegal actions outside of the company's control contributed to the problems that existed with the company, then they could, for the first time in history, prove the existence of naked short selling in a court of law. Once they established that, the SEC would have to deal with the criminal element that Martin, Frizzell, and thousands of others CMKX shareholders were certain was the real reason CMKX had never had a chance to succeed as a company.

Judge Murray: *Okay. Are we ready now for opening statements?*

Mr. Glynn: *Your Honor, we still have one pending matter, and that's the motion to exclude all evidence of naked short selling in the Respondent's securities. Does the Court have a copy of that?*

Judge Murray: *Let me just read the sentence. 'The issue: On or about May 2nd, 2005, the Division filed a motion to exclude all evidence of naked short selling. The Division asserts that I should rule in advance that I will not allow evidence of naked short selling at the hearing because the practice of naked short selling is wholly unrelated to whether CMKM Diamonds violated Section 13(a) of the Exchange Act and Rule 13a-1 and 9 13a-13.'*

CMKM Diamonds' answer does not allege that short selling was the reason CMKM Diamonds did not file the required reports. Accordingly, I grant the Division's motion. I will not allow extensive evidence of short selling into evidence because it is irrelevant to the issue that I have to decide in this proceeding.

Now, is the Division willing to stipulate orally that it appears that naked short selling has taken place in this stock?

Ms. Hakala: *No, Your Honor.*

Judge Murray: *You're not?*

Ms. Hakala: *No, Your Honor.*

Judge Murray: *Okay. If that's where we are, that's where we are.*

Then, after having the door slammed shut on the issue of proving that naked short selling was the root of all of CMKX's problems, Bill Frizzell tried to keep it slightly ajar.

Mr. Frizzell: *We're going to have witnesses, and in our cross-examination of these witnesses, we may be asking about the outstanding stock that's in this case. That may be important in the financial arena. I don't want, nor does Mr. Stoecklein want to violate the Court's motion because questions about naked shorting have to do with the outstanding stock. So will we be in violation if we talk about the outstanding stock when we're talking about the financial reporting?*

Judge Murray: *I will not consider it in violation unless something is latent. All I can suggest is, you ask the question. If I get an objection, then I will rule on it. Okay?*

Mr. Frizzell: *Thank you, Your Honor.*

After Judge Murray ruled against Bill Frizzell and the shareholders about naked short selling, and after the SEC pointedly refused to accept the existence of stock counterfeiting in CMKX, both sides presented their opening arguments, with the SEC's case basically hinging on a single issue:

On July 22nd, 2003, CMKM Diamonds filed a Form 15 signed by the company's president, Urban Casavant, in which Casavant represented that it was no longer subject to the periodic reporting requirements because it had approximately 300 shareholders of record. In fact, the Division anticipates the evidence will show that the company knew or should have known that, as of that date, it had 698 shareholders of record.

Hakala also said that they would prove although CMKX had publicly announced it was "working towards completing an audit of its financial statements," that "the Division expects the evidence to show that CMKM Diamonds does not have complete financial statements, and thus, that an audit of CMKM Diamonds' financial statement has not even begun." They went on to discuss the massive trading volume in the company's stock, the over 700 billion shares outstanding (to which Judge Murray asked "Isn't that extraordinary?") and that "certain individuals are liquidating substantial quantities of stock and pulling out the proceeds. People perhaps related to the company."

In his opening comments, Stoecklein seemed to want to place the blame on the past accountants hired by the company to bring their filings to date. He said the company paid $1.5 million to David DeSormeau as Chief Financial Officer over a two and a half year period, who produced only a 25 page document listing shareholders equity. Then, they paid $250,000 to D. Roger Glenn to bring the company's financial records to date, for which Stoecklein said that he received "a one-sheet letter that said, 'Dear Donald, We don't have any files.'" In this case, Stoecklein wasn't being facetious. The letter from Glenn actually did begin with "Dear Donald":

Dear Donald,

In response to your letter dated May 3, 2005, we do not have any documents related to CMKM Diamonds Inc. other than copies of those on file with the Nevada Secretary of State, which I'm sure you have. We never received any documents related to CMKM Diamonds. I was always informed that Brian Dvorak and someone named Ginger had all the company records. All we produced to the SEC were our billing records which had the description of work performed redacted.

Very truly yours,

D. Roger Glenn

Finally, they hired accountant Neil Levine to complete the job that neither DeSormeau nor Glenn managed to finish, paying him a $100,000 retainer on January 8, 2005. Stoecklein told the court "on Friday last week, the company gets a letter from Mr. Levine saying he's terminating his position as the auditor."

In the end, Stoecklein's argument was basically that the company was *trying* to get their financial reports together, closing by saying that "this process is moving forward, and it's just damned unfortunate that this company has hired some professionals that haven't supported it."

And then it was Bill Frizzell's turn:

I would like to make just a couple of brief remarks. Number one, Judge, there are records that were stipulated to in this evidence. There are 60,000 shareholders in this company. And what this Court does, of course, is going to affect those shareholders in that company. The SEC counsel has said there are 700 billion shares that have been issued by this company. I'm going to suggest to the Court that there are trillions of these shares that are in shareholders' hands.

This Court asked the question of the SEC counsel, who benefits from this large amount of stock. I'm not going to use the word 'naked short selling' because this Court has said it may not be relevant in these issues. I will say short sellers benefit by the millions it has in this stock at the expense of these shareholders. These shareholders have invested money and taken it down to a broker and said, 'Here's my money,' and that money never got to the company or never got to someone who had a right to shares to invest.

Frizzell closed with:

I'm saying there's some victims out here, too. I think, Judge, when you hear the testimony today, you're going to have some concerns about some motives as to why some of these reports haven't been filed and what are some problems within this company that may give this Court some reason to be concerned, and I think it's going to relate back to short selling. And I'd just ask the Court to keep an open mind in that regard.

And, Judge, we have at the helm of this company now a new cochairman of the board, Bob Maheu. He's going to be one of the witnesses who's going to testify for this company. I think the Court would be well to receive his testimony, and some problems that have gone on that have put this company in this position where it is today will be resolved. And on behalf of the shareholders, I look forward to the Court keeping the new people in charge now in mind when this Court renders a decision.

That's all I have at this point...Judge.

And with those final words from Owners Group attorney Bill Frizzell, Judge Brenda Murray introduced the first witness, and the hearing for revocation of CMKM Diamonds' stock began.

Chapter 21 – Witnesses for the Prosecution

"I think you're putting words in the witness's mouth. He's told you he doesn't know."

> ~Judge Brenda K. Murray, in response to a question directed at U.S. Canadian Minerals CEO Rendal Williams,

*"**Somebody** needs to put some words in his mouth."*
> ~CMKX Owners Group attorney Bill Frizzell

After the opening arguments, SEC attorney Leslie Hakala introduced the prosecution's first witness in the hearing that would decide the fate of CMKM Diamonds and its 50,000 plus shareholders:

Q. *Please state and spell your full name.*

A. *Neil Levine. N-e-i-1, L-e-v-i-n-e.*

Q. *And what is your occupation?*

A. *I'm a CPA.*

Q. *Mr. Levine, have you been hired to --- or your firm been hired to serve at CMKM Diamonds' outside auditors?*

A. *Yes, we have.*

Q. *What audit procedures have you done so far for CMKM Diamonds?*

A. *Currently no audit procedures have been performed.*

JUDGE MURRAY: *And when were you hired?*

NEIL LEVINE: *January 10th, 2005.*

MS. HAKALA: *Why haven't you done any audit procedures yet?*

NEIL LEVINE: *We're waiting for the company to provide their books and records so we could perform audit procedures as an accounting firm.*

Q. *When did you first request the books and records?*

A. *Well, we met with the company January 10th and we were -- about January 7th, 8th, and 9th we did a little due diligence, but from the first time we met the company, we told them what we would need to perform an audit.*

Q. *And what do you need to perform the audit?*

A. *General ledgers, books and records, cash disbursements, bank statements. All sorts of documents. Corporate documents.*

Q. *Have any of these records been provided to you?*

A. *No, ma'am.*

JUDGE MURRAY: *Could I just ask a question? Who have you been dealing with at the company?*

NEIL LEVINE: *I was dealing with the president, who we met, and we met the CFO, Mr. David DeSormeau, from the company.*

MS. HAKALA: *When you say you have been in contact with the company's president, who are you referring to?*

NEIL LEVINE: *Mr. Casavant.*

Q. *How did you first hear of CMKM Diamonds?*

A. *I think we heard of them around December of '04 when a -- we got a referral from a business -- a guy we did business with, and he said the company would be looking to hire an auditor.*

Q. *Who was that person?*

A. *Mr. John Edwards.*

Q. *What was his role with CMKM Diamonds?*

A. *I'm not sure. I think he was a business consultant, but his prior -- his accountant had resigned from their -- there's a new accounting - regulatory body that came around in October of '04 where, you know, there's only 900 guys like myself still licensed to do this type of work. And we did some work -- John had referred a couple accounts to us that his CPA had resigned, he was no longer doing that work. So that's how we came in contact with John. And I guess we did some good work with some of the companies he referred us to, and he referred us to this company.*

160

Q. *Okay. So what happened next after the referral?*

A. *I went with another partner of mine in -- a senior manager. We went to Las Vegas. We met with the company. It was a sales call for me. I explained to them what we could do for them. This is what we do for other public companies. And, you know, they retained us.*

Q. *When was that meeting in Las Vegas?*

A. *January 10th.*

Q. *And do you remember specifically where that meeting took place?*

A. *That was in the meeting in the prior accountant's office, David Coffey.*

Q. *Who was at that meeting?*

A. *I was there. One of my partners was there. I had a senior manager there. Mr. Urban Casavant was there. Mr. Edwards was there. And Mr. Coffey was there. And Mr. David DeSormeau was there.*

Q. *What did the company tell you about its plans at that meeting?*

A. *They explained that they were retaining us to bring their -- to bring themselves compliant, to move from the Pink Sheets back to the Bulletin Board or to another exchange. Another stock exchange.*

Q. *At that meeting did the company indicate that it wanted to prepare periodic reports?*

A. *Yes, they did.*

Q. *Who was doing the bookkeeping for CMKM Diamonds since January 1st of 2000?*

A. *Mr. DeSormeau. He's -- he was -- he said he would get us the books, that he was the inside accountant.*

Q. *What did he tell you about the state of the books when you first met with him on January 10th?*

A. *He said he would be able to get those books on QuickBooks and provide something to us.*

MS. HAKALA: *When did you return to Las Vegas?*

NEIL LEVINE: *I believe it was January 17th, 18th, or 19th.*

Q. *What did you do then specifically?*

A. *I spent three or four days at the transfer agent's office going through the transfer agent documents.*

Q. *Did you identify what documents you'd need in order to audit the stock issuances?*

A. *There were maybe, I think, five or six attorneys who had provided opinion letters on the stock issuances. And I met with Roger and I told him, and he said he would provide to us the backup to those -- Roger Glenn was the attorney -- to provide me the backup to the stock issuances.*

Q. *How many opinion letters did you need backup for?*

A. *I think -- there were numerous, but there were five or six different attorneys who had worked over that period of time.*

Q. *From those five or six attorneys, can you estimate how many letters? Fifty? A hundred? A thousand?*

A. *Ten.*

A. *Each time they did a dividend or each time they did some kind of -- they wanted shares issued, they would get -- they would rely on some opinion letter from an attorney.*

From there, Levine went on to explain the various exchanges with CMKX: how David DeSormeau sent him a list of who stock was issued to...but no stock prices to go with it, how the company issued over 3 billion shares to 390 entities on a single day on January 22, 2003 (which he described in response to Judge Murray's question as "very unusual"), and how DeSormeau failed to respond to repeated letters and phone calls from Levine asking for company records.

In March, 2005, Levine later met with Urban Casavant and new attorney Donald Stoecklein, who also promised to send him the company records. Instead, according to Levine, he received an email from Stoecklein saying that "they were making progress, things were slow, but they were making progress." Then, a week before the hearing, Stoecklein told Levine that he was "about to send him something"...but Levine said he never received anything. As a result, he said that he hadn't performed any audits because he "hadn't been provided with any books or records to provide any audit procedures."

Then, Levine read a letter that had been submitted as evidence to the court:

Dear Mr. Casavant: The Company has not provided the requested documentation and information required for us to perform our audit work. As a result, we hereby terminate our engagement with the company effective after the completion of our involvement at the administrative hearing scheduled for May 10th, 2005.

Donald Stoecklein cross examined Neil Levine for CMKX, which lasted less than five minutes and provided no new information whatsoever. Owners Group attorney Bill Frizzell then stood up to take a turn, prompting Judge Murray to comment "Mr. Frizzell is going to ask --- I assume because he's getting up -- some questions."

She then asked Hakala if she had any objection to Frizzell questioning the witness, since he was present as a "nonparty representative" for the shareholders. Hakala replied that while she didn't know what he was going to ask, that as a general matter "I don't understand why the shareholders would need to ask questions." Judge Murray overruled her vague objection.

MR. FRIZZELL: *You mentioned in your direct testimony that John Edwards referred you to this company; is that correct?*

NEIL LEVINE: *Yes, sir.*

Q. *Who is John Edwards?*

A. *John Edwards is a fellow that I met in Las Vegas a few years back that we did not do any work with until his accountant in October of '04 resigned or didn't want to go forward to do any work for the PCAOB. And there's a few accounts that we picked up from Mr. Coffey who has resigned and just stays on to do bookkeeping, and I think John is his -- he's John's personal accountant.*

JUDGE MURRAY: *Let's just --- for the record, that "PCAOB" is the Public Company Accounting Oversight Board.*

MR. FRIZZEL: *I guess you speak with Mr. Edwards on some basis -- some regular basis?*

NEIL LEVINE: *Yes.*

Q. *Does Mr. Edwards have any current stock position in this company?*

A. *I'm not aware of it if he does. I don't know.*

Q. *Back in the year 2003 or 2004, do you know whether or not Mr. Edwards had any stock position in this company?*

A. *I don't know. I've never seen -- I have not seen his name in the stock books, if that's what you're asking.*

Q. *And do you do accounting work for Mr. Edwards?*

A. *No, I do not.*

Q. *Would it surprise you that Mr. Edwards would own some companies, some LLC's or some companies that might have substantial stock positions in this company?*

JUDGE MURRAY: *Hold on just a second. Okay. Could you explain to me the relevance?*

NEIL LEVINE: *What do you mean by "surprise?"*

MR. FRIZZELL: *This immediate withdrawal of his services a day before this hearing, Judge, has us very concerned. Mr. Edwards has substantial holdings and has had, over the course of this company's development, substantial stock positions in this company. If there's some relationship between him and this sudden withdrawal of his services of this company, I would think the Court - it might be helpful to the Court.*

JUDGE MURRAY: *Let's ask the gentleman why he's terminating his relationship with the company.*

MR. FRIZZELL: *I was fixing to, Your Honor.*

NEIL LEVINE: *Okay. Basically in 25 years of doing accounting and asking for records, this isn't a company that me and my firm wants to continue to represent. I've asked for records over and over. I don't get any records. And I'll leave it at that.*

MR. FRIZZELL: *You testified, Mr. Levine, that you got no records after a certain point in this investigation; is that correct? No records from Mr. DeSormeau or not many records from the company, and that's the reason why you're no longer the accountant or the auditor for this company. Is that your testimony?*

NEIL LEVINE: *No. My testimony is this isn't the type of company that I want to typically represent, one where the owners take the Fifth Amendment and - when I do ask for records, and it's frankly become problematic.*

JUDGE MURRAY: *And, Mr. Frizzell, let me correct that, because I want to make sure I understand this. I heard the witness say he never received anything. Anything. He didn't get -*

MR. FRIZZELL: *I heard that also, Your Honor, but I want to make sure I didn't -*

JUDGE MURRAY: *But you're saying he received some. That is not the witness's testimony, as I understand it.*

MR. FRIZZELL: *Yeah. Okay. Well, my next question was going to be this, Judge.*

Q. *We were produced a file -- and I'm putting this in the form of a question to you -- by the SEC, approximately 400 pages of documents that came from Bagell, Josephs & Campbell* (the accounting firm Levine worked for) *with Bates stamp numbers. Did you help put those documents together and give them to the SEC?*

NEIL LEVINE: *I don't understand the question. When I was subpoenaed, anything I did have in my file that I did get from the company I turned over to the SEC.*

Q. *And how many pages was that?*

A. *254 pages, approximately, if I remember correctly.*

Q. *And those 254 pages were accumulated by you during a period of time, wasn't it?*

A. *They were sent to me by Mr. DeSormeau over a period of time. Up until March of -- March 2nd of '05.*

Q. *March the 2nd of '05 you were sent the stock transfer ledger by Mr. DeSormeau -*

A. *Which is a direct copy of the stock transfer records. There are records that are just a copy job that really cannot be audited at this point. It's just an Excel spreadsheet. Whatever he did, he copied the stock ledger book from the transfer agent.*

Q. *Is there any particular reason why you chose to withdraw your representation for this company or your attempts to audit this on the day before everyone is headed to Los Angeles for this de-registration hearing?*

A: *The timing is that we're a very busy accounting firm. I'm in the middle of a major season, which is the biggest May 15th deadline. And, frankly, you know, I'm done playing around with whoever I'm going to get documents from or I'm not, and I have to be on standby. And we just don't want to represent a company like this anymore.*

Q. *Does it matter that there's 60,000 shareholders that could be affected by your decision?*

MS. HAKALA: *Objection.*

JUDGE MURRAY: *Yeah, let me just say, Mr. Frizzell, you have a position, and the witness is trying to answer your question. That's kind of a loaded question.*

MR. FRIZZELL: *Yes, it is, Your Honor.*

JUDGE MURRAY: And *I don't think -- let's try to keep an air of civility.*

MR. FRIZZELL: *I understand. Thank you, Your Honor.*

REDIRECT FROM MS. HAKALA:

Q. *Did John Edwards have any impact on your decision to resign as auditor for CMKM Diamonds?*

A. *No.*

Q. *Did you discuss the matter with John Edwards before making the decision to resign?*

A. *No. I don't think anybody knows except for the company.*

In a recross-examination, Bill Frizzell attempted to walk through a door that Stoecklein had opened by asking Levine "if somebody were selling a share through their brokerage account and didn't have a certificated share, is it possible in your mind that through the electronic share process that there would be outstanding shares that would not be reflected on the issued shares from the transfer agent?" Even though Levine didn't appear to understand Stoecklein's question, it allowed Frizzell to continue along the same line of questioning:

MR. FRIZZELL: *If you receive documents -- let's say a company had a thousand issued and outstanding shares, and you got in your documentation some shareholder statements that reflected that there were 2,000 shares that had been in the hands of some 9 shareholders.*

MR. FRYDMAN: *Judge, I'm going to object. This is outside the scope of direct examination.*

MS. HAKALA: *I object as well.*

JUDGE MURRAY: *It's 2 to 1.*

MR. FRIZZELL: *I'm asking how he resolves that from an auditing perspective, because we have opened the door as to outstanding shares and how that's reflected in the auditing reports, Your Honor.*

JUDGE MURRAY: *I think the witness's testimony, as I understand it, is you can't have something outstanding that hasn't been issued.*

MR. FRIZZELL: *Okay. Let me ask this question, then. You're an auditor, you're a CPA, you have experience in this area. How are you trained to handle -- if that issue were presented to you or if you knew or had evidence that there was more stock out there than -*

MS. HAKALA: *Objection . Your Honor, I object that it assumes facts not in evidence.*

JUDGE MURRAY: *I'll sustain the objection. The gentleman's position is, he looks at - you correct me if I'm wrong. He looks at transfer documents that say "issued." He doesn't look in this bigger world that you're concerned about, shareholders, how much they say they own. He looks at actual records of where the company has issued securities through its board of directors. That's all he's concerned with. All this other shareholder stuff that you're aware of because of your clients, he only looks at the company's records and the transfer agents. He uses the transfer agent to confirm that, as I understand it.*

NEIL LEVINE: *That's exactly correct, Your Honor.*

After Levine's testimony, the prosecution brought in SEC informational technology specialist Christopher Wall. He testified about recording a web cast from *The Green Baron* on October 18, 2004 with CMKX's Urban Casavant and Rendal Williams from UCAD, which was then introduced into evidence by Leslie Hakala.

Wall was followed by an extremely nervous looking Helen Bagley, the transfer agent responsible for actually issuing shares of stock for CMKX and keeping track of shares issued. SEC attorney Leslie Hakala had Bagley confirm that there were 698 shareholders as of July 22, 2003 (well over the limit of 300 that would have exempted CMKX from filing with the SEC), and that there were just under 18 billion outstanding shares on the same date. Bagley also confirmed that on a single day, January 12, 2003, the Board of Directors held a special meeting where they issued a total of 994,083,000 shares to 360 people "for fieldwork in Canada," further proof the company knew that they had over 300 shareholders.

Finally, Bagley confirmed that by December 31, 2004, the outstanding shares had grown from 18 billion to a mind blowing 778,518,875,000. Judge Murray ended Bagley's testimony with the question "Could I just ask the witness, do you transfer stock for any other company that has over 778 billion outstanding shares?" to which Bagley answered simply, "No, we don't."

Next up was Suzanne Herring, who worked for CMKX through Stoecklein's law firm, and the latest in a long line of accountants who had tried to gather enough information about the company to bring their filings up to date. Her story was not that different from Levine's: repeated unanswered calls to David DeSormeau and unfulfilled promises of company records from office administrator Ginger Gutierrez, prior corporate attorney Brian Dvorak, and prior employee James Kinney. Herring *did* reveal that CMKX had no offices, and that the company was run out of Urban's home.

Herring also testified that Urban Casavant and his wife Carolyn had signatory authority to the company bank accounts, and that she had compiled a general ledger of cash flow. However, she had no idea where the cash flowing through the company and Urban's personal bank accounts came from, or for that matter, where it went.

Hakala then asked Herring about stock issued in 2003 for the jade collection. Herring had listed a debit of $56,885,000 worth of stock issued for the collection, which was later reversed...except that there were no records to show that the stock had ever been returned to CMKX. Then, Hakala pointed out another transaction in December of 2004, where stock valued at $60 million was traded for, according to Herring, "an additional purchase of jade." However, in response to Hakala's question "as of December 31, 2004, does the company have $60 million worth of jade?" Herring responded, "No, to the best of my knowledge."

Next, Herring testified in response to Judge Murray's questions about deposits made into CMKX's accounts, that all of the money coming in was personal loans to the company from Urban Casavant. Then, after Stoecklein objected, she put it another way:

> *When I am looking at the bank statements provided by Mr. Casavant, I have money coming in. I have a bank deposit. I know from Mr. Casavant that they are not doing anything to generate revenue. I know it's not revenue. I know that on occasion Mr. Casavant has lent the company money. I do not have loan agreements to support the money coming in. Most of that money is -- has been either treated as donated capital to the company without a loan document to support a loan.*

John Martin went out on to the front steps of the courthouse during lunch recess and called CT for his second live CFRN report, still not certain that he was even on the air. His "interview" was again posted on the message boards, this time transcribed word-for-word by a poster named `cruisecontrol`:

> Hello everybody, this is John Martin again. I just wanted to bring everybody up to date.
>
> We got in just one witness, whom Mrs. Hakala questioned, her name was Suzanne Herring. She reported that the books were essentially non-existent, that she's been working towards getting the books together.
>
> It is my understanding that in one hour we will reconvene. The Judge seems to think that we will finish this tonight. I have no idea what needs to be done, there's still a great deal of material to go through.
>
> I hope everybody's hangin' in there. It seems as though there's going to be quite a bit of questioning by Mr. Stoecklein and Mr. Frizzell as soon as we reconvene from lunch.
>
> I hope everybody's having a good day, and I'll talk to you soon.

After lunch, Judge Murray called Rendal Williams, bulletproof vest and all, as the SEC's fifth witness. In answer to questions from Leslie Hakala, Williams confirmed he was the CEO of UCAD and they had entered into business agreements with CMKM Diamonds. He went on to describe how he was introduced to Urban Casavant by Ed Dhonau (CEO of Nevada Minerals) in January of 2004. He testified that Urban told him at least "ten to twelve times" during 2004 that "he was hoping to be able to announce that he was reporting at the shareholders' appreciation party."

During Don Stoecklein's cross-examination for CMKX, he asked Williams if *his* company, U.S. Canadian Minerals, was current on their required reports to the SEC, to which Williams replied, "No, I'm not." He then revealed that Roger Glenn was UCAD's attorney as well as CMKX's former attorney. Stoecklein and Judge Murray spent the next forty-five minutes trying to sort out the details of the business agreements between UCAD, Nevada Minerals, and CMKX. After repeated questioning, explaining, and re-explaining, the agreement looked something like this: CMKX owned the American Mine shaft in Ecuador, which was operated by Nevada Minerals, and split the revenue (after expenses) from the mine with UCAD, who processed the gold ore from the mine. After all of the hoopla surrounding the joint ventures between UCAD and CMKX, the total 2004 revenues from the American Mine was, according to Williams, "somewhere between 90 and $120,000, which of that, 50% goes to CMKM Diamonds." CMKX's total revenue from the venture was between 45 and $60,000, and that was put back into the mine for expenses. As for UCAD, their *total* revenue for

2004 was..."somewhere between 90 and $120,000, which of that, 50% went to CMKM Diamonds."

When Stoecklein was finished questioning the witness, Judge Murray asked a few questions of her own:

JUDGE MURRAY: *What is your educational background?*

RENDAL WILLIAMS: *I have a BS degree in mechanical engineering.*

Q: *BS degree in mechanical engineering from what school?*

A: *And mathematics.*

Q: *Math. From what school?*

A: *Walla Walla College.*

Q: *I'm sorry?*

A: *Walla Walla College.*

Q: *Would you spell that? W-a-1-1 -*

A: *1-a. W-a-1-1-a.*

Q: *And where is that?*

A: *In Walla Walla, Washington.*

Q: *I should have known. I should have known. All right. And what is your work experience? Have you been involved in the mining industry or in business in some form?*

A: *I've been involved in the mining business industry for two years.*

Q: *Okay. And what did you do before two years ago?*

A: *I had a food company. We manufactured soy milk and infant formula.*

Then it was Bill Frizzell's turn. He focused the majority of his early questions on the business relationship between UCAD and CMKX, with Rendal Williams confirming UCAD had invested money in CMKX, and CMKX had received shares of UCAD stock which were distributed to the CMKX shareholders. Williams, however, couldn't remember how much money...or how many shares...changed hands.

Next, Frizzell tried to connect the SEC's temporary trading halt of UCAD two days before the shareholder's appreciation party with Urban's failure to make the anticipated announcement that they had become fully reporting:

MR FRIZZELL: *You testified that Mr. Casavant was hoping to announce at the shareholders party that they have become fully reporting; is that correct?*

RENDAL WILLIAMS: *That's right.*

Q. *And did you attend the party that was planned there in Las Vegas for the shareholders?*

A. *Yes, I did.*

Q. *What happened at that party? Why did that party -- or did anything unusual occur at that party?*

MS. HAKALA: *Objection. Vague.*

JUDGE MURRAY: *I don't know what you mean unless something big happened. Did something big happen?*

RENDAL WILLIAMS: *No.*

MR FRIZZELL: *When did the SEC investigation into your company begin?*

RENDAL WILLIAMS: *I don't know the exact date it started.*

MR FRIZZELL: *In relation to this shareholders party.*

MS. HAKALA: *I'm sorry. Objection. Calls for speculation.*

MR. FRIZZELL: *I understand, Your Honor. I've asked the witness if he knows when the investigation began in his company because it may very well relate to why Mr. Casavant is not -- was not able to announce about the reporting or some other things at that particular shareholders meeting.*

JUDGE MURRAY: *I think you're putting words in the witness's mouth. He's told you he doesn't know.*

MR. FRIZZELL: ***Somebody*** *needs to put some words in his mouth and -- I don't mean -*

MS. HAKALA: *Objection, Your Honor, move to strike.*

JUDGE MURRAY: *Yeah, hold on.*

MR. FRIZZELL: *I'm not trying to be disrespectful. I'm just trying to get an answer to the question, Your Honor. I'll try to ask it just a little different and this is just my last line of questioning, Your Honor.*

Was there anything that happened at that party or right before that party that might have caused someone not to be announcing things that they wanted to announce at that party? To your knowledge.

RENDAL WILLIAMS: *I don't know what other people were thinking. I wasn't planning to make any announcements at the party.*

MR. FRIZZELL: *Pass the witness, Your Honor. Thank you.*

MS. HAKALA: *Your Honor, I have brief redirect.*

JUDGE MURRAY: *Great.*

REDIRECT EXAMINATION BY MS. HAKALA:

MS. HAKALA: *Mr. Williams, are you aware of anything that CMKM Diamonds was planning on announcing to shareholders at that party in Las Vegas?*

RENDAL WILLIAMS: *No, other than Mr. Casavant said he was hoping to have his reporting done, but that's all.*

Q. *How far behind is U.S. Canadian Minerals on filing its periodic reports?*

A. *A couple weeks.*

Q. *Except for the Form 10-K for 2004, aside from that form, has U.S. Canadian Minerals filed all of its required periodic reports?*

A. *Yes, we have.*

After a few more questions about the mining venture in Ecuador, Hakala ended her redirect examination by asking Williams to elaborate about other business ventures between UCAD and CMKX. He confirmed the two companies had a joint venture in Canada, though it had not generated any revenue.

After Rendal Williams testimony, highlighted by the applause that Bill Frizzell elicited from the courtroom audience with his sarcastic asides while trying to get Williams to give a straight answer, it was time for the witness that every person in the courtroom had been anticipating since the trial began. Urban Casavant, CEO and President of CMKM Diamonds, was the person who, along with Iron Bob Maheu, could set the record straight. Judge Murray introduced Casavant, both attorneys still by his side, and the crowd broke into spontaneous applause again.

JUDGE MURRAY: *The Division's next and last witness is Mr. Casavant; is that correct?*

MS. HAKALA: *Yes, Your Honor.*

JUDGE MURRAY: *Is he present and we can swear him in? And I believe you've got your folks ready to go.*

MS. HAKALA: *Full name for the record.*

A. *Urban Armand Joseph Casavant. U-r-b-a-n, A-r-m-a-n-d, J-o-s-e-p-h, C-a-s-a-v-a-n-t.*

Q. *What is your occupation?*

A. *Fifth.*

MR. GRIFFIN: *I'm sorry, Your Honor. I explained at the break Mr. Casavant intends to assert his Fifth Amendment privilege with respect to all questions by the SEC.*

MR. CHESNOFF: *Your Honor, I think Mr. Casavant is prepared to read a statement.*

URBAN CASAVANT: *Upon advice of counsel, I respectfully refuse to answer the question pursuant to the Fifth Amendment to the United States Constitution on the grounds that the answer may tend to incriminate me and/ or subject me to fine, penalty, and/or forfeiture.*

MS. HAKALA: *Mr. Casavant, where do you work?*

A. *Fifth Amendment.*

Q. *What is the address there?*

A. *Fifth Amendment.*

Q. *And what is your role there?*

A. *Fifth Amendment.*

Within the first three sentences that Leslie Hakala asked Urban Casavant, the tone was set. The crowd suddenly turned dead silent, as if they had had the collective breath knocked out of them, and their hopes along with it.

To questions pertaining to whether information contained in company press releases was accurate:

Fifth Amendment.

To questions about how whether the company had ever done an audit to determine the number of real shareholders:

Fifth Amendment.

To questions as to whether he had even ever *seen* the press releases:

Fifth Amendment.

The proceedings stopped a couple of times so that the battery of attorneys could debate the legal ramifications of Urban pleading the Fifth, with the consensus finally being drawn that while he had every right to invoke the Fifth Amendment in order to protect *his* rights, that, as Judge Murray put it, "if the president of the company answered the questions truthfully, it would damage the company. It would be adverse to the company's position in this case."

And then the questioning continued. On four occasions, Urban even answered "Fifth Amendment" in response to questions about whether he would plead the Fifth Amendment on particular topics. When asked to turn the page on one of the exhibits in front of him Urban even refused that simple request, prompting Judge Murray to comment: "I think he's pleading the Fifth about even flipping to the page."

To Hakala's question about whether "CMKM Diamonds issued stocks to over 300 shareholders of record on January 12th, 2003":

Fifth Amendment.

Were those shares issued for field work in Canada?

Fifth Amendment.

What type of field work did those 360 people do?

Fifth Amendment.

It was the same to questions about whether Urban Casavant had signed and filed paperwork concerning CMKX's shareholders, whether he knew Rendal Williams, and whether he had done an interview with Williams on *The Green Baron* radio show: "Fifth Amendment, Fifth Amendment, Fifth Amendment."

All told, Urban Casavant invoked his Fifth Amendment rights "on the grounds that the answer may tend to incriminate me and/or subject me to fine, penalty, and/or forfeiture," a grand total of forty times. Other than stating and spelling his name for the court reporter, not one shred of information was revealed during his testimony, either in defense of, or incriminating the company or himself.

Finally, Hakala encompassed the entire testimony in one last question: "And is it your intention to assert the Fifth Amendment privilege against self-incrimination as to all questions regarding CMKM Diamonds?"

To which Urban replied:

Fifth Amendment.

Chapter 22 – The Defense Rests

"I don't know exactly what Mr. Casavant expected from me, but I can tell you what I told him. That if I took on this assignment, I would surround myself with a team that would hopefully clear up mistakes of the past that might have been made, and that I would insist that from hence on that the company be responsive and comply with all regulatory agencies."

~Bob Maheu, SEC Hearing, May 10, 2005

Within minutes, word of Urban Casavant pleading the Fifth Amendment made its way to the message boards and chat rooms, including *Raging Bull*, and was promptly met with…denial:

> rocketship0: Anybody that is reporting that Urban has taken the 5th at the hearing if full of S H I T in my opinion. And I would just love to slap around any individual that reports something like that without confirmation. He said, she said, it has been reported, etc, etc. Does anybody here really think that in a hearing like this that Urban is going to take the 5th. That is ridiculous! This is not friggin criminal court for goodness sakes. Incredible!

While the message boards were in the midst of the great debate about whether or not Urban Casavant could have possibly refused to speak out publicly in defense of his own company, Donald Stoecklein was presenting the company's side of the story as best he could, considering Urban's refusal to testify. The first witness Stoecklein called was Nevada Minerals CEO Ed Dhonau, whose company was one of the many that was announced in press releases as a business partner with CMKX.

MR. STOECKLEIN: *Can you explain to us the relationship between Nevada Minerals and CMKM Diamonds?*

ED DHONAU: *Well, it has a couple different facets. My first involvement was through Canada. I met Mr. Casavant in November of '03 and he actually is the gentleman responsible for my involvement in acquiring claims up in the Saskatchewan Forte á la Corne area in the diamond claims. And currently I'm the operator of another entity that CMKM Diamonds owns in Ecuador called the American Shaft.*

Q. *The diamond mines that CMKM owns in Canada, have you ever been an owner of any of those diamond mines?*

A. *Yes. On my first early flush of the diamond claims, I claimed approximately 500,000 acres during the early months of 2004.*

Q. *Do you have an idea of the numbers of acres that CMKM has claimed up in Canada?*

A. *From just what I've read and the maps that's available by the Saskatchewan government, not taking into consideration the interest that they have in the 500,000 that Nevada Minerals has, it's probably -- approximately about a million acres.*

Q. *Are you familiar at all with valuations of mining claims?*

A. *Well, just through my own experience as being in a private company, we do a cost basis. I do know, you know, some companies go out and they get independent evaluations done by the core samples or findings that they actually get in their own soil samples.*

Q. *Is there any way for you to tell the Court today in terms of the value, because one of the issues we have here today is valuation. Can you -*

MS. HAKALA: *Objection, Your Honor. Mr. Dhonau is not an expert in accounting for mining claims or anything else.*

JUDGE MURRAY: *I didn't know. One of the issues we have here today is valuation?*

MR. STOECKLEIN: *Yeah, yes, it is.*

JUDGE MURRAY: *I thought the issue was filing reports required by the SEC and whether or not they have been filed. And if they hadn't been filed, what to do about it.*

MR. STOECKLEIN: *We spent a lot of time on revenues with Mr. Williams. I don't see why we can't get a little testimony in as to the viability of this company and in terms of its reporting capabilities. I mean, is it viable? I would think Your Honor would want to know that information.*

JUDGE MURRAY: *We just had the president, the chief executive officer of the company, on the stand. He refused to answer a question. The best source of information refused to answer a question.*

After a short exchange between Stoecklein and Judge Murray, she sustained Hakala's objection. From there, Stoecklein questioned Dhonau at length about the relationship between Nevada Minerals and CMKX in Ecuador, which yielded no new information of significance, and attempted without success to get Dhonau to testify that the accounting process was made more complex because of the companies' business arrangement. Other than Dhonau telling Stoecklein that CMKX had invested a little over a million dollars in Ecuador and that Nevada Mineral had taken possession of some of CMKX's assets in payment of a debt amounting to $180,000, there was really no new information revealed from CMKX's first witness.

In fact, Hakala and the SEC seemed to get more mileage out of Dhonau than Stoecklein did, establishing that he had never seen any financial statements from CMKX, he had no idea when they might file any financial statements, and they had only received 80% of the 45 to 60 thousand dollars in revenue mentioned in earlier testimony (because of the percentage paid to Nevada Minerals). Even that revenue was used to buy air compressors for the mines by Urban, so no money ever made it into CMKX's accounts. Dhonau also testified that he had owned a substantial number of shares of CMKX, but had given them back to Urban in exchange for a promissory note that was due at the end of the year:

MS. HAKALA: *You used to own 75 billion shares of CMKM Diamonds stock, didn't you?*

ED DHONAU: *Yes, ma'am.*

Q. *What happened to that stock?*

A. *I surrendered them back to CMKM for a nonrecourse note in December.*

Q. *A nonrecourse note in what amount?*

A. *$2 million.*

Q. *Why did you do that?*

A. *In light of the investigation and what I had discovered in November, I just felt it was best for my company and my own well being to separate from the companies.*

Q. *The nonrecourse $2.2 million note, who issued that note?*

A. *CMKM Diamonds to Nevada Minerals.*

JUDGE MURRAY: *Did you cash it? Did you cash it? You actually got $2.2 million?*

ED DHONAU: *No, ma'am. It's not due until December of 2005.*

MS. HAKALA: *So in December of 2005 CMKM Diamonds will owe you -- or will owe Nevada Minerals $2.2 million; is that correct?*

A. *$2 million, yes.*

Q. *What did you discover in November that made you no longer want to own shares of CMKM Diamonds' stock?*

A. *It was just the -- it was a personal emotional reaction off of what was happening to the investigations.*

Q. *Can you elaborate on that?*

A. *It was just nothing more than a -- a gut feel of myself, and -- and after my deposition, I felt it was best for my company to stand alone as a private corporation.*

Ed Dhonau's testimony ultimately seemed to harm CKMX's case more than it helped. Since Judge Murray had disallowed Stoecklein's attempts to discuss the value of the company's assets *and* Bill Frizzell's efforts to bring the issue of naked short selling into the hearing, the company was down to two witnesses to somehow prove that they were on the verge of becoming compliant by filing their financial statements. The first of those witnesses was Iron Bob Maheu, who even at the age of 87, along with Urban Casavant and Roger Glenn formed the Holy Trinity of hope for CMKX shareholders. After his name was called, Maheu made his way to the witness stand, accidentally coming up the aisle at the far end of the courtroom, and having to maneuver his way around to reach the witness stand, prompting Judge Murray to comment "I think you took the long way around but..." Maheu might have been slow on his feet, but he was quick to respond, "I'll make it," eliciting appreciative laughter from the audience.

After confirming that Maheu was brought in by Urban Casavant as co-chairman and a director of CMKM Diamonds, Don Stoecklein asked Maheu why he accepted the position with the company:

MR. STOECKLEIN: *I'm a little curious now, in terms of CMKM Diamonds, why you would have taken the position of coming on as a board member.*

BOB MAHEU: *Well, I've always been challenged -- I mean intrigued with challenges and difficult assignments. I started at age 10 accepting impossible assignments. I'm also interested in the plight of stockholders wherever they may be. I happen to have lived my life in such a way that I've never feared a full background investigation, and I thought that I could make a contribution.*

Q. *What background would you have that you believe would help this company, CMKM Diamonds, to become compliant?*

A. *Well, I understand the necessity of a publicly held company to be compliant. And I'm not a novice in the world of being in compliance -- of an entity being in compliance. I had the privilege 50 years ago to set up the security and compliance divisions of the Small Defense Plant Administration. It was an entity that had been structured by the government to help start-up companies and small businesses. I learned very early on that you cannot help the ills of a small company or any company just by flowing money in their direction. I learned the value of compliance. And I made sure that the Small Defense Plant Administration was always in compliance. By that, I mean if, in fact, we made a contribution to a small business, we made sure that the money was used within certain parameters.*

Q. *What was the job that Mr. Casavant expected from you as a board member?*

A. *I don't know exactly what he expected from me, but I can tell you what I told him. That if I took on this assignment, I would surround myself with a team that would hopefully clear up mistakes of the past that might have been made, and that I would insist that from hence on that the company be responsive and comply with all regulatory agencies.*

Q. *Did you have any apprehension about joining the board of a company that had been under an SEC investigation?*

A. *No.*

He then went on to say that joining a company that "had problems" was not an issue for him, since he had "been there before," and again showed his quick wit when questioned about how much the company was paying him:

Q. *Are you being compensated for your position as a board member?*

A. *Yes, I am.*

Q. *I'm going to ask you, what is that compensation?*

A. *$40,000 a month.*

JUDGE MURRAY: *A month?*

BOB MAHEU: *A week. A month. Month. I'm sorry. I'm -- I was trying to get a raise.*

JUDGE MURRAY: *You did. You did.*

Stoecklein continued, trying to establish a pattern of progress since Maheu had joined the company:

> Q. *You mentioned a moment ago of the reasons why you joined the board. What has been accomplished, in your mind, in terms of compliance?*
>
> A. *I think that we have put together a team that has complied with my request and I hope that the work product that we're producing now will be evidence that we have tried.*
>
> Q. *Can you maybe explain to the Court individuals that you've had the ability to communicate with, and, as part of that, I'll ask it as a double question -- I know you don't like double questions -- but the time you've had to spend with these people?*
>
> A. *I've spent a lot of time with these people. And I might go back to my -- by the way, after the Small Defense Plant Administration, a new entity was formed called the Small Business Administration. And I also set up the -- and helped with the language that enabled the formation of that entity. After it was set up, I became an assistant to the administrator. And in continuity of what I discussed before, and my desire to make sure that the recipients were in compliance, I became known as the man with the whip. And I still have that whip.*
>
> Q. *And you've had an opportunity to use that whip in terms of helping this company develop its periodic reports for filing with the Commission?*
>
> A. *Yes, I have.*

Judge Murray pointed out to both Stoecklein and Maheu that prior witnesses had testified that they were requesting "data, books and records" from the company since 2005 but hadn't received anything as of the day before the hearing.

> JUDGE MURRAY: *How can they have given that testimony if you're sitting here and telling me that since February your team has made all this great forward progress towards fulfilling the reporting requirements?*
>
> BOB MAHEU: *To my knowledge, they have furnished the information that we have requested. I'm not aware of the testimony to which you refer.*
>
> MR. STOECKLEIN: *Are you suggesting that Mr. Maheu would have that information from three years before he joined the company?*
>
> JUDGE MURRAY: *Well, he should know that the accountants were looking for it and haven't been able to get it. Am I correct that you are unaware that*

accountants have been asking for information since February, March, and April and haven't been able to get it from the company?

BOB MAHEU: *I was unaware --- I was not unaware that they were asking for the information. But I was unaware that the information was not progressing.*

Again, Judge Murray herself seemed to be shooting down Stoecklein's line of questioning. At that point, he simply gave up: "Your Honor, we have no more questions for this witness."

Then it was Frizzell's turn to bat, trying to come up with some angle that Stoecklein had missed, or at the very least, continue along the same lines of questioning, hopefully with better results. He began by establishing that Maheu had a fifteen year relationship with Don Stoecklein, and that Stoecklein's firm had a team of attorneys, accountants, and auditors who were capable of putting together financial statements for CMKX. Then, he asked Maheu a question that slipped by the others in the courtroom, but contained the cryptic phrase "maybe you wanted something done but someone didn't":

MR. FRIZZELL: *Mr. Maheu, in your job as cochairman of the board, maybe you wanted something done but someone else didn't, who would -- and, by the way, the cochairman with you is Mr. Urban Casavant; is that correct?*

BOB MAHEU: *That is correct.*

Q. *Was there discussion about who would prevail if there was some dispute over what should be done between you and Mr. Casavant?*

A. *That I would refer any such -- any such instance to Attorney Don Stoecklein, yes.*

Then, he followed up by trying to at least confirm that Maheu, Stoecklein and their team were capable of bringing CMKX into compliance:

MR. FRIZZELL: *With this particular company, will you be able to assist and to get the reports that are needed to be filed? Will you be able to help the company get that done?*

BOB MAHEU: *I'm certain -*

MS. HAKALA: *Objection. Calls for speculation.*

JUDGE MURRAY: *Well, no, I'll overrule the objection. I mean, he's getting $40,000 a month, so of course he's going to help them, hopefully, to do something. I mean that's his job, isn't it?*

BOB MAHEU: *The answer -- the answer has just been answered.*

After Frizzell was finished with the witness, Hakala continued along the same lines Frizzell had established by asking about the company's financial reports, or more specifically about when they would be filed:

MS. HAKALA. *Do you believe that CMKM should promptly file its periodic reports?*

BOB MAHEU: *I most assuredly do.*

Q. *When do you anticipate those reports will be filed?*

A. *As quickly as we can.*

Q. *Can you set a date by which those reports will be filed?*

A. *As soon as they are ready, ma'am.*

Q. *Can you set a date by which those reports will be ready?*

A. *I cannot. But I assure you that I will do my best to comply with your request. I feel here that we have a partnership of sorts, I mean the government and we have a partnership to save these stockholders, and I will do my best to do that.*

"The government and we have a partnership to save these stockholders." It was perhaps the most relevant statement of the entire hearing and one purposely ignored by Hakala, who moved quickly on to another topic. After a brief discussion about who exactly was on Stoecklein's "team," Hakala went on the attack about CMKX's performance as a viable business. She first pointed out that CMKX didn't even have an office and spent the next few minutes trying to establish how many employees worked for the company. Maheu believed they had 22 employees, mostly in Canada, because he had been told that by Urban Casavant and Don Stoecklein.

Pointing out that Stoecklein wasn't on the board of directors, Hakala asked Maheu why he deferred to Stoecklein about business decisions regarding CMKX. Maheu answered without hesitation:

BOB MAHEU: *I didn't say that I deferred to him for business decisions. I -- my instructions to him -- excuse me -- my instructions to him are that we do everything we can to comply with the needs of the regulatory bodies.*

Hakala then took another approach, having Maheu read pertinent paragraphs from the various CMKX press releases, where the company announced the hirings of the various people who were supposed to bring them into compliance:

MS. HAKALA: *Please, would you read the first paragraph out loud.*

BOB MAHEU: *"Las Vegas, Business Wire, December 3, 2002. Casavant Mining Kimberlite International, Inc., announced today the hiring of David DeSormeau to implement a real time financial reporting and inventory control systems."*

Q. *As far as you're aware, was that financial reporting system ever put in place?*

A. *I am not aware of whether or not it was put in place.*

Q. *In the next paragraph, there's a reference to a Wesley Casavant. It says who was appointed secretary treasurer to ensure seamless integration with auditing practices. Is Wesley Casavant still secretary treasurer of the company?*

A. *I do not know whether he is or not.*

Next, she had him read from a June 4, 2004 CMKX press release:

BOB MAHEU: *"President and chairman of the board of directors Urban Casavant announced that the company has entered into discussions with a large New York securities law firm to represent the company and has paid a retainer to that firm to begin the process of bringing the company into full compliance in order to be fully reporting."*

MS. HAKALA: *Do you know why the company thought it needed to get into full compliance in order to be fully reporting in June of 2004? Do you know why they thought that?*

A. *I would think because they thought that that's what was supposed to be done.*

Q. *Okay. I'd like you to read the next paragraph, please, which starts out "Casavant and the board of directors."*

A. *"Casavant and the board of directors stated that, 'We are very happy and excited to be associated with a law firm of this caliber and are looking forward to their assistance and direction to become fully reporting in as short a time as possible.'"*

Q. *Do you know what happened with respect to that past statement; that they wanted to be reporting as soon as possible?*

A. *No, I do not. But I'd like to refer, if I may, to my first press release when I made it very clear that if there were deficiencies in the past, that we intended to hopefully correct them.*

Q. *Are you referring to the press release dated February 17th, 2005?*

A. *Yes, I am.*

Q. *Please would you read the first sentence of the fifth paragraph of this press release?*

A. *"CMKX is currently working toward completing an audit of its financial statements and the preparation of the necessary SEC filings. Investors and"*
-

Q. *That's enough. You're welcome to continue reading. My questions are about that first sentence. It says here that CMKX is working towards completing an audit. When this press release was issued, had CMKM ever even started its audit?*

A. *I read that differently. I read that they are working toward completing. Whether the start was pre this or they intended to do it the next day, I don't know, but I read it differently. I'm sorry about that.*

Q. *Has an audit of CMKM Diamonds financial statements even started?*

A. *As of now? I assume it has, yes.*

Q. *On what basis do you think that? Why do you think that?*

A. *Because that was my impression.*

Q. *What was your basis for that impression?*

A. *That I have been told that, yes, an audit had been started.*

Q. *Who told you that?*

A. *I believe it was Don Stoecklein.*

Q. *Does CMKM Diamonds have books and records and financial statements to audit?*

A. *I know that they are doing the very best they can to get all the records necessary for an audit, yes.*

Q. *Mr. Maheu, have you ever seen a general ledger for CMKM Diamonds?*

A. *No, I have not.*

Q. *Do you know how much CMKM Diamonds has in the bank?*

A. *No, I do not.*

Q. *Do you know what the liabilities of CMKM Diamonds are?*

A. *No, I do not.*

Q. *Do you know what the assets of CMKM Diamonds are?*

A. *No, I do not. Not -- no, I do not.*

Q. *Okay. I'd like you to turn to Exhibit 46. Exhibit 46 is a press release dated July 27th, 2004. This press release refers to the $3 million that CMKM Diamonds received from U.S. Canadian Minerals. Do you see that?*

A. *Yes, I do.*

Q. *Do you know what was done with that $3 million?*

A. *No, I do not.*

Q. *Do you know of any way for shareholders and the investing public to know what happened to that money?*

A. *I do not.*

JUDGE MURRAY: *Does the Division concede that CMKM Diamonds actually got $3 million?*

MS. HAKALA: *We're -- we -- we don't know. We're going to offer this press release.*

MS. HAKALA: *And my last question for Mr. Maheu is, if you turn to Exhibit 48, which is a press release dated September 13th, 2004. This describes $5 million that CMKM Diamonds received from St. George Metals, Inc. Do you see that? It describes a second payment of $2.5 million and refers to a prior payment of 2.5? Do you know what happened to the $5 million that CMKM Diamonds allegedly got from St. George Metals?*

BOB MAHEU: *No, I do not.*

Q. *Do you know any way that shareholders could find out what happened to this $5 million that it allegedly received?*

A. *If that is what you want to know, I will do my best to make sure that you get the information.*

Q. *But do you know of any way for shareholders and the investing public to find out what happened to this allegedly $5 million?*

A. *I certainly hope they do.*

Q. *Do you know of any way now that they could?*

A. *I do not, no.*

MS. HAKALA: *We have no further questions.*

A redirect examination by Don Stoecklein was for the most part ineffectual, establishing only that they had hired Suzanne Herring in January of that year to "prepare compiled financial statements." Judge Murray asked Maheu a question about why CMKX hired Maheu in the first place:

JUDGE MURRAY: *Okay. I want you to understand that sometimes I have to be blunt. Okay? Could you explain to me why I might think that they hired you and paid you $480,000 to give some color of legitimacy to this operation? In other words, you evidently have an esteemed biography. So did that thought ever cross your mind that this company brought you in just to make it look like there was some legitimacy to it and paid you this amount of money?*

BOB MAHEU: *First of all, Your Honor, I've only been paid, so far, $80,000.*

JUDGE MURRAY: *$80,000.*

BOB MAHEU: *And I would like to believe that, yes, that my background -- and I repeat. I can stand any, any full background investigation that any entity can do based on I already have. And I think that having spent a lifetime trying to be in that position -- and I do have a great record in business -- that, yes, I would like to believe that they would have hired me for my past experience.*

JUDGE MURRAY: *Has it ever crossed your mind that maybe you're being used?*

BOB MAHEU: *I don't think so, Your Honor. No.*

And that was the end of Iron Bob Maheu's testimony in the SEC revocation hearing CMKM Diamonds. Although Frizzell said Maheu "has a confident air about him, he's very deliberate and he's got very good diction," Iron Bob had appeared confused and out of touch on the witness stand at times, or at least out of the loop when it came to information pertaining to the company. In fact, Maheu would later describe his experience on the witness stand as "damned embarrassing."

After Maheu, only one witness remained to make the case for CMKX. Kristen Buck, who worked for attorney Anthony DeMint at Securities Law Institute, a subsidiary of the Stoecklein Law Group, had been assigned the unenviable task of overseeing the process of compiling financial reports for CMKX.

Stoecklein began by asking Buck about the infamous "Form 15" the company had filed in July of 2003 claiming they had fewer than 300 shareholders and were no longer obligated to file financial reports with the SEC. She then went on to describe a "discrepancy in the number of shareholders" between the official shareholder list they had received from the transfer agent (Helen Bagley at 1st Global Transfer) and the Form 15 that the company had filed with the SEC. While the filing showed less than 300 shareholders of record, the transfer agent records showed 698 shareholders at the time. Buck testified that they contacted the SEC and were told to file an amended Form 15, which meant that they would have 60 days to file all the financial statements to bring the company into compliance:

MR. STOECKLEIN: *Was there some concern obviously about the 60-day time frame?*

KRISTEN BUCK: *There was definitely some concern. We -- I hadn't, but others in our office had met with their former financial person and we needed to get information from them under whether or not we could actually comply with putting together reporting obligations.*

JUDGE MURRAY: *And who was this financial person?*

KRISTEN BUCK: *I believe it was David DeSormeau.*

MR. STOECKLEIN: *And can I ask what Mr. DeSormeau said about the ability to generate financial reports?*

KRISTEN BUCK: *It was my understanding that we hadn't received much information from him, so it became - the decision, I believe, was to retain somebody else that could prepare financial statements for the company.*

Q. *Are you at all familiar with the amount of money that was paid to Mr. DeSormeau to generate these reports?*

A. *I believe it was in excess of 1.5 million.*

JUDGE MURRAY: *1.5 million?*

KRISTEN BUCK: *(Nods head.)*

Buck confirmed that prior to her involvement the company had hired D. Roger Glenn of Edwards & Angell, LLP to bring their financial records up to date:

MR. STOECKLEIN: *Let me ask you, Ms. Buck, did you have any interaction with the prior law firm?*

KRISTEN BUCK: *There was requests sent out asking for information from them to be provided to us as well.*

Q. *And can you tell me what information you received?*

A. *We did not receive any information beyond one letter that was saying that they did not have any other documents except for what they'd provided under the subpoena which was some billing.*

Q. *And have you had an opportunity in reviewing documents to understand how much they've been paid to assist in the reporting process?*

A. *I don't know off the top of my head how much, but I know that it was -- they have been paid a fair amount.*

Buck went on to say that they had verified the mining claims in Canada and the business agreements in Ecuador and that although they were still missing substantial company financial records, they had enough information for "the process to begin" in compiling the periodic reports.

In Frizzell's short redirect, he asked Buck if the forty other clients that her company represented, the time spent preparing for the SEC hearing and the lack of adequate records provided by the company hindered their ability to make the 60-day filing deadline. She confirmed that all three things had slowed down the process and finished with "I think the filing could be done if everything was provided to us, yes."

Leslie Hakala began her questioning with a somewhat bizarre tirade about whether the information provided to the Securities Law Institute and forwarded to the SEC was "less than two banker's boxes" full. Buck responded repeatedly that she had received the information in file form and had no idea how many boxes it would fill. Hakala, not to be deterred, asked the same question eight different times in one form or another and finally had Gregory Glynn hold up a banker's box to refresh her memory:

KRISTEN BUCK: *So you're asking --- could you state the question again?*

MS. HAKALA: *Were the materials that you have been provided to prepare the CMKM Diamonds filings by the company more or less than would fill two of those boxes?*

KRISTEN BUCK: *I would say around two boxes or more.*

Q. *Which is it? Two boxes, less or more?*

A. *Probably more.*

Q. *Why weren't those provided to the Commission? I can represent, Your Honor, that the materials provided to the Commission did not fill two banker's boxes.*

A. *I believe we -- I know that we gave all the information that we had. Now, whether or not how you stack it and fill it in a box is, I guess, how you put the information together. I didn't put the boxes together myself.*

After the questioning had gone on for far too long, Stoecklein objected on the grounds that it was argumentative and "really ridiculous." Judge Murray ended the questioning by stating the obvious, that Buck had received records amounting to "around two boxes."

Hakala in rapid-fire fashion asked if Kristen Buck knew whether DeSormeau was paid in stock or cash (he was paid with stock), if Buck had seen any contracts with drilling companies (she couldn't remember), if she had seen any employment agreements (she didn't know "off the top of her head"), and if she had seen "contracts related to the $56 million jade collection that CMKM Diamonds has" (she had read the press releases, but didn't remember seeing any contracts). At times, Hakala seemed to ask the next question almost before Buck answered the one before it. She asked how much Securities Law Institute was being paid to prepare CMKX's filings (Buck "wasn't privy to that information") and finally culminated with the inevitable "Can you give a certain date by which CMKM Diamonds will be filing its periodic reports?" At that point, Judge Murray had to admonish her to "slow down."

Hakala repeated the question:

MS. HAKALA: *So, as you sit here today, can you give us a specific date by which it will be reporting?*

KRISTEN BUCK: *It would be speculation.*

The questioning moved on to the topic of the company's office, or rather their lack of an office. Hakala began by asking Buck if "CMKM Diamonds had any offices?" Buck replied that she had been given an address of 5375 Procyon Street, Suite 101, by Stoecklein, who she believed got it from Urban Casavant. She then confirmed her office was alerted in an email from Debbie Amigone to Anthony

DeMint, both of whom worked at Securities Law Institute, that CMKM Diamonds didn't have an office at that address. Hakala asked Buck to read the email aloud:

KRISTEN BUCK: *"Anthony, I was on the CMKX Net site and there are 21 pages of the fact that there is no corporate office. Apparently a stockholder on vacation went to the Procyon address and in Suite 101 is a hot rod shop. He spoke with a guy name Shawn who said there is no CMKX, Urban Casavant, Michael Williams, Robert Maheu, or anyone at this address. He has been there since September 2004 and the rest of the warehouse is empty. This guy that was there posted Shawn's phone number and other stockholders called him and he told them the same thing. The stockholders are saying that the company lied in its PR and SEC filings and they are now going to call Andy in the morning and then call the SEC. You may want to call Urban or Michael and have them move in and talk to Shawn at the hot rod shop and also tell Andy Hill what to tell the stockholders when they call him. Let me know if you want me to call anyone about this or if it is not important. Thanks, Debbie."*

MS. HAKALA: *No further questions, Your Honor.*

JUDGE MURRAY: *Is there any redirect for the witness?*

MR. STOECKLEIN: *No, Your Honor.*

JUDGE MURRAY: *Does this conclude CMKM Diamonds' direct case?*

MR. STOECKLEIN: *Yes, it does.*

JUDGE MURRAY: *Okay. Is Enforcement going to have a rebuttal case?*

MS. HAKALA: *No -- Division rests, Your Honor.*

JUDGE MURRAY: *I should say thank God but -- but I won't say that.*

Of the three witnesses Don Stoecklein brought in to defend CMKX, one said he sold his shares back to the company because he didn't want to be involved with them anymore, another (who was the co-chairman of the board of directors) seemed to have no idea what was going on with the company, the third witness testified that the company's office was actually a hot rod shop…and none of the three witnesses had a clue as to when CMKX might file their required financial reports.

After the hearing Bill Frizzell still couldn't shake the feeling that something wasn't right. The defense that Stoecklein presented for CMKX hardly seemed like a serious effort to save the company:

"I think that it was a joke; I think the judge wanted the shareholders to know that they were represented. 'We're glad you're here so that you can

hear what's going on. But other then that we're not going to get into naked shorting.' She did ask Leslie Hakala if the SEC was willing to acknowledge that there was naked short selling in the company, and Hakala said 'No.'

But the hearing itself was just a joke...what's an effective defense in that kind of a hearing? 'You didn't file your financials. We're going to revoke.' 'Ok, I'm trying to but it's really hard.' And that's your defense! So, who's going to win that? Of course you're going to lose."

The only thing left was the procedure of officially placing into evidence the various exhibits that both sides had used in their case. CMKX hadn't presented *any* evidence other than the files that the SEC had already admitted into evidence. It was a routine process, at least until it came to one piece of evidence, Exhibit 60. The SEC withheld that piece of evidence even though they had given it to Stoecklein and Frizzell in the first place, buried in the thousands of pages of other documents. SEC attorney Gregory Glynn described it as "a letter dated May 6th of 2005, to Ms. Anne Dansard Glowacki, NASD," and asked to withdraw it as evidence. Frizzell objected. Because it was provided as evidence by the SEC in the first place, Judge Murray sided with Frizzell and added it to the mountain of documents presented on that day.

The inclusion of that letter, which would soon become known simply as "the Jeffries letter," was significant. Bill Frizzell later explained it this way:

"The Jeffries letter is an apology to the NASD by the market maker that had been caught clearing 111 billion trades 'ex-clearing' which means the trades were not reported to the public and the market in general. They become short sales if the broker does not locate the security. No one apparently knows of these sales unless the NASD catches on. You see here they do nothing about it if the market maker apologizes. Now that is enforcement at its best. My question here is... Where are the securities represented by the buys? Were they ever delivered, or are they simply in electronic accounts somewhere? I bet they are. I bet E*Trade and Ameritrade have a butt load of these somewhere.

Forever after the SEC will have to support this letter and its content as truthful and authentic. When Leslie started trying to withdraw it, I obviously objected. This letter will forever after be referred to as the letter offered by the SEC in an official hearing of evidence of 'ex-clearing' and other dastardly things. I expect we will use this when we get to working on our claims against Jeffries and the other parties to those transactions."

The Jeffries letter was now included in the evidence and the infamous revocation trial for CMKM Diamonds, Inc. was officially adjourned. As Bill Frizzell and John Martin wearily made their way back to their hotel room, thousands of other CMKX shareholders were left with little else to do but speculate about the possible outcome...and hope for a miracle.

Chapter 23 – The Naked Truth

"I feel here that we have a partnership of sorts, I mean the government and we have a partnership to save these stockholders, and I will do my best to do that."
~Bob Maheu, SEC Hearing for CMKX

"I am not concerned about the present shareholders. I'm concerned about future investors in this company."
~Leslie Hakala, SEC

Back in their hotel room, Bill Frizzell and John Martin were exhausted from five nights of almost no sleep, but the boxes of evidence from the SEC were still sitting on the bed. Some files had barely been opened in the short time that Bill had to prepare for the hearing. Still running on pure adrenaline from the excitement of their day in court, they decided to look through the boxes for a bit before going to sleep. Bill sat on the bed and began to dig through one box, while John sat at the dimly lit table and sifted through another one. Although the day had been almost a blur to him, John remembered that night vividly:

> *"I was sitting at the table with my back to Bill, and Bill was on the bed, he had his glasses on and we were both looking through the files. I was sitting there reading and all of the sudden, I hear him behind me: 'Ooooohhhh shit!' And I turned around and said 'What?!' And he said, 'You're not going to believe this!' And that was when we figured it out."*

> Bill: *"Well, we were looking through the files that the SEC sent us. One of the things that they requested from Urban was copies of his bank statements. And one of these statements was titled 'PA Holdings, Inc.' which we thought was Prince Albert Holdings, Inc. It's like a holding company, and the account was in the name of Brian Dvorak, his attorney, but Urban would actually sign the checks. So we started looking at the deposits in relation to the times that a lot of the stock activity was going on. And we saw, for example, a 2.7 million dollar deposit into Urban's account from First Common Merchants, which was John Edwards' account. And on another bank statement we saw eleven deposits of $750,000 each in a two-week period in August of '04. Over eight million dollars in one month! We didn't know when the hearing was going on that there was this flow of money coming back into Urban's personal account. And we don't really know even to this day exactly where that money came from."*

> John: *"They're all cashier's checks!"*

Bill: *"So we went to the cert records that tell who was selling shares, and we saw that John Edwards was dumping all those billions of shares through NevWest in his 36 different trust accounts...and at the exact same time all this money was showing up in Urban's account!"*

John: *"At that point, Bill said it looked like Urban was giving shares to people he knew, they were selling the shares and sending him back 75% of the money. And it looked like Edwards was dumping shares, and Urban was getting a cut."*

Bill: *"But we didn't know for sure! That was the big thing; the deposit sheets that we had didn't tell us where the money was coming from. But every time, if you went back to the records from the transfer agent Helen Bagley...you took a cert number, and you multiply the number of shares times what it was trading for on that date, and it was almost to the penny: A certain percentage of it was going back to Urban.*

And then we started seeing all these shares issued to all these other people. For instance, 500 million shares were issued to Urban's secretary Ginger Gutierrez, and three days later they were surrendered. And tons of shares were issued to James and Jeannie Kinney, who Ginger also worked with at Part Time Management. Shares issued, dumped into the market, and at the same time, millions of dollars were flowing into Urban's account."

John: *"But then, we also saw money going to Rendal Williams and Ed Dhonau and all these other guys, and we were sitting on the bed, and I was looking at Bill, and I said, 'Oh my gosh, all these people are right here in town...and they're all in on it!'"*

The more John and Bill sifted through the boxes of documents the SEC had delivered to their doorstep, the more they began to realize that everything they thought they knew about CMKX up to that point was wrong. Their image of the company changed almost every time they opened another file, and the names that suddenly appeared as major players revealed a darker and far more complex side of the CMKX story. This was not the company they thought they had invested in, and although they still believed there was a serious problem with naked shorting in CMKX, they realized it was only part of the problem.

While the people who Bill Frizzell had checked out *before* he invested in CMKX all seemed to look good on paper, the facts that began to float to the surface during, and especially after, the May 10th SEC hearing painted a much more disturbing picture of the company's history. Bill recalled later that his first thoughts were regret that he didn't have all of this newfound knowledge just hours earlier:

"If I had a chance to read that stuff, if I had had just one more day before the hearing that all this stuff got here, and if the judge had let me...we would

still be in court!! What could I have done for the shareholders at this point? Well, we had Helen Bagley on the witness stand, under oath! I could have asked her, "Well, tell me about this? You got an opinion letter from a lawyer releasing 500 billion shares into the market place?' You know, they had Helen on these transfer records. Helen's name was all throughout this..."

John: *"...and Neal Levine!"*

Bill: *"Yeah, and Neal Levine...I mean the auditor who resigned in the middle of the hearing! He was aware of everything that had been going on! It was just a very ineffective cross-examination, simply because I wasn't prepared. I hadn't had the time to digest this information. All I could think about was these poor shareholders! I had put myself in a position of representing the shareholders and they were getting screwed! And I mean from every angle! And I was sitting there thinking, 'This person's in on it, this person's in on it, this person's in on it...And I know that the SEC knows...because I got this information from the SEC! And they don't want to hear about it. So who can help these shareholders right now?'"*

It wasn't just the revelation of shady dealings within the company that disturbed Bill and John. It suddenly seemed as if they had unknowingly walked into a situation that could jeopardize their own safety:

John: *"I'll never forget the feeling we had after figuring that out. I mean, all of these people suddenly looked like they were tied together, and we were stepping right in the middle of their mess! Bill had literally attacked Neal Levine and John Edwards in that hearing, without knowing if they needed to be attacked. He had no idea at that point."*

Bill: *"I had read John Edwards' deposition from before the hearing. I felt I knew where the SEC was going, so I kind of fed off of that. But I did not realize that there were 36 trading accounts that were opened in NevWest Securities. I didn't find that out until later that evening."*

John: *"Well I was sitting in Bill's room and I said, 'I'm checking out of mine.' So we got a totally different room..."*

Bill: *"I think we moved into another room that connects one room to another...I mean we were really nervous."*

John: *"We changed our name and everything on it! And we tried to get an earlier flight out!"*

Bill: *"We didn't even want to fly on the same flight!"*

John: *"These guys were right in the middle of it...and they had bullet proof vests and body guards!"*

Bill: *"The next day before we were supposed to leave, Don Stoecklein had set up a meeting with the SEC. And we were not excited about staying for this meeting, we wanted to get out of town, but Don felt like we were going to go talk to them about naked shorting. And that was the main reason that we were there in the first place, and I had all this evidence that I was hoping to give to the SEC, so we had to stay."*

When Bill Frizzell walked into the meeting on the morning of Wednesday, May 11, 2005, he saw every person in the room in a different light. He looked at the faces around him and began to wonder if he had a friend in the entire process. SEC attorneys Leslie Hakala and Gregory Glenn were there with someone else from the SEC, along with CMKX attorney Donald Stoecklein, Bob Maheu, and Mike Williams. Looking back at it later, Frizzell said:

"So I have all that knowledge while I'm sitting there at this meeting with the SEC. And I've got the corporate general council for CMKM, Don Stoecklein there, and Bob Maheu who was supposed to be cleaning everything up. I was seriously thinking 'You know, nobody wants me here. I don't even think the judge wants me here. The SEC damn sure doesn't want me here. The corporation doesn't want me here.' And I was thinking 'Oooo, this is ugly,' but I've got this information here and I'm trying to figure out what can I do with it."

Hakala had made every effort to exclude Frizzell and the shareholders from being represented from day one. In Bill's words, "Hakala and the SEC had the attitude of 'Why do the shareholders need a lawyer? Our job is to represent the investors... they don't need their own council.'" But in Frizzell's mind it was clear they were simply covering up their own mistakes: "Although the naked short position was not a central issue in the hearing, I had the concern that the naked shorting was so bad that the SEC was going to revoke this company in hopes of covering up the massive stock counterfeiting."

Hakala and Glenn introduced the person they had brought with them, Andrew Petillon, Branch Chief of Enforcement at the Pacific Regional Office. Frizzell was a bit taken aback; why were they bringing in the head of the entire Pacific region for this little diamond mine company?

Frizzell hoped that Maheu might side with him, especially with theories abounding that he was brought in specifically to deal with the criminals who were selling counterfeit stock into the market. Stoecklein wanted to buy time for the company to file their delinquent paperwork. Even if he was using Frizzell to drag out the process, at least he was siding with him on the issue of naked short selling. And who was Mike Williams? Frizzell still didn't know where Williams fit into all of this, since he had no official position with the company. Why was he there at all?

Sitting in the meeting with the three SEC officials, Maheu, Stoecklein, and Williams, Bill Frizzell wasn't certain how much of this newfound information he should divulge. He knew the SEC had access to it, and surely they had put two and two together and made the connection between the massive share dumping by Edwards and the other insiders and the money that flowed like water through Urban's bank accounts. But as far as the naked short selling, he knew he would have to lay his cards out on the table:

> *"I had a CD-ROM that had an actual picture of the broker's statements. And we had the database that actually totaled up what those statements were. So if they were inclined to do so, they could check out our numbers by just pulling up the data base, clicking on it, and there's a picture of the brokerage statement to see if it is authentic or not. In other words, this wasn't just a jokester conversation. We had a hard copy printout of every brokerage statement, who the broker was and what the number of shares were, a whole box full of statements with the CD-ROM sitting right there on top of it."*

In several conversations with Bill Frizzell, he recalled that Leslie Hakala had voiced her true feeling towards the more than 50,000 CMKX shareholders who had lost hundreds of millions of dollars:

> *"'I am not concerned about the present shareholders. I'm concerned about future investors in this company.' Those were her exact words! And I said, 'Leslie, that's 50 or 60 thousand people who have put their money in there. Your action is going to delist this security. All their investments go down the tube if this company goes under, and that's not a concern?' I remember having that conversation. She said, 'I'm just worried about future investors. I don't want anybody else investing their lives in this.' It was then that I realized that the SEC didn't want to do anything to help the shareholders of CMKX. They just wanted us to just go away."*

Still, Frizzell hoped to get Hakala and the SEC to consider the evidence he and John had put together with the help of the CMKX shareholders. Even though they had only a few days to solicit brokerage statements and put their case together, Frizzell was certain the information was enough to raise the question of naked short selling:

> *"It started off with Leslie asking 'What proof do you have of naked shorting?' 'Well, I have a CD and these are 5,050 brokerage statements that represent 350 billion shares. This has just come within the last five days. We also have a December 2004 report from the transfer agent saying that 2,033 people hold certificates representing 326 billion shares. That's 676 billion shares owned by only 7,083 shareholders. Since there are over 50,000 total shareholders total, it's obvious that the ones that haven't been counted yet will far surpass the 703 billion shares issued.'*

So, Hakala said, 'Well, how do I know that those brokerage statements haven't been altered?' 'Well...that can be verified through the brokerage house and we can get affidavits if we need to. But we're here to tell you that this is our investigation.' 'And she said, 'Well, if you prove the naked short, we will investigate it.'

The end result of all of this was that as I was walking out, we were all getting up, and Mr. Petillon, said, 'By the way, if this is an orchestrated short squeeze against the brokerage houses to make the stock price go up, we will come after those who are responsible.' And then he said, 'We would not look kindly on a cert pull because it would cause market manipulation.'

And this was the regional chief. I mean...it was a clear threat in my opinion from the SEC that if we did anything...well, I said something to the effect that if there are brokers out there with shares in their accounts that they haven't delivered, then...it is what it is."

Judge Murray had told Frizzell she would consider any evidence or exhibits offered until the time she rendered her decision, which was still two or three weeks away. As Bill Frizzell walked out of his meeting with the company and the SEC, the only thing he was certain of was that he wanted to continue the fax-in campaign and offer all information as evidence in the hearing.

The next morning, after trying unsuccessfully to book separate flights, Bill Frizzell and John Martin left Los Angeles, their heads spinning with the revelations of the past two days. The entire situation had changed dramatically, and they both knew they had to continue the investigation far beyond Bill's original agreement to represent the shareholders, at least until the judge rendered a decision in the hearing. Finally, still nervous and a little paranoid, they quit discussing the case on the flight back to Tyler, Texas and rode the rest of the way in silence.

There was one perplexing question that neither Bill nor John could answer after their eye-opening experience two days before. One of the most revealing files Frizzell had read through on Wednesday night was the one auditor Neil Levine had submitted to the SEC. He remembered trying to sort through the information, answering some questions while at the same time raising entirely new ones:

"The company hired Neal Levine to be their auditor, and when he was supposed to be beginning his audit he flew out to Las Vegas and met with everyone in David Coffey's office. He was fixing to audit all these books and give them to the SEC, so he had to find out about the company. And he actually took hand-written notes, and there was a page and a half of what they talked about in that meeting. The notes were dated 1/10/05, which was four months before the hearing. So up here at the top in his notes were the names of everybody who was at this meeting and it reads, 'Doc, comma, Urban Casavant, comma, Dave (who we know is Chief Financial Officer

Dave Desormeau), comma, Helen Bagley, comma, and David Coffey, the CPA.' So we were sitting there wondering 'Doc??? Who is this Doc?'

So we were reading along, and Levine wrote 'Mining claims out of the country.' Well that might have been a fifteen minute conversation, but he just wrote that down. Then, three sentences from the bottom it said, 'Expenses were paid by Doc's companies on behalf of the company.' You know, I was sitting there thinking 'We've got CMKM Diamonds. They've got 50,000 shareholders...it generated over $200 million worth of stock sales through the sale of this stock. And here is some guy named Doc? Expenses were paid by Doc's companies on behalf of the company?'

But then I saw that one of the things he said in his hand-written notes was 'Doc has the complete stock book.' I remember looking at that and thinking, 'Doc! What is Doc doing with the stock book?' For whatever reason, ol' Doc has got the stock book...and Doc is paying all the expenses...and I still don't know who Doc is!!"

Chapter 24 – The Plam

"The primary mission of the U.S. Securities and Exchange Commission (SEC) is to protect investors and maintain the integrity of the securities market."
~SEC Mission Statement, 2005

Back at work on Friday the 13th, John Martin and Bill Frizzell regrouped and looked around them, surveying the daunting task at hand. While they were gone, the brokerage statement faxes had continued to pour into Frizzell's Tyler, Texas office, but the events leading up to, during, and after the hearing had forced them to reevaluate their plans. Now Bill and John knew just how deep the problems with CMKX ran, and how far the SEC would go to bury not only the evidence of naked short selling, but of fraud within the company as well, along with the hopes, dreams, and investments of the 50,000 plus shareholders. They had already decided on the trip back to continue the fax-in campaign, at least until the information was submitted to Judge Murray. Frizzell sent out a letter targeting those shareholders who had yet to send in their brokerage statements in the hope of adding to the total numbers and prove there been more shares sold into the market than actually existed.

Although the SEC Hearing and the revelations immediately following had altered their perception of reality, their resolve was stronger than ever. The more they understood just how deep the corruption went and how badly the shareholders had been wronged, the more they knew they had to do whatever was necessary to uncover the truth.

After the hearing many CMKX believers began to openly question Urban's loyalty to the company and to the shareholders. A few messages appeared on the boards calling for his resignation while others quickly came to his defense, trying to somehow justify his lack of disclosure. It was clear their faith was shaken by the fact that he had refused to answer even one question in front of Judge Murray. What did he have to hide? Why was he worried about incriminating himself if he hadn't done anything wrong? How deeply did his refusal to testify harm the company itself (and by extension, the shareholders)? Urban Casavant, who had walked up the steps of the courthouse in Los Angeles to a hero's welcome of cheers and applause, was losing his hold on at least some of the CMKX faithful.

But there were still thousands of shareholders who were just as certain that it was all part of the plan. Although there were, as always, dozens of variations on the details, the basic premise was always the same. They still believed Urban, Glenn, and Maheu were toying with the real bad guys, setting up both the crooks who were manipulating the company's stock price and the brokers and market makers who were allowing hundreds of billions, if not trillions of shares of fake stock to flood the market.

With the brokerage statements still arriving, Bill Frizzell and John Martin continued to sift through the boxes of evidence the SEC had dumped on their doorstep just before the hearing. Frizzell was also working behind the scenes with Don Stoecklein and the company in hopes of brokering a compromise between CMKX and the SEC. In a June 16th phone call to Stoecklein, with Urban listening in, Frizzell voiced his concerns about the company's plans and the shareholders' reactions to the pending decision from Judge Murray:

Frizzell: *"I've been pleading with Urban. You've got to let me in on your plans, your secrets or something. I've got this shareholders' group. They're like a herd of cattle...when they get spooked, they just run off crazy. I can calm them down a lot, but right now whether it's the shorts, or whoever it is, they think they are going to lose everything the day this thing is delisted. It's got them spooked."*

Stoecklein: *"In terms of the overall plan...nothing has changed from day one. We are going to file a brief tomorrow. The SEC has until the 29th to reply to that brief. The judge has until the 17th of July to file her initial decision. We have 29 days to file the appeal brief, which frankly I'm going to start preparing early in the game, knowing that it's going to go in. I'm just going to anticipate that the initial decision will be for revocation. Our plan is to have our financial reports filed with the SEC the latter part of August. This plan cannot be shared with the shareholders. There was a little bit of a problem when I said before that we have an auditor. We had not engaged him and when that went out Leslie called me immediately wondering why we hadn't filed our 8-K. Since that time we are now engaging a different auditor. I will let you know when that engagement letter has been executed."*

Frizzell: *"Let me ask you a question: Is there just absolutely no ability to go to the SEC, go to Leslie and/or go to the judge and say, 'We want to share with you what's going on.'?"*

Stoecklein: *"I don't think it does you any good to talk to Judge Murray because she has made it very clear that she's only there for the purpose of the administrative hearing, for a specific issue and that is the revocation of the securities of CMKM, based on failure to file reports. That's all she's addressing."*

Frizzell: *"Don, we may be overlooking some help here. I think she would really like to help the shareholders in some way. You know how you could really put together some figures and some numbers, and maybe guesstimate something. Maybe we could do it in a confidential disclosure, some unaudited financials or something. Not only does this help me control this flock, it scares the beegeebers out of some shorts if it looks like we might actually defeat being delisted. I'm just terrified that you're going to lose about half your shareholders, law suits are going to start flying, not from me, even though that might be part of my obligation to these shareholders. You've got a flock that wants to believe, Urban, that all is right with the world. They just want us to show them that this money that you are spending is not some kind of front but that it's actually going toward the production of these records, which will ultimately save them and let them make a little money on this stock. I'm about to go after the SEC on the way they've handled this thing. But I need some help from the company on what you are doing. We've got to think outside the box. We need to do something a little differently to buy us some more time with this judge."*

Stoecklein: *"Are you suggesting, Bill, that we go to the SEC and cut a deal so the judge never has to issue her initial decision of revocation?"*

Frizzell: *"If that's a possibility. I don't know their parameters. I think the SEC is sensitive to these shareholders' plight. I've had to tell Leslie 'my shareholders are a little upset with management. They can't believe that no filings are going to be done.' She kind of chuckled, 'oh finally we got the shareholders mad at management.' The only reason I'm saying that is that I think she would be open to discussing any way to see if there is something we can do. They don't want the wrath of these shareholders either. What does the SEC need to get out from under this deadline?"*

Stoecklein: *"The only thing I can think of is negotiating a settlement with the SEC at this point. They've got to realize by now that we are going to appeal the decision and buy time. They've got to realize that the only reason we went through that hearing was to buy that time."*

Frizzell: *"The shareholders don't understand that it's okay for us to do that. The fact that we appeal it is not very soothing to them."*

Stoecklein: *"The only consideration we have to offer the SEC, or why the SEC would want us to do this, is to avoid us from filing the appeal order. In my mind, the SEC doesn't care about the shareholders."*

Frizzell: *"They want to have the appearance that they care. And I think the judge does care. Whatever the plan is for these shareholders, are we going to keep CMKX? Is it important that we keep the company CMKX as it is?"*

Stoecklein: *"I think the plan right now is to get this company reporting. Keep current. Keep reporting and ultimately go back onto the OTC Bulletin Board. If for any reason, this auditor won't sign off on a particular year we do have a backup plan to have an audit for '03 and '04, which gives us a 2 year audit to allow for a reverse into an existing reporting company which would cause the current shareholders of CMKM to suffer zero dilution. A share for share exchange. That can happen literally overnight.*

Now, that's all in place, ready to go. I don't think we can trust Leslie. This is going to be a big feather in her cap. She's got a whole different motivation. She made it very clear in the beginning to me. She said, 'we're not worried about the current shareholders. That's not our job to protect them. Our job is to protect prospective shareholders.' I took that as meaning, screw you, screw the company, screw the shareholders, we're protecting people in the future."

Three days later, on June 19, after accumulating over 10,500 total brokerage statements from CMKX shareholders, Bill Frizzell filed a post-hearing reply to Judge Murray that would eventually become known as "The Brer Rabbit Brief," on behalf of John Martin and the CMKX Owners Group, requesting additional time for the company to submit their financial reports.

He argued that the SEC had failed to fully investigate the accuracy of the infamous Form 15 filing that triggered the charges against the company, citing other cases where they had conducted investigations into Form 15 filings. He pointed out that Stoecklein had sought advice from the SEC on how to resolve the problem. Frizzell contended that since the filings of the company weren't due until April 17, 2005, the charges brought against CMKX were premature. He said "the shareholders remain confident that Don Stoecklein and Robert Maheu will be on hand to complete the filings and return CMKM to current filing status," and blamed the company's failure to file on those whose job it was to keep and produce accurate records:

"It is evident from the record that a host of accountants, financial officers, former management people and hired attorneys have created quite a nightmarish scene for any reputable auditor. We would ask this court to consider these factors while we admit reporting laws are currently being violated. To most shareholders, it appears the company has spent nearly two million dollars in less than 2 years on accountants, lawyers, auditors and other professionals who were supposed to perform the acts that clearly have not been done. It is shocking to hear we can't get proper accounting records gathered for an audit. Egads, doesn't the company keep books and file corporate returns to the IRS? Why are we in a position to have our registration revoked for non-filing when we hired an ex-SEC enforcement attorney a year ago for the sole purpose of making us compliant? We pay $100,000 to an auditor that bails out the day before our hearing on deregistration. His excuse for withdrawing is the company's delay in getting the records to him and he is busy with other clients. Can one company be a victim of such dumb, rotten luck? In the many exhibits proffered by the SEC, you will see David DeSormeau listed as our Chief Financial Officer for 2002, 2003 and 2004. He was paid 1.5 million dollars to run the business end of our company."

Frizzell went on to describe in detail the "dumb, rotten luck" CMKX seemed to have with every single person who was hired to put together their financial records: the original company auditor David Coffey, Desormeau, Neil Levine, and attorney Brian Dvorak. He cited the SEC's failure to bring several of those people to court:

> *"Why did the SEC fail to depose Mr. DeSormeau or subpoena him and his records to the hearing? Why was Mr. Coffey not questioned or subpoenaed to the hearing? An attorney regularly used by the company to issue letters of opinion to the transfer agent was Brian Dvorak, there is a subpoena for Mr. Dvorak, but there was no production of any materials by this witness. There was no deposition taken of Mr. Dvorak. Mr. Dvorak's appearance was not requested by either party. Does Mr. DeSormeau have the company's needed financial records and what actions did he take towards retaining an auditor? Why was there no evidence from this key witness presented to the Court by either the Company or the SEC? When Mr. Desormeau responded to Neil Levine's request for records, the response was on the letterhead of a company called Business Works. Business Works received 63 billion shares of CMKM stock in 2003 and 2004 according to the master shareholders list. By August of 2004 all stock belonging to Business Works had been sold or transferred out of this company. This highly paid chief financial officer seemed to be unimportant to these proceedings for some reason. Is the company's objection to revocation the equivalent of Brer Rabbit telling Brer Fox, 'Please, oh please, whatever you do, please don't throw me in that briar patch!'"*

Frizzell also used the brief to bring up the issue of naked short selling again, giving Judge Murray a crash course in the scandal that had been becoming more and more public over the past couple of years. Frizzell then described evidence submitted as "Exhibit 1," citing the 10,500 accounts totaling 455 billion shares documented in the monthly statements of CMKM shareholders. To that number he added the stock certificates from the transfer agent that totaled over 320 billion shares and another 67 billion shares held in brokerage accounts:

> *"This total of 837,359,968,295 exceeds the reported issued and outstanding 703 billion shares of the company by approximately 134,000,000,000. This alone is a staggering number of shares which have been sold by various third parties but do not exist except as electronic entries."*

He went on to point out that the totals didn't include stocks that had been through most overseas brokers or Canadian brokers. He also said that the stock had traded in 64 countries around the world, and that they had totaled only 10,500 accounts of a reported 52,676 accounts. Finally, he brought the issue of the suspected massive amount of counterfeit stock back to the legal problems of the company:

> *"We ask this Court to consider that revocation of this stock may have more to do with the naked shorted shares than a concern over late filings. This may explain what I perceive to be a rush to judgment. I have never seen a case*

with so much at stake where there has never been one word of negotiating a settlement. At least on the surface, the only problem here is the filing of some financial reports and obtaining the time necessary to prepare such reports. Why did the SEC choose the shortest possible time period to obtain a ruling from this court? Why does the SEC resist the company's request to view the 'open fails to deliver' which are given to them daily from the SEC? If the naked short position in this stock has any bearing whatsoever on this rush to judgment, I implore this court to slow down the judgment train."

On July 1, the SEC halted trading in another company that CMKX had touted in its press releases. St. George Metals (SGGM). SGGM had purchased 5% of CMKX's claims for $10 million dollars and 200 billion shares of SGGM stock to be distributed to shareholders as a dividend. That news had caused SGGM's stock to run from less than a penny to over seventy-five cents a share. It dropped almost as quickly as it had gone up. As in the case with CMKX, those who accumulated shares when the price was low and sold into the buying frenzy made a huge profit. On the other hand, those who bought at the top weren't quite as lucky and owned worthless stock that they couldn't sell at any price.

Two weeks later, on July 12, 2005, Judge Brenda K. Murray issued her initial ruling in the matter of CMKM Diamonds. In a thirteen-page ruling, she never mentioned the omitted evidence or naked short selling, instead focusing entirely on the case as it was presented during the May 10th trial. After a summary of the company's history, Judge Murray detailed the only area where CMKX seemed to exhibit prolific growth – the issuance of shares of company stock. She described how the trading volume grew from millions of shares traded per day up until August of 2003, when it suddenly began to trade billions of shares a day. She cited the range in price from $.0135 per share to a low of $.00013, and arrived at an average selling price of $.00071.

Judge Murray described how the company raised its authorized shares from 200 billion to 500 billion on March 1, 2004, and then upped it again to 800 billion five months later. She laid out an ugly pattern of accountant after accountant repeatedly asking the company for documents and records so they could compile financial reports. Instead, the only thing the accountants ever seemed to receive was huge payments in the form of either checks or billions of shares of stock issued by Urban Casavant. Her summary of Urban's testimony was short and to the point:

"Casavant refused to testify at the hearing, and asserted his Fifth Amendment privilege against self-incrimination to all questions asked by the Division. Nonetheless, I have not drawn any adverse inferences from Casavant's refusal to testify, because the evidence in the record is more than sufficient to decide this matter."

Judge Murray's description of Maheu's involvement was in stark contrast to the stories of Iron Bob's firm control of the company's destiny, and in fact, painted a picture that was much different than that presented in CMKX's press releases during the short-lived Maheu era:

> *"Maheu has no background in the mining business, and does not know how many employees CMKM Diamonds has, if any, who they are, how much they are paid, or what kind of work they perform. He has never seen CMKM Diamonds' general ledger and does not know what the company's assets and liabilities are. Maheu incorrectly assumed that an audit of the company's financial statements had started as of the date of the hearing. Maheu was unaware that CMKM Diamonds had not responded to requests for financial information and, at the hearing, he learned that CMKM Diamonds had not provided auditors and bookkeepers with documents they requested from Casavant months earlier."*

From there, she went on to discuss the share structure, saying that: "On January 12, 2003, CMKM Diamonds issued 994,083,000 shares to 360 people for 'fieldwork in Canada.' CMKM Diamonds also issued almost 3 billion shares to twenty-nine companies on January 22, 2003. As sole director, Casavant has authorized the issuance of an unbelievable number of CMKM Diamonds' shares."

Then Judge Murray turned her attention to the company, and in particular CEO Urban Casavant's continued assertions that they were on the verge of completing their financial reports to become fully reporting. She listed dozens of times between January and October of 2004 that Urban told associates about their plans to become fully reporting.

After thirteen pages detailing imaginary offices, nonexistent financial records, a revolving door list of accountants who accomplished little or nothing, a Board of Directors Chairman who seemed lost and confused during most of his testimony, and a CEO who refused to testify at all, it was painfully obvious what Judge Murray's decision would be. Before issuing her ruling, she summed up the company's current status and future prospects:

> *"CMKM Diamonds has no independent auditor and no financial statements to be audited. Furthermore, no drafts of CMKM Diamonds' missing reports have been prepared and no witness could specify a date by which the company would file any of its delinquent reports. As such, it is highly likely that CMKM Diamonds will continue to violate the periodic reporting provisions in the future.*
>
> *The public hearing was an opportunity for CMKM Diamonds to address the allegations in the OIP. It failed to do so. Casavant seems to be the only person running the company and he refused to testify. Several witnesses testified that they tried to get financial information from Casavant and he failed to supply it. CMKM Diamonds has been out of compliance since 2002, and has made no good faith effort to remedy the situation. CMKM Diamonds' failure to file required periodic reports has deprived the investing public of current, reliable*

information regarding its operations, purported million-dollar transactions, and financial condition."

And then, Judge Brenda K. Murray made her initial ruling official:

"Based on the findings and conclusions set forth above:

IT IS ORDERED THAT, pursuant to Section 12(j) of the Securities Exchange Act of 1934, the registration of each class of securities of CMKM Diamonds, Inc., is hereby REVOKED."

Chapter 25 – Dr. Mitchell, I presume?

"The stories that we got from our researchers were that John Edwards would come in the back door of all the offices, he'd never come in the front, he was always in the meetings for a very short time and then he was out of there...it was very strange, he just always seemed to be elusive. Two of our researchers said that John Edwards is a ghost, and another one said that she didn't think he even existed."

~John Martin, CMKX shareholders' advocate

While the brokerage statements continued to pour in, John and Bill, assisted by George Stephenson and Kevin West (who was commuting from San Antonio to help out), expanded their investigation into those people in and around the company who seemed most suspect. They focused their efforts on John Edwards and his thirty-six NevWest trading accounts, looking for connections between the massive sale of stock and the millions of dollars flowing through Urban's bank accounts. They pored over the boxes of documents the SEC had sent to Frizzell, searching for red flags that would help them put pieces of the puzzle together. Each morning, they would exchange ideas and discuss what had transpired the day before, while George Stephenson recorded every word. Several shareholders were recruited to gather invaluable information based on what Bill and John had learned. All along, John or Bill would issue regular updates to the shareholders on behalf of the CMKX Owners Group. Bill always ended his updates with the single battle cry of "Onward!" which eventually became yet another catchphrase on the message boards. At the same time, he was still trying to negotiate a compromise between CMKX and the SEC, and maintained frequent contact with Don Stoecklein.

As they dug through the SEC files, the nagging question from their earliest revelations haunted both Bill and John. Who was Doc, and how did he fit into all of this? It seemed ludicrous that an entirely anonymous individual could be pulling the strings from somewhere behind the scenes, not only financing the company, but walking around with the all-important stock book. He who controlled the stock book controlled the flow of money. John Martin recalled when Bill called him in to discuss the first of a series of bizarre discoveries:

"He called me into his office and said, 'Look here, this is strange!' He had two pieces of paper side by side, one of Neil Levine's hand-written notes from the meeting where it said 'Expenses were paid by Doc's companies on behalf of the company,' and 'Doc has the complete stock book,' and in the other hand he had Levine's testimony about the same meeting from the hearing. Bill said 'Who's on this list that's not on the other list?' And sure enough, Levine testified during the hearing that John Edwards was at the meeting, but on his

hand-written notes, there's no John Edwards listed...only Doc! I said 'Oh my Gosh, John Edwards is Doc! He has to be!'"

While it didn't seem incredibly significant to either Bill or John at the time, the "Doc" connection did lead them to research whether or not John Edwards was a licensed physician. Frizzell also knew Edwards had signed documents passing himself off as an attorney, but they could find no records that he was either a doctor or a lawyer. John vividly remembered the next piece of the puzzle falling into place:

"Three or four days later, while we were still researching this Doc thing, we happened on to a Xerox copy of Urban's black book with all his phone numbers in it that the SEC had given us. So I was looking through it, and there was no John Edwards in the book, but lo and behold, there's Doc! Just Doc and the phone number, and I said 'Bill...Doc! Here's Doc! It's in the book!' So we were trying to find out who Doc really was, and Bill immediately did a reverse search on the phone number, still thinking it was John Edwards, but instead, it was this guy by the name of Dr. Michael Mitchell, and we're all just really confused, because this Michael Mitchell is a pediatrician.

I remember that all of the sudden, I just blurted out 'Doc is John Edwards, he's both guys! John Edwards is Michael Mitchell!' And Bill looked at me and said, 'That's the craziest thing I've ever heard.' And I said 'You mark my words.' Because Edwards was elusive, in every case that we were researching him he was elusive, we could never really pin him down. The stories that we got from our researchers were that he would come in the back door of all the offices, he'd never come in the front, he was always in the meetings for a very short time and then he was out of there...it was very strange, he just always seemed to be elusive. Two of our researchers said that John Edwards is a ghost, and another one said that she didn't think he even existed."

For the next two days, Frizzell followed the trail of Doc, tracing Michael Mitchell as far in every direction as he could. He was originally tipped off to Edwards' involvement in CMKX by his refusal to answer the SEC's questions during the April 14, 2005, US Canadian Minerals (UCAD) investigation, and by their dogged pursuit of him during depositions. It was the questions about his connection to various bank accounts that led Frizzell to grill auditor Neil Levine about John Edwards at the SEC hearing against CMKX. Leslie Hakala, who handled the UCAD case for the SEC as well, had repeated a lengthy series of questions pertaining to the flow of either money or stock into or out of trading or bank accounts, trusts, and individual accounts that Edwards controlled. To every question during the UCAD depositions Edwards replied "Five," indicating of course that he was invoking his Fifth Amendment rights against self-incrimination:

Do you provide investment advice to anyone?

Do you have or control any bank accounts?

Do you have or control any bank accounts at Silver State Bank?

Do you have or control any bank accounts at Bank of America?

Do you have or control any bank accounts at Wells Fargo?

Do you have or control any bank accounts in Canada?

Since January 1ˢᵗ, 2003, have you ever wired money to or from, or written any checks on any accounts at Silver State Bank?

Since January 1ˢᵗ, 2003, have you ever wired money to or from, or written any checks on any accounts at Bank of America?

Since January 1ˢᵗ, 2003, have you ever wired money to or from, or written any checks on any accounts at Wells Fargo?

Since January 1ˢᵗ, 2003, have you ever wired money to or from, or written any checks on any accounts at any other bank?

Have you ever used any assets or funds from any corporate or trust accounts to pay you or your family's personal expenses?

Are you affiliated with PA Holdings?

Did you ever receive from anyone the proceeds of their trading in CMKM Diamonds?

Even though Hakala knew he would answer every question with "Five," she asked John Edwards almost 1,500 questions, including questions about his business associations with CMKM Diamonds, CMKXtreme, UCAD, Nevada Minerals, and all of the other various companies CMKX was reportedly connected to. She also asked about his association with twenty-seven different individuals, and if he had any conversations or business dealing with any of them concerning CMKM Diamonds. The list read like a Hall of Fame of people involved in one way or another with CMKX, including, among others, convicted stock manipulator Shawn Hackman, David DeSormeau, Ed Dhonau, Rendal Williams, Richard Taulli, Gary Walters, Mike King, Ian McIntyre, James Kinney, Brian Dvorak, Helen Bagley, Roger Glenn, and Urban Casavant. If Hakala had included Michael Williams and a few of the latecomers, she would have made a clean sweep of the major players in the CMKX Gang.

Hakala also questioned John Edwards about every one of the thirty-six trust and trading accounts he controlled at NevWest Securities, and as well as a number of companies he was associated with. It seemed that while Edwards might have been a ghost as far as his comings and goings were concerned, his fingerprints were all over the various alleged crime scenes.

It was this convoluted trail of money, stock, and questionable companies, trusts, trading accounts and associations with even more questionable individuals that interested Bill Frizzell. His reasons for pursuing the Doc/Mitchell/Edwards connections were motivated by his desire to uncover the trail of fraud that seemed to wind through the entire history of CMKX. He believed, "If we could show that Edwards was really Mitchell to the SEC and *prove* it, then every single stock transaction related to CMKX is an absolute fraud on the shareholders." *Everything* with John Edwards' name on it would be a complete fraud.

The trail began by tracing Michael Mitchell to his home in Mahopac, New York, where he was, or is, a pediatrician married to a Lynn Mitchell, with two children. His background at first seemed sketchy, but Frizzell gradually filled in the details of Mitchell's life. John Martin recalled how Edwards and Mitchell, originally tied together only by Neil Levine's notes and the phone number in Urban's black book, began to overlap at every turn:

"We had copies of two driver's licenses for John Edwards, one from Las Vegas and one from Grants Pass, Oregon, which we had received from the SEC, and in both photos he's making a weird face, like he's trying to look different or something. But we could never find a picture of Michael Mitchell, and we didn't know how to track him through family or anything else. Bill had called and talked to the New York State Medical Board, and they sent his file, but they blacked out his picture, of all things.

Then Bill found out that Mitchell was an author, who wrote a book about children's prescription medicine, so he had Goldie order the book, and there wasn't even a picture of him in his own book. But one of the things Bill noticed was that Michael Mitchell dedicated it to his children. Now, we already knew that Dr. Michael Mitchell lived in Mahopac, New York, so Bill began to track his kids, and as he dug up information on his son Chris Mitchell, he put his name into his search database.

I'll never forget the phone call. Bill called me up and he said 'You are not going to believe what I just found!' I said 'What?' and he said 'I got the book, I realized that the kids names were in there, I punched in his oldest son Chris, and the first thing that came up was Grants Pass, Oregon.'

So we started researching. We found out that Michael Mitchell grew up there, he went to high school there, his son was born there, but even in his high school yearbook, there was no picture of Michael Mitchell. Everything seemed to lead to one bizarre coincidence after another. Everywhere we turned, we found connections between John Edwards and Michael Mitchell, some real, some imagined, and some just eerie. We could have kicked the computer across the room and something pertaining to Edwards and Mitchell would have popped up. That was the way it seemed to be happening, everywhere we looked something was popping up between these two guys, but we could never pin them to the same location at the same time. No dates, no events, nothing ever coordinated together."

And that was how it continued, every door that was opened on Edwards and Mitchell, every bit of information, seemed to connect the two of them either as business associates...or as the same person. When Edwards was in action doing something, Mitchell seemed to just disappear, and when Mitchell could be traced to events and times Edwards was nowhere to be found. They never overlapped.

While the CMKX saga played out, so did the John Edwards/Michael Mitchell investigation. The series of events that unfolded over the next few months were remarkable, and made John and Bill, as John put it, "99.99% certain that John Edwards was really Michael Mitchell." After the Doc revelation led to the Grants Pass, Oregon connection, Frizzell uncovered more and more information on Dr. Michael Mitchell and the elusive John Edwards, but no information seemed to exist for Edwards before the mid-80's. He had two children with his first wife Deborah - or was Deborah his second wife? He then left Deborah to marry Diana Lee Flaherty, whose former husband Robert Flaherty had suddenly died after both he and Diana had been charged with stock fraud. From there, the information began to come together in a bizarre entanglement of the two lives. Besides the known facts connecting the two, and the fact that Dr. Mitchell was born and raised in Grants Pass, Oregon, the same small town that John Edwards had a driver's license from, they soon learned that:

- John Edwards, his then wife Deborah, his two children, and two business associates all had social security numbers issued from Grants Pass, Oregon...and all applied for on the same day. Afterwards, his two business partners did a series of real estate transactions between themselves to establish a credit history.

- Deborah Edwards (then Deborah Compton) was raised in Grants Pass, Oregon, directly across the street from a family with the last name of Mitchell.

- Dr. Mitchell, although he was a licensed pediatrician, was also heavily involved in the stock market, and ran a now defunct stock picking website.

- The president of Mitchell's pediatric clinic was a man named Lee, whose two sisters were doctors in the clinic, and whose families originally immigrated from a small province in China called Guangdong. That same province also happened to be the home of fifty-five CMKX shareholders, the only ones in all of China, and they all worked for the same company in Guangdong.

- John Edwards' wife Diana Flaherty's maiden name was Lee.

- Several of John Edwards's trust accounts listed Dan Lee as the principal trustee.

- Dan Lee was also the general manager of Steve Wynn's Mirage Resort in Las Vegas, and Wynn was a good friend of...Bob Maheu.

- Dr. Mitchell and his wife Lynn had a Las Vegas trust account called LM Family Partnership, established by the same agent who set up several of John Edwards' trust accounts.

- Michael Mitchell and John Edwards both signed their names above the signature line on legal documents, and in fact, Edwards signed his name, which looked suspiciously like a scribbled M. Mitchell on more than one document.

Although Bill Frizzell and John Martin couldn't connect Diana Lee Flaherty to Dan Lee, and neither could be tied to the Lee's who worked for Mitchell and whose relatives traced back to Guangdong and CMKX, there was plenty of evidence to connect Mitchell and Edwards. At times it was difficult to tell what was coincidence and what was a valid connection, but the sheer volume of information was in itself convincing. It seemed almost certain that they were one and the same.

In fact, Bill and John tracked John Edwards, the *real* John Edwards, back to his origin...in England. They found a birth certificate for Edwards, but were never able to find the man himself. However, they later connected John Edwards' birth certificate to a man registered as Edwards' father in a Los Angeles, California nursing home...owned by Dan Lee...under a social security number belonging to Deborah Edwards. The natural conclusion was that the senior Edwards was really Michael Mitchell's father, registered by Edwards/Mitchell under an assumed name using Deborah Edwards' social security number.

The ties between Mitchell and CMKX didn't stop with his employees' ties to China. Dr. Michael Mitchell was also the President, CEO, and sole director of a publicly traded company called Conversion Services International (CSII). Originally known as LCS Golf, the company issued shares to purchase other golf-related companies that all had one thing in common: they failed within the first year or two after the deals were completed. The company also entered into, and subsequently defaulted on, a series of contracts for financing, often issuing large amounts of CSII stock to cover the deals. Eventually, the company collapsed, and now lists as its sole intellectual property a patent for an animal pillow with a pouch, to be sold under the name "Adorables." The company never trademarked, manufactured, or marketed Adorables. CSII later changed hands and became a legitimate data warehousing business...without Michael Mitchell.

Frizzell later discovered that CSII, under the control of Mitchell, did attract at least one major investor. In November of 2004, CMKXtreme invested $2.25 million in Mitchell's company in exchange for CSII stock. However, unfortunately for CMKX shareholders, CMKXtreme was a private company owned by the Casavant family (with Urban's brother Ron Casavant as the CEO) even though it was financed with CMKM Diamonds' money and stock. And while Mitchell might not have been running CSII when it changed hands, Urban still owned stock in the company when it moved to the American Stock Exchange a year later, and bragged to Bill Frizzell that he "had just made a million dollars in one day."

Also, among the records supplied by the SEC to Frizzell was a $10,000 personal check written from Urban Casavant to Michael Mitchell's LM Family Partnership in 2004. Frizzell later questioned Casavant about the check, saying, "The conversation came up, and Urban stuttered and stammered around, and he said, 'Uh uh uh I think we were gambling together one day, and he loaned me some money.'" And after another trademark Urban hesitation and slight stutter, he told Frizzell that Mitchell was a merchant banker. Urban's wife, Carolyn, also inadvertently admitted to Frizzell "everyone calls John Edwards Doc."

In yet another bizarre turn of events, one of the most famous families in America was pulled into the Michael Mitchell investigation. On June 8, 2005, while the investigation was in full swing, Kevin West received a bizarre email from Michael Pickens, the son of Oklahoman turned Texan billionaire, oilman, and famed corporate raider T. Boone Pickens. West, who worked for stock market reform through his website, was also talking with Hugo Cancio about a tentative Fuego Entertainment documentary about stock market fraud. Michael Pickens claimed to have evidence of massive stock market fraud along with his father, saying that:

"I have been involved with several microcap companies that were REAL companies until their stock was shorted to death.

I have been involved in the Securities industry since I was a teen and my father has also been heavily involved most of his working life. His name is Boone Pickens and we are from Texas.

We did some investigating and found some very interesting things going on in the shorting world. This is a different SCAM than the mm's shorting naked all day long every day, which is a very simple thing to explain how they get away with it.

I would like to discuss this with you guys and tell the story of what we found out. We have exact names of people who are doing this and have ruined companies.

The reason I believe that this is so important is that it is completely different than the mm's shorting. We believe that Reg SHO was so lax because of all of the lobbying by this huge firms. The other slant that we have discovered will shed a new light on the subject and should be included in your Documentary."

Because of the typo in the email referring to "this huge firms," it was impossible to tell whether Pickens was talking about one or more firms in his claims that he and T. Boone Pickens had evidence of massive stock market fraud and lobbyists influencing landmark SEC regulations. Kevin responded to Pickens by email, and then tried to call him at Michael Pickens' company M3 Hedge, LLC. The phone number was disconnected, and he received no reply to his emails. Just five weeks after Michael Pickens' extraordinary email to Kevin West, the Wall Street Journal reported that the SEC in conjunction with federal prosecutors arrested Pickens... for stock fraud:

> *"According to documents provided by federal prosecutors, Pickens works as a stock promoter and is president and CEO of a company called M3 Research LLC. He promotes stocks through research reports and 'tout sheets' distributed to investors via bulk faxes.*
>
> *Federal prosecutors contend Pickens and an associate falsely inflated the value of stocks in four companies from July 2004 until January 2005 by offering fictitious stock tips to potential buyers. He then sold his own shares in the companies for inflated values. Typically, the value of shares increased from less than $1 per share to $5 to $6 per share."*

The complaints against Pickens said he would send out millions of hand-written faxes made to look like "misdirected confidential notes from a stockbroker to a client, a Dr. Mitchel." He would accumulate stock when it was cheap, send out faxes advising Dr. Mitchel to buy because it was getting ready to triple in value, and then dump the shares after the price ran up. Pickens allegedly defrauded the shareholders of at least $300,000.

Then, while Bill Frizzell was investigating their Dr. Mitchell, he found another connection between Mitchell and Pickens. After his suspicions were aroused by the "Dr. Mitchel" heading on Pickens' faxes, he discovered that Michael Pickens' hedge fund had invested a million dollars into CSII, the same Mitchell company that Urban had sunk $2.25 million into. Frizzell tracked down the federal prosecutors' complaints against Pickens, and immediately noticed that not only were the fake faxes addressed to "Dr. Mitchel," they were usually signed as being from "Chris." Frizzell decided that if properly persuaded, Michael Pickens might lead him to Michael Mitchell.

> *"It was not easy, but I end up going to Boone Pickens office, and saying, 'I want to talk to Michael Pickens.' And I just left a little message talking about his SEC problems, and saying I was thinking about helping him. And I got a call from Michael Pickens. I said, 'Michael, this may be pretty far fetched, but I think this Michael Mitchell is John Edwards.' And then I said, 'All I want is a photograph of Michael Mitchell. And we could go to the SEC and I think it would help you in the justice department. I know you put a million dollars into CSII.*
>
> *He said, 'Well, I've never seen him before.' I said, 'I don't understand it, you invested a million dollars...'*

'Yeah, I put a million dollars in this business, but we just talked on the phone several times. He was just a guy always looking for money, and he seemed pretty straight up, so we put $1 million in his pocket.'

What the...is it that easy to get one million dollars in your damn deal? Pickens and I were going to be in New York at the same time and I asked if he could arrange a meeting with Michael Mitchell. He said 'yes.' I said, 'You'll never even know that I'm there, but I can get a picture.' I was at a soccer game in Dallas, where Michael Pickens lived, and I suggested we get together for lunch or something. And he said, 'Well, I've got to go feed the cows' or something like that. 'I'll have to give you a call back.' And I never heard back from him. I called him a couple of times, and he never responded."

In August of 2005, Bill Frizzell and John Martin made their trip to New York to continue their investigation of Dr. Michael Mitchell, without any help from Michael Pickens. They spent the first day in downtown New York City going to the various clerk's offices and digging through records for Mitchell. What they found was motive:

"What we found out was that Michael Mitchell had a $600,000 lien against him from the Taj Mahal in New Jersey, so he obviously had a huge gambling problem. He had IRS liens in huge amounts, and tons of credit card companies after him. And he was being sued in Florida over several hundred thousand dollars he owed in a lease agreement in the LCS Golf deal. That gives him motive to not be Dr. Mitchell. That gives him a motive to be John Edwards, because all these creditors are after him."

Early the next morning, while John Martin took the train back into the city to continue searching through legal records for information about Michael Mitchell, Bill Frizzell had different plans. He decided to head north to Mahopac and check out Mitchell's hometown and neighborhood. He retold the story in true East Texas fashion:

"I was thinking that maybe I could meet somebody up there in Mahopac that could get me the skinny on him. I was almost afraid to hire an investigator. I didn't know who to trust, so I decided to go do it myself. We were in New Jersey, and I had the rental car, and I got my map out, and I plotted where Mahopac was...it's only an hour north. And I leave early, like 5:00 a.m. so I could beat the traffic and be there by six or seven o'clock. I saw where you could go on the west side of the Hudson River and go up and make one turn on the George Washington Bridge, and hit a little turnpike, and go all the way to Mahopac, basically. So I got up, and got in the car, with my map beside me...and it was already full... those freeways were already full at five o'clock! Anyway, I got on the George Washington Bridge, and I was looking for 84 North. I was cutting across the bridge and it said George Washington Bridge Upper, and George Washington Bridge Lower. And I was thinking 'I don't know if I need Upper or Lower!' So I just picked one, and then there's

18-wheelers everywhere. And there were like 3 lanes and I was doing sixty-five miles per hour, bumper to bumper, and I just saw this sign go by that said, '84 North'... and I was thinking 'Oh crap!!!' I was heading over to Manhattan!. You know we learn to drive in East Texas, we miss an exit, what do we do? We take the next exit! Make a U-Turn and come back around. Common sense.

So I started trying to get over, I must have driven for miles. No exit! 'Oh crap!!' So sure enough here comes an exit, so I just came off, and I was thinking, 'Take a left! Go under the freeway, go back and take it back to where I messed up.' So I took a left, but there's no service road that takes you back up on the freeway. So I was heading into this neighborhood. Now it was 6:00-6:30 in the morning, and here's ol' Billy white boy in his rental car, and I was thinking 'Well, I've taken a left, so I'm going north.'

And I was driving, and the neighborhood started deteriorating fast. And all of the sudden I started seeing 'Harlem Auto Body' and I was thinking, 'Oh crap! I'm in Harlem!' I was driving around, by myself, quite annoyed, in a big ol' rental car... first block, there were two buildings boarded up, second block there's three boarded up, and then, there's plywood everywhere! Everything's boarded up! And there's no highway markings or anything. I'm fixin' to have to ask somebody. Pull over in Harlem, 'I'm lost! I'm from East Texas, and I've got a little bit of money in my pocket, but I'm lost! Would you mind telling me how to get out of town?'

So I just kept winding around, and I finally found something that was a freeway type sign. 'Get me on the freeway! If it's got a number on it, I'm happy.' I finally got on 84 North, and I'm thinking 'I'm going to Mahopac, New York!'

I finally got there, and the first place I stopped was at the address that we had for his office. Croton on the Hudson. I wanted to go see if he had a place that looked like an office. If you've ever seen these little villages on the Hudson River, just north of New York City, I mean it's really just picturesque. I pulled into a little place and they got me a cup of coffee and a donut, and I was sitting there. I was just going to read the local paper, like I was waiting for someone. I was thinking that maybe there was some realtor there that I could talk to, and sure enough there was a realtor's office next door. And the lady was coming in, and I just said, 'I'm just looking for some property around here. Are there many doctors here? I've got a couple small kids, and I was just curious.'

(In a female voice) 'Well, there's one pediatric clinic down the street here on the right.' So I called them and they had no idea who Michael Mitchell was. No one had heard of him, no one knew him, even though that was the address

listed with the medical board. He was using this address in Croton on the Hudson, and it was a false address. There was just nothing there.

Then I went to Mahopac, and I drove through Michael Mitchell's neighborhood, and there were two lanes, literally not even a shoulder. I wanted to see whose cars were in the driveway. I wanted a license plate number. I wanted to know who the neighbors were, because we had some names of some neighbors. And I was thinking 'If I just had my jogging gear on, I could just jog by. Nobody would know.' So, I went to a Wal-Mart looking for shorts and shoes, and didn't find exactly the size I wanted, but I thought, 'well, hell, I can just leave them here if I want.'

So I got me some jogging gear, and I had my camera with me. And I had already been up in the cul-de-sac; this house had a long driveway that went down there to it. You could see a Mercedes parked right there, but you couldn't make out the license plate. So I drove about a half a mile past this cul-de-sac, and I pulled off on the side of the road. I walked back down there with my camera, and I remember going up in there, and thought 'joggers are not looking like this.' You know, they're jogging, they're not looking like they're doing something else, so I had to just kinda look a little bit and keep jogging, you know. So I made a little circle around here, and I stopped and I walked, real slow, trying to get in front of the house. And I was dying to know whose license plate was on that car, for some reason I just thought that would be important. I got about one step on that and I heard a car start. And I thought, 'Oh, crap!' And so I just kinda kept walking past that driveway, and then I started heading back in the direction of my car. And I had my camera, and I had already taken a couple of pictures of the house but they didn't show much. Just as I passed the driveway, the car just literally came racing up that driveway! And I'm thinking, 'Maybe they're going to pick up their kids at school, or something like that. But the way they came at that driveway, it was like a racecar...and then it stopped.

And I'm walking and thinking, 'Joggers don't look back!! Do joggers look when a car is coming around? Only suspicious people that are investigating things will stop and turn around and look in that direction!' That's exactly what I was doing. And the car pulled out and it stopped right there and it ended up turning left. I thought, 'Oh my gosh, they're going to drive by me. They're going to, you know...I don't know what. They're going to shoot me or something!' But instead, they just drove off."

From there John Martin took over the story: "He called me on the phone, and I could just hear him, and he's all out of breath."

Bill: "Well, I had to do a little jogging to make it look real, you know? I was scared! It was a scary deal! We heard that John Edwards is mob connected, here's some guy that we think is Edwards living in a million dollar home on this lake, and he doesn't even work! That scares you! And I'm out there jogging by his house taking pictures. I'm just thinking that this was not a safe situation."

Although the trip to New York didn't give Bill Frizzell and John Martin *all* the information they needed, it filled in more missing pieces to the puzzle, and made it clear that Mitchell was not who he seemed to be. Upon their return to the familiar surroundings of Tyler, Texas, they followed another trail that led in the opposite direction to Las Vegas, where John Edwards had set up shop and pieced together the scheme that would eventually cost CMKX shareholders hundreds of millions of dollars.

After following the leads that had taken them from Mahopac, New York to Grants Pass, Oregon, and from there to Las Vegas and all the way to Guangdong, China, they decided to focus on John Edwards and his *new* wife, Diana Lee Flaherty.

Diana Lee's story was, and still is, almost as interesting and complex as Edwards' sordid tale. In 1993, Diana Lee and her husband Robert Flaherty started a company called Phoenix Metals USA II, Inc. In 1996, claiming they possessed proprietary technology that enabled them to extract gold, platinum, and other precious metals from volcanic cinders, they attracted investors who pumped millions of dollars into the company. They hired promoters and financial investment writers to pump the company, claiming they had acquired control of "volcanic cinder cones" holding recoverable gold reserves worth twenty-five billion dollars.

In 1997, the SEC brought a civil suit against Robert Flaherty claiming the company was issuing fraudulent claims, and in January of 1998, a permanent restraining order was issued barring Flaherty and Phoenix Metals from "making false statements and engaging in fraudulent business practices regarding the sale of securities." In August of 2001, the U.S. Department of Interior determined their claims had "no scientific or technological validity and the cinders contained no valuable mineral content."

In December of the same year, Robert Flaherty died, and Diana Lee took over control of the company with a man named Michael Gardiner. Ignoring the cease and desist orders from the SEC, they continued to pump the so-called cinders to precious metals technology. Then, a series of parallel but unrelated events took place that eventually merged together:

- December 29, 2001: Robert F. Flaherty died; Diana Lee took over Phoenix Metals.
- February 19, 2004: John Edwards filed for divorce from his wife Deborah.
- March 2, 2004: Diana Lee Flaherty and Michael Gardiner were indicted by the U.S. Department of Justice for stock fraud; Diana Lee was arrested the following day at her home.

- April 1, 2004: One month after her indictment, Diana Lee married John Edwards in Las Vegas. Then Edwards realized that his divorce from Deborah wasn't final and the marriage to Diana Lee wasn't valid.

- April 15, 2004: Michael Mitchell filed the agreement for the LM Family Limited Partnership, in Las Vegas.

- September 10, 2004: John Edwards's divorce from Deborah was finalized, although she later claimed that she never signed off on the divorce agreement, and that it still wasn't valid.

- September 16, 2004: John Edwards married Diana Lee (again), this time with Jeff Turino as his best man. Turino was the CEO of PCBM, the company that had been rumored in late 2002 and early 2003 to be a takeover target of CMKX, bringing an influx of thousands of PCBM shareholders into CMKX. Incidentally, Both Turino and Edwards were said to have used Helen Bagley's transfer agency as an "office" when they were in Las Vegas.

- October 18, 2004: Urban Casavant wired $10,000 to LM Family Partnership in Mahopac, New York.

At one point in Frizzell and Martin's investigations, even Robert Flaherty's death began to look suspicious. He died on a Saturday, the services were held the following Friday, but he wasn't buried until Monday, three days after the funeral. His obituary listed a gravesite at Southern Nevada Memorial Cemetery, but there was no record of him ever being buried there and no death certificate on record. Plus, pictures of Flaherty and Edwards showed a striking resemblance between the two con artists. Was it possible that Flaherty was really another Edwards' alter ego, staged his own death to escape prosecution, and then, as Edwards, "remarried" Diana Lee…twice? It wasn't until late 2006 that U.S. Attorney Timothy Vasquez said that DOJ attorneys had spent time with both Flaherty while he was in the hospital, and Edwards during Diana Lee's trials, and that they were indeed two different people. It was just another oddity in an ongoing series of trails. Some led to valuable information, while others led to either another trail, or, as in the case of the Robert Flaherty/John Edwards connection, to dead ends.

Chapter 26 – Trust the Team

"The problem is, you can't tell on the spider web, which ones are spiders, and which ones are flies."
~Bill Frizzell, Attorney, CMKX Owners Group, November, 2006

Doc wasn't the only problem with CMKX; Bill Frizzell knew the list of names involved was almost as long and convoluted as the money trail itself. The same characters appeared over and over throughout the life of the company and many of those names had a history of showing up together in one questionable penny stock company after another. Most significant was the hundreds of billions of shares that were sold into the market and the money trail that accompanied them. By calculating the shares issued to a handful of individuals, and adding in the shares issued to Urban Casavant and 26 of his relatives, Bill and John were able to account for an incredible two-thirds of the total shares sold:

- John Edwards alone accounted for 289 billion shares of stock dumped through his various trading accounts, trusts, and companies.
- Urban and 26 of his family members received over 104 billion shares.
- James Kinney, who was hired by Urban as a "consultant" in April of 2003, and his wife, Jeannie Kinney, received a total of over 89 billion shares.
- Ed Dhonau received 80 billion shares of stock (later returned in exchange for cash payments) for the deal with Nevada Minerals.
- David DeSormeau (through Business Works) received over 63 billion shares as Chief Financial Officer of CMKX, hired "to implement a real time financial reporting and inventory control systems" that never materialized.
- Ginger Gutierrez, Urban's personal secretary and DeSormeau's business associate, received almost 40 billion shares of stock issued either to her name or to Part Time Management, the company apparently controlled by James Kinney and David DeSormeau, where she held the position of secretary/treasurer.
- Emerson Koch and his family were issued over 49 billion shares, presumably because of his involvement in protecting the mining claims from the bad guys.

**Ed Dhonau, Urban Casavant, Emerson Koch, and Rendal Williams in action.
Courtesy of Jason Webb and Anthony Pullicino.**

Also, substantial amounts of shares were issued to a number of people who seemed to have no connection to the company whatsoever:

- Dave Gutka and his family received 56 billion shares of stock.
- Peter Dunn received 54 billion shares.
- Grant Hodgins received 54 billion shares.
- Wallace Geibelhaus received 32 billion shares.
- Vince Mazzei and his family received 20 billion shares of stock.

The first week of July in 2006, John and Jill Martin made a trip to Las Vegas, the epicenter for most events surrounding CMKX. Armed with a list of forty to fifty addresses of CMKX related companies and residences, they set out to fit a few more pieces into the puzzle. With little more than a rental car, a digital camera, and a map of the city, they made the rounds, looking for addresses connected with John Edwards, Ed Dhonau, Rendal Williams, Urban Casavant, David DeSormeau or anyone tied to CMKX. One of their due-diligence contacts was on the phone with them, researching each address, which invariably led to yet another address... and to yet another. What began as a simple list grew to a never-ending path from one site to the next.

After their experience at the SEC hearing, and believing there were truly dangerous characters involved in the CMKX story, they hoped to avoid being recognized. Goldie booked the hotel room for them under an assumed name, and they actually went as far as to dress incognito, with John wearing shades and a hat, and Jill dressed in what he would later jokingly describe as "hooker clothes." At times, Jill would wander into buildings asking about addresses, playing her role to the hilt, complete with bad accent, chewing gum, and exaggerated mannerisms.

They took pictures of everything, and soon realized that most addresses given as legitimate offices were nothing more than UPS Store drop boxes. Several John Edwards' companies would often be housed in the same office. The Martins would photograph one office, phone it in to their researcher, and he would in turn call back with as many as twenty to twenty-five other Edwards' companies listed with exactly the same address. Other times, the addresses were convenience stores, churches, or other businesses totally unrelated to the ones listed, and many addresses were simply nonexistent.

At one building that housed dozens of Edwards' companies, John Martin went inside to take pictures of the office directory, when someone who looked exactly like Edwards' drivers' license photos walked right past him, brushing his arm as he went by. It was an eerie moment for John and Jill; a close encounter with the man so many people feared.

Many of the homes they hoped to photograph, including Urban's house and several homes that Edwards owned, were in gated communities. John and Jill would wait around the corner until someone entered through a back gate and drive in just before the gate closed. They took pictures of the various homes and cars in the driveways, always on the lookout for who was coming and going. Just as it was with the offices, many homes turned out to be vacant. The titles had changed hands multiple times, and were often sold from one insider to another for unusual amounts of money far below the actual value of the home.

Clark County	90 INNISBROOK AV	$ 3,450,000

Ref #: 405629

Bedrooms:	5	PropSubType:	Single Family Residential
Full Baths:	3	Subdivision:	EST AT SPANISH TRAIL #6
3/4 Baths:	2	Year Built:	1997 / Resale
Half Baths:	1	Garage:	4 / Attached
SqFt:	9,461	Carport:	0

ELEGANT CUSTOM ESTATE IN SPANISH TRAIL ON GOLF COURSE END OF CUL DE SAC OPEN VIEWS NEW POLISHED LIMESTONE SPACIOUS RMS FLOWING FLOOR PLAN 2 MSTRS 1 DOWN 5 FPS 5TH BDRM USED AS OFC B-INS T/O 2 STORY VOLUME LIV RM 3 BDRMS DN LG ISLAND KIT GRANITE HUGE MSTR W/BALCONY HIS&HERS BATHS + W-IN CLOSETS ABSOLUTELY PERFECT HOME

Urban Casavant's home on the market for just under $3.5 million. Real estate ad.

In the evenings they would try to spend a little time enjoying themselves, and in fact, celebrated their anniversary during the trip. With only $500 dollars allotted to cover all their expenses, including the rental car, gas, food and what little entertainment they could afford, it was truly a low-budget experience. Only six months removed from the fateful Christmas when the Martin family hit rock bottom, money was still scarce. On their anniversary, they decided to splurge by dining at a moderately priced Italian restaurant in their hotel. Before dinner, they bought a ten dollar ticket for the nickel slots in the casino, taking turns pulling the lever, winning a dollar, then losing it one nickel at a time and repeating the process.

To make it more interesting, they moved from one nickel machine to the next and worked their way through the entire casino. With less than five dollars remaining on their ticket, John bet it all in the quarter poker machine. He hit the button, and won $868. He turned around, put the $868 ticket into the machine behind him...and won $500 more. Then he put that ticket into the next machine and won another $235. Instead of the ninety dollars they had set aside for their anniversary dinner, they spent triple that amount on food and a couple of shows. Along the way, they continued to place bets with their winning tickets. They climbed aboard the plane the following morning with $1,200 in their pockets, enough to make their house payment when they returned to Tyler, Texas.

Bill Frizzell, John Martin and Kevin West continued their exhaustive investigation, combining information supplied by diligent shareholders with their own research. Dissecting the records from the SEC was a huge undertaking, and their perception of the truth was constantly transformed as they moved from one box of evidence to the next. Interestingly, even though all three had access to the same information, decidedly different opinions began to emerge. In many ways they represented the three divergent factions that had evolved from the once unified CMKX shareholder base.

To John Martin, everything was black and white. While he once believed the company was locked in a battle against short sellers who wanted to kill the company, and the SEC, who wanted to bury the body, he now saw things in a totally different light. The more evidence they uncovered, the more cynical and negative he became, not just about CMKX, but also about the ethics of business in general. There was no middle ground; to him corruption seemed to permeate all levels of business, especially in the stock market.

As an attorney, Bill Frizzell was more pragmatic, but he was still an optimist at heart. He wanted to believe that at the very least, Urban Casavant, Don Stoecklein, and Bob Maheu were working on behalf of the shareholders. He required irrefutable evidence before placing them in the same category as John Edwards. He did concede that Urban had most likely made some serious transgressions when it came to running the company, but it seemed plausible that he had simply hooked up with the wrong people.

Kevin West was the polar opposite of both Bill and John in his beliefs, but was especially at odds with John. Kevin truly believed that Urban, Iron Bob

Maheu, and Roger Glenn were executing a plan that would not only make the shareholders rich, but would clean up the entire stock market. Like other True Believers, his theory was complex and implicated brokers, hedge funds, and short sellers who were defrauding the shareholders.

In October of 2004, Kevin had posted a message on the *Sterling's Classroom* message board that spoke both to his faith in God and his almost obsessive devotion to Urban Casavant:

To all Bashers...

Do you sleep well at night? Did you ever wonder why, with all the money you make, that things just don't seem to go well for you?

Money isn't everything. And when you make your money without regard to mankind or the goodwill of all, you are not doing things according to the codes of life. Look at it any way you want. Karma, if that's your magic word. You reap what you sow, and I am sure many can tell you from experience.

No matter what you believe, Urban Casavant is a Godly man and God is using him to re-distribute the wealth on this earth. If you are one that tries to mess with this plan, may God have mercy on your soul?

I wish everyone well, and I hope and pray that those of you that work on behalf of those that wish to rob America and its many beautiful people of all races of their hard earned money have a change in your heart and realize just what you are doing.

If you do not change your ways, than you get your just rewards in the end. Again, may God have mercy on your soul.

To all others, those of you that plan to do the right things with your wealth. You will benefit and reap rewards well beyond your wildest imaginations. My fellow brothers and sisters, we are one and we are all part of the same spirit.

May God Bless you

KW

Despite their different viewpoints concerning CMKX, the three of them shared a common goal of doing what was best for the shareholders. Bill held off on filing lawsuits against the company because he wanted to be 100% certain he was accurate in his beliefs. He also knew a lawsuit filed on behalf of shareholders was more difficult to win. As a result he was always working behind the scenes acting as an unofficial mediator, hoping to engineer a compromise that would save the company.

In the meantime, the company's stock was still trading, pending Judge Murray's final decision. The price dropped to an all-time low, sometimes selling for as little as .00006, or $60 for a million shares. While some shareholders were obviously dumping their stock in fear of permanent revocation, others were actually buying more. The rumors that a cash settlement had already been brokered by Maheu and Urban continued unabated, with only the dates and amounts revised to explain away every missed deadline.

The company finally hired a new auditor on July 11, the day before Judge Murray issued her initial decision. Stoecklein assured Frizzell auditor Brad Beckstead would complete the task well before Murray rendered her final decision. Frizzell hoped this would convince the judge they were making a bona fide effort to comply with SEC regulations.

Eleven days later, Beckstead and Watts, LLP resigned as the auditor of CMKM Diamonds, Inc. In a letter to the company dated July 28th, they stated, "In performing our audit procedures, we have become aware of information relating to possible illegal acts." Among the possible illegal acts they found was the "improper personal use of company funds," specifically citing the four million dollars Urban Casavant diverted from CMKX accounts to CMKXtreme. While most shareholders had assumed that CMKM Diamonds owned CMKXtreme, it was in fact a private company owned by the Casavant family and run by Urban's brother Ron.

Beckstead and Watts went on to describe numerous loans that the company made to its officers and to insiders in violation of SEC regulations, "significant monetary and stock transactions with individuals and entities who appear to be CMKM shareholders and/or prior officers and directors of the Company," and questionable transactions with U.S. Canadian Minerals.

They ended their letter, which was also filed with the SEC, by saying:

"The apparent violations of the securities laws described above may result in SEC enforcement action against CMKM which could result in a significant expenditure of corporate assets in defense, and may result in fines, penalties, and damages;

The apparent violations may result in civil litigation or criminal enforcement, which may also result in fines, penalties, and damages.

We are unable to quantify the amounts involved because we have not been provided sufficient information to do so, and because CMKM's books and records are, in their current state, inadequate and unauditable."

It was another stunning blow to CMKX shareholders, who had watched their dreams of riches unravel into an ugly morass of fraud and deception in a few short months. At the same time that Beckstead was exposing the questionable arrangements between CMKX and CMKXtreme, Urban was cutting ties with NHRA drivers Jeff Arend and Connie Cohen. A few weeks later, they abandoned their sponsorship of driver Tony Barone. With Judge Murray's final decision due within weeks, things looked hopeless for the tens of thousands of investors who had once believed in Urban Casavant's claim that he wanted to create a million millionaires.

Not surprisingly, there were still those who continually undermined Frizzell and Martin's efforts to uncover the truth about who had wronged CMKX shareholders. Andy Hill was still posting messages in *Paltalk* claiming to have inside information from Urban Casavant:

> Hello, CMKX'rs..I spoke at length with UC today about Mr. Frizzell and Mr. Martin. Loyal CMKX shareholders should ignore anything said by the OG and demand a full refund. The OG is misrepresenting facts and making wrong subjective assumptions about CMKX.

If any shareholders chose to ignore Bill Frizzell because of Andy Hill's admonishments, it didn't deter Frizzell, who was still single-minded in his pursuit of the truth. After working so closely with Stoecklein trying to save CMKX, Frizzell was shocked by Beckstead's resignation. Frizzell had been formulating a plan of his own based on their extensive investigations into the company and decided to take a proactive approach and force the issue. On September 9th, Frizzell sent Stoecklein a nine page "shareholder derivative rights" letter. He demanded the company take legal action against six individuals and one brokerage firm he claimed had defrauded CMKM Diamonds and its shareholders of hundreds of millions of dollars:

- John Edwards was accused of opening 36 trust accounts at NevWest Securities and another 20 companies domiciled in Langley, B.C., all of which were simply "mail drops" with no real physical addresses whatsoever. He dumped hundreds of billions of shares of company stock through the various accounts, much of it restricted stock. Edwards also tried to buy a majority stock position in Crown Financial, who was one of the main market makers who facilitated the sale of CMKX stock.

- NevWest Securities, already under investigation by the NASD, was accused of helping Edwards dump his stock and launder the money from the sales.

- Neil Levine and the accounting firm of Bagell, Josephs and Company were accused of professional negligence for their abrupt resignation during the SEC hearing, especially since John Edwards brought Levine into the company to begin with.

- David DeSormeau was accused of professional negligence for failing to institute promised accounting systems for the company, a project for which he received 63 billion shares of CMKX stock worth over $1.5 million.

- James Kinney was accused of fraudulently selling over 100 billion shares of CMKX stock issued to either him, his wife Jeannie, or to Part Time Management.

- Ginger Gutierrez was accused of being the signor on many checks written on the various CMKX and CMKXtreme bank accounts, and of personally receiving 23 billion shares of stock along with stock issued to Part Time Management.

- Brian Dvorak was accused of legal malpractice for writing the opinion letters that released hundreds of billions of shares of company stock, and for approving the illegal 100-1 forward split that only selected shareholders received.

On October 20, Entourage Mining Ltd. (ETGMF) announced that they had entered into agreements to purchase all of CMKX's claims in the Hatchet Lake, Forte Diamond, and Smeaton property in exchange for 45 million shares of Entourage stock to be distributed to CMKX shareholders. It was described as a "wind-up distribution" in CMKX's press release, indicating that CMKX would effectively cease to exist after the distribution. They appointed a task force comprised of Bob Maheu, Don Stoecklein, and Bill Frizzell to conduct a cert pull to determine the legitimate shareholders of CMKX. Frizzell was aware of SEC Pacific Office Chief Andrew Petillon's comments after the hearing: "If this is an orchestrated short squeeze against the brokerage houses to make the stock price go up, we will come after those who are responsible," and "We would not look kindly on a cert pull because it would cause market manipulation." But Frizzell also knew that because the company's stock no longer traded, and the Entourage distribution gave them a valid reason for the cert pull, there was nothing Petillon or the SEC could do to halt the process.

On the same day that the Entourage deal was announced, they appointed former CMKX executive Corey Klassen to their board of directors. Unknown to shareholders at the time, others connected to CMKX were acquiring Entourage stock before the announcement of the CMKX agreement. Urban's brother-in-law Eric Reid (who had already been issued almost 21 billion shares of CMKX stock) received 132,500 shares of Entourage stock as a finder's fee in a private placement agreement. That agreement closed on December 31, 2004, ten months before the Entourage/CMKX deal was consummated. In the private placement, Entourage distributed 2.8 million shares of stock priced at fifteen cents a share to various individuals, including:

- Emerson Koch, who received 666,500 shares of ETGMF.
- Urban Casavant's son Wesley received 666,500 shares of stock.
- Urban's daughter Cindy Dwyer also received 666,500 shares.

- Rick Walker of United Carina Resources, TSX Ventures, and Consolidated Pine Channel Gold Corp. received 153,000 shares of stock.

The following day, on October 21, 2005, without responding to Frizzell's shareholders' derivative rights demands, Donald Stoecklein submitted a one-paragraph letter to Judge Brenda Murray:

"CMKM respectfully requests that the Commission withdraw CMKM's Petition for Review and institute the Initial Decision of the Administrative Law Judge revoking the registration of the common stock of CMKM pursuant to Section 12(j) of the Exchange Act, effective immediately."

On November 4th, CMKM Diamonds released an update to its shareholders:

"On or about Oct. 28, 2005, the Securities and Exchange Commission, in response to CMKM's withdrawal of its appeal, declared Administrative Law Judge Brenda Murray's initial decision final. This effectively revoked CMKM's reporting status under the Securities Exchange Act of 1934, as amended. As such, it is currently unlawful for any broker dealer to effectuate a trade in CMKM's common stock."

On October 28, 2005, the last share of CMKX was officially bought and sold on the stock market. In all, 703,518,875,000 real shares were in the hands of company insiders and 50,000 individual shareholders. The final closing price was $.00008, eight-one thousandths of a cent. Whoever bought the last shares paid a grand total of $80 for the rush of owning a million shares in a diamond mining company.

On the same day, the SEC also permanently revoked St. George Metals (SGGM), who had invested $10 million dollars into CMKX during the height of the stock buying...and selling...frenzy.

It was difficult to tell exactly how much money flowed through the company coffers and other insider bank accounts during the approximately two and half years that CMKM Diamonds traded. If the $0.00071 average trading price Judge Murray cited in her initial ruling was accurate, then the 703 billion shares sold by CMKX to shareholders amounted to just under $500 million. Those same shares, now in the hands of over 50,000 shareholders, would have been worth a grand total of $56 million, or one-tenth of what was paid for them...if the stock was still trading at all.

It was the most shares ever sold in the history of the stock market, in a company that had almost zero revenue, never filed a financial report, and hadn't even revealed to their stockholders the total number of shares issued until after trading was temporarily halted prior to the May 10, 2005 SEC hearing.

Chapter 27 – Waiting on a Sign or From Here to Eternity

"This is a time for the CMKM stockholders to look forward towards the future and forget the past. Working as a united front will allow us to extract all available sources of value for distribution."

~Robert A. Maheu

If the revocation of CMKX wasn't enough of a blow to the shareholders, a week before Judge Murray's decision became final, and the day before Stoecklein withdrew the company's appeal, a filing with the SEC revealed even more bad news. Effective at exactly 10:00 A.M. on October 20, 2005, Robert "Iron Bob" Maheu resigned as a board member and co-chairman of CMKM Diamonds. The filing not only announced Maheu's resignation, it laid out the game plan for what sounded like the dissolution of CMKX:

> *"CMKM believes it is in the best interest for the company to accept Mr. Maheu's resignation as a director due to CMKM's current lack of funds to continue its operations and in anticipation of a distribution to CMKM stockholders of the anticipated receipt of the Entourage stock, whereby Mr. Maheu has agreed to lend his assistance to CMKM and its stockholders as a consultant, trustee, or in any other capacity as needed during the winding up of CMKM's affairs. Additionally, Mr. Maheu has agreed to waive his rights to any past financial obligations due him from CMKM.*
>
> *Mr. Urban Casavant will remain as the sole officer and director of CMKM until the affairs of CMKM are wound up. As a result of health concerns, Mr. Casavant intends to resign as the sole officer and director effective immediately upon a determination that all shares and other assets of CMKM have been properly disbursed to its stockholders."*

Although it wasn't announced publicly until over two weeks later, and then only because Iron Bob was referred to as "former CMKM Co-Chairman and the designated trustee of the Task Force," most shareholders had already begun to spin the bad news, claiming the only plausible reason for Maheu's resignation was that they had already won. It seemed obvious to Urban and Maheu's loyal followers that a settlement had already been brokered. The message board and chatroom gurus' predictions, most of which seemed outlandish to anyone who looked at the public information in a logical way, only reinforced the hopes of those who had pinned their dreams on Urban Casavant's promises of creating a million millionaires. As usual, there were grandiose plans to spend the riches waiting just around the corner, and the fact that many shareholders had invested in CMKX as a matter of faith made them even more certain that God would reward their patience.

Posting as WWJDthrume (or "What Would Jesus Do thru me"), Debi Kiontke posted a "budget" on January 16, 2006, three months after Maheu resigned as Co-Chairman due to the company's lack of funds. Based on rumors being spread by the Belgians that a huge cash payout was on the way, Debi claimed she would "sponsor 1,000 children through World Vision, fund a special project or two, invest in a 'fat farm'/retreat center, pay any taxes due and have something left over to invest, after paying my bills and getting a house. And of course tithing to my home church and giving to my favorite Christian Ministries that I haven't been able to do anything financial for in a long time."

Like most CMKX shareholders, her dreams were grandiose and noble, but unfortunately hinged mostly on unproven rumors from gurus who always batted zero. The Belgians were the main messengers of incredible claims of massive wealth, and posted under names like Wodan, Mano and flugalbinders0. Mano in particular was persistent, naming dates that were usually just days away and payouts so outlandish that even the most gullible believers took his predictions with a grain of salt. Others, like e1o54 and the ever-present Accadacca, only added to the steady flow of misinformation and unsubstantiated rumors.

One self-professed prophet who went by Roddy56 set up his own private message board, where he would personally approve every member and hold court as he told his followers (always posting in all capital letters) to "BELIEVE AND BE FAITHFUL TO MY VOICE," and saying "I LEAD WITH TRUTH NOT BY POPULAR CHOICE." His followers would in turn respond with "yes I am faithful roddy," and "you are a great leader roddy." It was eerily reminiscent of extremist religious cults that had made headlines for their manipulative behavior.

While the gurus were busy setting…and then postponing… and then resetting date after date on which the shareholders would be paid their hundreds of billions or trillions of dollars, others waited to be paid by the company as well. Two weeks after CMKM Diamonds signed over their Canadian mining claims to Entourage on October 20, 2005, CMKX defaulted on their deal with Nevada Minerals. Urban yielded all rights to the American Shaft Mine in Ecuador, after acknowledging the receipt of multiple notices of default.

For the next several months, most shareholders spent their time trying to obtain their CMKX certificates in order to receive their Entourage distribution and watching the counter on the CMKM Task Force website move slowly towards the magic number of 703 billion shares. Shareholders who didn't receive certificates would be holding counterfeit shares, even though said shares had been paid for and credited to their brokerage accounts.

While Maheu and Stoecklein might have officially been on the CMKX Task Force, it was left up to Bill Frizzell, John Martin, and Kevin West to once again mobilize Frizzell's office and oversee the process. Their prior experience with the brokerage statement fax-in campaign helped them deal with the logistics of receiving, counting, and tabulating the thousands of incoming stock certificates. This time, Kevin's wife Angela took over Jill Martin's role in organizing the help, and Johnny was once again in charge of seeing that nothing went wrong from a technical standpoint.

While the cert pull continued, John and Bill were still following leads and gathering evidence. They hoped that the research they and others were conducting could eventually be used in legal actions against the ever-growing list of people who appeared to have profited at the expense of the company and the shareholders.

On a subsequent trip to Las Vegas during the height of the cert pull, John and Jill staked out 1st Global Transfer in an effort to see who was frequenting Helen Bagley's transfer agency. Bagley had complained that she was overwhelmed by the task of issuing certificates for the thousands of CMKX shareholders, and claimed to have hired extra employees who were working in shifts around the clock. 1st Global had recently moved to a larger office, undoubtedly funded by the substantial revenue Bagley was generating from the cert pull. However, When John and Jill staked out 1st Global late one afternoon, there were only two cars parked outside of the office, nowhere near the ten to twelve people who Bagley had claimed were working around the clock. They stayed into the evening to document the arrival of the night shift, but by the time they gave up their vigil at nine o'clock that night, no one else had arrived, and only one car remained from earlier.

Another revelation of the second Las Vegas trip was the discovery of a second transfer agency located less than a block away from 1st Global…owned by John Edwards' son Toby Edwards. It just tied Bagley and John Edwards together even more closely, and raised suspicions about who was in charge of the issuing of stock in CMKX and other companies that Edwards was connected with. Along with information that Jeff Turino and Edwards both used 1st Global as their personal offices, Edwards had reportedly been seen carrying what appeared to be boxes of stock certificates out of Bagley's office during the height of the CMKX selling frenzy.

With 1st Global and the brokerage firms apparently doing whatever they could to slow down the process of issuing stock certificates to CMKX shareholders, the original deadline of December 31, 2005, set by the Task Force was extended to March 31, 2006. Then, *that* deadline was extended to May 15, 2006, and many shareholders still hadn't received their certs.

On May 31, 2006, Bill Frizzell sent a complaint letter to the NASD, SEC, Nevada state securities regulators, and several key members of Congress, claiming there was "indisputable evidence of large numbers of failed deliveries in this stock," and that brokers are trying to undermine shareholders' rights by denying them their rights to ownership, stating that:

"Nevada law NRS 78.235 mandates that each shareholder has the right to request and receive certificates of ownership from the company for their stock. Specifically, the statute states, "Every stockholder is entitled to have a certificate, signed by officers or agents designated by the corporation for the purpose, certifying the number of shares owned by him in the corporation."

Excuses brokers gave CMKX clients for failing to deliver stock certificates were taken from Frizzell's complaint letter and reprinted as a David Letterman style top ten list in an article on *The Faulking Truth* titled "The CMKX Story: When Too Much Isn't Enough":

1. *"We had your cert, but it is now lost. It will take us another 6 to 8 weeks to obtain another one."*

2. *"This stock purchase was a book entry only and no certificate is available."*

3. *"Your stock was classified as a worthless security and is no longer in your account."*

4. *"Our clearing firm has not been able to deliver these certificates due to a backlog of requests at the transfer agency."*

5. *"I have been instructed we are no longer pulling certs for CMKM and there is nothing I can do. You need to contact the company."*

6. *"CMKM Diamonds has a "K" code next to it, indicating that it is being held in safekeeping for the client. The clearing agent has made the decision not to issue certs but rather fax a copy of the certs it holds to the transfer agent."*

7. *"Attached herewith is evidence of ownership of shares held electronically by XYZ clearing for ABC broker. ABC to confirm receipt of this proof of shares of CMKM and related companies are held with XYZ."*

8. *"In light of the lack of cooperation (by the transfer agent), your May 15th, 2006 deadline must be bogus and must be extended, and Entourage shares could of course still be sent to ABC for the benefit of XYZ."*

9. *"MNO said they had discussed with the Task Force the acceptability of the affidavit as proof of ownership in lieu of the certificate, and that it would be accepted."* No such conversation ever occurred with the Task Force members.

10. *"We ordered your certificate, and it has been lost. You must now fill out a loss certificate."* The transfer agent confirms that no certificate was ever issued.

Each quoted statement above is taken verbatim from a shareholder's letter or from a broker's written response to a shareholder's request for a cert. I could continue with pages and pages of documented incidences of these broker responses to the requests of the shareholders if such is necessary to establish the need for a full investigation.

The article went on to discuss a potential shortage of billions of shares of CMKX stock, and pointed out that the DTCC claimed the amount of failed deliveries has never exceeded 500 million shares for the *entire market*, which made it likely "that the failed deliveries in this one little company...that no longer even trades...could surpass the entire number of fails claimed by the DTCC for the entire stock market."

There were other questionable tactics brokers used to circumvent the likelihood they didn't have enough CMKX shares to go around. Some brokers tried to have the certificates delivered in their own names instead of those of the rightful owners, so they could collect the Entourage shares themselves, and do a "book entry" of those shares in the accounts that were short, effectively trading one non-existent stock for another one. *The Faulking Truth* article put it this way:

"They want to trade their short position in CMKX (which can't be covered because the stock is no longer available) for a short position in Entourage Mining, which they can then go out and buy on the open market (because it is trading). Voila! No more short position, and hopefully, no more massive legal liability against the brokers for robbing the shareholders blind.

There's only one problem: the brokers don't own the stock, the shareholders do. Since CMKX is now a private company, the brokers should no longer hold it in street name. They were only the custodians of the stock, holding it until such time that the real owners, the shareholders, the ones who bought and paid for the stock in the first place, requested that the stock be handed over to them.

In all reality, the brokers should have delivered the CMKX stock within three days after they made the sale, as required by law. Instead, the stock hasn't even traded for the past seven months, and many of them still can't deliver."

While it was impossible to tell exactly which brokers would be caught without enough shares to go around, both Ameritrade and E*Trade still hadn't delivered shares to many clients. In fact, the Positions Report Frizzell obtained from the DTCC in April showed that E*Trade had only 38,594 total shares left to distribute, while *The Faulking Truth* had received emails from E*Trade customers claiming they were still waiting on tens of millions of shares in certificate form. Where were those shares?

The article closed by projecting the problems with the brokers and the regulatory agencies in the CMKX fiasco onto the broader market, and ended with a quote from Frizzell and the signature *Faulking Truth* closing line:

"This is nothing more than a shell game, a series of ploys and stall tactics designed to hide the fact that something is very wrong with our stock market system. Couple this little tale with the growing number of other companies now presenting evidence of their own of rampant stock market manipulation and stock counterfeiting, and you have a trail of corruption that is unraveling at a frightening pace.

Bill Frizzell put it in perfect perspective in his closing paragraph, one that I hope our securities regulators and elected officials pay close attention to:

'There was a time in the market place when shareholders rights at least co-existed with the rights of the broker/dealers. You have now been presented with evidence of shareholders who have demanded that their brokers issue certs for their holdings. Many shareholders have been flatly refused by their broker. This violates Nevada state law and the spirit, if not the letter, of federal regulatory law. I call on you to begin an investigation into this injustice.'

And that, my fellow patriots, is the Faulking Truth."

On June 6, 2006, the CMKM Task Force was officially dissolved, having succeeded in bringing the total number of shares issued as certificates to around 635 billion shares, but never reaching the magic number of 703 billion shares. To the very end, the brokers stalled at every possible opportunity, and finally just quit delivering shares altogether. Shareholders had hoped that the cert pull would force both the SEC and the brokers to deal with issue of counterfeit stock, but ultimately it left yet another unanswered question in the CMKX saga. It looked like the 50,000 plus CMKX shareholders had been given, as one poster put it, "the American Shaft," by both the company and the stock market system itself.

In the first official company press release in almost nine months, Urban Casavant thanked Maheu, Stoecklein, and Frizzell for serving on the Task Force, and announced that he had been "suffering from serious health related issues and is no longer able to carry on the day to day related activities of the company," and that he would announce new management within the next two weeks, and establish a new office "within 30-45 days."

As their final act, the Task Force recommended that the company file an interpleader motion to ask the court to help identify the bona fide shareholders in order to distribute the 45 million shares of Entourage stock. The press release closed by naming another attorney to handle the interpleader motion:

"Recently-retained legal counsel for CMKM, John T. Moran III of the Law Offices of Moran & Associates, a law firm whose residence is situated in the Great State of Nevada, will now proceed via the federal court system and, specifically, initiation of action in interpleader and for purpose of accounting and earmarking certificates to those shareholders presenting viable equity in the Company. As part of the Task Force's recommendation, the federal courts

have subpoena power which, if deemed appropriate, could ultimately be used to gain cooperation from brokers that have allegedly-refused to comply with the Company and Task Force's efforts to date. This interpleader action must take place so that the Company can move forward."

Chapter 28 – SOOn?

"I've had people say 'God led me to CMKX.' And I'll say, 'Well, are you sure God led you to this, or do you just think he led you to it?' 'No, I'm sure he led me to it.' 'Okay, well maybe he led you in to this to increase your knowledge, or maybe he led you to this to show you that what's important isn't money, it's family and friends. Or maybe he led you into it to be a part of bringing about positive change in the world.'

My greatest fear is that people will lose faith in God…not in Urban, not in CMKX, not in their dreams of getting rich, but in God, because they believe that God led them to CMKX, and it didn't work out. In their minds, God misled them, He let them down."

> ~Pastor DeWayne Reeves, Christian Financial Radio Network

With the end of 2006 rapidly approaching, many CMKX shareholders were still hoping for a positive resolution to the CMKX saga. Long since past were the daily battle cries of "To da moon!!!" and even the "Stock Play of a Lifetime" slogan had been altered on some message boards to read "The Stock Play *For* a Lifetime."

While some shareholders had managed to pull themselves together and move on with their lives, and others had turned their blind belief in Urban Casavant into a desire to know the truth, for the most part it was still just a waiting game. Unfortunately, many shareholders, running out of resources, time, and patience, were at the end of their emotional rope. John Martin, Kevin West, and DeWayne Reeves, along with the various message board moderators and administrators, were receiving desperate pleas from increasingly distraught shareholders.

With the gurus still spreading rumor after rumor on the boards and in the chatrooms, many shareholders still clung to the hope that one of the endless streams of unfulfilled promises would finally come to fruition. Accadacca appeared on *CFRN's The Faulking Truth Show* on August 4, 2006, and admitted he was hired to spread rumors about the company, none of which had come true in the prior year and a half that he had been active in *Paltalk* and on the message boards:

> *"I came into CMKX roughly in March of 2003. I was contacted by an individual and we talked and I met him and took a position…you know I can't really tell you who employed me to do this job but I will say it's been the most exciting job anyone could ever have. At this present time I am not compensated. Prior to revocation, I guess you could say I was."*

Using Accadacca's claim in March of 2005 that Citigroup was supposedly buying out CMKX the following week as an example, it was pointed out that all of his claims were inaccurate. Accadacca replied, "I understand that, my main objective was to hold the shareholder base together prior to revocation, I did not want people to sell."

It was a stunning confession. Accadacca had been paid to lie to shareholders to keep them from selling their stock before the SEC revoked the company. After dozens of unfulfilled rumors and outright lies, he pledged on *The Faulking Truth Show* to cease giving predictions of dates and payout amounts:

> *"I'm done with the dates. I know we're getting paid. I know that. We are so close that I'm not gonna state any more dates or any more price per share, because we are that close. I feel I don't have to at this point."*

One month later, Accadacca was at it again, posting "Money in hand no later than 10-31-06." To confuse the issue even further, Willy Wizard came on the March 4, 2006, show immediately afterwards and said that Accadacca had told him "I'll never tell you the truth."

Even Uncle Melvi made an appearance on the same show, reciting his favorite line, "Don't believe it unless it's in an official press release." Of course, he failed to mention that the only official press release the company had issued in the past nine months was the announcement of Urban Casavant's failing health and impending resignation as CEO of CMKM Diamonds.

It didn't seem to matter. For those who were desperate for hope, even false hope was better than nothing. Every time one predicted date failed to materialize, there was a ready-made excuse and a bigger, better payoff to appease the followers. Mano had raised his claims for a payout to a whopping $1.61 per share, which would bring the grand total buyout to well over a trillion dollars. And rumors about candidates to replace Urban Casavant as company CEO had grown in magnitude to include Microsoft's Bill Gates and legendary financier Warren Buffet. But for those who had waited years for empty promises to be fulfilled, outrageous rumors only served to create additional confusion in an already troubling situation. In many cases, early shareholder optimism had given way to outright despair:

> BrainDamage, one of the co-founders of the popular CMKX message board *Proboards66*, had "settled into a comfortable routine of teaching information technology seminars for computer programmers." After 9/11 and the crash of the technology industry, unable to find work, by 2004 he was getting "pretty desperate and depressed." Then a friend told him about CMKX, and he began investing just in time to ride the run from .0001 to .0011 in June, but never sold a share. Within a year he had invested $60,000 of his and his wife's regular and IRA brokerage funds, along with his kids' funds, into CMKX...and had subscribed to *The Robb Report* (a magazine about luxury lifestyles) to "prepare myself for having loads of money to spend after the next run."

After buying up almost 200 million shares of stock through the run and well beyond, BrainDamage was jolted back to reality by the shareholders' party:

> *"By the infamous shareholders' party, I began to face the fact I and tens of thousands of others had been skillfully bamboozled. By Christmas I was*

a nervous, miserable wreck. My marriage was hanging by a thread; I was almost, but not quite, suicidal, definitely not functional. I lucked out by finding a psychotherapist who could listen to my CMKX-oholism without judging me for it, and within a few months I more-or-less began coming to my senses. First step: resign as an administrator of the Proboards66 board. The CMKX community doesn't 'need' me more than my family does. Now, here it is mid-2007, and I'm still seeing the same therapist... and realizing how much about myself the CMKX debacle has forced me, and continues to force me, to come to grips with.

While I was still convinced we were all going to be filthy rich from CMKX, I felt my difficult life up to that point was all just some kind of test, and that soon I was certain to be well rewarded for my perseverance. Now I recognize that pain is not always rewarded; sometimes it's just there to be surmounted."

Like BrainDamage, many of the early supporters of the company had changed their viewpoint after the events of the past couple of years. Those who were now labeled as bashers had once been ardent followers of Urban Casavant. Chris1, who had heard Urban say "We are driving truckloads of diamonds out of there," became skeptical of the hundreds of unfulfilled promises and unsubstantiated rumors. Even Topogigio eventually admitted openly that he had been used to mislead shareholders. Sterling, who was arguably one of the most prominent early supporters of CMKX, realized that he too had been used to promote what now appeared to be a scam:

"I actually believed that CMKX was the Stock Play of a Lifetime. The things I posted, I believed. Maybe it seems like it's out in left field now, because it never materialized, but at the time, it seemed possible.

For instance the message I posted 'We've got diamonds, we've got gold,' when I posted that originally, Urban was talking to Topo, who was talking to Frank, and Frank relayed that message to me directly. So I posted my message, and Topo called Frank and said, 'Urban said to tell you that we forgot to mention, we got uranium too.' I talked to Topo afterwards, and he confirmed everything. He was all excited about everything at the races, saying that Urban told him 'we're gonna be rich.'

Now some of that is what Frank or Topo told me, but if I posted that Urban said it, then Urban said it to me. So where it says that 'Urban said that CMKX will be at .50 to .60 cents even without the covering of the naked short position!' then Urban said that to me. The stock was at .0001, the price didn't run up until a few weeks later, so if you bought then, you could have sold for ten times that in early June. I recommend that people take some profit when it runs up, not just with CMKX, but with any penny stock, and don't invest any more than you can afford to lose. I had that posted on Sterling's entire

Classroom, but everything was ignored when it came to CMKX. And I'm not putting anybody down, because I didn't sell any of mine during the run.

The problem was, I could go into Paltalk, and someone would ask me 'What do you think about the potential of a cash dividend,' and I would say 'I think the potential for a cash dividend is good, because that would force the short sellers to cover.' And the next thing you know, I'm hearing that 'Sterling said we're getting a cash dividend tomorrow!' So I'd have to go back and make it clear, 'I'm only speculating about what COULD happen, I'm not saying it will happen,' but it didn't matter. People only believed what they wanted to believe.

Then Urban asked me to go to Canada with several other shareholders, and I saw the drilling, we did all kinds of driving around, and Urban would say 'Here's all this land belonging to all you shareholders," and you're seeing all that...and all the money spent on all the races...and it was hard NOT to believe it. Even before the races, when you're hearing about De Beers and what they've got, and all the land CMKX had, and thinking about the potential valuation, it already looked like the stock play of a lifetime...that just solidified things when I went to the races and Canada.

Later, when we learned about how many shares were out there, and I began to question the company, they would get mad at me, and say I was a basher, and I wasn't one of the loyal longs anymore.

But the truth is, if I had to go back and do everything all over again, I would probably be just as stupid, because the same things that existed to make me see the opportunity for CMKX would have existed then, and I would be thinking the same way."

`Hillbillymajik` was one of many shareholders who placed his faith in the man himself, Urban Casavant. He told his twin brother, father, and mother about the stock later dubbed the Stock Play of a Lifetime, convincing them to invest in CMKX as well. This is how he described the excitement and hope CMKX brought him:

"This stock would answer all of my worries; it gave me hope. I had a rough couple of years, and, when I found this stock, it was like the answer to my dreams. At the time I had a wife and 5 kids. We were struggling to make ends meet. But I believed in the man who wanted to make one million millionaires. I spent countless hours researching the stock, following every little tidbit I could connect with CMKX. I felt I couldn't go wrong. Everything seemed to make sense."

Just like thousands of other CMKX shareholders, `Hillbillymajik` obsessed over the company and ultimately paid the price for it:

"I lost sleep staying up late at night when my family was sleeping. I would wake up in the morning to read the message boards. I checked the message boards like a crack addict. My brother and I took the trip to Las Vegas to the shareholders meeting. I reported back to the board I posted on with any tidbit of 'if you're in, you win' from our room. I dreamed about how this man would change my family's life. I spent every last penny of savings of over $3000 and would have bought more if I could have.

I ended up with over 31 million shares and 780,000 shares of the spin off company. To make a long story short, I lost my wife and 4 of my children due to the neglect and financial recklessness caused by my investment in CMKX. Now I am a broke, single dad of a beautiful 12-year-old daughter. I'm working 50 hours a week and struggling to make ends meet on a printer operator's wages.

The loss I have suffered may never truly be known to me, for it is my daughter Jessica and the rest of my family that will ultimately suffer the consequences of what I've done. And for that I am sorry."

Ruby Reese and her husband told a story that paralleled many shareholders, one of hope for a better future, based in large part on the promises of message board gurus:

"We have owned a business for 20 years; due to the computer revolution, the business has slowly reduced in size to just the two of us working as brokers in the art printing industry. And when we had the opportunity to invest in CMKX, and were told it was a 'stock play of a lifetime,' I sold a life insurance policy and we invested about $8,000, which was huge for us. We were not making enough money to live on, and this was our chance to have some sort of retirement. We KNEW it was going to happen very 'soon', so when our business failed, we looked the other way because of CMKX. We both went out and got temporary jobs just until we hit pay dirt. Stress was high, very high because we had not much income and huge debt - but we refused to believe that we were in trouble."

For Ruby Reese and her husband, hope soon gave way to debt and stress, and the inherent pressure led to greater problems:

"My husband had trouble with heartburn all of the time due to stress, and ended up in the VA hospital with a triple bypass. Was it stress of a failed business? Was it stress of not enough income to pay bills? Was it stress of wondering if we would ever see anything from the only investment we had ever made? I believe it was a 'yes' to all of these.

We are both still working for much less than we are worth, we still have huge debt that we try to pay, and we have lost our dream of the only thing that we both truly believed in, that this investment would give us something to retire on. I am especially sad because I feel we could have done things much different had it not been for the pipe dream, and we would be in a better place today."

Ruby signed her story as "A very sorry investor."

Terrence Simmons (Tmoney) was a college football standout who played semi-pro ball before returning to school to study architecture and engineering. He coached the 2006 Champion Bay Area Gambler Football team in Texas. He believed God and his faith led him to the Stock Play of a Lifetime. "It's all about the hope I have for others."

Terrence, like Hillbillymajik, lost everything: "I had a great job and lost it, my wife, even my dog left too." But to Tmoney, it was still about the hope: "I have to live and to die with hope, and I do hope for CMKX and my family as well."

Stockseekerok was earning $130,000 annually in the Oklahoma City oilfields when he bought 47 million CMKX shares. Struggling with sudden bouts of vertigo, he needed an income when he could no longer work. Eventually, "caught up in the hype of the promised .07 and .54 per share payout," he spent all his time with thousands of other shareholders on the message boards.

It was the eternal waiting for the anticipated payout that exacted an emotional toll:

"By November of 2004 the stress had taken such a toll on me physically that the vertigo attacks were coming almost daily, I was afraid to drive a car for fear of killing myself, or worse, some innocent person that just happened to be in my way if an attack came on.

I was finally diagnosed with Meniere's disease. That ended my career in the oilfield. I went from a prosperous person to a disabled man dependent on SSDI for my living. No, CMKM did not cause the disease, but the doctors told me the stress accelerated the progress by tenfold. I lost my home, I lost my new car, and I had to move to an area where I could survive on my SSDI. Medical bills ate my home; all the testing, specialists and then a medicine bill of 700 dollars per month drained my nest egg rather quickly."

Lorraine Knudson heard about CMKX from her son who bought a million shares for a hundred dollars. Lorraine invested a little, found *Paltalk*, and experienced the excitement that captivated other shareholders:

"I fell in Love. 1.9m acres of the most diamondiferous land in Canada. With the stories of green stuffium, Roger Glenn, we kept investing more, twenty million shares and 10 thousand dollars. I just wanted a better life for my family and friends."

For Lorraine the events that elapsed between her and her family's initial investment in CMKX and late 2006 were significant:

"Some have now died; some are dying as I type. My mom has lost her vision and needs help...the stories could go on. At times we are in great despair; I'm unemployed, unable to work due to back injury, with no medical insurance."

Surprisingly though, Lorraine stopped short of wishing that she'd never become involved with CMKX, but not because of the hope of wealth, but because of the relationships and knowledge she gained from the experience:

"I have made some truly great friends through CMKX. I have learned all about the corruption in the marketplace. 'Never love a stock and never invest more than you can afford to lose.'

God help us all...for believing in a dream."

Ed Kelley invested $45,000 into CMKX hoping to help those who needed it the most. It wasn't long before he had serious regrets about his decision to invest in Urban Casavant's diamond mining company:

"My life was destroyed by Urban and his cronies. He stole every penny I had and I was stupid enough to let him. Now I am bankrupt, terminally ill with no way to pay for the care I need to stay alive, no hope for the future. My eyes were opened right after the shareholder party when he claimed we were ready to file but we were nowhere close to doing so. I should have taken a loss and bailed out while I could, but stupid me, I thought maybe, just maybe, those guys were right. So I continued to hold on to my shares rather than dump them. $45,000 hanging on a wing and a prayer.

I started questioning Urban in the forums and I became a pariah. People started calling me a basher, accusing me of being paid to do so. No matter how many predictions these guys made, I denounced every one of them, and every prognostication failed. Yet, to say anything bad about the person who made the prediction was heresy, and when I did, I was blasted and banned from a number of forums.

I may never recover a single cent of my investment but it doesn't matter anymore. All I want now is justice and to see Urban's butt in jail for a very long time with every single asset he owns being turned over to us shareholders so that when he finally gets out, he is old, sick and penniless, just as he made me. Rot in hell Urban Casavant!

I am alone. I have no wife, no kids, and no one to remember me when I am gone. It could have been otherwise. I had great plans to help others when CMKX paid off. People would have remembered me as a kind, giving man who helped so many. Now, no one will remember me, for anything at all. All because some thug stole my future from me."

The story Lan told was so tragic as to be almost unbelievable. Lan invested in CMKX with hopes of performing good deeds, but then, made financial commitments long before his ship came in. Having invested $100,000 in over half a billion CMKX shares, he bought a house for nearly one million dollars. He promised loans and help to family and church members, all based on the predictions of the chat room and message board gurus. He was left penniless:

> *"I lost everything I owned. Because I was told the money was coming in any day now since Oct 2004, I didn't pay or file my corporate or private income tax and could go to jail. I told my local church leader I would get him a full time nurse for his ailing wife in 2005, but she died still hoping a nurse would come. One elder in the Church who was depending on me had to dump his $650,000 house for half the price because he bought a 1.1 million house before he sold his old house. Now he can't pay for the new house and had to borrow money from his brother just to have a place to live. I told my small church that I would buy them a building, and 150 people had no place to meet while everyone was waiting for the diamond mine to come in. The whole Church thinks I am a nut case and a scumbag for leading them on. They will have nothing to do with me.*

> *I promised my mother a penthouse apartment and the finest nursing care money could buy after she fell and broke her hip. She now has to live on government assistance. My relatives told me not to have anything to do with them, and one relative said don't come to his funeral. He died before I could redeem myself.*

> *I do not even have enough money to get my teeth fixed. I am now living in a camper on the back of a truck in a friend's field, paying $1 a day for electricity, so the IRS can't serve me, and to buy time while waiting for the diamond mine to come in."*

A strong believer in Urban Casavant and CMKX, `silverbulletgirl` described herself as a "13 year breast cancer survivor and a 7 year naked short fighter-survivor." She wanted to provide a better life for those closest to her, including her two children. `silverbulletgirl` never wavered in her belief that CMKX would pay off. She encouraged others to fight naked short selling in the stock market:

> *"I feel so blessed everyday in my life and thank God everyday for the things I do have and am not upset for the things I don't. I leave you with the famous words of my father 'Big Jack' who died in 1988 of yes, cancer, he always said 'NO ONE EVER SAID IT WAS GOING TO BE EASY' when he spoke of life, and guess what? HE WAS RIGHT!"*

Along with those who shared their experiences, there were thousands more whose stories remain locked behind closed doors. Some, like the two brothers who used their interest in CMKX as a common bond to strengthen their relationship, found positives in their investment decisions. Howie Romans, like Kevin West before him, was motivated to become a stock market reform advocate, creating a group called the "CMKX Shareholders Coalition for Market Reform."

Still, many shareholders' losses were considerable, leaving many hopelessly in debt, their personal lives in shambles and teetering on an emotional cliff. Threats of suicide weren't uncommon. Those who were on the receiving end of despondent emails from shareholders often had little more to give in the way of support than a few kind words of sympathy. In a letter posted to CMKX shareholders, John Martin detailed some of the reasons that Bill Frizzell was dedicating so much time and energy towards salvaging something positive for the shareholders:

> *"We have calls almost daily from those who fear they have lost everything. Widows who have no one to rely on who have dumped all their money into this company; people with cancer who are trying to make one last effort at supplying income for their family before they die; seasoned investors who have in excess of a million dollars at risk. The stories go on and on and on. We are almost in tears some days with the stories, as well as the cries for help."*

They could feel the pressure, stress, and resentment building steadily on the boards, and wondered when it would reach a breaking point. As someone posting under the name of Marino so aptly put it, those spreading the unfounded rumors of riches and massive payouts "may not be the cause of the people standing on the cliff, but they are pushing them over the edge."

pro Mi se!!!

IF it is proveN THaT THis CmKx THiNg HaS been a well orchestrated

Scam!

THose Responsible will be HUNTED down (urban, mchen ect.) will be HUNTED down + SHOT TO feel

DeATH!!!

A fax sent to Bill Frizzell's office. Courtesy of CMKM Diamonds, Inc.

Chapter 29 – I Have a Bad Feeling About This...

"Has anyone seen the truth? I seem to have lost it three years ago."
~teamplayersbc, *Sterling's Classroom*, July 18, 2006

By September of 2006, discontent on the message boards had given way to despair, frustration, and outright anger. The shareholder's comment that unfounded rumors of riches and massive payouts could be responsible for pushing some sharheolders over the edge of the cliff seemed to be coming true. Bill Frizzell's office even received death threats. They were mostly directed at company insiders, but the anger often extended to Frizzell and John Martin, and even at times to those who were simply trying to cover the story from a journalistic viewpoint. Any disparaging comments about CMKX were taken as a direct affront to the shareholders themselves.

The Bill Gates as CEO rumors were still circulating, but most shareholders would have been happy with any major player who Urban brought in to finish the job that should have been completed months, or even years ago. After a year in which the company only issued three press releases, compared to over fifty PR's during CMKX's glory days of 2004, the rumors and speculation proliferated. The promises of imminent wealth and riches continued, and one enterprising person even issued a press release (quickly exposed as a fake) reportedly from CMKX. It claimed that "certain parties" had been arrested for attempting to defraud shareholders, and that they would receive $1.61 per share in the negotiated settlement, along with "additional future cash distributions."

At the other end of the emotional spectrum, there were those who were losing patience with the barrage of unsubstantiated claims and unfulfilled promises, and tried to expose the Accas, Manos, Wodens and Jay-Adobes of the internet world as purveyors of false hope and rumors. A poster called Primate on the *CMKX.net* message board said:

> I would just like to know what makes the promise of news
> by the end of May any better than the promise of news at
> the end of April, and the end of March, and the end of
> February, and the end of January, and the end of December,
> and the end of November, and the end of October, and the end
> of September, Oh, and lets not forget the news in between
> at about two week intervals we've been promised. All
> these clowns need to be b!tch slapped by each and every
> shareholder multiple times at the very least. Does it
> make them feel special to outright lie to people and play
> on their last bit of hope? To what end is this big game
> going to come? I may not be the sharpest crayon in the box,
> but I am pretty confident that I am not going to become a
> millionaire off my thousand dollar investment.

Then, on September 19, 2006, Urban finally came through on his promise of hiring a new CEO. After rumors of legendary business icons Warren Buffet or Bill Gates taking over the company, Urban's choice to act as interim CEO was someone that no one, including those closest to the person chosen, could have possibly predicted:

LAS VEGAS--(BUSINESS WIRE)--Sept. 19, 2006--CMKM Diamonds Inc. has named a shareholder, Kevin West, as the new Interim Chief Executive Officer of the Company.

Mr. West has worked for the past 18 months in an effort to help determine those shareholders that are holding viable equity in the Company. First, through a brokerage statement fax-in campaign initiated by attorney Bill Frizzell and the CMKX Owners Group, and then the most recent cert pull conducted on behalf of the now-dissolved CMKM Task Force. The knowledge gained during this process will prove invaluable in helping the Company to move forward.

'I would like to welcome Mr. West as an Interim Officer of the Company,' stated a Director and Chairman of the Board, Urban Casavant.

'Mr. Casavant has asked me to help him with the day-to-day operations of the Company. The details before us are going to require a bit of time and complete focus to make sure that they are done correctly,' stated Mr. West.

Interim company CEO Kevin West. Courtesy of CMKM Diamonds, Inc.

As always, the boards reacted immediately. In this case, the reaction wasn't entirely favorable, especially since many had hoped for a high-profile name in the CEO position. Those who actually knew Kevin trusted him to add integrity and honesty to the company's front office, something that seemed to be sorely lacking up to that time. But it wasn't long before his almost reverential devotion to Urban was brought into question. His "Urban Casavant is a Godly man and God is using him to re-distribute the wealth on this earth" comment was reposted on several message boards, often with opinions that Urban had purposely hired a True Believer to appease the shareholders and stall for more time. The fact that Urban had pulled both Uncle Melvi and Andy Hill from the shareholder ranks and made them a part of the company did little to soothe apprehensions.

On the same day, Bill Frizzell issued an update of his own, supporting Kevin as interim CEO, and reassuring shareholders that Urban had picked the right man for the job. He said they had known for a couple of weeks that Kevin was in negotiations with Urban, but hadn't spoken with him in detail. He called it "a good day for the shareholders of CMKX stock," and described Kevin as knowledgeable and a "dedicated advocate for the shareholder." Frizzell went on to say:

> *"Hiring Kevin tells me the company is dead serious about the matters that were covered in the last press release of the company. It is clear evidence to me that an interpleader will be filed. It is an indication to me that efforts are being made by the company to have its stock trade again. How long it will take is anyone's guess, but I believe Kevin will move as quickly as he is allowed to move.*
>
> *There will be some who will criticize Kevin's hiring. Some will say this is a stall tactic or another token gesture to appease the shareholder group we have put together. This would be quite an error in judgment on the part of CMKM management if Kevin were hired for such reasons."*

He closed his update by acknowledging that "Kevin may not be Bill Gates or Warren Buffett, but he has a unique ability to calmly analyze troublesome situations and apply common sense solutions." He cited his honesty and moral character more than once, saying he had "never lived a lifestyle that we often see when corporate greed overtakes the obligations to work in the best interests of the shareholders."

Behind the scenes, the talks had been detailed and in depth. After Urban first approached Kevin in the middle of August, he set up a conference call with Michael Williams, who suddenly seemed to be involved in every CMKX decision. It was Williams who first told Kevin they were interested in hiring him as the new CEO, saying that Urban needed to "step away from the position."

Kevin went to John Martin and Bill Frizzell and told them about the offer. Bill and John recalled the meeting when Kevin first broke the news about being contacted by Urban:

> John: *"Kevin asked Bill and me to come downstairs because he wanted to talk to us about something. He told us that he had been contacted by Urban about going to work for CMKX, but he didn't mention the CEO job. I remember*

being very angry at first and spouting off something, and Bill just leaned back in his chair, and then he said 'Now, wait a minute John.'"

Bill: *"I think it's fair to say that we were for him getting involved, but we certainly had concerns about what it was he was getting involved in. I remember saying 'What are you being asked to be CEO of? Satisfy yourself that there are real assets in the company that you're being asked to take charge of, and not just liabilities.'"*

John: *"Of course, we were going at it from an entirely different angle. Kevin firmly believed that he was going to find everything that the shareholders had been promised there. Bill and I were scared to death for him, but at the same time, we wanted to make certain that Kevin realized they might be setting him up, and that he went in knowing that that could be the case. And even though we knew that Kevin believed in the company, we also were confident that if he went in there and found out that things weren't right, he would come back and share what he learned with Bill. Plus, this was going to be a way for us to be certain that we weren't stepping on toes if we were to do something proactive."*

Bill: *"In my mind, I was thinking 'Could these people be so arrogant that they could pluck someone like Kevin out of our office and use him... to have him take a position just to pacify the shareholders for their own purposes?' In my mind, I was thinking 'No, they couldn't be that stupid.' It was inconceivable to me at that time, so I thought I had reason to be optimistic. There was a time period before he accepted the job of interim CEO where we would email back and forth, we'd be asking him for information, and he was stonewalling us. John and I were still continuing our quest to get information for the shareholders. And there was a little period there where it was like 'What the hell's going on?'"*

John: *"Bill always understood it from a legal standpoint, and from Kevin's standpoint of being loyal. I remember several conversations where I verbalized to Bill that I thought we had lost him. I really felt like he had turned that corner. There were times that we were getting emails saying that he couldn't tell us anything, but there were a lot of times where we got no communication for months."*

Even after going through boxes and boxes of evidence from the SEC, and accompanying Frizzell and Martin on investigative trips, Kevin still hadn't lost faith in Urban Casavant. On September 6th, the morning before Kevin was to sign the contract with Urban and after a couple of weeks of soul-searching with his wife Angela, he sent Urban an email pledging his loyalty and commitment to the job:

"My wife and I have been talking a great deal over the last two weeks about where we are in our life and what we believe is to be our destiny now and in the future. We believe in our hearts that we were meant to be part of helping to bring your dream about for all of these shareholders and their families. As you said before, it is fate.

That said, we believe and trust in whatever decisions you make today...any decision, even if you choose for us not to be involved from this point forward. Although, we feel we are supposed to be and very much want to be part of this. You must do what you feel is the right move as you have been working on this for many years of not only your life, but also the lives of your family.

We are aware of the length of the journey ahead and the bashing and threats that will come our way. This does not concern us as we are very strong willed people. It would be easy to stay here and go back to work for John and Bill going through the week on a normal schedule from 8am to 5pm, Monday through Friday and always be together at night."

He ended his email by pledging his loyalty and support, saying they were "ready to pick up and move wherever you need to move us to make this work." He said he was willing to leave his family in Texas and travel most of the time if necessary, or that they would "move down the street from you in Canada," if that was what the job required. He ended with "Total dedication to help make this work is what you will get, you have not only my word, but our word as husband and wife," and signed it from "Kevin and Angela."

It became immediately apparent to Kevin that Michael Williams was an integral part of every decision, almost to the point where at times he seemed to exert more control than Casavant himself. Every trip to Las Vegas would entail waiting for hours until Williams arrived at meetings or to pick Kevin up at his hotel. Some days he wouldn't show up at all. When he did, he made it a point to mention the names of famous people he knew, and was constantly on the phone. During one phone call right after the first time he picked up Kevin, Williams left a message that said "It's really important, Bob's been trying to get ahold of me all day." Kevin of course assumed he was trying to get in touch with Bob Maheu. In a later phone call, Williams mentioned Global Intelligence partner Kevin Ryan, saying "Well, make sure you get some for Kevin Ryan too, I know he'll want some of that." It just reinforced what Kevin West already believed, and seemed to confirm that Maheu and the Global Intelligence organization were still behind the scenes taking care of the shareholders.

The next morning, Williams took Kevin West to meet with John T. Moran III, the attorney working on the interpleader motion. Kevin later recalled the first thing that caught his eye as they walked into the conference room in Moran's office:

"I should've known something wasn't right just by the picture on the wall. Basically, it was these people that are looking devilish, their ears are all pointed and they're red and they're picking on their clients, taking money from them. This was in the conference room, a big huge picture. J.T. walked in and the first thing he did was give Michael a hug and shake my hand, the double hand shake thing, 'The pleasure is all mine.' He turned around and he had a little rip in his pocket and said 'Can you believe these $4,000 suits rip just like the cheap ones?' And that was the second thing that struck me as wrong; I was like 'Here I am wearing my brand new $89 blazer from J.C. Penny's.'"

Before every meeting, Williams would spend fifteen minutes in private with the attorneys before allowing Kevin to join them, and in the attorneys' offices it was Williams calling the shots. He would go on about how they were going to file the interpleader and save the company, but then he mentioned for the first time that they were planning to "sell off about half a million dollars worth of the Entourage stock" to pay additional attorneys' fees and reimburse Urban. Even though Kevin voiced his opposition to the plan, they told him Urban had no money, and that was the only way to finance the legal work required to file the interpleader. They said they wanted to complete the paperwork within the next two weeks and have it filed by mid-September. At least that was something he could count on. Finally, a definite date that would move the plan to the next phase.

The scenario that the hundreds of billions of shares authorized by Roger Glenn and the other CMKX attorneys had either never been sold into the market or had been repurchased by the company seemed as plausible as ever to Kevin. And since Maheu was still involved, it was obviously only a matter of time before Iron Bob would expose Edwards and his cronies, as well as the world's largest brokerage firms who had been flooding the market with hundreds of billions of shares of counterfeit stock.

At the urging of Bill and John, Kevin pushed the company to issue a press release about the interpleader, the first news released by CMKX in over five months. Kevin even wrote the PR with Williams, while Moran edited the section describing their plans to file the interpleader to force the brokers to open up their books and reveal who actually held real shares of CMKX stock. He finalized his contract with Urban and Michael Williams in early September, giving up $1,500 per month of the salary they had offered him in exchange for a promise that they would rent office space and hire a secretary.

After signing the contract with Urban, Kevin flew back to Las Vegas to meet with Moran, eager to move forward with the interpleader. He drove to Moran's office with Urban Casavant's brother Ron, but as they were walking up the front steps of the office building, Moran's secretary called Kevin on his cell phone and cancelled the appointment, saying he had a last minute meeting with another client. A phone call from Kevin to Moran ended in an argument, with Kevin already feeling as if they were stalling him. He returned to Tyler the next day without meeting with Moran in person and without seeing either Urban or Michael Williams.

It was a couple of weeks later that Kevin returned to Vegas, with meetings arranged once again with Urban and Moran, except this time J.T. set up the meeting without Williams present. Kevin immediately noticed a difference in Moran's demeanor:

> *"We went to see Moran, he got us into his office on schedule and was being really courteous and acting professional, this was the only time Michael wasn't there. He said 'Urban, I'm ready to put my staff full time on this. The interpleader was a little more complicated than we thought and it's gonna take me two weeks and I'm gonna put everybody to work on it. But I need 150 grand and I need it before I can start.' Urban looked really nervous and I couldn't understand what was going on. I still had this idea that there might really be a sting going on. I was thinking 'he must be nervous because he's hiding something from me,' all these things kept going through my head. Urban, in every conversation with me, would say 'I gotta take you through this one step at a time, we can't get ahead...' Urban, sat there and thought for a minute, and the first thing he said was 'Well, I can do that in payments, right?' Moran said, 'No, I've got to have that $150,000. It's just like running a business, if you're under a budget...'"*

In the meantime, Urban still hadn't given Kevin the money to rent an office or hire a secretary. Kevin paid for the cell phone he was using as a temporary company phone, with promises from Urban that he would be reimbursed. Even on his trip to Vegas to finalize the contracts, Kevin was staying at a "low rent hotel on the bad side of town, where I was even afraid to walk across the street to the convenience store." On later trips to Vegas, when Urban was there from Canada, he and Ron Casavant would pick up Kevin from the airport and drive directly to the bank. Urban would withdraw stacks of hundred dollar bills, which would be gone by the time the trip was over.

In October, Urban called Kevin and told him that Moran had been paid and was serious about finishing the interpleader. Kevin returned to Las Vegas but once again, he spent most of his time in the hotel room with both Urban and Moran seemingly avoiding him. Urban later expressed his own frustration with the situation, saying that both Moran and Williams were avoiding him as well. Kevin West was beginning to question the motives of those who surrounded Urban, especially Michael Williams and J.T. Moran, who both seemed to be manipulating Urban for their own personal gain. Kevin recounted that trip to Vegas, which unfortunately set a pattern of events that seemed to happen every time he was there:

> *"Urban had been calling J.T. all the time. Mike was telling us one thing and J.T. was telling us another, and then J.T. would cancel meetings. Then Michael would do his usual thing where he wouldn't return phone calls, and Urban was just getting more and more frustrated. But there were things I didn't know*

yet. *Michael was money-motivated. If Urban didn't have any cash, Michael was hard to get ahold of. When Urban had cash it was an entirely different story. Urban even told me one time that when he was 'cashed up,' as he called it, that 'he humps my leg like a puppy dog.' The interpleader was supposed to be finished and I hadn't even done anything on it yet...I hadn't even seen it.*"

PART FIVE

"The gem cannot be polished without friction nor man perfected without trials."
~Confucius

NASD Charges NevWest in CMKX Saga...
Justice at Last?

By Mark Faulk
September 26, 2006
www.faulkingtruth.com

In a saga that many thought was dead-on-arrival, the NASD today filed charges against NevWest Securities Corporation of Las Vegas, and company President Sergey Rumyantsev and Vice President Antony M. Santos. They charged the company and its officers with violating NASD's Anti-Money Laundering Rule, saying that they failed to file Suspicious Activity Reports ('SAR'), or cease trading in multiple accounts owned and controlled by JE, NevWest's customer, regarding over 500 transactions. Edwards traded over 250 billion shares of stock issued by CMKM Diamonds, Inc. totaling over $53 million. In the 28-page complaint, the NASD also charged NevWest with failing to file SARs or halt wire transfers "involving $43 million through 139 separate wires from at least 28 of the accounts JE had opened at NevWest to various bank accounts."

They were the first charges brought in a story that began in late 2002 (or even earlier including the earlier incarnation of CMKM Diamonds), and might have come to an end on October 28, 2005, when Administrative Law Judge Brenda Murray officially revoked CMKM's (commonly referred to by its trading symbol CMKX) reporting status, after the company withdrew its appeal of Judge Murray's initial ruling against the company for failure to file required financial reports with the SEC.

However, this was one company that simply refused to die. Bolstered by over 50,000 shareholders and an advocacy group begun by CMKX shareholder John Martin and represented by attorney Bill Frizzell, the CMKX Owners Group worked their way into the SEC hearings, and continued to press for action against the various people involved in what they perceived as a massive fraud extending into every corner of the financial market process, including not only numerous individuals who took advantage of a system rife with loopholes and poorly enforced SEC regulations, but implicating nearly every major brokerage firm in the U.S. and Canada.

In fact, in a letter to then CMKX attorney Donald Stoecklein over a year ago, Owners Group attorney Bill Frizzell called for the company to take legal action against several of the people who he named as being involved in the scheme to defraud tens of thousands of CMKX shareholders, with John Michael Edwards, or "JE," at the top of the list. He specifically cited the 36 NevWest trust accounts, along with another 20 additional companies that have addresses in Langley, B.C., and are owned and controlled by Edwards. In addition to Edwards and NevWest, Frizzell named company auditor Neil Levine (who was brought into CMKX by Edwards), CFO David DeSormeau, "consultant" James Kinney, secretary Ginger

Gutierrez, and attorney Brian Dvorak as individuals who were involved in the problems with CMKX.

NevWest President Sergey Rumyantsev said today "In our perception, we believe that we have fail-safes in effect that go far above and beyond the industry standards. We feel completely wronged in this particular case." Rumyantsev also questioned the NASD's action against their company, saying "We were singled out, why were we the only one charged when hundreds of billions of shares were sold by other brokers?"

Another source close to the story echoed Rumyantsev's sentiments, citing the serious problems with other major brokerage firms, including Ameritrade and E*trade, and the long and drawn out process of trying to issue stock certificates to bona fide shareholders. Many have still not received stock certificates over a year after the company initiated a cert pull in an attempt to determine if there were more shares sold than actually existed.

In the meantime, many questions remain in the CMKX saga. Why has it taken so long for regulatory agencies to take action against those who defrauded over 50,000 shareholders, and why hasn't the SEC taken any action whatsoever? It was reported last week in a court document involving John Edward's wife Diana Lee Flaherty's own stock fraud trial that Edwards himself is still under investigation for stock fraud, and there are unconfirmed reports of a major sting operation targeting dozens of others involved in the CMKX scandal.

In the broader sense, the sheer scope of this scam, and the reported massive selling of counterfeit stock into the market that accompanied it, raises serious questions as to the system of checks and balances that protects our stock market. Let's just hope that the investigations don't stop there, and that the major brokers are held responsible for their part in this financial train wreck, and that the SEC itself is made to answer for their ineptitude and failure to "protect investors and maintain the integrity of the securities market."

Chapter 30 – The Wheels of Justice

"I don't want to say dates because it's very complicated, but I'd like to say that we're weeks away from completing our investigation and issuing indictments."

~ FBI Agent Ryan Randall, discussing federal investigations into CMKX

While Kevin West was pushing the company to complete and file the interpleader, other events were transpiring behind the scenes on the federal level. Department of Justice prosecutors filed a motion in mid-September protesting the release on bail of John Edwards' wife Diana Lee Flaherty. They noted that Flaherty might be a flight risk, but even the fact that Edwards himself was under investigation didn't stop the judge from granting Flaherty's bail. The attorney representing Diana Lee Flaherty was Sherwood Cook, who was also appointed to be Flaherty's third party custodian to assure she didn't flee the country while free on bail.

On September 29, 2006, it was confirmed on *The Faulking Truth Show* on *CFRN.net* that "the FBI and two other federal agencies" were conducting an extensive investigation into CMKX and several people involved with the company. FBI agent Ryan Randall of the Las Vegas division said "the FBI and two other federal agencies had been working together for quite some time" independently of the SEC, taking a team approach to bring charges against those who had defrauded investors in the company. It was the first real indication that justice might be realized. Randall had a long list of people targeted in their investigation, a list that included, among others, John Edwards, Mike King, Gary Walters, Rendal Williams…and Urban Casavant.

In a private interview, FBI agent Randall said there were "thousands of investors who didn't want to admit that they would never see their money again," and described it as "a scam from the very beginning." He said "there isn't a whole lot that we can do to fix the damage, but we can make sure it doesn't happen again." Randall also said groups like the one who scammed CMKX shareholders had "pretty much destroyed the microcap market," and followed up by saying "I believe that if we can bring down this group that it will eliminate 80% of the fraud in the state of Nevada." Randall said his goal was to help "take down every one of these guys, and then take a long vacation." As for Urban Casavant's involvement in the scam, agent Randall didn't mince words: "He's as bad as the rest of them. At the very least, he's right in the middle of it, even if he didn't mastermind the whole thing."

Another federal agent, Timothy Vasquez of the Department of Justice, who headed the investigation into Robert and Diana Lee Flaherty in the Phoenix Metals stock fraud case, said when it came to dealing with fraud in the penny stock market, "they had serious issues with the way that the SEC handled their investigations." Ryan Randall agreed, saying that the SEC had only supplied them with partial documentation in the case, implying they didn't have access to the thousands of documents Bill Frizzell had at his disposal while representing John Martin and the CMKX Owners Group. Vasquez did confirm that CMKX was under formal investigation by both the FBI and the DOJ. FBI agent Randall later said that agent Charyn Aldred was heading the efforts for the IRS Criminal Investigation Division.

But the FBI, DOJ, and the IRS weren't the only people interested in the world of CMKX. Shareholders raised questions about the NASD's singling out of NevWest while ignoring potential violations by larger firms such as E*Trade and Ameritrade. NevWest's CEO Rumyantsev raised valid concerns that they alone were charged "when hundreds of billions of shares were sold by other brokers."

Bill Frizzell had also voiced questions about the Jeffries letter admitted as evidence in the SEC revocation hearing for CMKX. While NevWest brokered the sale of the 250 billion shares of stock, those same sales had to be cleared through a larger broker or clearing house. Frizzell stated:

> *"The letter from Jeffries and Co. brokerage firm was sent to the NASD after the CMKX Owners Group began the brokerage statement fax campaign four days before the revocation hearing of May 10, 2005. The letter was a response to requests from the NASD concerning 'Jeffries failure to report certain transactions' specifically 'two broker dealer customers approached Jeffries requesting that transactions in CMKX be settled on an ex-clearing basis.' Jefferies said that they made a 'business and operational risk decision to allow a limited number of broker dealer customers' who were long sellers of CMKX to settle the trades 'Ex-Clearing.'"*

Frizzell went on to say that since the brokers traded the huge number of shares outside the system to avoid putting up the substantial deposit required for such large volume, Jeffries should have filed a "Suspicious Activity Report" of their own. He also asked:

> *"If the NASD knew about the suspicious trading activities because of the Jeffries letter in May of '05, why did they wait over a year to file charges, and why didn't they file similar charges against Jeffries? Why would the NASD allow the major brokers like Jeffries to circumvent the rules, while instead singling out the 'little guys' like NevWest? If anyone should know the rules and be held accountable, it should be the major brokers. I don't think that the NASD ever intended to expose them. Surely the SEC and NASD have a system of checks and balances whereby they share information to make sure that the markets run smoothly and efficiently."*

Frizzell also speculated about whether NevWest was one of the brokers who approached them about clearing the trades outside of the trading system, as required by law:

> *"The trades occurred from March through September of 2004, which corresponds with the time frame and number of shares dumped by NevWest*

during this period. If NevWest is in fact the client that Jeffries cites in their response letter to the NASD, then Jeffries clearly violated the very same regulations that NevWest was charged with violating.

In the month of July 05 alone, Jeffries did 80 transactions involving CMKX through Ex-Clearing. Jeffries announced record revenues for the third quarter ending Sept 30, 05, with total revenues up 29% and net earnings up 20% over the prior year. Jeffries is the clearinghouse, were they responsible to determine that any trades cleared through their firm were legal?"

While neither the NASD nor the SEC took action against the larger brokers and the clearinghouses, the SEC didn't file charges against John Edwards or *any* of the other individuals involved. Instead, it was left up to the federal government's criminal branches and the industry's own regulatory organization to clean up their mess.

The CMKX story itself was finally attracting some national attention because of the NASD charges, with articles printed in the *New York Times* on September 29, 2006, and in the *Denver Post* a couple of weeks later. *The New York Times* article, written by Floyd Norris and entitled "Selling Shares by the Billions to Racing Fans," opened by asking questions no one seemed able to definitively answer:

"Was this stock being traded by crooks? Should the brokers have noticed? How about the regulators, who now charge that the brokers missed 'red flags' but may have missed a few themselves?

The story of a tiny Nevada company that claimed to be in the diamond mining business but spent the little money it had on sponsoring a race car, sheds light on the market for small stocks that can fly below the radar for years."

Norris later posted in an online blog that he was deluged with emails from irate CMKX shareholders. He added details that weren't included in his earlier article, and linked John Edwards to former company auditor Neil Levine and transfer agent Helen Bagley. Then, Norris responded to angry CMKX shareholders who claimed he ignored the issue of naked short selling:

"So who are shareholders mad at? The management? The man who sold more than a third of the shares outstanding without ever filing a form saying he owned more than 5 percent, and who may have been an insider? The S.E.C. for letting this go on for a couple of years before revoking the company's registration, or for having not yet brought any charges against J.E. for selling them shares that may well be worthless?

No, not any of them. A few shareholders who contacted me today were furious about my column because it failed to identify the real villains, as they saw it — the naked short sellers who they say sold the shares without borrowing them."

By contrast, the *Denver Post* article printed on October 15, 2006 and written by Will Shanley, dealt directly with the stock counterfeiting issue, using the term in the title: "Outcry Grows Over Naked Short Selling." That article detailed the story of a CMKX shareholder named Carol Pederson, who invested $15,000 in the company after hearing on the internet chat rooms about the one million plus acres of mineral rights they held.

In what many shareholders saw as a validation of CMKX's rumored naked short selling problems, Shanley quoted SEC Chairman Christopher Cox's comments in a July, 2006 speech. Cox said that naked short selling is a "serious problem" that can "drive down a company's stock price to the detriment of all of its investors." Shanley also quoted Overstock.com CEO Patrick Byrne, who asserted "The system is rigged...I've gone from golden boy to public enemy No. 1 for trying to expose this." Byrne also said "Brokerage firms sometimes short-sell more shares than have even been issued."

Shanley went on to address the other side of the issue that fraudulent companies had begun to use the possibility of naked short selling as a cover for dumping *real* shares of stock into the market:

"Yet some companies claiming to be hurt by naked short sellers have other problems and are perhaps using short sellers as an excuse to cloak their own mismanagement or fraud, experts say. Some company executives even naked short-sell shares of their own firms as new investors buy in, a twist on the classic pump-and-dump scheme, they say.

'You have two separate types of companies that talk about naked short selling', said Mark Faulk, an Oklahoma City-based author preparing to release a book later this year about CMKM. 'This company, by my estimation, is not a good poster child for the problems associated with naked short selling.'

The company, Faulk said, used unusual promotional tactics to create an 'obsessed' legion of investors. The company plastered its stock ticker on billboards and on the side of a racecar and even handed out free shares.

Faulk estimates that investors lost $250 million or more and that at least three government agencies are investigating it. He said it's unclear whether CMKM knowingly defrauded investors; the company owned mineral rights to some land in Canada that initial tests showed could contain diamonds, he said. Attempts to contact CMKM officials were unsuccessful."

Shanley ended his article with an ominous quote from CMKX shareholder Carol Pederson, who said "I wouldn't put my money in Wall Street until there are changes. This is bigger than anyone realizes."

Chapter 31 – Revelations

"Urban, I have three words for you: Switzerland, Germany, Austria. Those are countries that don't extradite back to the U.S."

~John T. Moran, III, in a meeting with Urban Casavant and Kevin West

Christmas was nearing again, and for the shareholders of CMKX, it was a bitter reminder of the struggles and unfulfilled promises of the prior two years, and a beacon of hope that this Christmas would be different. None of the main players in the CMKX saga had been arrested or charged with any crimes, and it began to look as if the entire process was stalled. Adding to the frustration, the company went silent again after the announcement of Kevin West's hiring. The tension on the message boards seemed to be reaching a breaking point.

Kevin West, hindered by the company in his efforts to communicate with the shareholders, felt the pressure most of all. With every trip to Las Vegas he felt more isolated, always spending the majority of his time waiting in hotel rooms. Even staying at the opulent Venetian Resort Hotel and Casino didn't help, especially since the rooms at the Venetian were comped. At the Venetian they called it the Venetian Players Club, with the slogan "High class play with higher class pay." Up to this point, Kevin had never seen Urban after eight in the evening. He had no idea how he spent his nights…or how much company money he gambled away to "earn" his membership as a high-roller in the Venetian Players Club.

On one of his early trips to Vegas after yet another fruitless meeting with the attorneys, J.T. Moran gave Urban a stack of cards that had been sent by shareholders for Urban's birthday. There were over fifty cards ranging in size from standard-sized to the huge novelty cards. It was obvious to Kevin that the people who had sent the cards had put real time, money, and effort into sending their best wishes to Urban. Kevin later said:

> *"When we got into the Lincoln Navigator, I picked up the cards and I set them neatly in the seat thinking he's going to go home and read these tonight. Then, about a month later, I was back in Las Vegas and Ron picked me up at the airport again. I put my luggage in the very back and I saw all the cards sitting back there unopened, just thrown back and piled every which way, so it was obvious that Urban never even looked at them. It really bothered me."*

Even if Urban neglected to read the cards from his many followers, at least one persistent shareholder claimed to reach him by phone. In a message posted on *Proboards29*, `JoeRockss` recounted a conversation with Urban on December 7, Urban's 50th birthday:

> `Just talked to the man himself. The call lasted about 15 minutes...In one word....unreal.`

> To start, this man is genuinely nice and shared many personal things about his life with me this time and gave me a reason to be excited about CMKX again.
>
> I said "Mr. Casavant, you must feel like you have the weight of the world on your shoulders."
>
> Then he said, "That weight is about to be lifted, shortly. Did you ever see a U-Haul truck following a hearse?"
>
> I said, "No, what do you mean?"
>
> He said, "You can't take it with you and I plan on spreading it around."
>
> He said, "I love waking up in the morning with no enemies."
>
> He also said that he, Carolyn and the attorneys are working on this thing relentlessly.
>
> Just like the last conversation, he said, "Everything's gonna be fine. Just be patient."

"Just be patient." It had been the battle cry of the CMKX faithful, including Kevin West, for almost four years. While Urban was promising to spread the wealth among the CMKX shareholders, he was months behind on Kevin's salary, and had run up a $1,600 cell phone bill that Kevin was paying for out of his own pocket:

> *"One of those trips to Vegas, he knows he's got to give me at least a couple of months pay and he comes in and pulls out a billfold full of cash. He goes, 'I've got something that's taking place today, tonight, I'll be able to get you your pay tomorrow. Go ahead and get your room and stuff and I'll be over here in this little room.' I met him over there and he was feeding $100 bills in these machines. It was the high-rollers room, where all the big gamblers were. Ron was there sitting next to Urban, and Urban was feeding hundred dollar bills one after the other into his machine and Ron's machine...'"*

Because it was the first time Kevin had seen Urban gamble, he tried to write it off as an isolated incident. He spent the rest of the week with Ron, waiting for the interpleader to be finished. The excuses became more creative as time went by. There was the usual "two days away from being finished" excuse, or the time an assistant had it on his laptop and his mom was sick so he left the office. Another time, they were connected with someone who was supposedly doing the actual interpleader...and he turned out to be an assistant still in law school:

> *"Later that night Urban said they sent him the first few pages and he was sure everything was on the right track. All they had sent him was Urban's statement, and the two pages that I had put together as a Task Force statement.*

I knew that Urban had borrowed $80,000 using the Juina Mining stock as collateral, which was supposed to go into the bank account but never did. I called him every day, 'we're out of money, I don't have money for the kids' Christmas,' and then all of a sudden, two days before Christmas, Urban said, 'I just put $7500 in your account. I'm sorry buddy, that's all I've got. I'm going home with a dollar in my pocket.' He was always going home with a dollar in his pocket."

The week before Christmas, Kevin decided to force the issue. He had his brother call a close friend who posted regularly on the message boards, and started a campaign to bombard Moran's office with phone calls, emails, and faxes from CMKX shareholders in an effort to motivate Moran to finish the interpleader by the end of January. The effect was so overwhelming that the shareholders basically shut down Moran's office, making it impossible for them to do anything but answer phones, emails, and faxes.

In response, the company issued a press release on December 20, 2006, stating they had "met with their corporate attorney, John T. Moran III" and "discovered additional Company information that dictated further investigation and due diligence" so the interpleader could be filed. Then they promised follow-up releases every thirty days, which only made matters worse. After years of pent-up frustration, no one wanted to wait another thirty days for the interpleader to be filed, much less for a monthly status report. According to Kevin:

"Some of the shareholders got pissed off because of the PR and they bombarded his office with phone calls and emails again. His secretary got a message to me to call J.T.'s office immediately. I called and J.T.'s dad was screaming and yelling at me, ripping me up one side and down the other, because his office was being shut down. When he finally quit ranting and raging I said, 'Look, I have no control over these shareholders, they're frustrated.' He said, 'We agreed to take you guys on as a client...and if we don't get this stopped right away we're backing out.' Then J.T. jumped on the phone to show off for daddy and he said, 'Here's exactly what's going to happen, you're going to release another PR right now, you're going to put a phone number on there, you're going to call it a hotline and we're going to get these phone calls stopped to our office.' So after four months of no PRs at all, we put out two in one day."

The obvious reason for releasing the first PR was to convince the shareholders to quit harassing Moran. An hour later, they released another:

"CMKM Diamonds, Inc. has set up a new phone number that will be answered by Interim CEO Kevin West during regular market hours to help address shareholder questions and concerns."

Kevin spent the next couple of weeks fielding phone calls from one shareholder after another, with every conversation immediately relayed back to the various message boards. One phone call in particular had a major impact on Kevin:

271

"I was talking to shareholders and they were crying their hearts out to me on the phone. I had a few people that started out irate but they asked their questions and I answered them, and they would calm down.

Then I got a message from somebody named Marc. When I returned the call someone named Connie answered. I said, 'Connie who?' She said, 'Connie Cohen, the motorcycle racer.' At first she started off very hostile but then she realized that she was yelling at the wrong guy. She told me the whole thing, that Urban guaranteed them a three-year contract. He talked them into selling their business and buying a motor home, trailer, and motorcycles on credit. You have to realize with what they were doing there are a lot of expenses. With the bikes you have to change the engines out after two or three runs. Although she got some money from Urban, he ended up not paying her most of the money he promised.'"

The Cohens ended up owing $250,000, with an additional $30,000 in credit card debt. Ron Casavant would regularly promise them that money was on the way, eerily reminiscent of the "checks in the mail" rumors shareholders had been hearing for years. According to Marc Cohen, Ron and Urban were worried that if they quit racing, "shareholders would know the company was falling apart."

After almost four months of empty promises from Moran and Williams culminating with the phone call to Connie Cohen, Kevin knew he had to take matters into his own hands:

"I called Urban and I said, 'You know how we always talked about wanting to bring somebody in and go after the people that screwed the company in the past? I think we need to bring Bill Frizzell in.' Urban says, 'Yeah, you tell Bill that's my idea...you tell him.' I wasn't going to tell him that.

The second week of January, Bill came out to Vegas. We went to the meeting with J.T. and Urban on one side, and Bill and me on the other side of the table. As usual, nobody wanted to start the meeting because Michael Williams wasn't there yet. Bill couldn't figure that out either, he was going, 'What's Michael Williams got to do with anything?'

Michael showed up and he had a can of Go Fast. He sat down at the table and he said, 'What do you think of the new label?' He was showing Urban. I said, 'what's that?' And Michael said, 'Urban saved this company, he put two or three million dollars into it at a time when they were on the verge of either making it or not and now they just signed a contract with Wal-Mart.' Urban said, 'Yep, now I'm getting twelve cents per case for life.'"

Frizzell remembered the meeting as being nothing more than a way for Moran to pacify him after he asked the company to take action against John Edwards and other company insiders. He had been talking to Kevin sporadically over the past few months, putting pressure on him to make something happen for the shareholders. Kevin said that after a while, he had begun to feel like he was letting both Bill and the shareholders down. By the time Frizzell found himself sitting in Moran's office, listening to them talk about how much money Urban was going to make off of the Go Fast deal with Wal-Mart, he knew they were wasting their time:

> *"There was no doubt in my mind that the interpleader was not going to happen. I thought it was a big joke. Nothing good came out of it for the shareholders and I knew something bad was going on at that point. They were talking about putting the company in bankruptcy, distributing the stock through an interpleader and paying all these lawyer fees to Moran and David Chesnoff, paying back Urban, and just draining the only resource that the shareholders apparently had at that point. It was just sickening to me. They said that they had talked to the judge and they thought they could sell off a third of the shares. Mike Williams was going to be appointed trustee and he was going to get paid for that, all this crazy stuff that made no sense to me at all. I kept telling Kevin, 'That's not how judges do; they'll lose their seat on the judiciary by having ex-parte meetings with parties. That has absolutely never happened, period, end of story.'*
>
> *It was another classic case of keeping your friends close and your enemies closer, and bringing me into the conversations to make me be less aggressive in whatever I was trying to do. They invited me out there because I was making a noise about going after John Edwards. Little did I know that there was no difference between what they were doing and what John Edwards was doing. I don't think for one minute that they imagined that I would ever get my hands on subpoena power and go after their bank records. Had they known that, I don't think I would've even been invited into that room because now that we've seen the records, it's just ridiculous what they were doing with the shareholders' money."*

The constant stalling from the attorneys and the tragic stories from the shareholders weren't the only warning signs that disturbed Kevin. He felt personally responsible for what happened to the shareholders, as if he had the fate of 50,000 people in his hands.

On the same January trip that he and Bill had met with Urban, Moran and Williams, he also met Emerson Koch for the first time. Koch had been holding the mineral claims in his name for longer than CMKX had even existed, reportedly to keep the bad guys from stealing them away from Urban and the shareholders. Kevin had always believed that he was one of the protectors of the shareholders; someone who, like Urban, could be trusted:

> *"I met Emerson at the Venetian, and while we were waiting for Urban I said, 'I think we need to fire J.T. Moran and get Mike Williams out of the picture.' And Emerson was like, 'Man, I like your way of thinking.' So we hit it off, and we got to talking. He said, 'By the way, I have to ask you a question. Did*

Urban catch you up on money right before Christmas?' I said, 'Partially, why?' He said, 'Well, how much did he pay you?' I told him, 'Seventy-five hundred, but that included us paying for the phones and other expenses. Why?' 'Well, I sent twenty thousand dollars to catch you up.' Of course later I found out that he had also just received two personal loans for $400,000 and $80,000 using Juina Mining stock as collateral, but the money never made it into the company accounts. He had paid Moran $150,000 in October which would have come out of the loans. The rest of the money was supposed to go to pay expenses and attorneys' fees, but he wasn't paying anything, he wasn't even paying the phone bill.

That same week while Bill and I were there, some guys came in from Vancouver. One of them was Les Kjosness, who is the president of Golden Arch Resources. I was getting suspicious that they were doing something with some of our claims but I wasn't going to ask at this point because Bill and I had our own objective to find out what was going on.

I called Phxgold *because on January 22nd, Golden Arch Resources puts out a PR that said something about zinc. I went back to old CMKX PR's and it was the exact same type of wording. We came to the conclusion that they had exactly the same claims that were in the Canadian Mineral Resources records. Every single thing was the same except they changed the name of George Lake to Wakefield Lake. It was exactly the same as the CMKX PR announcing the zinc claims for CIM.* Phxgold *actually traced the directions on the claims maps and they were the same claims.*

Bill was there, and he had even asked Emerson at dinner, which by the way Bill didn't know he was paying for until Urban said, 'Bill, I hope you brought your credit card' and then turned to the waiter and said, 'bring me another lobster tail.' At dinner, Bill asked, 'Whatever happened to the zinc claims?' Emerson said 'Oh, they just disappeared. You have to have all this money to keep the claims up and they just...disappeared. They just lapsed.' You could just see Bill's expression."

Disappearing zinc claims that magically reappeared in deals with other companies. CMKX claims that lapsed from a lack of funds while millions were invested in a company that produced energy drinks. Hundreds of thousands of dollars that were supposed to go into company accounts that ended up who knows where? And of course, there was the never-ending litany of lies about the interpleader. Kevin was beginning to re-evaluate his entire belief system, to face a reality that many shareholders had already accepted:

"I spent the entire week with Urban, and saw an entirely different side of him. Every day, I saw him get totally blitzed, but not only off of alcohol. He would bring a backpack from Canada every time he came to Vegas, and it was just full of drugs. They were prescription, but they were very strong

narcotic drugs for pain. He would pick me up every time he came down from Canada and he'd be slurring his speech. He would say things like, 'Man, I fell off the step this morning and my back is really hurt.' He was taking 2 or 3 or 4 times the prescribed dosage, mixing them all, and getting drunk. Those guys would start in the morning, have one beer here, go another place and have another beer there, and then go somewhere else and have 5 or 6 beers. It was like that every day, I just hadn't known about it before."

It was during another trip around that same time period that yet another issue surfaced, one that had been hinted at since the first day of Kevin's involvement with the company. On every trip to Las Vegas, Urban would mention someone in Europe who was interested in buying out the entire company, with the story growing more elaborate and detailed with each telling. According to Urban, this person was willing to give every shareholder two cents a share for their stock. At first, Kevin didn't even think twice about the offer, seeing it as nothing more than an option of last resort:

"For 703 billion shares it came to fourteen billion dollars total. And you know what? Because two cents was such a small number, we were used to hearing a $1.54 and stuff; it didn't even cross my mind.

It was on one of those trips, we were sitting eating at the Peppermill, we were on the little barstools and it was just me and Urban and Ron. I said, 'Urban, you keep telling me you've got this guy in Europe that wants to give us two cents a share.' And he said, 'Yep, yep, yep, he's calling me every week.' And I said, 'Do you realize that's fourteen billion dollars?' And there was this long pause, and then finally Urban said, 'Huh?' 'Do you realize that's fourteen billion dollars?' 'Yup, yup, they are going to make so much money off of it that it doesn't even matter.' And then I was thinking, 'No way.'

We talked about it again later because it really bothered me. Urban said, 'Well, it wasn't going to be cash. It was going to be a share swap and their shares are currently trading at two cents a share.' I knew at that moment that it never existed. That was kind of a defining moment."

During the month of February, Kevin and Bill were busy putting together evidence while still holding out a slim hope that the interpleader might eventually be filed. By then, they were in regular contact, and at Bill's urging, Kevin had begun to tape record his conversations. Certain that he could step in and stop it if necessary, Frizzell told Kevin not to worry about the possibility of Moran, Urban, and Williams selling off the Entourage shares.

In the third week of February, after weeks of soul searching and endless late-night talks with his wife Angela, Kevin West, who just months earlier had been one of Urban's most loyal followers and an almost rabid believer in the Stock Play of a Lifetime, made one of the most difficult decisions of his life. He called Bill and told him that he wanted to resign. The pressure was too great, and he felt as if the shareholders had lost faith in him. Even though Bill kept telling him that he needed to "hang in just a little longer," Kevin had reached a breaking point. He sat down at his computer and began to type, and wrote Urban an email, but didn't send it for two days. After a little over five months as interim CEO of CMKM Diamonds, Kevin West, frustrated with the lack of direction and results from those who really in charge of CMKX, finally hit the "send" key on his computer, turned off his cell phone, and for the first time in months spent the entire day uninterrupted with his family.

From: *Kevin West*
Sent: *Saturday, February 24, 2007 8:02 AM*
To: *Urban Casavant*
Subject: *Very important.... need to open today Urban*
Importance: *High*

Good morning Urban,

I know you are under the most stress that you could possibly be under at this time. I too, am under a tremendous stress and I am taking a huge beating from all sides. I have told you that I would be loyal to you, honest, hard working, responsive, dedicated and that I loved you like a brother. All of those things I have done and my love for you and your family goes without saying. Likewise, my love to all of the hurting shareholders and their families is weighing very heavy on my shoulders. I truly thought I could help you to help them when I took this assignment with you.

I have talked to several of the people out there on the boards that will again (the very last time) go to bat for us with the masses of shareholders to TRY and give us a few more days before the lawsuits and such begin to hit. All I have to do is say the word, and they will try to help us ONE LAST TIME. I do not know if even their pleas will help us this time. This is all the time we have Urban to make this right. I will only put these dear friends out there to go to bat for us if I can be allowed to deliver on my promises. Otherwise, I cannot in good conscience ask them to do so.

So far, my hands have been tied by our corporate attorney, by his not delivering on the interpleader as promised and paid to do. The last week in September, he promised us both in his office that he would have the interpleader done in two weeks after receiving a payment of $150,000 from you. You delivered it to him within one week at a great financial loss to yourself by going in debt to do so. I believe that you have even given him much more than this by now. J.T. has not even helped out by allowing an approval of a PR with an explanation of why the delays. J.T. won't return phone calls or emails... not even one. I *do not believe any of his excuses any more and will not tell lies to anyone by telling them there is a good reason why the interpleader is not done yet. Now I am even to the point that I will not put out a PR unless it is to tell the world that the interpleader is filed and can be seen online. When I was talking to shareholders on the phone in the past weeks, I honestly believed that we were just a few days away from filing the interpleader and that there was a real reason that we had to wait for... this is no longer the case. I don't believe one word that is coming out of Vegas.*

*Right now your decisions are being made out of fear Urban, and that is not good for you, your family or the shareholders. **I am begging of you one last time to let me help.** You told me just last week to never doubt your trust in me. You have told me that you do not trust Mike or J.T. and that in fact you believe that you are now being scammed yet again. You can't go on this way Urban.*

You know without one doubt in your mind that you can trust me to do the right things for these shareholders, and that will in turn be the best thing for your situation and for your family. If you don't make the right decision at this juncture, this group of shareholders will become an angry mob and want to lynch you and me both, and you know that is just around the corner. I am told that lawsuits begin flying by Monday-Tuesday morning. The angry mob starts when the lawsuits hit!

If you want me to do the right thing here, you have to give me the full reign to do so. I will take the bull by the horns and try to buy a few days to make the necessary arrangements. I will get attorneys (that are shareholders) to get the interpleader done. You can stay on as director and give me a signed resolution of the board for me to do as I see fit to do what needs to be done, or you can put me on as sole officer and director and go fishing so that you can claim that you had nothing to do with it so J.T. won't come after you. Your choice! I won't ask you for a single penny from this point forward except for the cell phone bill if you want to keep that phone.

***If you won't do this Urban, then at least do the right thing for myself and my family and officially remove me from my position by noon Saskatoon time on Monday and I will not hold you any longer liable for the rest of my contract.** I have put my family through too much in hopes of helping you and the shareholders and it is not fair to make them suffer any longer if you can't let me do what needs to be done.*

Either decision is up to you, but I need a signed resolution from the board on either decision. (I will send them tomorrow (Sunday) in another email) If you want to resign as director and assign me, I will get the right forms drawn up by an attorney for you to sign within a couple of hours on Monday morning.

I have put my family through too much in hopes of helping you and the shareholders and it is not fair to make them suffer any longer if you can't let me do what needs to be done. You know that I am only trying to help. You have not seen even one selfish motive from me and I have never taken advantage of you in any way.

I hope you understand the love with which I write to you and how hard it is to write this letter to you today Urban. You are my friend and I want you to be safe for not only yourself, but your wife, kids and grandchild. I also have a loving wife, two boys, a granddaughter and a grandson on the way..... I need to do what is best for them above all else and I know you understand that. I want to help you to help everyone, but the ball is in your court to make the decision to allow what needs to be done. I am laying my job on the line here by asking you to terminate me by noon Monday, but I have no choice if you won't let me help you. I can't go past noon on Monday without your decision Urban. Please make the right choices for everyone.

I am leaving my phone shut off today, my wife would like to have ME for the day without CMKM. I will turn it back on tomorrow (Sunday) morning.

With the love and sincerity of a TRUE friend,
Kevin

The following Monday, Kevin waited until just after noon to call Urban, completely in the dark as to what decision Urban had made after reading his email:

"I said, 'Did you not read my email?' He said, 'Oh no, I saw it but I didn't read it.' I said, 'Urban, it was very important, I suggest you go read it and I'll call you back in about an hour.' I called him back in an hour and his whole tone had changed. He was no longer hyped and he was very solemn, very somber. He said (quietly), 'I can't do this without you.' I said, 'Urban, you're not taking any advice from me; you're not letting me make any decisions. You're letting these jerks run this company. Meanwhile, these shareholders are wondering what's happening and we can't tell them anything. I'm just tired of it; I'm not going to put my family through it anymore.'

He asked if he could call me back in an hour. He called me back and said, 'I just got off the phone with Michael and here's what we're gonna do, I'm not firing you, you're not going to quit. Michael's guaranteeing me we're going to have the interpleader by the end of the week.'

He just brushed me off again."

By the end of the following week, there was still no indication that the interpleader filing was any closer than it had been the month before, or the one before that, or even six months ago. Kevin called Urban every single day. He had given up on addressing the personal issues with Urban, who was still depositing money into the company bank account one day, only to take it out the next.

On March 27, 2006, in what amounted to a warning shot across the bow of the company, Bill Frizzell sent a follow-up letter to his September, 2005 Shareholders' Derivatives Letter. Addressed to Urban Casavant, Kevin West, and John T. Moran, III, he said that the company had failed to "take legal actions against a securities broker and various individuals for damages caused to the company." He then got straight to the point of the letter: "A suit will be filed this week on a party or parties named in this letter as a result of the Company's refusal to act on such shareholders' request."

Frizzell went on to state: "In my opinion there still remains huge 'fails to deliver' of Company stock in brokerage accounts around the country. I have the benefit of various NOBO and OBO lists that existed before the cert pull. As you know I have a wealth of documentation from several brokers who refuse to issue certs to their customers in CMKX. The documentation that has been sent to this office will be very helpful to the Company and shareholders as we work towards trading status."

He presented a summary of the First Derivatives Rights letter, a list that made it seem impossible for any rational person to question the magnitude of the corruption that existed in CMKX. He said that continued investigation had confirmed the facts laid out in the first letter, and recommended that:

> *"The Company should pursue its remedies against all third parties that have harmed the Company. Shareholders have asked me to pursue these individuals and others. I will do so on their behalf for the benefit of the Company.*
>
> *Shareholders demanded legal action by the Company in September of 2005 against John Edwards and NevWest Securities. The NASD has now completed its investigation into the Edwards' trades and filed a complaint against NevWest in September of 2006. The facts set out in the complaint confirm the shareholders' concerns regarding the acts of Mr. Edwards. The NASD complaint states that 250 billion shares of CMKX stock was sold through the Edwards trading accounts. Shareholders concerns were validated by this complaint."*

He summarized the remainder of the miscreants' list, which included former accountant Neil Levine, former company treasurer and CFO David DeSormeau, consultant James Kinney, who received almost 100 billion shares of CMKX stock, and former secretary Ginger Gutierrez, who received 23 billion shares of stock.

And then there was Brian Dvorak, whose laundry list of dirty deeds spanned a full page in the first letter, including the issuing of numerous opinion letters that allowed over 200 billion unrestricted shares of CMKX stock to be dumped into the market. He also authorized the forward split that gave certain individuals 100 times the number of shares held prior to the split. It was later revealed that in several of the opinion letters, Dvorak actually miscalculated and issued 1000 shares for every share that was purportedly already owned. In a letter dated December 15, 2003, Dvorak issued 4 billion free-trading shares of CMKX stock to Emerson Koch, who he said had purchased 4 *million* shares of CMKI stock. To make it even more confusing, the opinion letter first claimed that Koch originally purchased his shares on November 4, 2001, then said that corporate records showed that he purchased them on February 21, 2001. Either way, Koch received his financial windfall based on Dvorak's "fuzzy math." Not only did Dvorak authorize the issuance of an extra 3.6 billion shares of stock, neither Koch, Urban, or Helen Bagley from 1ˢᵗ Global Transfer caught the error. Koch received, sold and pocketed the money from extra shares worth hundreds of thousands, and possibly millions of dollars.

Frizzell reiterated his recommendation that the company should pursue legal action against everyone named in the first shareholders' rights letter. Then he added Roger Glenn to the list of those who he believed should be sued, a name that for a lot of shareholders formed one of the three points of the Holy Trinity of CMKX.

Frizzell laid out his case against the man who most shareholders had heralded as a savior to the company when he came on board in June of 2004. It was the trumpeted entrance of Glenn that almost single-handedly triggered the massive price run that sucked in thousands of shareholders when the stock rose over a thousand percent in a matter of days…and then dropped back to its original price of one one-hundredth of a cent. He ended his list with the most damning fact of all, that "Mr. Glenn had authored 11 opinion letters in a three-month period resulting in the issuance of 300 billion plus shares," which were immediately sold to thousands of unsuspecting shareholders by John Edwards, David DeSormeau, James and Jeannie Kinney, and a host of others.

At another meeting with Urban, J.T. Moran and his partner Jeff Bendavid, only the second one where Michael Williams wasn't present, Kevin realized why Urban really wanted to walk away from CMKX. Moran brought up the idea of putting the company into bankruptcy again, and Kevin immediately protested:

"Moran told us that they had been talking to a securities firm in New York that specialized in bankruptcies and said, 'They said we should forget about the interpleader and put the company into bankruptcy. That way we can sell off a third of the Entourage shares, we'll all get paid and you can leave.' Then he turned to Urban and said 'You know you're going to jail, right?'

Urban was shaking so badly that you could see it…his hands were shaking so much you could hear his watch rattling. He told J.T. 'I talked to Chesnoff and he said he'd get me off.'

Moran told him 'You might skate on some of the charges, but they'll get you on a couple. You'll get a minimum of 13 years in prison.'

Then he turned to me and said 'Kevin, cover your ears for a minute.' I said 'What?' He said 'Cover your ears for a minute.' I told him that if he wanted to speak to Urban in private that I'd leave the room, but I wasn't going to cover my ears.

So then he turned to Urban, cupped his hands over his mouth and mouthed something to him, but Urban shook his head that he couldn't understand him. Finally, Moran just said it out loud, 'Urban, I have three words for you: Switzerland, Germany, Austria. Those are countries that don't extradite back to the U.S.'"

As the meeting ended, Kevin asked Moran to submit his bankruptcy proposal to him in an email, and followed up with another request a few days later. Moran never responded or submitted anything in writing, and the subject was never brought up again.

By the end of March, after receiving the Second Shareholders' Letter from Bill, and after one last unproductive meeting with Moran, Williams, and Urban, Kevin was once again ready to resign. He met with Urban on March 27th, and laid it on the line with him, suggesting that Urban needed to get his life together, find some kind of spiritual direction, and ask God for guidance. Urban finally seemed to pay attention to what Kevin was telling him in that conversation. Actually breaking down and acting visibly upset, Urban talked about "returning to Canada and never coming back." He confessed to Kevin that he was once again broke, and said that he didn't know how he would ever be able to explain to his wife Carolyn that he had "wasted millions of dollars." Kevin set up a meeting for the following morning between himself, Urban, and Bill Frizzell, who was in town on other legal business, and left Urban to contemplate what they had talked about.

Frizzell remembered the phone call he got from Kevin that evening: "Kevin called me and said, 'You know, it's really kinda scary. It looks like he's fixin' to assign me permanent CEO and president and he's going to resign. I've never thought about being in this position. You gotta be careful what you ask for.' But I could sense some real concern on his part, that's when I knew he needed my support."

The next morning, Bill and Kevin waited for Urban well past the time of their scheduled meeting in the lobby of the Venetian. Finally, Urban showed up, looking like a completely different person than the one who Kevin had met with the night before. Ironically, in describing the scene later, Kevin used the exact same phrase as the shareholder who had called Urban on his birthday:

"Urban came into the hotel lobby and looked like a man who had the weight of the world lifted off his shoulders. He was smiling from ear to ear, his whole persona was different. I thought maybe that he had spent the rest of the night

and the following morning reassessing his life, but instead we found out that he was down in the casino trying to beat a slot machine that he had won $112,000 from the year before. That's where he was the whole time. That evening we went to dinner and had a nice conversation and talked very little about CMKM. Sometime during the evening Urban said, 'I want to resign so if you want to take over...'

According to Bill:

"Urban offered to resign. Kevin had said, 'if you're not going to let me run the company then I'm going to resign.' Then it came full circle: 'Not only do we not want you to resign, we're going to give you the company.' Urban was acting like he was anxious and scared to death and couldn't wait to get on a plane back to Canada. He said he had a meeting with his attorney David Chesnoff and they were going to indict him and he was really worried about that."

Kevin picked up the story from there:

"Later in the evening Bill said, 'Before we finalize this, Kevin wants to take you up on your offer to fly him to Canada to see the core samples.' Urban was still pushing the idea that it could be a world class diamond mine. He said, 'I'll get a geologist to meet us there, the whole nine yards, everything you want.'

The next morning I had an attorney of mine draw up the paperwork for the board resolution which named me as chairman of the board, director, CEO, president, secretary, and treasurer of the company. Bill met us for breakfast at the Golden Nugget, then Bill left when it came time to discuss the new contracts. Urban's brother Ron was with him, I had three copies of the contract. Urban and Ron looked them over, they asked me a few questions and I answered them. Urban said, 'It all looks good to me,' Ron said, 'Yup.' Urban signed everything in triplicate, we got our copies straight, I called Bill and he came back. While we were sitting at the table, I called for my tickets to Canada and Ron called for his but I had to pay something like $50 for his tickets, too. Urban confirmed that there would be a geologist there; we had everything worked out.'"

Within three hours of signing control of CMKM Diamonds over to Kevin West, Urban Casavant was on a plane headed for Canada, vowing to never return to the United States, and afraid that he wouldn't even make it to the border without getting indicted or arrested. As Kevin put it: "He kissed the ground when he got to Canada."

Chapter 32 – The NEW CMKM Diamonds

"We've been conned by pros."
   ~ stonecrusher, *Proboards66*

Urban Casavant officially resigned on March 29, 2007, due to "health reasons." His last official quote was issued in a press release as he fled the U.S. for Canada, convinced he was narrowly escaping federal authorities:

> *"My health issues are forcing my resignation, but I believe that I have finally found the right man to take over at the helm. Mr. West has proven his tenacity along with his care and concern for the shareholders of this company over and over again through an extremely difficult time. I want to thank you all for your continued loyalty and trust in spite of no news coming from the company for extremely long periods."*

And then he was gone, leaving market reform activist and CMKX advocate Kevin West in control of the company bank accounts, one cell phone...and no office. After selling well over $250 million of CMKX stock in less than three years, how much money did Urban leave in the company coffers? When Kevin took over CMKM Diamonds, Inc, there was a grand total of $558.50 in the bank accounts. It was the first of many stunning revelations Kevin West and Bill Frizzell would encounter on a regular basis.

Kevin ended the press release by saying "I look forward to the coming weeks and months ahead, as WE the shareholders finally move forward together. More information to begin immediately."

After Urban abandoned the United States (and CMKX) for the familiar terra firma of his native Saskatchewan, and within hours of the first March 30th press release, new CEO/President Kevin West issued a second PR. It was clear there would be no more extended periods of company inactivity and "More information to begin immediately" wasn't an overstatement:

CMKM Diamonds, Inc. Hires Frizzell Law Firm to Start the Process of Recovering Assets

LAS VEGAS--(BUSINESS WIRE)--CMKM Diamonds, Inc. is in receipt of the Shareholder Derivative Rights Demand letter that was prepared on behalf of the shareholders by Bill Frizzell. We are currently investigating many facts that will help us decide the best order of filing lawsuits in a quest to recover monies and assets that belong to the shareholders of this Company.

The first order of new business was to hire the Frizzell Law Firm. The investigations conducted by the firm have uncovered many facts which have revealed the reasons for the issues that the Company now faces. The Company expects the first suit to be filed against two individuals. This suit is only the first of many suits that are being prepared. The details of these suits will be made available once they are filed.

'It is my understanding that these first two lawsuits will be filed in Las Vegas before the end of the day.' Mr. West continued, 'I have known and worked with Bill Frizzell and know, beyond a shadow of doubt, that his full intent has always been to work on behalf of the best interests of the CMKM shareholders. I am excited and honored to have his help.'

The Frizzell Law firm has hired Las Vegas attorney George Cromer as local counsel to file these first two lawsuits on behalf of the Company. Los Angeles attorney, Al Hodges, will be assisting the legal team as it proceeds.

While the message board posters mostly seemed ecstatic that *any* action was being taken, there were still those who criticized both Frizzell and Kevin West, accusing them of hindering The Plan many still believed would lead to riches for those who remained patient. Others questioned both their methods and legal authority in the so-called "takeover" of CMKX, triggering speculation they had masterminded, along with John Martin, the takeover of CKMM Diamonds months before. Still other shareholders speculated that Bill and Kevin were part of The Plan all along, and were just the next players brought in by the real masterminds, Bob Maheu and Urban Casavant, to both clean up the stock market and help create a million millionaires. The battle cry of the month was "If you're in, you win." Incredibly, rumors of imminent payouts still persisted, and board gurus like Accadacca, Jay-Adobe, and the Belgians simply adjusted their predicted payout amounts, dates, and excuses to explain away each missed deadline. Even former head of investor relations Andy Hill resurfaced to defend Urban, echoing the "If you're in, you win" refrain and claiming Urban was still in control and setting up the big payout from behind the scenes.

Despite those who still chose rumor over fact, the overall response to West and Frizzell's involvement was overwhelmingly positive. It had been on the boards for over a week that Frizzell was planning to file some type of lawsuit against the company, including a March 13th email from Frizzell that was posted on *Proboards66* ending with "If things go as planned, some very significant litigation is about to begin. Let's hope it is helpful to us." With West's appointment as permanent company CEO, it looked like the lawsuits would originate from within the company itself. It was a stunning turn of events.

When Kevin took over the company reins it had several lawsuits pending against it, including one from shareholder Francisco Carrano, who named both Urban Casavant and John E. Dhonau, along with CMKX and Dhonau's companies U.S. Minerals and IB2000.com as defendants. Another lawsuit filed by shareholder Gene Hurd, who owned 200 million shares of CMKX stock, named CMKM Diamonds, Inc., Urban Casavant, Robert Maheu, David DeSormeau, Rupert

Perrin, Carolyn Casavant, Wesley Casavant, and Cindy Casavant as defendants. A third lawsuit filed by shareholder Jay Rutherford named CMKM Diamonds and included attorney John T. Moran III.

It didn't take Kevin and Bill long to figure out the lawsuits were the least of their problems. Aside from the $558.50 in the company bank account, the certificate for 45 million shares of Entourage stock comprised the grand total of the assets of CMKM Diamonds, Inc. Everything else was apparently gone, either squandered away or stolen outright by who knows how many con artists and swindlers. Frizzell recalled the days following Urban's resignation:

"By default, Kevin took over the company. Then we began to figure out what we were going to do next. When they finally signed everything over, the next few days were spent talking to Urban. Kevin realized that 'I've got $558 in the bank and I've got a bunch of lawsuits against the company, and that's it.' He had the Entourage cert out there and it finally dawned on him that 'We've got some major problems here to resolve and the only way we are going to do it is to go back and find out where all the money went.' At that stage we knew there were people who needed to be sued, we just didn't know that how widespread the corruption was.

Remember, what I was having to do without Kevin being CEO was to file what's called a derivative action. That's legally a lot more complicated because you're bringing the legal action as a shareholder and not as the company. Once Kevin became the CEO, I could actually come in and represent the company. That made it a lot easier to file the lawsuits.

I thought that Kevin might have acquired a lot of information, at least a lot more than what he did, but it didn't take us long to figure out that we just didn't have a lot of additional information. If any records existed no one wanted to turn them over to us, but we certainly had enough to pursue the first lawsuit."

While the message boards were buzzing with speculation over who the company would go after first, to Frizzell, the answer was clear. Only a week before Urban resigned, the NASD negotiated a settlement with NevWest Securities for their part in the massive dumping of shares by John Edwards, referred to only as "JE" in the charges. They were cited for "failing to adequately implement and enforce anti-money laundering (AML) procedures" in violation of NASD regulations. The settlement said that:

"NevWest failed to adequately perform due diligence, file Suspicious Activity Reports (SAR) or cease trading in multiple accounts owned and controlled by JE, NevWest's customer, regarding over 500 transactions, involving more than 250 billion shares of sub-penny stock issued by CMKM Diamonds, Inc. (CMKM) totaling over $53.0 million. As a result of these sales, NevWest earned commission revenue totaling $2.5 million, which accounted for

approximately 36% of the firm's total revenue during the relevant period. Moreover, between January 2003 and December 2004, NevWest failed to adequately perform due diligence, file SARs, or cease effecting wire transfers involving $43 million through 139 separate wires from at least 28 of the accounts JE had opened at NevWest to various bank accounts."

According to the NASD settlement, Edwards sold 207 billion shares of CMKX stock through his 36 NevWest accounts in 368 separate transactions, profiting over $49 million dollars in 2004 alone. That same year, he wired funds totaling $41.5 million from those accounts into his various bank accounts, including one wire transfer totaling over $4 million. The NASD said NevWest President Sergey Rumyantsev and Vice President Antony M. Santos were "aware or should reasonably have been aware of 'red flags', which should have individually or collectively triggered NevWest's AML obligations," and that they should have filed Suspicious Activity Reports with the NASD and/or put a freeze on Edwards' accounts. Edwards had hand delivered the stock certificates to the firm, many of which weren't registered to a specific name. Incredibly, NevWest allowed John Edwards to sell over a third of the total shares issued by CMKX through their firm alone. Not only that, through those accounts, Edwards had already sold over 6 billion shares of Pinnacle Business Management (PCBM) stock before it was revoked, and millions of shares of Barrington Foods stock, which later became U.S. Canadian Minerals (UCAD).

NevWest made over $2.5 million in commissions from the sales, accounting for 36% of their revenue during the period Edwards was dumping stock. So what was their punishment for helping to embezzle $53 million from CMKX shareholders while they pocketed $2.5 million? The NASD fined the company a paltry $100,000, suspended Rumyantsev and Santos for three months, and forced them to take 32 hours of AML training over a two-year period. And, as had become the norm in most SEC and/or NASD fraud settlements, the company was allowed to pay their fines "without admitting or denying the allegations of the Complaint." What amounted to a mere slap on the wrist for NevWest felt more like a slap in the face of the CMKX shareholders, who received absolutely nothing in compensation for the $53 million stolen from them by Edwards and enabled by NevWest. It was typical of the fines the SEC had been levying against brokers for the past decade, negotiating settlements that allowed the perpetrators to keep the vast majority of their ill-gotten gains while paying a small fine and promising not to do it again.

For the shareholders of CMKX, their only hope for justice lay in the hands of Bill Frizzell and Kevin West. While the SEC allowed the criminals, including John Edwards, to walk away scot-free, Frizzell prepared to take action on his own. Several shareholders stepped forward to help finance the legal battles that lay ahead, some investing large sums of money to aid in Frizzell's and West's efforts to see those who had wronged so many innocent people brought to justice. It was agreed that any money loaned to the company would be repaid out of any assets or settlements the company managed to recover and Frizzell signed on the loans as a personal guarantor. It was a calculated risk on his part, based solely on his ability to recover part of the $250 million was stolen from the shareholders.

On March 30, 2007, Bill Frizzell, with the help of their Las Vegas counsel George Cromer, filed the first lawsuit on behalf of the "NEW" CMKM Diamonds, Inc. The two individuals named in the lawsuit were none other than John Edwards and former CFO David DeSormeau, and included up to fifty other individuals and fifty corporations to be named later. Even though it was the single biggest event that had transpired since the company was delisted almost two years earlier, Frizzell saw it as simply a starting point in the process he hoped would finally bring justice to a tragic saga:

> *"We had the information from the NASD complaint that was relatively new, and DeSormeau was a negligence case where obviously if he was the Chief Financial Officer and he couldn't get a set of books together it was a no-brainer that he was negligent. Those were two things that I could use to get subpoena power to get litigation started. I had to start somewhere. I had to get the courts to give me the ability to go after these people. I wanted them to know that we were coming after them, and also that would be helpful so that Kevin could show the shareholders that we're doing what we can."*

The 24-page lawsuit laid out in excruciating detail an ugly pattern of manipulation, massive stock dilution, and fraud engineered by Edwards, DeSormeau, and other insiders yet to be named. The lawsuit claimed that:

> *"The Defendants, and each of them, conspired with other officers and insiders of CMKM to dilute the stock and reap huge profits personally causing damage to CMKM. Defendant DeSormeau (also referred to in public filings as company treasurer and financial systems consultant) failed to keep accurate and complete accounting records of CMKM. This failure, and DeSormeau's refusal to turn over CMKM records resulted in CMKM's ability to obtain audited financials as required by the regulatory agencies."*

Frizzell then detailed the SEC hearing resulting in CMKX's delisting after over 700 billion shares of stock were sold to unsuspecting investors:

> *"From January of 2003 through August of 2004, various stock dilution techniques were employed by Defendants to inflate the issued and outstanding stock of CMKM by over 700,000,000,000 shares. It has taken the concerted effort of a group of lawyers, accountants, financial advisors, brokers, market makers, insiders, professional stock manipulators, and corporate fiduciaries to inflate those shares. The investing public was unaware of the insider trading, self-dealing and market manipulation that was ongoing while press releases presented CMKM in a positive light. Press releases from CMKM suggested that CMKM was buying back stock by the billions when insiders such as Defendants Edwards and DeSormeau and certain officers and affiliates of CMKM were well aware that while a few billion shares were being retired, hundreds of billions were in fact being sold through the public markets by*

287

insiders. The two named defendants were liquidating CMKM stock by the hundreds of billions shares unknown to the general public investor. Hundreds of millions of dollars were paid by CMKM shareholders to acquire stock as a result of the positive press releases issued by CMKM. Only a small portion of the proceeds of the sale of this stock were used to further the legitimate business of CMKM because of the trading techniques orchestrated by Defendants."

Many shareholders were paying attention to the research done by `Pedro2004`, `Ric`, `GeorgeBurns`, `Phxgold` and a handful of others who were instrumental in compiling the information posted on the message boards over the past couple of years. Although most were aware of the fraud perpetrated on them, the lawsuit laid it out in graphic detail.

Besides noting that "DeSormeau was the financial controller and worked with John Edwards to direct all stock trading activities of the corporation," and that he "was present at each and every significant meeting regarding the sale of company stock," the lawsuit also claimed:

- Since the acquisition by CMKM of CMKI in 2002, there has not been a single page of audited financials filed with the SEC nor made available to company shareholders, despite numerous press releases detailing efforts to obtain audited financials.

- Bank statements, auditor Neil Levine's handwritten notes, and stock records of John Edwards and David DeSormeau received by Frizzell before the SEC hearing revealed "disturbing facts of massive dilution and manipulation of CMKM stock."

- DeSormeau, through his two companies Part Time Management, Inc. and Business Works, Inc. was issued 79 billion shares of CMKM stock, of which all but 380 million shares were sold into the market. Four other companies controlled by DeSormeau sold another 12.5 billion shares of CMKM stock.

- DeSormeau, "although compensated in extraordinary sums, breached the duties owed to company by losing, destroying, or hiding company records from company officials and regulatory agencies."

Based on an average selling price at the time, David DeSormeau would have "earned" somewhere around $30 million from the sale of the more than 92 billion shares issued to his companies. It was an incredible amount of compensation considering that in return the company got, as Stoecklein phrased it during the SEC hearings, "25 sheets of paper that is merely shareholders' equity."

From there, Frizzell laid out the case against John Edwards, painting a picture that placed Edwards in control of the company almost from the very beginning:

"In late 2002 or early 2003, Edwards convened a meeting at his office and invited many stock promoters and eventual insiders of CMKM. At such

meeting, Edwards agreed to raise $100,000,000 to allow CMKM to develop the mineral properties owned by CMKM in Saskatchewan, Canada. At this meeting, John Edwards began control of CMKM. Records produced at the administrative hearing described above show that John Edwards' companies paid all the bills of CMKM. Company management gathered prior to the institution of the SEC 12j proceeding with an auditor hired by CMKM to audit the records of CMKM. John Edwards attended the meeting with the auditor and company management. The auditor, Neil Levine, had worked with Edwards in other companies and was brought to CMKM by John Edwards. Neil Levine accepted a six-figure retainer from CMKM but withdrew from the audit in the middle of the SEC hearing, thus hindering the efforts of CMKM to present audited financials to the SEC."

And then, as he did with DeSormeau, Frizzell listed off one fact after another concerning Edwards. After promising to help Urban and CMKX raise a hundred million dollars, Edwards instead:

- Set up the 36 trading accounts at NevWest and began to systematically sell off hundreds of billions of shares of CMKX stock, kicking back part of the money to company officials and diverting the rest to various bank accounts. In fact, a handwriting expert said that it appeared that a single individual signed several of the names on the trading account applications.

- Set up post office boxes and mail drops for the trusts used solely as a means of laundering money from the sale of stock. Twenty companies were traced through transfer agent records to Langley, B.C., and were nothing more than mail drops used to liquidate CMKX stock.

- Kept physical control of the stock ledger, even though he had no official title or position with the company.

- Refused to testify in depositions taken during the UCAD investigation, instead invoking his Fifth Amendment right against self-incrimination.

In summarizing the incredibly complex web of lies, deceit, and manipulation, Frizzell and West condemned not only the crooks themselves, but indicted the entire financial system. They painted a picture that was a microcosm of every penny stock fraud in the U.S stock market, extending into many larger companies as well:

"The facts uncovered during the investigation of those responsible for the delisting of CMKM has shown this case to be a textbook case of market manipulation. The early financiers of CMKM including John Edwards and associates of his are well known in the market place for their fundraising activities. It is not clear if previous CMKM management was aware of the toxic financing built into the fundraising promised by John Edwards. It is clear that billions of shares of stock has been paid out to individuals who

had no relation to CMKM Diamonds, Inc. Billions of shares of stock were distributed in 2004 to people based on claimed debts of CMKM in 1998. This stock was distributed to known short sellers and firms that consistently prey on thinly traded stocks like CMKM Diamonds, Inc.

The sophistication of these so-called seed money investors is frightening. The average investor and for sure the novice investor has no awareness of the control over the market price that can be exerted by unscrupulous manipulators. These manipulators, many who attached their talons to the CMKM stock, are known to the SEC but the regulators simply do not have the manpower to police the corruption in the penny stock market.

In a sense the facts of the CMKM saga represent the 'perfect storm' in a penny stock dilution. CMKM has a somewhat dynamic and charismatic CEO who is convincing in his story about the discovery of valuable mineral deposits. A promoter (sometimes referred to in this case as a merchant banker) aligns himself with management with promises of raising millions for this new company. Immediately appears the known short sellers, profiteers, and toxic financing agreements...The grip on CMKM by these sophisticated manipulators resulted in a delisting and almost a destruction of CMKM. A look at the early stock distributions in CMKM shows recipients of stock to be people from the area known as 'maggot mile' in Boca Raton, Florida. An area where short sellers and market manipulators have access to hedge funds and finances that can control and cripple a small cap company.

Stock dilution on the CMKM scale cannot occur without stockbrokers ignoring the trading rules put in place by the regulators. Market makers control the bid and ask and virtually dictate the fortunes or losses that occur during a normal trading day. The price of the stock is not guided by Company success or problems, but by sheer manipulation from the key players in the market. Brokers must ignore SARs reporting requirements and allow activities like the John Edwards trades for the CMKM story to unfold. Trades are allowed 'ex-clearing' and accepted in the marketplace as a simple accommodation to the parties. It takes individuals like those who attended the initial meeting of the funding group in CMKM who understand how to dilute a stock and make fortunes in the process. It takes cooperation with every entity in the financial marketplace for dilution to occur on the scale that was accomplished in CMKM stock.

In order for large quantity trades like those occurring in CMKM a promoter must have lawyers, auditors, a transfer agent, and market makers who are willing to bend their own ethical rules and in some cases industry standards to facilitate such dilution. The naming of Does 1-50 represents the individuals that will be pursued by CMKM for the acts of stock manipulation, self-dealing and professional negligence. The naming of Roe Corporations 1-50 represents the companies that will be pursued by CMKM for their involvement in this massive dilution and market manipulation."

Chapter 33 – The Maheu Factor

"When that hearing took place in Los Angeles I was so damned embarrassed because they ended up asking me the same questions that I'd been asking without getting any answers for about two plus months. Frankly, like Urban, I was tempted to take the Fifth Amendment but that's not my style."

~ Robert Maheu, March 11, 2007

As Bill Frizzell and Kevin West plotted their next move after filing the initial lawsuit, it became increasingly obvious to most shareholders CMKX had been a scam of epic proportions. However, for those who chose to cling to hope instead of facing an unwelcome reality, there was always the Bob Maheu factor.

Even though Maheu officially resigned from CMKM Diamonds in October of 2005, the belief that he was still firmly in control from behind the scenes fueled the hopes of thousands of shareholders. Since he hadn't spoken publicly about his role in CMKX since the May 10, 2005 SEC hearing, the stories had flourished unchecked for over two years. It didn't matter how far-fetched the rumors sounded on the surface; with Bob Maheu in charge anything seemed possible.

In a series of interviews conducted in March and June of 2007, a year and a half after he resigned, and after two years of complete silence about CMKM Diamonds, eighty-nine year old Bob Maheu told his side of the story.

An early morning phone call prompted Maheu to comment, "I've always said that if you go to bed with a clear conscience you don't need much sleep." After first giving his word, twice, that he wouldn't lie or in any way deceive the shareholders to cover up some covert plan, he began, as he often did, by relating his past experiences. He detailed his involvement in the attempt to overthrow Fidel Castro, his years as the alter ego of Howard Hughes, and his role in aborting a contract between Aristotle Onassis and the King of Saudi Arabia that would have given control of the world's oil to Onassis.

He then told the now-famous story about how he met his wife Evette, leading into his lifelong reputation of taking "impossible assignments":

"At age eleven, I came home and told my Mom that I had just met the little girl that I was going to marry. And after she said it was impossible for the third time, I said "Mom, I love you very dearly, but I'm going to prove you wrong." And I married that little girl not once, but four times. We were remarried on our 25th, on our 50th, and on our 60th without telling the kids we eloped to Seattle, just the two of us, and we were remarried in the same little church where we had first been married sixty years earlier. And all through my life... when I was in school, if someone said we have to drop this program, I'd say "Why?" In college it was the same thing."

Then, he dropped a bombshell about his involvement in the CMKX saga, "But this one...this one was a mistake. It was an impossible deal."

After talking about his early FBI career, and how he had received a meritorious raise for his first assignment, Maheu said "I took this one (CMKX) on with the same enthusiasm, I should've checked it out a hell of a lot more carefully before I did."

In early interviews with Maheu, he said his involvement with CMKX began with Mike Williams. Maheu described Williams as someone who "kept popping up now and then with ideas, and we never ended up doing anything of the business sort, nothing ever came to fruition that I can think of except this one." He also said he couldn't recall how he met Williams and that "I get so damn many of those, people come up with ideas and very seldom are they worth following."

Williams called Maheu in late 2004 and asked to bring over an associate, Urban Casavant, for a meeting at Maheu's home office. Maheu said that he had never met Urban Casavant before that first meeting. After meeting once, Williams contacted Maheu again at a later date, and again brought Casavant over to discuss a business proposal. The offer Williams and Casavant made to Maheu was to become Chairman of the Board of Directors for CMKM Diamonds, and to deal specifically with straightening out CMKX's compliance and regulatory issues.

After the second meeting, Maheu agreed to help CMKX, with the stipulation he could bring in his own attorney. After accepting a salary of $40,000 per month for his involvement, Maheu brought in Donald Stoecklein to oversee the job. Maheu said "I made it very clear that I couldn't guarantee what I could do about the past. But I would insist that from hence forward that they would be in compliance."

The company announced Maheu's hiring amidst considerable fanfare on January 31, 2005, giving an overview of his qualifications and then saying "to list all of Maheu's accomplishments would turn this brief announcement into a novel."

Although Bob Maheu didn't know Casavant before the meetings in late 2004, Kevin Ryan did. Unknown to Maheu, filings with the SEC showed that in September of 2004, CMKXtreme loaned $2 million to Crystalix, a publicly-traded company whose CEO was Kevin Ryan. The deal called for the loan to be converted to Crystalix stock at a later date. Shortly afterwards, Urban Casavant and Michael Williams talked Bob Maheu into joining the CMKX Board of Directors. Then, on April 11, 2005, CMKXtreme loaned another $1 million to Crystalix. Urban Casavant personally signed both checks.

Over the next couple of months, Stoecklein worked closely with Urban Casavant and CMKX, reporting to Maheu about what progress was, or wasn't being made. When the SEC issued the temporary trading halt of the company's stock on March 3, 2005, the focus shifted to the hearing itself. When Bob Maheu made his way to the witness stand he already knew that Urban Casavant hadn't answered a single question in defense of the company or its shareholders:

"When that hearing took place in Los Angeles I was so damned embarrassed because they ended up asking me the same questions that I'd been asking without getting any answers for about two plus months. Frankly, like Urban I was tempted to take the Fifth Amendment but that's not my style. And for the sake of the stockholders I didn't want to allow the only two directors to both take the Fifth Amendment.

I didn't have the information; I realized that there were decisions made, or non-decisions made, with which I was not contacted or appraised. Anyway, then I really started putting the heat on the law firm. And you know 'crunch out the numbers that I need here.' I kept getting reports that they could not crunch the numbers. Finally I told Don, 'Don, when and if you are absolutely convinced that we cannot crunch the numbers enabling us to be compliant, I want you to tell me.' And when he did is when I submitted my resignation.

They kept trying to get the numbers; that I know. They'd get the accounting group, and then their own people, and they'd asked for numbers, and there was always some kind of delay. When Don said to me categorically, he said 'Bob, there's no doubt about it, we're not going to be able to get the numbers together enabling us to comply.' That's the day I submitted my resignation."

In the March 2007 interviews, Maheu gave his reasons for serving on the Task Force:

"I stayed on the Task Force until we came up with the recommendation that they get an attorney, a trial attorney, and go to court... and I've not had anything else to do with it, and as I've told you, when I resigned about a year and a half ago, I forfeited all my back salary and everything.

Unfortunately...or fortunately, I started handling impossible assignments when I was eleven years old, and I've always been challenged. And as you know... you can't make them all. When I tell you that I resigned and forfeited all the back pay that they owed me, frankly, I just wanted the hell out."

On October 26, 2005, five days after announcing that CMKM Diamonds was flat broke, Crystalix, the company headed by Maheu's partner and good friend Kevin Ryan, converted the $3 million Crystalix loan from CMKXtreme into Crystalix stock. Those 47 million shares, which had been paid for with company funds, were instead deposited into Urban Casavant's personal trading account.

At almost the exact time that Urban walked away with over $3 million worth of Crystalix stock that should have gone into the company bank accounts, CMKX defaulted on four agreements, all of which were hyped during the period that hundreds of billions of shares of CMKX stock were sold into the market:

- They lost all rights in the deal with United Carina Resources because they couldn't afford the $500,000 payment on the Hatchet Lake mineral claims in Canada.

- They defaulted on the deal with Emerson Koch for the Smeaton Forte á la Corne claims in Saskatchewan because they failed to pay for maintenance, drilling, and exploration expenses.

- They lost their rights to the American Shaft gold mine in Ecuador because they didn't make the required payments to Nevada Minerals.

- They defaulted on a second Nevada Minerals agreement because they failed to provide required funding for maintenance, drilling, and exploration on the Forte Diamond mineral claims.

After CKMX defaulted on their various contracts with other companies, the only asset remaining were the shares the company received when they traded the rest of their mineral claims to Entourage for stock. Bob Maheu stayed on to work with the Task Force, with fellow Task Force members Bill Frizzell and Don Stoecklein, and shareholders' advocate John Martin. Maheu spoke highly of current CEO Kevin West and advocate John Martin's efforts on behalf of the shareholders, but he saved his highest praise for Bill Frizzell. After acknowledging that his own involvement was limited, he discussed Frizzell and Martin's roles in the Task Force:

> *"I trust Bill with anything. There's never been a doubt in my mind that his whole participation was to protect the stockholders. Compared to what Bill was doing, if you compare it to that, and what John was doing, my involvement would've been a real little bit. I concurred with everything they were doing... but they were doing it. Bill has worked damn hard, as you know."*

In his most direct statement about his tenure with CMKX, he described his decision to work with the company as "the biggest mistake I've ever made in business," and confirmed that he "had no involvement with the company for well over a year." Although he had heard the rumors he was still behind the scenes controlling the situation, he seemed a little perplexed that "they can't seem to be convinced that I'm not still involved."

It was clear from Maheu's own retelling of the story that his actual role in the CMKX saga bore no resemblance to the rumors spread on the message boards and chat rooms. He dispelled rumors about Peter Maheu's alleged involvement in the Bermuda Short sting ("Peter was not involved at all."), about whether he had a nephew who was involved with CMKX ("It was worse than that, it was a grandson wasn't it? Whatever. No, there is not."), or that he was brought in by Steve Wynn ("Steve is a good friend, but no; he was never connected to my knowledge."). As for the rumors he is somehow related to Urban Casavant, he said that his mother's maiden name was Casavant, but he didn't know whether his family was related to Urban Casavant, and it had no connection to his involvement with CMKX.

("My mother was born in Maine, and her name was Casavant. That's an odd name...they could be related.")

As for the rampant rumors that had seemingly grown in scope each time they were repeated, Maheu said, "I know how these things evolve. The unfortunate thing about it is, as I was telling someone just the other day, the repetition of a lie becomes the truth, if it's repeated often enough."

Although Maheu couldn't say for certain whether he knew John Edwards, he said he "might have met him once," and stated all he recalled about Edwards was "that he was involved...he was buying stock or selling stock. Again, a lot of these things were never passed by me."

In fact, Maheu said he wasn't involved in many decisions concerning CMKX. "I was left out of a lot of things...I kept saying 'When are you going to get an office?' Decisions were made without consulting with me."

It was a recurring comment in Maheu's story, and one that led him to speculate they might have been using him for his name only, in an attempt to lend credibility to the company:

"I had to have that feeling. Although I answered affirmatively when the judge asked me that question at the hearing, I didn't mean to. That was at the inception of this whole deal. I was what? Two plus months aboard at the time of the hearing, and not a hell of a lot longer."

When it came to Urban Casavant, Maheu had mixed feelings. In answer to the question "Do you really believe he had the best interests of the shareholders at heart in this?" he said:

"As strange as it may seem, I do. I think he's very naïve and shoots from the hip. And truly... many times I feel sorry for him."

He then followed with a rhetorical question about Urban:

"How many people in your life have you seen, who without even realizing, live in a world of wishful thinking?"

And expanded on it with a comment that included both Urban and many of the CMKX shareholders:

"Reality does not exist in their world. I have been kinda weaned in that world because when Hughes... I was his alter ego for 15 years. When he went to the point of isolation I saw what lack of reality can do; it causes a lot of problems. It gets to the point where if they remove themselves from reality, unfortunately from that aspect reality exists in their minds... luckily, reality still exists outside. That happens, unfortunately."

Just as he had always done in the various statements or comments released during his short tenure as CMKX's Chairman of the Board of Directors, he emphasized his concern for the shareholders. When asked what his hopes were for the shareholders of CMKX, he replied:

"I'd love to see them get whole plus. I decided early on that I did not want any more salary and I continued on because there is nothing that would please me more than to see them come out whole plus."

No matter what Bob Maheu says in any interview, there will be some who still see it as all part of the Master Plan, and write off any statements he makes as simply more disinformation and sleight of hand. This is clearly not the case. Although it is possible, and maybe likely, that Maheu himself was misled by Michael Williams and Urban Casavant, and possibly his own associates, Maheu presents himself as a man of his word, and his reputation reinforces that view. While he has clearly utilized disinformation during his illustrious career, deceiving 50,000 innocent shareholders for over two years isn't in his character. He answered every question sincerely and without hesitation, with an awareness that most people half his age would envy.

In a follow-up interview in June of 2007, one year after Maheu and Stoecklein resigned from the CMKX Task Force, Bob Maheu once more addressed the issue of his involvement in covert sting operations, forced negotiations with brokers or government agencies or massive cash settlements:

"Did you at any time have any involvement, directly or behind the scenes, with any Federal enforcement agencies orchestrating any type of sting operation, or trapping naked short sellers?"

"Absolutely not."

"No involvement with naked short selling or negotiating any type of cash settlement for CMKX shareholders, or any type of settlement?"

"Absolutely not."

"And no current involvement?"

"No."

When told that the continued efforts of Bill Frizzell and Kevin West might possibly result in a positive outcome for the shareholders, Maheu said softly:

"You don't know how much I pray for that."

Chapter 34 – The Train of Truth

"In my opinion, we're going to learn that Mr. Casavant is paying for all of this. If he were the bad guy and was going to be the eventual target of Mr. West's legal actions wouldn't you think he would have identified Mr. Casavant by now? The fact that Mr. West has not fingered Mr. Casavant makes me suspect that the two gentlemen are working together on this."

~CMKXhope, *Proboards 70*, April 21, 2007

For Bill Frizzell and Kevin West, the CMKX saga had been a series of defining moments, just as it was two years earlier for John Martin, and just as it had been for almost every CMKX shareholder. What seemed to be reality one minute could be irrefutably changed the next minute as each new shred of information or evidence opened another door. In a few short months, Kevin had gone from True Believer to filing lawsuits against former company insiders. Bill, in the meantime, had moved from representing the shareholders as an outsider, to serving on the CMKX Task Force for Urban Casavant, and then to suing former company officials as the attorney representing CMKM Diamonds.

The months leading up to and immediately following the filing of the first lawsuit were a whirlwind of activity for West and Frizzell. They spent long hours sorting through thousands of documents separating what was relevant from what was merely a distraction. After the first lawsuit, Kevin immediately contacted anyone who might have information that could possibly explain how a company that sold in excess of $250 million in stock could have nothing to show for it...no diamond mines, no real assets, no accounting records...no money. He spoke with Urban Casavant on a regular basis, asking him to assist them in going after Edwards, Desormeau, and whoever else had defrauded the shareholders. Bill Frizzell recalled that while Urban was somewhat co-operative at first, the relationship between Kevin West and Urban soon became strained:

"Kevin had been pleading with Urban: 'Urban, we've got to go after the bad guys. Can you help us get some funding into the company?' Those kinds of questions were going back and forth between Kevin and Urban. And Urban just ended up basically saying 'That's all there is buddy, have fun.'

I remember one phone call where Kevin asked 'Urban, what happened on the Crystalix deal?' We knew something had happened, we saw a note in the records that we got from the SEC right before the hearing in May of '05, showing where Urban had loaned Crystalix a million dollars cash two weeks before the hearing, and six months earlier in September of '04, he had loaned Crystalix two million dollars...but we never saw where that money came back to the company. Urban said, 'Oh, that was my personal deal,

*that didn't have anything to do with the company, and yeah, I got paid back.'
Well, we looked back and there had never been any announcements when the
money was loaned out, but then we looked at the trading records, and all of
the sudden, Crystalix stock is being traded by Urban in his personal trading
account. We knew right then that there was a lot of hanky panky that went on
that we were fixin' to find out about. We put two and two together, and we got
a problem here, folks."*

Urban's connection wasn't the only revelation from the Crystalix deal. As
was often the case, every event seemed to connect in a never ending trail, and one
by one the players came together as well:

*"The Crystalix deal also made us start to connect Michael Williams to a lot
of things. The company had put out a press release that he was going to be
appointed to the Board of Directors, but then we never heard anything about
it again. The fact of the matter is that he's a convicted felon, and he couldn't
serve on a board. We knew that Mike Williams was involved with CMKX
way back in December of '02, we recently found a check where Urban paid
Williams some money then. I don't know whether Bob Maheu knew anything
about it, but Mike Williams...or somebody...pitched Urban on Crystalix, and
it just so happened that Kevin Ryan was the CEO of Crystalix and was also
a partner with Bob Maheu's son Peter Maheu, so you can put that together
anyway you want to. That just doesn't sound like a coincidence to me. If Bob
Maheu didn't know about the Crystalix loans, then there's a problem with the
fact that his own lawyer Don Stoecklein didn't point out the potential conflict,
or at least the appearance of conflict of interest in that deal."*

Although the issues with the Crystalix deal and Urban's sudden reluctance to
offer any help whatsoever in pursuing the CMKX criminal element were obvious
red flags to Kevin and Bill, it was an email to Urban's former personal attorney
Elizabeth Baird that provided the next, and possibly the most significant defining
moment. At first, she responded to Kevin's request for records pertaining to
CMKX with a curt "I don't have any company files; I represent Urban Casavant,
not the company."

Within an hour, she seemed to have a change of heart, emailing back to
confess, "Well, I might have a couple of files."

Two days later, a DHL truck pulled up in front of the new CMKM Diamonds
office, and the driver unloaded seven boxes. Not knowing what they contained or
who they were from, Kevin signed the delivery receipt, and they carried the boxes
inside and opened them to find hundreds of files...from Elizabeth Baird.

For the next few days, they pored over the seven boxes, each one revealing a
wealth of new information. It wasn't long before their perception began to change
once again as they looked at company bank account records and trading records
for company insiders, and tied that information in with what they already knew.
Bill Frizzell saw it as a pivotal time period in his and Kevin's understanding of
just how widespread the fraud was:

"One of the things that stands out in my mind was that these records looked like they'd been picked over. For instance, you'd have some bank statements, but the supporting pages that had the checks in them were gone. Or there would be board resolutions, and then there would be months that were missing. There was no continuity whatsoever to what we received. It looked like it had been gathered up and just thrown in a box. And this was supposed to be four years of company records. With all these hundreds of millions of dollars of transactions there was no bookkeeping going on. It became quickly obvious that contrary to what they said at the SEC hearing, there was never any attempt to do a real financial audit. The whole SEC hearing was nothing but a sham on the part of CMKX.

Until after we got those records from Lizzie Baird, it wasn't apparent to me how much the insiders had wasted the assets and invested in their own little personal deals. Up until then, I still thought that it was mainly a John Edwards' deal, that he was running the scam from outside the company. For awhile, I at least thought that maybe they had plans to develop the claims, so even if they all got rich, at least the shareholders might have something to show for it in the end...some value for their money.

The information from Lizzie Baird also made us turn around and look at the records that we already had differently. We would go back and look at the shareholder records again, and the other records, it just filled in a lot of blanks. Once we went through the boxes, it didn't take long to realize that the actual CEO and his inner circle were the biggest culprits of all."

For Kevin, the realization that much of the fraud originated within the company itself was emotional. The bank account records and checkbooks they were sorting through left him with a sinking feeling… the truth was far uglier than he had ever dreamed. Three million dollars in company funds were paid to Crystalix, whose CEO Kevin Ryan was Bob Maheu's business partner at Global Intelligence, over two million in checks written out to CSII, the company controlled by the elusive Michael Mitchell, and millions more to companies that had absolutely nothing to do with CMKX.

At the same time company insiders were living like kings, many shareholders were going through financial trauma. While John Martin was driving through a blizzard on Christmas Eve trying to sell enough sleds to keep his utilities on and buy a few presents for his family, Urban and his family were depositing millions into their own accounts.

Every page seemed worse than the one before – a million dollar check to Urban in July of 2004, another million dollar wire transfer in September, over three million each deposited into his, Carolyn's, and his son Wesley's accounts in October…and on and on. And at the bottom of every page in all capital letters was the phrase "CONFIDENTIAL TREATMENT REQUESTED BY URBAN CASAVANT."

Despite the incoming cash flow from shareholders, CMKX was neglecting the financial welfare of the company. Kevin listed the assets CMKX was losing while everyone but the shareholders seemed to be getting rich:

"When we got the files from Lizzie Baird, there were some board resolutions that we hadn't seen before. They showed that Urban signed over every last remaining asset that we ever had. In Stoecklein's office he signed over the American Mine in Ecuador to Nevada Minerals and Ed Dhonau, he signed over all the rights to any claims in Canada to Emerson Koch, he signed over our 50% interest in United Carina back to Rick Walker, Plus, we had just found out a few days earlier that they had sold all the zinc claims to Golden Arch Resources and Les Kjosness, and that money was gone too."

Even the companies that Urban was connected with before CMKX were simply vehicles to provide a stream of money to Urban and his cohorts. Several companies he had created in Canada including Diamond Quality, Buckshot, and Commando Mining were the same ones whose shareholders received shares of CMKX, often getting one-hundred times the number of shares they held in the prior companies, if they had ever held shares at all.

Kevin called Urban to break the news that they were going to go after all the assets they believed belonged to the company and its shareholders. Urban and Emerson offered to pay Kevin to "help with his personal expenses" in what Frizzell would later say amounted to nothing more than a bribery attempt. Kevin emailed Urban and told him that any money that Urban or Emerson wanted to put towards helping the company would have to be deposited into CMKM Diamonds' bank account. Urban never responded.

It was clear what had to happen next. As they continued to receive records from subpoenas issued based on the first lawsuit, the picture continued to change dramatically. Frizzell suddenly saw the big picture more clearly then he ever had, and knew exactly whose name would be at the top of the next lawsuit:

"We were looking for direction on who to sue and what to sue for, and there was no way we could avoid suing Urban. It was just all of the things in total. Remember Urban had this thing about having total control over all the checkbooks. I think we subpoenaed about forty bank accounts...and Urban's a signatory on every bank account. Ginger Gutierrez was the secretary who signed on a couple of accounts, but all other accounts were totally controlled by Urban. He might have been manipulated by someone else to some degree, but he was sure writing the checks out."

At the same time, Kevin and Bill had been taking steps to halt the ongoing sale of company stock. Incredibly, even though CMKX hadn't traded on the public market for over a year-and-a-half, shares were still being bought and sold behind the scenes based on the never-ending rumors still being spread about impending payouts and settlements. Delidog, a poster by the name of Marco Glisson who owned a hot dog restaurant in Wisconsin, alone was buying and selling billions of shares of CMKX stock. Delidog was rumored to be buying shares for the various brokerage firms who hadn't been able to deliver what they had sold years earlier. Kevin West ordered Helen Bagley at 1ˢᵗ Global Transfer to stop issuing stock certificates. She informed him that she had one stock certificate ready to ship out to E*Trade, one of the brokers who Frizzell and John Martin were convinced had a massive short position in CMKX. It seemed clear the brokers were worried about their involvement in the scam and were still trying to cover their own tracks. Kevin stopped the transaction and addressed the issue in an April 20ᵗʰ company press release that also detailed what they had learned from the Elizabeth Baird files:

> *"The Company has recently halted the transfer of a large bulk certificate to a major brokerage firm from a third party. A specialist will be hired to completely research and investigate both sides of this transaction along with the many recent transactions of possible insider sales of large bulk certificates."*

In the same press release, he spoke candidly about how his perception of the truth had changed over the past few months:

> *"When I first accepted the position of Interim CEO, I made a promise to myself and my family and friends that if I found there was not a real plan in place for the benefit of all shareholders, then I would come forward with the information I found. Not only am I going to share this information with you, the shareholders, but will do everything in my power to make sure that these individuals and entities will never be able to harm others in this same way again.*
>
> *When I started to work for CMKM in September of last year, I had high hopes and aspirations of making positive changes and forward progress in the evolution of this Company. Like so many of you, I believed that there was a plan in place that could not be revealed for one reason or another. However, after many months of failed promises, it was clear there was not a plan and no forward progress for our Company would ever happen until massive changes were implemented."*

Weeks earlier, Frizzell and West had also cut off all ties with J.T. Moran and Associates and asked them for an accounting of the money they had received from CMKX. As was becoming the norm for the new company, they immediately released that information to the shareholders. Kevin received his first threatening phone call from Michael Williams, who questioned his firing of Moran and his request for records of their expenditures. Williams ended the phone call by saying "You guys are making mistakes that you just don't believe."

On April 25, 2007, two and a half years after describing him as a Godly man who "God is using to re-distribute the wealth on this earth" and nine months after he asserted that "Many will be surprised as to who the 'good guys' actually are,"

Kevin West filed a lawsuit against Urban Casavant for defrauding the 50,000+ CMKX shareholders of more than $200 million dollars. The lawsuit Bill Frizzell and Kevin West filed on behalf of CMKM Diamonds against Urban, Michael Williams, former company attorney Brian Dvorak, James Kinney, Ginger Gutierrez, and several others said:

> *"During the last several years, CMKM has sold over $200 million in corporate stock to the public, but as of this writing, only $558 remains in the corporate bank accounts. Rather than use the funds raised through equity sales for the benefit of the corporation, Urban Casavant and his cohorts have funneled the money into their own personal bank accounts and trusts for their personal use, all at the expense of the corporation."*

It was an almost prophetic twist on Kevin's comment in August of 2006 that "many millionaires will be made from this stock play." One of Urban Casavant's most loyal devotees, handpicked to preside over CMKM Diamonds while the perpetrators fled with the shareholders' money, had instead helped trigger Casavant's downfall.

Chapter 35 – The Lawsuit

"Although the company has received millions of dollars from the sale of securities during the preceding several years, those funds are now gone. The question remains, where did the millions of dollars invested in this company go?"

~Lawsuit filed by CMKM Diamonds, Inc. on April 25, 2007

The second lawsuit filed by CMKM Diamonds described, as phrased by Bill Frizzell in the first lawsuit, "a textbook case of market manipulation." It expanded on the saga laid out in the claims against John Edwards, David DeSormeau, and the trail of "lawyers, accountants, financial advisors, brokers, market makers, insiders, professional stock manipulators, and corporate fiduciaries" that conspired to rob those who invested their money in a dream. Urban Casavant, Michael Williams, Brian Dvorak, James Kinney, Ginger Gutierrez, and the trust PA Holdings, Inc. were added to the growing list of co-conspirators. DeShawn Wayne and Bucko LLC, also named in the lawsuit, were connected to various properties that Frizzell and West believed should belong to the company.

The second lawsuit recounted the story of how Urban Casavant came to Las Vegas holding the rights to over one million acres of land around Saskatchewan, Canada and met with a group of penny-stock promoters led by John Edwards and Gary Walters. Edwards and Walters promised to raise $100,000,000 for Casavant to develop the mineral claims.

The lawsuit laid out a trail of corruption that encompassed several players, but presented Urban Casavant as the main promoter of the company, working hand in hand with Edwards, DeSormeau, Williams, Dvorak and the other con artists to pump the company while they pocketed the profits. It was a textbook study of how shareholders in the penny stock markets can be fleeced by crooks while brokers and regulatory agencies appear to be either asleep at the wheel or help facilitate the crimes. Laid out in narrative form, the lawsuit divided the story into appropriately titled sections:

Casavant Promises One Million Millionaires

Urban Casavant began promoting the sale of stock in his new company through various means. Shareholders were told that promising kimberlite pipes had been discovered on the CMKM mineral lands. Casavant and company management also issued press releases telling the shareholders that CMKM had acquired zinc claims, uranium finds, and gold mines in South America. Casavant and CMKM claimed to have a goal of producing "one million millionaires." Rumors abounded that a major buyout of CMKM was forthcoming because of its huge diamond discoveries and skillful acquisitions being made by company management - a major buyout promising $1.54 a share to its shareholders was being touted throughout the investment community. Casavant and the company management refused to deny these rumors and in fact encouraged them. According to the promises and press releases issued or condoned by Casavant, individuals investing $100 to purchase stock at $0.0001 per share would become overnight millionaires when the huge merger took place. Casavant was aware of these rumors but made no efforts to deny or correct them. The result of the company's decision to fuel and/or permit such rumors to continue was a stock-buying frenzy by the public during 2004 and beyond.

Hundreds of Billions of Shares Sold into the Market

During this stock-buying frenzy, and as a direct result of the promotional scheme devised and implemented by Casavant and his cohorts, billions of shares of CMKM stock were being sold into public markets. Over a two-and-a-half year period, CMKM dumped over 700 billion shares into the marketplace. This scheme was perpetrated by Casavant along with highly paid lawyers and insiders of the company, including defendants Williams, Kinney, Gutierrez, and Dvorak. From the period January 2, 2003, through May 3, 2005, the public purchased more than $200 million of CMKM stock either from the company or through its agents.

Casavant and Prior Management Loot the Company

Rather than use the funds raised through the sale of stock for the benefit of the company, Casavant and the other defendants used the funds for their own personal purposes. The funds were channeled into accounts held by entities such as the UAJC 2005 Irrevocable Trust. Some of the funds were used to purchase real estate in the Spanish Trails development of Las Vegas, including a $3.5 million home located at 90 Innisbrook, Las Vegas, Nevada. CMKM is informed and believes that Casavant used funds obtained from CMKM in order to purchase the Innisbrook property, along with several other pieces of real estate.

Other company funds were used by Casavant to pay his personal gambling debts at local casinos, in particular the Venetian hotel. Cashiers checks, checks payable to cash and huge payments made to credit cards from company funds were customary methods of paying the gambling debts of Mr. Casavant.

CMKM's new management has recently obtained many company resolutions that were passed which allowed 703 billion shares to be dumped into the market. The resolutions demonstrate that billions of shares were transferred to friends and families of company management and insiders. Bank records confirm proceeds of a portion of these sales came back to the company, *but these funds were then invested in projects beneficial only to Casavant, company management, and company insiders personally.*

Casavant and former company management touted through press releases that CMKM had invested millions of dollars in joint ventures for the benefit of the company. Former CMKM management informed the company's shareholders of their company's ownership of zinc mines and royalties, gold mines, and other mining and exploration companies (USCA, GEMM, SGGM). Those investments and/or joint ventures no longer exist. Casavant and former company management have not provided any explanation for the loss of these other investments except to say there were no funds available to maintain those investments.

CMKM's new management has recently discovered that CMKM had been forced to close their accounts at three major banking institutions in Las Vegas in 2003 and 2004, due to banking irregularities. Banking records (only a small portion of which has been made available to current management) show that millions of dollars were transferred in and out of banks by wire transfers, cashiers checks and checks made out to cash...CMKM is informed and believes that over 33 bank accounts were opened by the company or its related affiliate companies.

CMKM hired Dave DeSormeau in November 2002 as its chief financial officer. As CFO, DeSormeau transferred company stock through a maze of third-party companies. New management has discovered a letter from DeSormeau to Casavant dated April 5, 2004 demanding $1,500,000 for "his work in the past three years," including "time spent working on forming corporations" and completing "real estate transactions" such as those referenced above. When these demands were made, DeSormeau had already sold approximately 20 billion shares of CMKM stock through his company, Business Works. Following this letter, the company transferred an additional 40 billion shares of stock to Business Works. These shares were immediately sold into the market place.

CMKM's new management has located invoices showing purported purchases of equipment and vehicles with corporate funds. No equipment or vehicles are now owned by the company with no explanation for their disappearance.

CMKM has also recently located a trust account held by a Canadian law firm, which has been used to receive and send several million dollars to various CMKM insiders and to pay other personal expenses. For example, $932,180 was sent by wire transfer to the UAJC 2005 Irrevocable Trust from this account on January 31, 2005. These funds were company funds being held in this trust account. This wire was sent just two weeks after the opening of the UAJC 2005 Irrevocable Trust account.

In 2004, it became public knowledge that the SEC was seeking administrative action against CMKM for its failure to file financial reports. The company made several major press releases announcing the hiring of Roger Glenn, a former SEC attorney and CPA, with a major law firm in New York City, to "help the company become fully reporting again."

On June 14, 2004, the price of the last trade was .0010 indicating a 10 fold increase in the share price. The announcement of Mr. Glenn's involvement alone caused a major spike in stock sales at a time when company management was engaged in self-dealing and investing in the stock market, real estate and other ventures.

In fact, Mr. Glenn did nothing to help the company resolve its SEC problems. It has been discovered in the last few weeks that Mr. Glenn actually wrote legal opinions authorizing billions of free trading stock and assisting the company to increase its authorized shares from 500 billion to 800 billion shares. The only information released to the public about Mr. Glenn was his hiring to help with the SEC reporting problems.

Similarly, the company made a major press release touting the appointment of successful businessman Bob Maheu to the Board of Directors. Mr. Maheu was quoted as saying "we ...anticipate working with the SEC to ensure our compliance with all federal regulations." A large retainer was paid to Mr. Maheu by the company, yet no beneficial action came as a result of Mr. Maheu's hiring. Many shareholders increased their purchases of CMKM stock based on the news of Mr. Maheu's appointment to the board of directors. In 2005, the SEC revoked the registration of CMKM stock for the company's failure to file financials.

On March 29, 2007, Casavant resigned as sole officer and director of CMKM and appointed Kevin West as Chairman of the Board of Directors and also appointed West to be the president, vice president, secretary, and treasurer of CMKM. On March 29, 2007, CMKM had only $558.50 in its corporate bank account.

At the time of Casavant's resignation, CMKM was, and is, the named defendant in three separate lawsuits brought by a shareholder, by an alleged creditor, and by two prior joint venture partners. CMKM had no attorneys actively defending CMKM in the lawsuits on March 29, 2007.

West was informed by Casavant that there were no assets owned by CMKM with the exception of 45,000,000 shares of Entourage Mining (ETGMF) common stock which is to be distributed to shareholders per agreement with Entourage Mining. Entourage stock currently trades at .20 per share. This block of stock represents approximately 50% of the ownership of Entourage.

There are presently in excess of 50,000 shareholders of CMKM stock. The cost of distributing share certificates to its shareholders will exceed $250,000. An interpleader action was recommended to CMKM in 2005 by a task force appointed to identify its 50,000 shareholders. The task force recommended seeking help of the courts in identifying all of the bona fide shareholders of the company due to the refusal of certain major brokerage houses to issue stock certificates to CMKM shareholders.

West was left with no funds to begin an interpleader action or to distribute Entourage shares to its shareholders. Based on representations by Casavant to Mr. West, the company has no other assets. Accordingly, even if the company found the resources to file an interpleader action and distribute the Entourage shares, there would be no assets remaining in the company after the distribution of Entourage stock.

Following Casavant's resignation a few weeks ago, Mr. West flew to Canada to inspect the core samples that purportedly supported the early promotion of CMKM stock. Records now available to CMKM indicate that several million dollars was purportedly paid to a drilling company in Canada. Core samples exist as evidenced by photos in the attached Exhibit G. Casavant continues to maintain the opinion that the kimberlite formations existing on the claims owned by the company (now in the hands of Entourage) will yield the largest and most prolific diamond field ever discovered.

New management plans to return CMKM to trading status and work with Entourage in the development of the remaining mining claims. The waste of corporate assets, self-dealing, and malfeasance of Casavant, former CMKM management and insiders may prevent such occurrence, however, unless corporate funds are recouped from Casavant and his associates.

The Disappearance of Company Funds

Although the company has received millions of dollars from the sale of securities during the preceding several years, those funds are now gone. The question remains, where did the millions of dollars invested in this company go? In 2002, the shell which eventually became CMKM was current in reporting its audited financials. From the third quarter of 2002 until the present, however, CMKM has never filed nor had prepared any company financials, audited or otherwise. No corporate income tax returns have ever been filed for the company since 2002.

Upon receiving the appointment as Chairman of the Board on March 29, 2007, Kevin West immediately contacted one of Casavant's personal attorneys and requested all company files. On or about April 7, 2007, Mr. West received 7 boxes of company records. Upon review of those records, CMKM has learned that among other purchases, company management, either directly or through specially created limited liability companies, corporations or trusts purchased the following real estate with corporate funds:

> *a. 90 Innisbrook Avenue, Las Vegas, NV ($3,500,000) (Spanish Trails)*

> *b. 30 Princeville Lane, Las Vegas, NV ($775,000) (Spanish Trails)*

> *c. 7146 Mission Hills Drive Las Vegas, NV ($349,000) (Spanish Trails)*

CMKM is informed and believes that Casavant and his associates have purchased other real estate holdings purchased with company funds.

Casavant and his associates formed P.A. Holdings, Inc. as a vehicle to use company funds to invest in outside ventures and fund certain select company activities. The company was formed by Casavant and Attorney Brian Dvorak. Casavant signed all checks on the P.A. Holdings account. Brian Dvorak is listed on state incorporation records as holding all offices of the corporation. The registered agent for P.A. Holdings, Inc. is Globalwide Investment Company, LLC., an LLC owned by Brian Dvorak.

CMKM is informed and believes that money was funneled through P.A. Holdings, Inc. to fund CMKXtreme, the UAJC 2005 Irrevocable Trust and a host of other companies and ventures. P.A. Holdings, Inc. had no revenues and no discernible business operations but received in deposits millions of dollars. During the brief span from July through August 2004, P.A. Holdings, Inc. received over $14,000,000 in deposits, but the checks accompanying these bank statements have never been produced by prior management. These funds came during the time that CMKM stock sales were at an all time high following the announcement that Roger Glenn was on board to solve all the problems with the SEC.

Casavant and his associates formed UAJC 2005 Irrevocable Trust with corporate funds and or funds derived from the sale of corporate stock. Through this trust, several pieces of real estate had been purchased, stocks are traded on an ongoing basis, and other investments have been made. Casavant refers to this trust as his personal trust account. Defendant Mike Williams is the purported trustee of such trust and is charged with making investment decisions on behalf of the trust. This trust was created and run by Casavant. The millions of dollars used to fund this trust magically appeared when stock sales were at the highest in CMKM history. CMKM had no revenues and had no offices at that time. The trustee of this trust, Mike Williams, is known to be a business partner that was given billions of shares of CMKM stock but had no official position with the company other than serving as a financial advisor to Mr. Casavant.

The UAJC 2005 Irrevocable Trust entered into a contract to purchase four office buildings in 2005. A specially created limited liability company "Four Vegas Properties, LLC." was created to purchase the buildings. The trust had no assets but was formed solely to purchase the four buildings by the UAJC 2005 Irrevocable Trust. A check was tendered for $1,000,000 dollars to secure the property. Casavant used the address of CMKM as the address for these buildings on public filings.

A lawsuit resulted from the attempted purchase of these buildings with corporate funds. In that suit in July 2006, Mike Williams testified in a deposition there was in excess of $8,000,000 dollars and more in the UAJC Trust account. Casavant and Williams have personally received substantial sums from a settlement with the building owner over the purchase of such buildings. No funds have been turned over to the company resulting from such purchase.

Mike Williams is the trustee on the UAJC 2005 Irrevocable Trust and is thus a fiduciary to the corporation. Mr. Williams was the subject of a press release at one point naming him as a director of CMKM. Mr. Williams has received billions of shares of CMKM stock through his MDW and GRW Irrevocable Trust and his company Lifeline Entertainment for reasons unknown to current management. No documents have been made available to new management explaining such stock transfers. Mr. Williams claims to be the investment advisor to Casavant.

With millions in cash coming from stock sales, company management began to invest heavily in the stock market. Investments were made in penny stocks belonging to other company insiders such as Broadband Wireless, Inc., which belonged to Mike Williams. Another $2,000,000 was invested in or loaned to a company named Crystallix. Crystallix stock was bought and sold heavily in Casavant's personal stock trading account. In or around May 2005, Casavant made an additional $1,000,000 loan to Crystallix bringing the total loaned to $3,000,000. When he was asked about that loan, Casavant indicated that it was his personal money and it is all taken care of.

New management has also recently located check stubs indicating loans or purchases of stock totaling $2,250,000 in Conversion Services International, Inc. (CSII). These checks were written on a CMKXtreme account on or about February of 2005.

CMKM also invested $1,000,000 of company funds in Mobile Wireless Security in July 2004. There has been no accounting of this advance or loan or purchase made by CMKM.

> *New management has also discovered a wire transfer indicating a purported purchase of eight diesel trucks from GMC in Canada. The wire totaled $371,100.86 made payable to Owens and Sweitzer. As of the date of this lawsuit, CMKM has been unsuccessful in locating the vehicles that were purportedly purchased.*

> *It is also clear that Casavant and his associates directed the expenditure of millions of dollars of company money on joint venture agreements with companies like USCA, GEMM, SGGM and Golden Arch Resources. The company intends to pursue any recoveries it may have for any failed investments it has with these and other companies.*

The April 5, 2007 lawsuit told a sordid tale of greed and corruption and total disregard for the interests of the 50,000 shareholders who trusted Urban Casavant and the other major players in CMKX with their dreams and their money. In a press release a week later, Kevin discussed the near-term company focus on recovering stolen company assets and addressed the issue of E*Trade's attempts to buy shares of company stock years after it had ceased trading:

> *"The near-term focus of management will be to take action in pursuit of the following goals:*

> - *Find lost / misappropriated Company funds, and return them to the Company;*
> - *Locate those who have wronged the shareholders, recover assets from them, and if appropriate, their insurers;*
> - *Thoroughly evaluate all pending contracts and current legal obligations to expedite the Company's return to trading.*

> *In the first of two CEO updates on 4/18/07, Mr. West mentioned an ongoing investigation by attorney Bill Frizzell 'into the sale of bulk certs.' To this subject, Mr. West now adds, 'We have evidence of the attempt by at least one specific large brokerage firm to purchase for itself, rather than simply transfer, such certificates. However, we will have an expert examining several suspect transactions.'"*

The expert mentioned in the press release was Susanne Trimbath of STP Advisory Services, who was hired to wade through the mountain of documents that showed a trail of unsettled trades, shady stock purchases, and trades cleared outside the system. Trimbath's credentials included twenty years as an economics and financial expert, teaching stints at New York University, Stern School of Business and the New York Institute of Finance. She was a senior research economist with Milken Institute, Director in operations at Depository Trust & Clearing Corporation (NY); and an economic briefings Editor with the Federal Reserve Bank of San Francisco. She was also a frequent speaker on the issue of naked short selling, a prolific author, and a regular contributor to academic and business publications and referees technical articles for academic journals.

Three days later, on April 25, CMKM Diamonds filed an application for a temporary restraining order to keep the defendants named in the lawsuits from "selling, trading, encumbering or transferring identifiable funds and certain real estate and other assets that are rightly the property of CMKM; and hiding, altering, or destroying any documents or records belonging to CMKM Diamonds, Inc.." They asked for a temporary restraining order to be issued against all of parties involved in the lawsuit, and listed the properties, trust accounts and other assets that they believed should be frozen until it could de determined which ones were in fact the rightful property of CMKX. They closed by emphasizing the importance of the restraining order to the company's survival:

> *"There have been 30 to 35 different accounts located at various banks since 2003 which need to be reviewed. If this court does not enter an order restraining third parties from destroying records and from transferring assets belonging to CMKM Diamonds, Inc., irreparable harm will come to the company because the company will be unable to continue operations."*

While the lawsuit presented Urban and John Edwards as the main characters in the CMKX conspiracy, Michael Williams had emerged as an important connecting thread between several of the major names who were used to promote the company. The February, 2005 CMKX press release named Williams as an incoming board of directors' member, and presented him as a consummate professional "with a world of experience." His background included his position as Chairman of the Board of Broadband Wireless, which would eventually become one of the many unauthorized recipients of CMKX shareholders' money. He was also touted for his extensive background in the entertainment industry, which included administrative and career management for artist ranging from Snoop Doggy Dog to Wesley Snipes and stints at A&M Records and Island Records. He even had his own prominent record label as an artist, songwriter and producer at Warner Electra Asylum.

While the others named in the second lawsuit had no response to the accusations leveled against them by Frizzell and West, Williams decided to take a direct approach. He had already voiced his displeasure with Bill and Kevin's actions when they fired Moran, but his follow-up call was the one that showed his true colors. Kevin missed the May 9th phone call, but Michael Williams left a message on his answering machine that was in stark contrast to the picture of Williams painted by Urban Casavant two years earlier when he was introduced to the CMKX shareholders:

"Hey Kevin, Michael Williams.

I found out that you guys named me in a case against Urban.

And I knew you were a piece of shit. I knew all along you had something up your sleeve. I knew all along you were out to fuck Urban.

You know what? This game is going to backfire on your little fat faggot ass.

You take that message to your fucking bank. This is Michael Williams.

I knew your ass was a piece of shit. I knew you were up to some conspiracy.

You and your good friend Bill Frizzell are going to wish you never took that road.

Mark my words!!"

Chapter 36 – Operation Surround

"Rumors of trust accounts with money and other assets that have been established for the benefit of shareholders or rumors of dividends to be paid to shareholders are absolutely not true. Those that are demanding the Company to pay out monies held for shareholders are feeding off of this false information. Rumors that our Company was set up as a sting on the markets are false. Any rumor that has not been identified by this press release should be considered to be untrue."

~ CMKM Diamonds, Inc Press Release, April 20, 2007

Even the most vocal critics applauded Kevin West and Bill Frizzell's aggressive action against Urban Casavant. Pedro2004 from *PB66*, one of the more diligent shareholders who had uncovered and helped to piece together much of the information about the shadier side of CMKX, actually posted a public retraction of his earlier derogatory comments about Kevin. He titled the May 2nd post "Kevin now has my respect" and ended it with:

KW completely surprised me with his actions the past few weeks.

KW was able to see the light and woke up.

And KW's immediate actions were to stop the injustice from continuing!

Several others echoed Pedro2004's sentiments about Kevin West, especially his willingness to go after the same person who he had once placed upon a pedestal. Still, there were those who were so desperate that they would go to any extreme to convince others...and themselves...that even the lawsuits were still part of some incredible Master Plan. The *International Room* in *Paltalk* was one of the most fanatical forums that still entertained the delusions of massive cash settlements stashed safely away in top secret trust accounts. It didn't matter that the lawsuits laid out a deplorable story of greed and corruption, Urban, Maheu and Roger Glenn supporters still packed Ines's chat room to hear Accadacca and the Belgians spout off about impending payouts, trust funds with trillions of dollars in them, and companies within companies.

A rash of new articles about CMKX brought even more attention to the plight of those who lost everything in the Stock Play of a Lifetime. A May 24th *Hedgeworld* article by Christopher Faille entitled "Diamonds (and Conspiracy Theories) are Forever" highlighted the differences between the company's actions against Urban Casavant, and the unsubstantiated claims of riches and sting operations orchestrated by Urban himself.

Over the next few months, Bill Frizzell and Kevin West continued to issue one subpoena after another. The players in the CMKX scandal who at first seemed at odds with each began to overlap in a complex spider web of deceit that was epic in its scope. Frizzell's comment from two years earlier that it was difficult to tell the spiders from the flies in reality had a simple solution. With the notable exception of Brad Beckstead, the accountant who took one look at the company's records and walked away, every single person on this web was a spider. The only real flies were the 50,000+ shareholders who had been lied to and robbed blind by Urban Casavant, John Edwards, David DeSormeau, Michael Williams, Ed Dhonau and a cast of predators that included attorneys D. Roger Glenn, Brian Dvorak, Sherwood Cook, and J.T. Moran III.

Frizzell and West have uncovered a trail of deceit and lies that leads in a dozen different directions, a trail that has no end in sight. Of those named in the first two lawsuits, only DeSormeau responded. His defense? He never worked for CMKM Diamonds and had nothing to do with the company whatsoever:

Comes now Respondent, David DeSormeau, and for his Affirmative Defense states and alleges as follows:

1. That at no time was he an Officer or Director of CMKM Diamonds and was under no duty or obligation to resign or inform shareholders or the general public of any activities of CMKM, its officers or directors.

2. That said David DeSormeau was neither compensated as an officer or director nor ever held himself out to be an officer or director of said CMKM or granted authority to any person or persons to notify the general public or individuals to the contrary.

3. That any listing or representation of the Respondent serving as a Director or Officer was done without his permission and knowledge.

4. That at no time was said David DeSormeau in any position to have knowledge of the planning, inter-workings or strategies of CMKM, its Officers, its Directors or any actions of individuals that are part of this action.

A letter from DeSormeau to Urban Casavant on April 5, 2004 painted a much different picture. At the height of the pump, just as CMKXtreme was announcing its sponsorship of the Jeff Arend race team, DeSormeau was demanding more money from Urban Casavant and CMKX:

"In case you need a memory jogger, the money is due for time spent working on forming corporations, paying the Secretary Of State fees for the past three years, and travel and meals for you and associates that were charged to my credit card. As your request a number of friends and relatives received free tax returns and financial planning that would normally been billed at a substantial fee...

Bottom line is that all the real estate transactions are completed and everything you have requested of me is done. I have lived up to my part of the deal. Your part is to pay the $1,500,000.00 that is due me. I know if we make another payment plan it just won't happen. So, I am willing to take 15 billion shares of CMKM in exchange for the fees due my company. I will not wait a week or a month. This must happen NOW.

Take this seriously. I am the one who has been through everything with you from the beginning. If I do not have the stock in hand by Friday, May 7, 2004 I will go after every legal option available. If you think the shareholders have been upset in the past, what do you think it will be like if they see the former CFO filing suit for nonpayment?"

Two weeks after DeSormeau's demand letter to Urban, Brian Dvorak wrote an opinion letter authorizing the issuance of 24 billion shares of CMKX stock, and added another 46 billion on May 13. Of those shares, 37 billion were signed over to DeSormeau by Urban Casavant. If he sold those at the average price for that month, DeSormeau pocketed over $11 million after claiming that Urban and CMKX owed him $1.5 million. Including shares that were issued prior to his demand letter, DeSormeau and his company Business Works received 63 billion shares of stock for his role with the company.

Frizzell and West took advantage of the fact that no one else even showed up in court to defend themselves by freezing any assets they could trace back to company money. The ever-expanding list included trust funds, trading accounts, stock purchased in other companies, bank accounts, and commercial and residential property.

Even the crooks began to turn on one another. Gary Walters and Richard Taulli, who have yet to be sued by CMKM Diamonds but are clearly on their radar, traded what appeared to be drug or liquor induced attacks against each other on the *Raging Bull* message board. Walters' tirades were particularly bizarre, and implicated Edwards and Taulli in schemes to defraud investors in other companies as well, including Nanosignal (later Microsignal) and Exxcode. He tied them in to CMKX attorneys Brian Dvorak and Sherwood Cook, and convicted stock fraudster Shawn Hackman as well, and took the credit for introducing Edwards to Urban Casavant. He always posted in all caps with little punctuation, horrendous spelling and rambling commentaries that managed to paint everyone but himself as a crook:

IF YOU KNOWE AT ALL EVEN THAT DAM RICK TAULLI STOLED HUNDREDS OF THOUSANDS FROM ME AS WELL, ANY WAY TAULLI STAYED ON WORKING FOR URBAN CASSAVANT WHO I DID MEET EDWRDS FROM A FRIEND DON DICKSON WHO INTRODUCED US AND I TURNED EDWARDS ON TO. I WORKED HARD AND THEN CSAME RICK INTO THE PICTURE A FEW WEEKS AFTER I HAD A CONSULTING CONTRACT WITH CASSAVANT MINING.WE RAISEED URBAN 2.5 MILLION IN CASH IN 2AND OPNE HALF WEEKS, ANY WAY WHEN TAULLI TOLD EDWARDS I

WAS GOING TO BRING IN THE COPS, EDWARDS FREAKED OUT AND
THAT IS HOW WE DEPARTED, TAULLI STAYED AGAIN CIRCUMVENTING
ALL OUT CLIENTS AND CONTACTS AND WENT WITH EDWARDS ETC,
THEY KEPT MILKING THE PUBLIC AND TAULLI ROBBED THE MARKETS
AND DEALS AS WELL.SO NOW THIS IS WHERE WE ARE AT. THEY
HAVE NO IDEA HOW I HAVE REACHED OUT AND THE LORD HAS
BROUGHT ME GOOD PEOPLE NOT CROOKS LIKE HACKMAN DEVORAK
COOK AND TAULLI/EDWARDS.

On July 17, 2007, the company targeted the numerous attorneys who had helped to facilitate the fraud against the shareholders. They sent an eight page letter addressed to fourteen attorneys and their law firms, some well-known to CMKX shareholders, such as D. Roger Glenn, Brian Dvorak, Donald Stoecklein, John T. Moran III, Thomas Cook, and Steve Oshins, and others who no one had ever heard of. After insisting that he wasn't singling out any attorney in particular and briefly laying out the scandalous history of the company, CEO Kevin West addressed the real purpose of the letter:

"It is clear now from the results of our discovery that many bank accounts were set up to facilitate the diversion of funds which should have been used for valid corporate purposes. In addition to CMKI and CMKM accounts, we now have bank records of P.A. Holdings, Inc., CMKXtreme, Inc., Diamond Quality, Inc., Canadian Diamond Fields, Inc. and Spirit of Las Vegas, Inc. We have also obtained numerous bank accounts from insiders that used these accounts and their own accounts to divert company funds. Real estate, stocks and other investments were made with millions of dollars of company funds.

You are receiving this letter because I have located cancelled checks, wires, cashiers' checks or other evidence showing that you or your firm has been paid to represent CMKM Diamonds, Inc. at various times since 2002. Your checks may have come from any of the above named accounts or directly from insiders of the company. We have located checks payable to some of you from stock trading accounts belonging to various insiders and trusts created by these insiders. It is clear that much legal work was done by you since 2002 resulting in documents which the company must obtain to complete the audit work which I have undertaken.

I have been hired to run a company without being provided with records which are absolutely necessary in our efforts to become a trading company again. We have hired forensic accountants that have agreed to assist us in preparing our books for a full audit as we proceed.

It is very disturbing that we have located millions of dollars in payments to various third parties but the records needed to document such dealings are noticeably absent. We have been told these documents were created by many of you and I am requesting that you provide me with copies of such documents. We are seeking from your records, including but not limited to, all documents, agreements, promissory notes, copies of checks, memos, emails or other written correspondence pertaining to:

1 check payable to Urban Casavant for $3,000,000 on 9/21/04, 1 check payable to Carolyn Casavant for $3,000,000 on 9/21/04 and then 1 check from Urban Casavant to US Canadian Minerals (USCA) for $3,000,000 on 9/21/04 and 1 check from Carolyn Casavant to USCA for $3,000,000 on 9/21/04. 1 cashiers' check payable to USCA for $3,000,000 on 9/7/04, 1 check payable to USCA for $3,000,000 on 9/22/04, 1 check payable to USCA for $3,000,000 on 9/27/04, 1 check payable to USCA for $500,000 on 9/28/04, 1 check payable to USCA for $500,000 on 10/15/04 and 1 wire transfer to USCA for $200,000 on 12/9/04."

West and Frizzell listed 95 total checks and wire transfers totaling over $52 million. They ended with a comment that summed up the entire seemingly never-ending CMKX saga:

"This list does not represent a complete list of the records we are requesting. This is a partial list of transactions which are lacking in documentation. The list grows daily as we continue discovery into the company's past business dealings."

In September, one of the final pieces of the puzzle fit into place. Even though most shareholders now accepted that Urban Casavant had fallen prey to his own greed, the popular belief was that he had most likely succumbed to the lure of money as the scam progressed. The fact that he had been so visible in the early stages of CMKX seemed to indicate that he had initially believed his own promises to the shareholders. Who could possibly be so brazen that they would put up billboards advertising a scam? It seemed far more likely that Urban became caught up in the money grab that was initiated by Edwards and associates. It was true that while Edwards essentially took the money and ran, Urban stayed on and actually helped fund the cert pull and the never-filed interpleader. Was it because he truly cared? Or was it just a series of ploys to drag out the process until the company could be forced into bankruptcy and the statute of limitations ran out on potential lawsuits against him and others involved in the scam?

A search of past corporate records in Nevada by one of the company's investigators provided the answer. While recent records could be found online, older records had to be researched by hand at the Secretary of State offices in Carson City, Nevada. It was there that the articles of incorporation for Part Time Management revealed the true intentions of both Urban Casavant and David DeSormeau. Part Time Management had been issued almost 24 billion shares of CMKX stock, and had been portrayed as an accounting firm solely owned by DeSormeau. In reality, Part Time Management was incorporated solely as a vehicle to facilitate the illegal sale of CMKX stock on March 29, 2001, almost two years before John Edwards and company helped to set up CMKM Diamonds

Front of Item #:172601002008568, Amount:$3,000,000.00, Date:09/21/2004

Account:8207582367-F, Item:200090105, Amount:$300,000.00, Date:10/01/200

Account:8207582367-F, Item:200040267, Amount:$500,000.00, Date:09/27/2004

Checks written by Urban to himself and his wife.
Courtesy of CMKM Diamonds, Inc.

Front of Item #:167101002006618, Amount:$1,000,000.00, Date:07/28/2004

Front of Item #:173601002007450, Amount:$100,000.00, Date:10/01/2004

Front of Item #:172601002008568, Amount:$3,000,000.00, Date:09/21/2004

Checks written by Urban to himself and his wife.
Courtesy of CMKM Diamonds, Inc.

as a publicly traded entity. While DeSormeau was originally listed as the resident agent, the president, secretary, treasurer and sole director of Part Time Management was none other than Urban Casavant. Urban's name was dropped from later documents so that he could covertly issue billions of shares to Part Time Management as CEO of CMKM Diamonds. That single document was absolute proof that the groundwork for defrauding the CMKX shareholders was being laid far in advance. Urban and DeSormeau planned it from the very beginning. Every move after that moment was nothing more than another step in the perpetuation of one of the largest financial frauds in history. In fact, another Urban Casavant company called Full Time Management had been involved in charges of stock fraud and manipulation in Canada in 1999.

In the end, it was Urban Casavant's refusal to testify in a court of law, not once but twice, that was the true indication of his lack of loyalty to the over 50,000 shareholders that he promised to turn into millionaires. While Edwards was stealing his money anonymously, Urban was shaking hands and gaining the absolute trust of those he would eventually betray. He squandered most of the stolen money on expensive hotels, liquor, and a gambling habit that pumped millions of dollars of shareholders' money into the casinos of Las Vegas. Even his legendary acts of charity were financed by shareholders' money, most likely to feed his own desire to be seen as a hero to the masses while he robbed them blind.

Urban Casavant seems to have fallen victim to his own carefully constructed false reality. When he hired Kevin West as the interim CEO of CMKM Diamonds, he made the ultimate miscalculation: he underestimated the power of morality and honesty. Urban Casavant and those around him wrongly believed that everyone has a price, and in the end, that was his undoing. The simple fact that Kevin West refused to be bought off was the beginning of the end for Urban Casavant, Michael Williams, John Edwards, and the others who conspired to commit one of the largest and most complex frauds ever perpetrated in the stock market.

Chapter 37 – Leaving Las Vegas

"Today's action demonstrates that we will aggressively pursue individuals who ignore their obligations as gatekeepers to our markets and instead collude with their clients to violate the federal securities laws."
~ Linda Thomsen, Director of the SEC's Division of Enforcement

A trip to Las Vegas by Kevin and Angie West to Helen Bagley's 1st Global Transfer office in October of 2007 revealed even more evidence of fraud. Kevin noticed that several stock certificates were obvious forgeries, and many contained Edwards' signatures that were altered to look like other people's names. They spent an entire day looking through boxes and making photocopies of any suspicious looking documents. As a result, the company was able to trace many of the assets that Edwards purchased from the sale of stock back to forged stock certificates.

Six months later, during the second week of April, 2008, CMKM Diamonds was preparing to officially file some of the forgeries with the court. Frizzell was concerned that once Edwards and Bagley realized that they possessed copies of Edwards' forged stock certs, it was possible that records might begin to mysteriously disappear. According to Frizzell:

> *"If it came as some kind of revelation to Helen Bagley or John Edwards that we had that information, if there was ever going to be a time that they were going to do something to get rid of the evidence, it would be then. We felt as if it was essential that we had those records in hand before that was filed. I didn't want John Edwards calling Helen Bagley up and saying 'Hey, remember you were the one who got that $225,000 from me? That sure is gonna look bad when those forged certificates show up...Are you sure you can find all those?' 'Oh, I get the message, John.' 'Okay, see ya...'*
>
> *Next thing you know, there's a fire at the warehouse, or the records just kind of disappear or something."*

Realizing how vital the original forgeries were to their cases, and how much vital evidence was stored at the 1st Global office, Kevin contacted Helen Bagley and made arrangements to drive out and pick up all of the CMKX records the following Monday.

On the morning of April 5, Kevin and Angie West rented a van and left Tyler, Texas. They drove thirteen hours the first day, spent the night at a cheap hotel, and left at 5:30 A.M. the following day, finally arriving in Las Vegas late Sunday evening. They awoke again early on Monday, calling Helen Bagley's office at 7:30 A.M. and talking to her son Jeff, who in turn contacted Helen and told them to come to the office. Kevin and Angie made the short drive to 1st Global Transfer, and were escorted to the storage building where the CMKM Diamonds records were stored. While Kevin loaded the twenty-nine boxes into the rented van, he had Angie watch for suspicious vehicles, camera in hand. He had already told her that John Edwards reportedly drove a distinctive-looking yellow Hummer, and instructed her to take pictures of anything she saw. They loaded the van without incident and left about an hour after they arrived, pulling off the highway at a nearby IHOP…to see a yellow Hummer flash by on the highway, only a few cars behind them. Like John and Jill Martin's sighting from almost three years earlier, there was no way to tell if the unusual yellow Hummer following them was the elusive John Edwards, but it was enough to give them both chills.

After leaving the IHOP, they passed an address that triggered another moment of realization. 7500 W. Lake Mead, which was the address where John Edwards had rented mail boxes for several of his fraudulent companies, was less than six blocks away from Helen Bagley's office.

What happened next, however, was something that Kevin could only attribute to an act of God. After months of delays while working out the details for turning over the 1st Global Transfer CMKX records to Frizzell and West; after suddenly deciding that it was essential that they pick up the boxes on that day, at that hour, an event happened that shareholders had been hoping for since the company was delisted almost two years earlier, and that many had begun to think would never happen. Three and a half years after the company was delisted, and over two and half years after the NASD filed charges against NevWest Securities in the same scam, the SEC finally filed charges in the CMKM Diamonds fiasco:

SEC Charges 14 in $64 Million Penny Stock Scheme

FOR IMMEDIATE RELEASE
2008-54

Washington, D.C., April 7, 2008 — The Securities and Exchange Commission today charged 11 individuals and three companies, alleging they conspired to illegally issue and sell unregistered stock in a purported diamond and gold mining company and lined their pockets with more than $64 million from 40,000 investors nationwide.

The SEC complaint alleges that CMKM Diamonds, Inc., with assistance from a transfer agent and an attorney, fraudulently issued hundreds of billions of shares of purportedly unrestricted stock to the scheme's mastermind. The complaint also alleges that CMKM's CEO Urban Casavant generated investor interest in the company through false press releases, Internet chat boards, and "funny car" race events across the country without disclosing that he ran the company from his house in Las Vegas and that CMKM's primary activity was to issue and promote its own stock.

Linda Chatman Thomsen, Director of the SEC's Division of Enforcement, said, "The perpetrators of this massive scheme include several securities professionals and an attorney. Today's action demonstrates that we will aggressively pursue individuals who ignore their obligations as gatekeepers to our markets and instead collude with their clients to violate the federal securities laws."

Rosalind R. Tyson, Acting Regional Director of the SEC's Los Angeles Regional Office, added, "The allegations in this case highlight the significant investor harm that results from abuses in the penny stock market. Although CMKM's stock sold for well under a penny a share, the defendants were able to reap millions in profits by conspiring to flood the market with billions of unregistered shares while falsely promoting CMKM's value."

The SEC's complaint charges CMKM, the broker-dealer and transfer agent involved, and 11 individuals including Casavant. The mastermind of the scheme, John Edwards, who was living in Las Vegas, and others allegedly sold their unregistered shares into the public markets for a profit of at least $64.2 million, much of which was paid to Casavant to support his extravagant lifestyle. The complaint alleges that Edwards profited by approximately $26.4 million from sales through a single broker-dealer. Casavant profited by approximately $31.5 million, and others Casavant recruited profited by approximately $6.3 million, according to the complaint.

The SEC's complaint, filed in U.S. District Court for the District of Nevada, alleges that from January 2003 to May 2005, CMKM improperly issued up to 622 billion shares of purportedly unrestricted stock. These issuances allegedly were based in large part on both written authorizations and attorney opinion letters prepared by Brian Dvorak, CMKM's lawyer, which were often inadequate, suspect, and inconsistent. Nonetheless, the complaint alleges that based on these faulty documents, CMKM's transfer agent, 1st Global Stock Transfer LLC, and its owner, Helen Bagley, issued stacks of stock certificates without restrictive legends.

The SEC's complaint alleges that Edwards, his associates Kathleen Tomasso and Anthony Tomasso, and Casavant's cohorts James Kinney and Ginger Gutierrez then deposited the certificates with various broker-dealers and sold the shares into the market. NevWest Securities Corporation and its employees, Anthony Santos, Sergei Rumyantsev, and Daryl Anderson, are alleged to have sold more than 259 billion shares of CMKM stock for Edwards, despite numerous red flags indicating a massive unregistered distribution.

The SEC charged all of the aforementioned participants with violating the registration provisions of the federal securities laws. In addition, the Commission charged CMKM and Casavant with violating the antifraud and various reporting, record keeping, and internal controls provisions.

The SEC seeks a permanent injunction against all defendants and an accounting, disgorgement with prejudgment interest, and civil penalties against all of the defendants except CMKM. In addition, the Commission seeks a penny stock bar against each of the individuals and an order prohibiting Casavant from acting as an officer or director of any public company.

The Commission acknowledges the assistance of the Financial Industry Regulatory Authority (FINRA) and the Saskatchewan Financial Services Commission in this matter.

The SEC's investigation is continuing.

Finally, it appeared that justice might be served on a government level as well as from the efforts of Frizzell and West and those who supported them. The incredible irony of the situation was that as Kevin and Angie West were leaving Las Vegas with 29 boxes of forged stock certificates, company stock records, and Lord only knows what other damning evidence, Helen Bagley was being charged with securities fraud. If West and Frizzell had waited even one more day, or if Kevin and Angie had arrived at Helen Bagley's office a couple of hours later, Helen Bagley most certainly would not have handed over 29 boxes of damning evidence. In fact, Bagley was one of the primary targets of the complaint, prominently featured on six pages of the 27 page complaint.

The SEC went into explicit detail about her involvement with John Edwards, and her part in facilitating the epic fraud against CMKX shareholders. The SEC contended that:

- Bagley had known Edwards since the mid-1990s.
- Bagley received a "purported loan" for $200,000 from Edwards.
- Bagley "directly and indirectly through her son received payments in excess of $344,000" from Edwards' associates Kathleen and Anthony Tomasso during 2003 and 2004.
- 1st Global illegally issued "more than 589.7 billion shares of CMKM stock in certificate form without a restrictive legend to the Edwards Entities, Edwards' nominees, Casavant's nominees, and others."
- Stock issuances were "based on obviously incomplete and suspicious and, in some cases, forged documentation," including "substantial amounts of stock certificates" based on forged attorney opinion letters.

The SEC detailed dozens of stock transactions that Bagley okayed. Along with the forged opinion letters, she issued stock authorized by attorneys who weren't licensed at the time, attorneys who listed offices that they didn't move into until months later, certificates that didn't identify the recipients, and in one case, the same opinion letter used three different times with only the date changed.

Among the most egregious violations were a number of stock issuances to Edwards or his associates authorized by former CMKI CEO Ian McIntyre, who signed off on the stock as a company trustee long after he had turned over CMKI to Urban Casavant. In other cases, McIntyre, who Bagley had never even met, authorized stock issuances to Edwards as a board member, even though he never held that position for the company. Several of Edwards' trading accounts at NevWest were listed in McIntyre's name as well.

So why did McIntyre sign off on billions of shares for Edwards and his associates? According to the SEC, the answer was simple, but it was a revelation that took everyone else by surprise, including John Martin, Bill Frizzell, and Kevin West. In describing the early history of the company, they said:

> *"In late 2001 or early 2002, Edwards acquired the then-empty corporate shell, reincorporated it, and listed "Ian McIntyre" as its president and director in Nevada and Commission filings. The Commission believes, and on that basis alleges, that "Ian McIntyre" is an alias used by John Edwards."*

Other than the shocker about yet another alleged alias for John Edwards, the SEC charges mostly mirrored the two shareholders' rights derivative letters and the subsequent lawsuits filed by Bill Frizzell on behalf of the company. They listed Brian Dvorak's considerable violations, saying, "Over a ten-month period, Dvorak wrote at least 464 opinion letters, the vast majority of which contained baseless or fabricated justifications for the issuance of unrestricted CMKM stock." They said that NevWest Securities pocketed over $2,575,000 in commission from their dealings with John Edwards, and that NevWest broker Daryl Anderson alone made $2,300,000 for executing the trades.

While the SEC listed a litany of charges against Edwards, Casavant, Dvorak, Bagley, and their associates, for many shareholders it seemed to be a case of too little, too late. The complaint raised many questions about who wasn't charged and why the SEC waited so long to act.

Notable on the list of those who weren't charged was former SEC attorney D. Roger Glenn, who wrote opinions letters that allowed hundreds of billion shares to be sold into the market based on little more than Brian Dvorak's claim that the issuances were legitimate.

Another individual who wasn't charged by the SEC was CFO David DeSormeau, who profited an estimated $30 million from the more than 92 billion shares issued to him and his companies, and who helped Urban set up the framework for the scam from the very beginning.

So why didn't the SEC charge DeSormeau? While it's possible that he is on the "SEC's investigation is continuing" list, a comment that J.T. Moran made to Urban in the presence of Kevin West could explain why he wasn't named in their complaint. According to Kevin, as they were leaving the meeting where

Moran recommended that Urban flee the country to avoid prosecution, he also said, "By the way, I was down at the federal courthouse and I saw your fat buddy down there with three boxes marked CMKM." West also noted that DeSormeau wasn't called as a witness in the May 10, 2005 SEC hearing, and speculated that DeSormeau supplied evidence to avoid prosecution.

Among the other prominent players not charged were convicted felon Michael Williams, U.S. Canadian Minerals CEO Rendal Williams, Nevada Minerals president Ed Dhonau, and Casavant associate Emerson Koch, who made millions for simply holding the claims to the 1.9 million acres of mineral claims that were used to entice prospective shareholders to invest in the company. In addition, the SEC again ignored charges that brokers failed to deliver hundreds of billions of shares of stock in addition to the 703 billion shares that company insiders dumped.

Brian Pugh of the DOJ declined to comment on the ongoing joint investigation into CMKM Diamonds by the FBI, the DOJ, and the IRS. He said that any criminal investigation within those departments would have to originate from a grand jury. FBI agent Ryan Randall again confirmed that the investigation was headed by the IRS, but had no knowledge when...or even if...criminal indictments would be filed.

For CMKX shareholders, it was a bittersweet victory. The national media in both the United States and Canada finally began to cover the story in depth, but shareholders still felt betrayed by a system that seemingly abandoned them years ago, ignoring their pleas for help.

Back in Tyler, Kevin West and Bill Frizzell began to pore over the 29 boxes from Bagley's office. Kevin described an early discovery from the 1st Global files:

"In the very first box of paperwork handed to me from 1st Global stock Transfer last Monday, I came across a letter from the Salt Lake District Office of the Securities and Exchange Commission asking for the following:

Re: In the Matter of CMKM Diamonds, Inc.

Dear Ms. Bagley:

The Salt Lake District Office is requesting a copy of your firms stock issuance control log for the above company. In particular, it would be helpful to obtain copies of any stock certificates, transfer instructions, shareholders list, corporate resolutions, or other back up documentation with stock being issued to Mr. James Kinney personally or to any entity he is associated with from 1/1/03 to the present. Please provide copies of any transfer instructions or requests provided to your firm by Mr. Kinney as well."

The letter, signed by an SEC staff attorney, was dated May 26, 2003, but the fax date was May 26, 2004. West soon found additional documentation that provided confirmation that the SEC had evidence of fraud in the company at least a year and a half before they halted trading in the stock:

"Handwritten notes dated 6/7/04 in a file marked with the 1ˢᵗ Global attorney's name indicate that there was enough information asked for to have knowledge of the underlying stock fraud being perpetrated on innocent investors by this date at the very least. This coincides with Roger Glenn's hiring timeframe. Although it appears that the SEC letter may in fact have be written and sent in 2004 instead of 2003 because of the fax time stamp and the handwritten notes with a date in 2004, this was still before the major run up in stock and before at least 300 billion shares of the stock was dumped.

In another folder that was actually held together by a rubber band with these first two mentioned folders, there is an unmarked folder that has a yellow sticky note on the inside flap that states, 'These were copies SEC made.' Some of the documents include:

1. Corporate resolution of a John Edwards shell company used to move illegally issued and sold stock with 'John Edwards' written on a sticky note with arrow pointing to his name.

2. Several opinion letters from Todd C. Smith

3. Various corporate resolutions signed by Urban and one signed by Ian McIntyre

4. Other paperwork associated with stock issuances in summer 2003"

West and Frizzell have already uncovered a wealth of forged stock certificates and fraudulent documents in the boxes from Helen Bagley's office, along with new evidence that implicates several of Wall Street's largest clearing firms and brokers in the epic robbery of hundreds of millions of dollars of shareholders' money. The accumulated evidence shows a clear pattern of gross negligence and outright fraud. Although they have spent years trying to cover their tracks by wiping out stock in customers' accounts and buying non-trading shares from individuals, many brokers are still guilty of failures to deliver stock to their customers.

Chapter 38 – This Bird has Flown

"Everybody knew it was the end of the line, for Big John. Big Bad John."
~Lyrics to Big Bad John, by Jimmy Dean and Roy Acuff

As of April 15, 2008, Bill Frizzell and Kevin West are still sorting through the boxes from Helen Bagley's office, accumulating more evidence on a daily basis. They are cooperating with Federal authorities to provide information in hopes that eventually the FBI, DOJ, and IRS will follow the SEC's lead and issue promised indictments against the dozens of players who conspired to defraud 50,000 shareholders. Worst of all, the vast majority of those involved already had a history of either outright fraud or associations with companies that were exposed as fraudulent. While they continue to pursue the crooks and the assets stolen from the company and its shareholders, many have simply disappeared:

Urban Armand Joseph Casavant:

Urban Casavant, CEO of CMKX. Courtesy of Jason Webb and Anthony Pullicino.

Urban Casavant was charged with fraud by the SEC on April 7, 2008. After avoiding all efforts to be served in the Nevada lawsuit filed by CMKM Diamonds, Inc., Casavant or his attorney filed a Waiver of Service of Summons in the SEC case, which gives him 60 days to respond to SEC charges. Casavant's stock dealing career goes back to October 18, 1993 as evidenced in a lawsuit filed by Fred Tham in the Supreme Court of British Columbia. He went on to become president of a public company called Petro Plus. Petro Plus was halted by the Alberta Stock Exchange in 1996 and Urban Casavant resigned from the company during the same time. Urban's brother, Victor Casavant, settled with the Alberta Securities Commission on August 15, 1995 for selling unregistered securities. In a December 12, 1999 lawsuit filed in Alberta against Urban Casavant by White Bear Construction, LTD., Casavant and certain family members were accused of other improper stock related transactions. Casavant is believed to still be living in Canada. Process servers sent to his home were met by a woman fitting the description of his wife, Carolyn Casavant, who told the process servers that no Casavants lived there.

John Michael Edwards:

Drivers license photo of the elusive John Edwards. Public information.

John Edwards was charged with fraud by the SEC on April 7, 2008. Edwards has been sued in a Nevada lawsuit filed by CMKM Diamonds, Inc. and is currently avoiding all efforts to be served in this case. On May 4, 2006, Edwards' wife Diana Lee Flaherty was found guilty of conspiracy to commit securities fraud and money laundering in the Phoenix Metals scam. After lengthy delays and stall tactics, she began serving her 90-month prison term in September of 2007. Although it has never been proven that John Edwards and Michael Mitchell are indeed the same person, massive circumstantial evidence still links them in dozens of ways As is the case with most mysteries surrounding CMKX, only time will reveal the truth. West and Frizzell continue to uncover numerous legal documents (including forged corporate resolutions and transfer of stock powers) transferring CMKX certs to other entities. The documents are obvious forgeries where John Edwards' signatures were altered so it appeared to be the signatures of various other individuals, allowing Edwards to anonymously sell billions of shares of CMKX stock. Among the documents is a recently discovered CMKX stock certificate issued in Mitchell's name that appears to contain another forged signature by Edwards. The whereabouts of Edwards are currently unknown, although he is rumored to have fled to China.

David James DeSormeau:

David DeSormeau and Roger Glenn. Courtesy of Jason Webb and Anthony Pullicino.

David DeSormeau has not been charged by any federal entities for his role in defrauding 50,000 CMKX shareholders. DeSormeau still lives in Las Vegas and has been served in a Nevada lawsuit filed by CMKM Diamonds, Inc. DeSormeau was served with an Order of Prohibition and Revocation by the Division of Securities Department of Financial Institutions for the State of Wisconsin on December 2, 2003 for his role in the eBait scam. If he sold his 63 billion shares of CMKX stock at the average selling price when they were issued, his profit would have been $30 million. Not bad for a chief financial officer who never filed a single company report with the SEC...and who later claimed that he was never compensated or held any position with the company. DeSormeau currently holds the position of CFO for Switzerland-based AMDI Petroleum. Their website claims that DeSormeau has acted as "a consultant to companies in the areas of financial controls, international banking and compliance with the Securities and Exchange Commission" for the past ten years. His duties there include setting up financial controls and conducting internal audits for AMDI.

Michael David Williams:

Michael Williams mugshot after being arrested on 99 charges in 1999. Arrest photo, Public information.

Michael Williams has not been charged by any federal entities for his role in defrauding 50,000 CMKX shareholders. Mr. Williams is currently avoiding all efforts of being served in a Nevada lawsuit filed by CMKM Diamonds, Inc. Williams was last known to be involved as President of Products for WORLDVUER, a company from American Fork, Utah, where his picture and bio are still on the company website. Previously, Williams was an officer for a public pink sheet company by the name of Broadband Wireless International Corporation. Prior to teaming up with Urban Casavant, Williams was arrested and booked on February 23, 1999, in the LA Superior Court, with Judge Ito presiding. Williams was charged with 99 counts of Grand Theft and other securities violations. He was released on January 19, 2000 to a lengthy probated term following his incarceration. While on probation, he conspired with Urban Casavant and others to rob CMKX shareholders. The whereabouts of Mr. Williams are unknown at this time, but it is believed that he is still in the Las Vegas area.

John Edward Dhonau:

Ed Dhonau, CEO of Nevada Minerals. Courtesy of Jason Webb and Anthony Pullicino.

Neither the SEC nor CMKM Diamonds has filed any lawsuits against Ed Dhonau for his role in defrauding the company and its shareholders. Ed Dhonau was censured in 1998 in his home state of Ohio for selling unregistered securities. Dhonau, who has ties to nearly every major player in the CMKX scam, has served as an officer or director of twenty Nevada companies, several of which had connections to known stock manipulators. Convicted fraudster Shawn Hackman served as secretary and treasurer of four Dhonau-headed companies: Horizon Prime Inc., Western Sky Inc., Red Bluff Corp., and Silver Stream Corp. Others with ties to Dhonau who have been either convicted or charged with stock-related crimes are Barclay Davis, his wife Loretta Davis, and Laurent Barnabe. Dhonau showed up in the courtroom at the first CMKM Diamonds hearing with a man who he identified as a U.S. Treasury agent. Bill

Frizzell subsequently discovered that Dhonau was the trustee on Urban Casavant's UAJC trust account named in the second lawsuit as one of the major vehicles used to launder shareholders' money. Frizzell planned to call Dhonau as a witness at the following hearing, but Dhonau wasn't present. His whereabouts are unknown.

Brian Dvorak:

Brian Dvorak was charged with fraud by the SEC on April 7, 2008. Dvorak has been served in a Nevada lawsuit filed by CMKM Diamonds, Inc. He now lives in Boulder, Colorado and owns Boulder Black Belt Academy. He continues to write opinion letters for public companies in Nevada, including one as recent as March 7, 2007 for Biocrude Technologies, Inc., issuing retroactive free-trading shares. Edwards' associate and convicted felon Shawn Hackman also worked for a time as a paralegal for Dvorak. Dvorak filed for bankruptcy on October 29, 2007, after transferring the title of his house to his wife in 2006. He listed over one million dollars of debt and only $37,000 in total assets. Among the debts listed was a loan for $160,000 from CMKM Diamonds and another one for the same amount from Urban Casavant. He also listed a "potential claim" from the SEC against the CMKM loan, $283,000 in taxes and debt owed to the government, and over $273,000 in unpaid student loans. The bankruptcy trustee in the case is looking into the undisclosed transfer of property and the almost one million dollars of unsecured debt in the case. According to the U.S. Bankruptcy Code, a debt cannot be discharged in bankruptcy if it was obtained due to fraud.

Rendal Williams:

Rendal Williams, CEO of USCA. Courtesy of Hugo Cancio.

Neither the SEC nor CMKM Diamonds has filed any lawsuits against Rendal Williams for his role in defrauding the company and its shareholders. Williams resigned as the CEO of US Canadian Minerals in May of 2006, shortly before it was delisted by the SEC. It is been rumored that Williams has fled to Europe to continue in stock market related manipulation by signing up US companies on a foreign market. The scam is said to involve using foreign markets such as the Berlin-Bremen Stock Exchange to free up shares of stock in companies that are restricted so that they can be sold in the U.S. stock markets.

D. Roger Glenn

Neither the SEC nor CMKM Diamonds has filed any lawsuits against D. Roger Glenn for his role in defrauding the company and its shareholders. Glenn is still an attorney at Edwards Angell Palmer & Dodge LLP. In May of 2007, Roger Glenn, along with his law firm, was sued for malpractice by BCI International Holdings in a multi-million dollar lawsuit that alleged that Glenn was negligent in performing due diligence in a series of stock purchases and asset acquisitions that cost the company millions of dollars. That case is still pending. He was contacted during a *Faulking Truth Show* on *TogiNet.com* which aired live on October 26, 2007. When requested to answer questions about CMKM Diamonds, he replied that he couldn't comment and abruptly ended the call. A CMKX shareholder by the name of LED sent a tape of the show to Glenn and the CEO of his law firm Jeffery Hunt, vowing to "make D. Roger Glenn's life miserable." The tape included Mark Faulk's commentary after Glenn hung up, listing the 313.5 billion shares that were released into the market as a result of Glenn's opinion letters, and referring to Glenn as "a crook." There has been no response to these allegations from either Glenn or Jeffery Hunt.

Gary W. Walters:

Neither the SEC nor CMKM Diamonds has filed any lawsuits against Gary Walters for his role in defrauding the company and its shareholders. Walters is currently a resident of Las Vegas and is involved in six currently active lawsuits in the Nevada State court system. In one case, he was charged with 36 counts of theft and fraud. The residing judge in the case is Joseph Bonaventure, who although his last name is spelled differently is the uncle of Nevada county assemblyman John Bonaventura, who was heavily connected to Walters through Ramoil Management, Energy Ventures Organization, and Nanosignal. Walters was convicted in a Nevada state court on February 7, 2008 of 19 counts of theft, forgery and falsifying records and a bench warrant was issued for his arrest. Until recently, Gary Walters was an active poster on the NNGB (NanoSignal) message board on Raging Bull, where he professed his innocence while implicating Edwards, Richard Taulli and others.

Robert A. Maheu:

Neither the SEC nor CMKM Diamonds has filed any lawsuits against Iron Bob Maheu to date. Maheu recently wrapped up interviews for a documentary and movie based on his life story. Maheu was a defendant in a February 20, 2007 lawsuit filed by CMKX shareholder Gene Hurd, which was dismissed in September of the same year. Recent stories have surfaced claiming that Maheu was originally contacted about CMKX by second generation mobster Louie Ippolito, and that it was Ippolito who introduced him to Michael Williams. Maheu confirmed in a followup interview on January 18, 2008 that he knew Ippolito, but denied that Ippolito was the one who introduced him to Williams. Interestingly, although Maheu had stated in earlier interviews that he didn't recall how he met Williams, when asked if Ippolito first approached him about Williams, he said, "No, I don't have that recollection at all. My recollection is that Donald Stoecklein had done some work for Michael Williams and that is how I was introduced...that's my recollection." CMKM Diamonds has recently uncovered three checks from John Edwards' company First Colony Merchant written to Ippolito. The checks, totaling $105,000 and signed by Edwards, were issued between July and September of 2004 – four months before Maheu was appointed to CMKX's board of directors.

Donald J. Stoecklein:

Neither the SEC nor CMKM Diamonds has filed any lawsuits against Donald Stoecklein to date. Stoecklein currently owns the Securities Law Institute and is working out of an office in Las Vegas while being licensed to practice law in California. On August 1, 1995, the SEC entered a cease and desist order against him for his role in selling unregistered securities. The SEC alleged that Stoecklein was involved in a fraudulent scheme to raise capital for Softpoint. Stoecklein was ordered to pay a disgorgement of $19,975 plus interest and to cease and desist from any committing further securities violations.

John T. Moran III:

Neither the SEC nor CMKM Diamonds has filed any lawsuits against John T. Moran III to date, who has refused to turn over records pertaining to the company. Moran was appointed to the State of Nevada Ethics Commission by Nevada Governor Jim Gibbons on January 18, 2008. "The State of Nevada will be well served by John T. Moran III, who has an exemplary record of service to the State of Nevada and Clark County," said Governor Jim Gibbons. A failed attempt to contact Moran on the February 25th *Faulking Truth Show* prompted a return call on March 6th. In that off-air exchange, Moran stated that although he had not read *The Naked Truth*, "I am waiting for the book to come out so I can sue for defamation of character." After bragging that he was rich enough to back up his threat of a lawsuit, he said "I'd rather set a dog on fire and watch it burn than kill it and put it out of its misery." Moran denied any wrongdoing, but declined repeated offers to tell his side of the story, citing attorney/client privilege with Urban Casavant.

Melvin O'Neil:

CMKX Investor Relations Melvin O'Neil at the CMKX/ UCAD Shareholders' Party. Courtesy of Jason Webb and Anthony Pullicino.

Neither the SEC nor CMKM Diamonds has filed any lawsuits against Melvin O'Neil to date. O'Neil recently had a short stint as the spokesperson for Golden Arch Resources, but was let go after CMKX shareholders bombarded the company with phone calls protesting his hiring. He is known to still be making appearances in various chatrooms claiming that he is speaking with a "Special Friend" who some shareholders are convinced is Urban Casavant. He was last heard singing the Jimmy Dean/Roy Acuff song *Big Bad John* in a surreal response to questions about Urban Casavant on *The Faulking Truth Show* on November 1, 2007...all eight verses and choruses. He later called and apologized, claiming that he hasn't spoken with Urban Casavant in months. Taking a cue from David DeSormeau, he also claimed that he was never the head of Investor Relations for CMKX, even though he stated a year earlier that Urban had appointed him to the position in April of 2003.

Ron Casavant:

Ron Casavant, Urban's brother and CEO of Casavant International Mining. Courtesy of Jason Webb and Anthony Pullicino.

Neither the SEC nor CMKM Diamonds has filed any lawsuits against Ron Casavant for his role in defrauding the company and its shareholders. Ron Casavant has been seen at NHRA races promoting other questionable companies, and is reportedly claiming that Kevin and Bill got Urban drunk and talked him into signing over the company...even though Ron was with Urban the morning the papers were signed. According to Marc Cohen, Ron Casavant spent all of his money and at one time was sleeping in his car in the Cohen's NHRA racing pit after CMKX was halted. On August 14, 2007, Ron bought a $265,000 home in Las Vegas, NV.

Among the other players in the CMKX saga:

- Jeff Turino is said to have fled to Russia to avoid possible prosecution in the PCBM scam.

- Richard Taulli has been supposedly posting sporadic responses to Gary Walters' accusations on *Raging Bull*.

- Ex-CMKX spokesperson Andy Hill still posts on CMKX message boards and frequents *Paltalk* chatrooms.

- Emerson Koch was recently contacted by phone during the October 25th *Faulking Truth Show*. When asked what services he provided to earn the over 48 billion shares of CMKX stock that he and his family received from the company (including the 3.6 billion share "bonus" he received from the Dvorak/Bagley error), he immediately hung up.

While many of the so-called gurus on the message boards have slipped quietly into the shadows, Accadacca and a few others still frequent the *Paltalk* chatrooms, reciting failed deadlines, unsubstantiated rumors, and inaccurate predictions to an increasingly skeptical audience. Accadacca's real name is reportedly Roger Stelma, who has been charged with failure to pay back child support, but female visitors to the chatrooms have still been known to profess that they "want to have his baby."

Kevin West and Bill Frizzell are moving forward with their lawsuits against Urban Casavant, David Desormeau, John Edwards, Michael Williams, and others who they believe defrauded the over 50,000 shareholders of CMKM Diamonds. They have plans to file many more suits in an effort to keep the Company alive and restore some of the assets that belong to the Company. So far, they have located several properties, upwards of 50 bank accounts, numerous trust funds and stock holdings in dozens of other public companies that have traced back to CMKX shareholders' money. Every one of the major players lived in lavish homes funded by CMKX shareholders' money, and Urban owned at least three different homes. Even Emerson Koch had a huge lake house and a 5,000 sq. ft. boathouse.

Including the earlier investigation initiated by John Martin, Frizzell and West have already accumulated over 250,000 pages of documents. The records sent over by the NASD on the NevWest Securities/John Edwards investigation alone amount to over 25,000 pages of documents. It is a remarkable feat considering the fact that CMKM Diamonds never filed a single financial report and turned over no records whatsoever to West when he became CEO. Along with the records they are pursuing from attorneys and others related to CMKM Diamonds, Frizzell and West have recently issued subpoenas to acquire bank records from Go Fast Nevada in an effort to track "checks in substantial amounts from individuals and companies related to former CMKM management payable to Go Fast Nevada and other Go Fast entities."

They are, in the simplest terms, following the money. It is likely that they will eventually pursue many of the attorneys and brokers who were involved in robbing the company coffers, and are considering their options in the still unresolved naked short selling or fails to deliver issue. Frizzell has been interviewing attorneys to assist the company in the next phase of litigation, which could involve as many as 100 lawsuits. He is looking for specialists in both research and litigation, specifically attorneys who have had success in winning large settlements in other cases. His hope is to expand the scope of their efforts and to move forward in pursuing what he describes as several "slam dunk" cases against the criminals who perpetrated a massive fraud against so many innocent victims.

John Martin and Bill Frizzell. Courtesy of The Owners Group, Inc.

Chapter 39 – Diamonds are Forever

"CMKX should have used the money to build mines, to at least give the shareholders something worthwhile. They could have built a beautiful mine."

~ Marc Cohen, husband of CMKXtreme motorcycle race driver Connie Cohen

The most ironic part of the CMKX saga is that while John Edwards, Urban Casavant, and their cohorts were stealing every penny they could get their hands on from their own shareholders, other diamond mining companies in Canada were actually spending their resources on looking for diamonds…and finding them. The appeal of non-conflict diamonds has intensified after a 2007 film called *Blood Diamonds* depicted the ruthless methods often used in African diamond mining, and recent concern over terrorism has only heightened the interest. Canada is now the third largest diamond producer in the world, trailing only Botswana and Russia.

There are over 30 diamond exploration and mining companies in Canada, some legitimate, and others most likely scams. Three Canadian mines producing over $3 billion worth of diamonds a year are currently in operation, with three more scheduled to begin production over the next few years. One company, the Rio Tinto Group, recently approved funding of $563 million for the Diavik diamond mine, which has produced over 8 million carats of diamonds per year since 2004. The Diavik Mine is projected to produce over 110 million carats of diamonds worth $25 billion over the next fifteen to twenty years.

As of November of 2007, another Canadian diamond mining company, Shore Gold, was announcing extremely favorable results from core samples taken from the Forte á la Corne area of Saskatchewan, finding a total of "689 commercial sized diamonds, collectively weighing 205 carats." Thirty-three diamonds greater than one carat have been recovered so far, and on June 27, they announced that they had recovered one diamond weighing 49.50 carats, and another one weighing over 22 carats, the two largest diamonds found in the area so far.

In comparison:

- CMKX issued and sold 703 *billon* shares of stock, while Shore Gold has issued and sold a total of 182 *million* total shares.
- CMKX squandered over $250 million of shareholders' money and had only $558 in the bank when Urban handed the company over to Kevin West; Shore Gold had $76 million in the bank as of November 23, 2007.

- CMKX found two micro diamonds in the entire history of the company, while Shore Gold has recovered a total of 7,500 carats of diamonds worth an average of $135 per carat just from their test drillings.

- Finally, while CMKX's stock price went from over a penny a share in 2003, and lost over 99% of its value, Shore Gold's stock price has risen from a low of seventy cents to around four dollars a share, an increase of over 500%.

Did the CMKX claims contain diamonds? According to Marc Cohen, the husband of CMKXtreme race driver Connie Cohen, there appear to be diamonds in the core samples that Ron Casavant was showing off to shareholders at the races:

"I have one of the kimberlite core samples from a CMKX core drill. I have two pieces; I split it in half with a hammer the other day so I could look inside of it. They're supposed to be from the Carolyn Pipe. Ron carried it around as a sample.

I'm telling you man, this thing has diamonds in it...you can see it with a ten-power magnifying glass. They're glistening. I showed it to people at the races all the time. I didn't pump it, Ron would just say, 'Hey, show them the kimberlite,' and I'd take it out of my toolbox and let people look at it. He kept losing it. I said, 'Ron, don't lose it, give it to me, I'll take care of it.'

I've never had anyone look at it to confirm it, the only way to check diamonds in kimberlite is through x-ray. I've been holding on to it the entire time. There's diamonds in there...they may be all industrial grade diamonds, but that's a business in itself. Isn't that weird? I've got a chunk of kimberlite that says he had the goods."

Cohen also confirmed stories that drillers were breaking bits when they hit kimberlite while drilling on property that was held by CMKX:

"I was at Urban's, and five of his Canadian friends were there in Las Vegas. And this one guy was talking to Urban, and he said 'Yeah, we're drilling for oil on the property and we keep hitting this green stuff.' Urban looked at him and said 'I don't know what that is, it might be a big rock or something.'

It was kimberlite. That's what the guy was hitting with his drill. I heard that story so many times from those Canadians. They're trying to drill for oil, and they're hitting diamonds, and they don't even realize it."

After taking over CMKM Diamonds in March of 2007, Kevin West visited Canada and viewed the core samples, but Urban reneged on his promise to have a licensed geologist present. Instead, Kevin was met by Urban's sister-in-law Sharon Halderston, who appeared to be knowledgeable about diamond mining but was far from being an objective licensed geologist. While it was impossible for

Diamond claims in Canada held by Emerson Koch for CMKX; called
"cow pasture" by some writers. Courtesy of Jason Webb and Anthony Pullicino.

Rundown mine site used to convince CMKX shareholders that CMKX had
"the goods." Courtesy of Jason Webb and Anthony Pullicino.

Urban Casavant and Jeff Arend, holding kimberlite core sample.
Courtesy of Jason Webb and Anthony Pullicino.

Kevin to evaluate the samples, he had every intention of pursuing the search for diamonds…at least until he discovered that Urban and his cohorts had ruthlessly robbed the company and its shareholders.

Do the core samples held by Marc Cohen contain real industrial-grade diamonds? And were the samples that Ron Casavant showed to CMKX shareholders and potential future shareholders at the races even from the Carolyn Pipe test drillings? Are there diamonds in any of the core samples sitting stored in the 2 ft. by 4 ft. wooden box in Saskatchewan? As usual, those are questions that can only be answered over time, if at all.

One disturbing discovery was a letter from a creditor in 2002 that claimed that Urban Casavant owed him money for providing a "parcel of rough" for the company, which is a bag of rough cut diamonds. Why would Urban buy rough cut diamonds if he was on the verge of his own massive diamond discovery in Saskatchewan? Were the rough cut diamonds intended to be yet another sales tool to entice potential shareholders? It makes the question about whether the core samples are even from the CMKX claims even more relevant.

So did the CMKX controlled claims actually have the potential to yield substantial amounts of diamonds? It appears that much of the 1.5 million acres of land that they held the mineral rights to was most likely, as *Stockwatch* put it, "moose pasture." After Entourage took over the rights to the claims held by Emerson Koch for CMKX, they allowed the majority of them to lapse. According to research done by Pedro2004 on *Proboards66*, Saskatchewan records showed that as of September, 2007, only 23 diamond and four uranium claims remained. A total of 35,487 acres is all that is left of one of the largest diamond mining claims in the world. According to Craig Doctor, who handles communications for Entourage, they retained the rights to the claims with the greatest potential of being diamondiferous and allowed the others to lapse. Among the claims that were allowed to lapse, the infamous "Carolyn Pipe" was restaked and is now controlled by United Carina and Consolidated Pine Channel (renamed Star Uranium Corp. and United Uranium Corp. and under new management).

There is a chance that CMKM Diamonds could actually regain control of the remaining claims that Entourage currently holds. In September of 2007, Entourage Mining filed a lawsuit against Emerson Koch's company 101047025 Saskatchewan LTD. and CMKM Diamonds to cancel the distribution of the 45 million shares of Entourage stock to CMKX shareholders. A CEO update from Kevin West on September 28th said:

> *"Our records show substantial money was paid for the claims and for drilling on the claims. It is the company's firm belief that these remaining claims should belong to the company because of the money spent to maintain these claims."*

Perhaps the greatest tragedy is that so many shareholders bought their CMKX stock at least partially because of the very real diamond potential that exists in Canada. If Urban Casavant had spent his time…and the company's considerable resources…searching for diamonds instead of squandering millions in the casinos in Las Vegas or on an extravagant lifestyle, the outcome might have been significantly different for the company and its shareholders. If he had taken the high road and exposed Ed Dhonau and John Edwards and their cohorts to the legal authorities instead of joining in the money grab, it is possible that CMKM Diamonds might be a legitimate mining company today. Instead, it is little more than a shell of a company trying to resurrect itself by suing its former officers and insiders in an attempt to recover stolen assets.

Despite the major obstacles that lay before them, Kevin West and Bill Frizzell still believe that "The New" CMKM Diamonds, Inc. will once again become a viable company, and will trade in one form or another at some time in the future.

Chapter 40 – A Blueprint for Corruption

"You have to kill the company to hide the crime."
~ Bill Frizzell

This story is about CMKX, but it could just as easily be about any of hundreds, or even thousands of penny stock companies. Shareholders invest their hard-earned money only to watch helplessly as potential turns into disaster, and dreams of wealth and riches become nothing more than so many empty promises. This ongoing scheme has been growing unchecked for decades.

It is a complex and well-oiled machine where every component from the paid shills on the message boards to the highest levels of Wall Street represent an important cog in the scheme. None of this is by accident. Every entity and person involved plays a role in the orchestrated scheme to defraud America. Those who are not involved in the actual act of defrauding the middle class are either helping to facilitate the robbery, or destroying the evidence after the fact.

This conspiracy has no clear beginning, and up to now, no ending; it is both carefully planned and self-perpetuating. This example revolves around CMKM Diamonds simply because it is the largest single fraud ever perpetrated in the world of penny stocks. It is the central flashpoint where 50,000 shareholders were unwittingly led into the epicenter of corruption. CMKX was indeed the Perfect Storm. It was a feeding frenzy of excitement evolving into obsession, hopes lapsing into despair, and dreams turning into nightmares.

It's been said that a person can rob more money with a pen than with a gun. But with the advent of electronic trading, stock message boards, and spam emails, it is the click of a mouse that is the most deadly weapon of all. The details might differ from one scam to another, but the basic strategy is always the same. Stock fraud is a carefully constructed step-by-step strategy designed to rob shareholders, destroy the evidence, and cover the robbers' trails:

The Blueprint: In the set-ups of the late 1990s and early 2000s, the companies were often victimized by unscrupulous lenders, naked short sellers, and offshore hedge funds, but now the con seems more often than not to emanate from within the companies. The same individuals appear in numerous companies as corporate officers, members of the board of directors, consultants, or simply major shareholders of the various scams that populate the penny stock market.

In the case of CMKX, the wheels of fraud were in motion long before the scam began. John Edwards was setting up fake companies, trust accounts, and trading accounts to launder his share of the spoils. Urban Casavant and David DeSormeau were setting up fraudulent companies like PartTime Management as vehicles to funnel shares of stock and money. Ed Dhonau and Rendal Williams

347

were creating their own "mining" companies to partner with CMKX. Each person involved in the scheme was there for a specific reason, either to set up, facilitate, or perpetuate the robbery. In some instances, their role was simply to provide a distraction before, during, and after the fraud.

The Sucker: It is important for the perpetrators to know who their victims are far in advance. The core group of victims in most cases is comprised of the victims from the just completed scam. The prior scheme often overlaps with the new scam or is carried out as a parallel scheme at the same time.

The core group of shareholders in CMKX originally came from PCBM, a company that cost its own shareholders tens of millions of dollars in losses. In this instance (as is almost always the case), the PCBM scam was fronted by some of the same people who later showed up in one form or another in CMKX, most notably John Edwards, Jeffrey Turino and Adam Barnett. They also shared the same transfer agent – Helen Bagley at 1st Global Transfer. This was not by accident.

The Pitch: The pitch can be as subtle as a few people pumping the company on popular stock market message boards and sending out spam emails or as blatant as a 50-foot billboard at a racetrack. Surprisingly, these techniques are not only utilized in the penny stock market, but are common in larger companies as well. Because the criminals have gotten away with murder in the loosely regulated pink sheet and OTC stock markets, they have become more brazen and worked their way up to companies listed on the larger exchanges.

As the PCBM scam began to play itself out, the CMKX buzz was just beginning. A few pumpers began posting on the PCBM and other popular penny stock message boards, hyping CMKX as the next big thing. Volume in CMKX was already beginning to pick up, which is usually a sign of buying interest. This is essential, and is often nothing more than an illusion created by the same group of people buying and selling shares to each other.

The Pump: The key to a successful pump is simple – raise the excitement level until emotion supplants rational thinking in the investment decision-making process. The perpetrators often use message boards, misleading or bogus press releases, and a rumor mill that is tightly controlled and fed behind the scenes to set up one glorious run on the stock. The price goes to astronomical heights, pulling in more buyers as it increases to several times its original value. The perpetrators, however, are selling into the pump, dumping shares both on the way up, and later, on the way back down as well. Often they can dump shares at a huge profit on the way up, then overwhelm the buying pressure by shorting the stock at or near the peak and all the way back down to below its original price. Then, they create another buying frenzy by buying back the shares that they shorted at a fraction of the cost.

In the case of CMKX, the pump was taken to new heights. It began with the usual posters planted to promote the company's stock on other message boards, in particular PCBM. At the same time, Urban Casavant began to put out press releases that were filled with vague promises that were easily spun by the planted posters. It's no coincidence that many of the most avid CMKX pumpers, including Wodan from the later infamous "Belgian connection," had also pumped PCBM. They were the foot soldiers in this con, turned loose to spread rumors that always seemed to emanate from a secret source inside the company, a broker or banker, or someone else in the know. They appeared to possess inside information that gave them credibility on the boards and in the chatrooms. Some, like Accadacca, ultimately achieved guru status, with hundreds of followers who obediently spread their predictions and words of wisdom even further. Unfortunately, this was all orchestrated as well. The foot soldiers were purposely fed their information by those at the top. For example, Urban would put out a press release saying that the company was looking at merging with another company…but didn't name the company in question. He didn't have to name names. That was the job of the foot soldiers, who quickly let it leak that the company in question was none other than…PCBM. It was a process that was repeated for as long as there were shareholders gullible enough to believe it.

CMKX and its shareholders alike coined hyperbolic catchphrases such as Urban's legendary "Million Millionaires" pledge, and the subsequent "Stock Play of a Lifetime" and "Perfect Storm" catchphrases. The races were the ultimate promotional events, complete with photo ops featuring big names and celebrities like rock icon Sammy Hagar, who had no idea that he was being used to add glamour and luster to a scam. Nevada Secretary of State Dean Heller's involvement with CMKXtreme, however minimal, sent a clear but misguided message to shareholders that the company had to be clean.

While the races and billboards were building the excitement at street level, the press releases continued to feed the frenzy, and in some cases, led shareholders unknowingly into other scams. What seemed to be partnerships with other companies usually turned out to be introductions to a parallel con designed to bilk even more money out of unsuspecting investors. What looked like bonuses in the form of stock dividends from other companies were really just free samples designed to whet the shareholders' appetites for that stock as well.

Remember the CMKX agreements with UCAD? Over $15 million in CMKX shareholders' money was pumped into UCAD. At the same time, Urban and Carolyn Casavant, and their children Wesley Casavant and Cindy Dwyer, along with Corrine Ward, received 600,000 shares apiece in return in late September of 2004. While CMKX shareholders were buying into UCAD at or near the high of $19 a share, Casavant and company (along with Rendal Williams and everyone else who had a piece of the action) were dumping their shares.

Then, they repeated the same scenario over again. Casavant International Mining (CIM), UCAD, SGGM, Nevada Minerals, and CMKXtreme were all created for the sole purpose of creating an illusion of legitimacy while stealing more money at every turn.

Even the deal to transfer CMKX's assets to Entourage Mining appeared to be just another way to deliver the shareholders to that company...where Urban and several of his family members already owned shares of stock. Send 50,000 shareholders to Entourage, pump that company, create a buying frenzy...and sell at the high.

Finally, there were the "names" brought into the company to add fuel to the fire. Ex-SEC attorney Roger Glenn's involvement at the height of the buying frenzy was perhaps the most significant catalyst that convinced thousands of shareholders to continue to buy stock at ten times the original price. Instead of saving the company from being delisted, Glenn issued seven opinion letters in a single month that allowed over 300 billion additional shares to be dumped into the market. Even the legendary Bob Maheu turned out to be nothing more than a high-profile diversion to keep the shareholders placated while the crooks pocketed their money. And all along, many shareholders continued to idolize Urban Casavant, who was eventually exposed as perhaps the biggest crook of them all.

The pump worked so well with CMKX that it actually did take on a life of its own. The most avid shareholders, like `Topogigio` and `Willy Wizard`, were fed information that was dutifully passed on to others, while `Sterling` and *The Green Baron's* Ed Miller were given preferential treatment because of their access to other potential investors through their message boards and chatrooms. In fact, CMKX even "promoted" the most dedicated believers to actual positions within the company, pulling both Andy Hill and Uncle Melvi from the ranks to handle investor relations. There is nothing more convincing than a pumper who truly believes.

Even Kevin West began his epic journey in CMKX as a true believer in CMKX, in Urban Casavant and his dream of a Million Millionaires. Until his eyes were opened to the ugly reality of the situation, Kevin was at one time 100% convinced that the company was the Stock Play of a Lifetime.

Battered Shareholder's Syndrome: Once the mind defines something as absolute truth, it is difficult, and in many cases almost impossible to redefine that truth as a fallacy. The human brain needs things to be laid out in black and white, absolute truth on one side, easily defined lies on the other. To reach that conclusion, information is needed, and in the absence of factual information, any convincing and well-thought out rumor or theory will suffice.

CMKX took it a step further by purposely feeding false information to the victims, thus creating a core group of shareholders who truly believed in the lie. Many of those same shareholders were convinced that God had led them to CMKX, making it practically impossible to shake their belief in the company and its charismatic leader. Even when warning signs began to appear, the shareholders had become too disoriented and confused by the conflicting information to make rational judgments about their investment. They had begun to question their own decision-making abilities, and taking no action whatsoever.

The Dump: While the shareholders are being told to buy, buy, buy, those in control of the stock are in the sell, sell, sell mode. This is commonplace in the world of penny stocks, but it's another technique that can be used in almost every stock in the market. On his show, "Mad Money," former hedge fund manager Jim Cramer has described how he and others in the industry feed misleading and false information to the media about companies that were often household names. It was another tactic to manipulate the stock price so a profit could be made on a short sell. Other times, they would create rumors that would drive the price up if they held long positions in the company's stock.

Piling on: In stock fraud, everyone wins...that is, everyone except for the shareholders. The brokers are raking in record revenues and multi-million dollar bonuses from the sale of stock, and even more when they don't have to deliver it. The market makers receive a fee as the middleman whether the trades settle or not. The transfer agents profit from keeping track of the shares and issuing certificates, even if the company dumps 703 billion shares into the market. Attorneys issue questionable opinion letters, accountants play fast and loose with the rules, paid promoters hype, message board posters pump, and the captured media dutifully either praises or bashes the companies. And every one of them makes a profit from hefty fees, shares of stock, or both. With help from all of the above, hedge funds and/or company insiders manipulate the stock price up and down at will to fit their current position.

Burying the Body: To perpetuate the perfect fraud, the evidence must be destroyed. Once the con artists have finished milking the shareholders dry, the company will most likely conveniently fail to file one form or another with the SEC, or violate some obscure rule. In all likelihood, the SEC will simply bury the body and all the evidence with it.

Like many other penny stock scams, CMKX was designed to fail from the very beginning. The very same fraudulent business deals that were set up to fuel the pump had built-in mechanisms that guaranteed their failure once they outlived their usefulness. Missed payments voided existing contracts and returned assets to the original owners. Eventually, devoid of any value whatsoever, the company was supposed to either be delisted by the SEC and left to die or bankrupted from the built-in mountain of debt. It was only the intervention of Kevin West and Bill Frizzell that short-circuited the process.

The same scenario is being repeated over and over again on a continual basis. If the company dies, then the evidence dies with it. The records are destroyed, the money trail is obliterated, shares in brokerage accounts are wiped clean, and short sellers are free and clear.

Risk, uncertainty, and ignorance: Ignorance is not necessarily a reflection of a lack of intelligence on the part of the investor. It is more often a lack of information, which is usually by design, and an excess of misinformation, which is always by design. When it comes to investing, what one doesn't know can not only hurt them, it can be financially fatal.

Misinformation, on the other hand, is something that is often nearly impossible to sort out from fact. Investors need to educate themselves to recognize the techniques commonly employed by con artists trying to steal their money. Otherwise, sooner or later, they will find themselves in the same boat as the shareholders of CMKX, and millions of investors like them, hoping that a miracle will turn their investment into prosperity. Until the regulators do a better job of policing the stock market in general, and particularly the world of penny stocks, "buyer beware" will continue to be the golden rule of investing.

Epilogue: The Naked Truth

"The primary mission of the U.S. Securities and Exchange Commission (SEC) is to protect investors and maintain the integrity of the securities market."
~ SEC Mission Statement, 2003, www.sec.gov

"In 2005, Chairman Cox requested that the mission statement be changed to better reflect the current goals of the SEC."
~ SEC Senior Counsel Chris Wilson

"The mission of the U.S. Securities and Exchange Commission is to protect investors, maintain fair, orderly, and efficient markets, and facilitate capital formation."
~ SEC Mission Statement, December 23, 2005, www.sec.gov

Unfortunately, the story of CMKM Diamonds, like most stories in real life, doesn't end up as a package held together by a ribbon tied neatly in a bow. For many Americans, there is no pot of gold (or in this case, wheelbarrow full of diamonds) at the end of the investing rainbow. As of November 30, 2007, not a single indictment has been issued against those who robbed over 50,000 shareholders... correction; make that "50,000 people"...of their hard earned money, and more importantly, their belief in the American Dream. Tens of thousands of lives have been changed, for better or worse. As *Proboards70* moderator Kranker put it, "Shareholders quit their jobs, ran up their credit cards, got divorced, and even died while all the rumors were circulated that we would be rich *tomorrow* at 9:27am, everyday... No amount of money in the world can bring back what they lost along the way."

Are the thousands of companies that dot the landscape of the penny stock market legitimate enterprises trying to realize their own version of the American Dream? Or are they part of the scam, set up from the start to bleed shareholders dry? What about the thousands that have already been destroyed? Were they victims of a system gone wrong or predators using that same system to line their own pockets at the expense of investors hoping to better their own lives? In the end, it will turn out that it was a little of both extremes, and everything in between. Unfortunately, regardless of who the criminals are, the victims are always the shareholders.

As of this writing, the corruption not only still exists, it has in fact escalated. Despite considerable progress made by advocates of stock market reform, our financial system is dangerously close to reaching the point of no return. What began as a limited giveaway to a few well-connected ultra-wealthy friends of Wall Street and Washington has turned into a worldwide money grab.

If one organized group of criminals can wreak this much havoc in our financial markets for decades, just imagine how bad the corruption must be system wide. How many John Edwards and Urban Casavants are out there, aided and abetted by their own cartel of hardened criminals bent on destroying our entire system? And why were they allowed to steal hundreds of millions of dollars from shareholders in company after company without repercussions for decades?

Ultimately, the responsibility rests with the SEC, who has designed a system of checks and balances that accomplish neither goal, and with a Congress who has turned a blind eye to the pleas of their own constituents. The regulations that should protect the millions of shareholders who have invested their money and lives into the American Dream instead have been abandoned in favor of big money and greed. Our financial markets are controlled by criminals and driven by heartless greed, and the SEC has given away the keys to the vault. The system that is now in place in our stock market not only allows corruption, it is actually set up to facilitate the countless robberies that take place on a daily basis.

While breakdowns in the federal system and at the SEC were largely responsible for the CMKX scam, there are other factors that facilitate corruption of this magnitude as well. A 2005 U.S. Department of the Treasury report cited Nevada as one of three states that invites fraud through lax corporate regulations. The report stated:

> *"Legal jurisdictions, whether states within the United States or entities elsewhere, that offer strict secrecy laws, lax regulatory and supervisory regimes, and corporate registries that safeguard anonymity are obvious targets for money launderers. A handful of U.S. states offer company registrations with cloaking features – such as minimal information requirements and limited oversight – that rival those offered by offshore financial centers."*

The report went on to describe shell companies, such as the ones the John Edwards, Urban Casavant and others involved with CMKX used to launder money stolen from shareholders, as entities that "have no physical appearance other than a mailing address, employ no one, and produce nothing."

A corporate planning company publishes a list called "16 Reasons to Incorporate in Nevada" touting the state as the most "corporate friendly and pro-business" state in the country. Beginning with "Nevada Protects the Corporate Veil," which refers to corporate officers being held personally liable for company debts, the list includes:

- ***Nevada Protects the Corporate Veil.*** *Nevada appears like an iron fortress to your creditors. In fact, the corporate veil has only been pierced two times in Nevada in the last 24 years!! In comparison, in one out of two cases, the corporate veil is pierced in California.*

- ***Nevada Protects the Board of Directors and Officers.*** *In 1987, the Nevada Legislature passed a revolutionary law that permits corporations* to place provisions in their Articles of Incorporation that would eliminate the personal liability of officers and directors to the stockholders of Nevada Corporations.

- **Nevada does NOT Exchange Information with the IRS.** Nevada is only one of two states that do not turn over corporate information to the IRS.

- **Nevada Offers the Best Protection of Board of Directors from Shareholders' Lawsuits.** In order to find the Board of Directors liable, the shareholders must prove gross negligence on behalf of the Board of Directors. The test to prove gross negligence in Nevada is to pierce the corporate veil. No other state has such a high test.

- **In Nevada, One Person Can Hold ALL the Corporate Offices.** One person can hold the offices of President, Secretary, Treasurer, and be the sole Director in Nevada. Many states require at least three (3) officers and/or directors.

- **Nevada does NOT Require Stockholders, Directors, and Officers to be US Citizens or Live or Hold Meetings in Nevada.** Directors need not be Stockholders and Officers and Directors of a Nevada corporation can be protected from personal liability for lawful acts of the corporation.

In 2005 alone, Nevada added over 40,000 new limited liability companies to its roles and collected hundreds of millions of dollars in incorporation fees. The same year, they led the nation in white collar crime committed utilizing the internet. Current Nevada Secretary of State Ross Miller recently began to make changes to the secretary of state's website. Under predecessor Dean Heller (now a Nevada congressman), the website enticed prospective public companies by asking "Why incorporate in Nevada?" Then, the website answered its own question: "Minimal reporting and disclosure requirements. Stockholders are not public record."

Stock market reform activist Bud Burrell, who has followed the CMKX story for years, commented on the efforts of the CMKX shareholders to find help at the federal and state level:

"These shareholders initiated tens of thousands of written and oral complaint communications to every single State and Federal entity, agency and many others, to include the Department of Justice, the Attorney General of Nevada, every level of the SEC, the DTCC, the NASD, their Congressmen, The House's Committee on Financial Services, their Senators, The Senate Banking Committee, and many, many more. They begged for help and they got one form of answer: "We don't have the resources." In every single incidence, not one of these organizations or their related officials discharged their sworn duties to protect individual investors."

The fleecing of over 50,000 CMKX shareholders should never have happened. Let me repeat that, because this is the real story here:

THE FLEECING OF OVER 50,000 CMKX SHAREHOLDERS SHOULD NEVER HAVE HAPPENED.

Just as they bear the brunt of the responsibility in the failure of our financial system, inaction by the SEC and our elected representatives in Congress is directly responsible for the suffering those 50,000 shareholders endured. Where were they over 15 years ago, when these same criminals were robbing shareholders in other scams? Where were they over four years ago when advocates began sounding the alarm about a system horribly out of control? And where were they when those same desperate shareholders were crying out for justice, only to have their cries fall upon deaf ears?

The ongoing joint investigation by the DOJ, FBI, and IRS into CMKX has dragged on for years, much to the dismay and frustration of the shareholders of the company. A phone call to Charyn Aldred of the IRS on November 5, 2007, confirmed that Brian Pugh was heading up the investigation into CMKX for the Department of Justice. While Pugh didn't return calls and the DOJ spokesperson who did couldn't comment on the CMKX investigation, she did discuss fraud investigations in general:

> *"There's such a shortage of agents at the FBI and the IRS to work such big fraud cases because they've been reassigned to terrorism and many other things. They're very strapped for resources and so are we. Las Vegas has grown so much over the last twenty years and our offices haven't grown much at all. The top priorities of the Department of Justice and this administration are fighting terrorism, violent crime, and crimes against children, so the fraud cases are not at the top of the list. Even if they were, they still take a long time to investigate and bring to the point of issuing charges. Sometimes they're never charged; just because we have an investigation doesn't mean we're going to have enough evidence to charge anybody. That doesn't mean that people haven't done anything wrong or that are criminal, it just means that we don't have enough evidence to prove it beyond a reasonable doubt. Every case is different obviously, but in my experience, especially with investment fraud and securities fraud cases, they take many, many years."*

Bill Frizzell said that while he couldn't comment on specifics either, CMKM Diamonds is willingly cooperating with all federal regulators and enforcement agencies. Frizzell and West have repeatedly expressed their desire to see all the perpetrators in the CMKX tragedy brought to justice, and I have repeatedly passed their names and contact information to the various enforcement agencies. Leslie Hakala of the SEC has continued to gather evidence as well, so there is hope that eventually fraud and criminal charges will be brought against John Edwards, Urban Casavant, and their cohorts.

If the only thing that this book accomplishes is to serve as a wake-up call to the problem of financial fraud then it will have been worth it. My hope is that it will act as a catalyst and put pressure on the federal agencies who have been investigating this scandal to finally make it a top priority. I hope that the outcry is loud enough and persistent enough to grease the wheels of justice. While it might not be possible for regulators to return what was stolen from 50,000 shareholders, at least let there be some retribution against those who did the crime.

On December 23, 2005, the Securities and Exchange Commission, after first eliminating the word "honesty" from their Mission Statement in their 2003 Annual Report, changed the Mission Statement again, without notice. Originally listed on their website as "The primary mission of the U.S. Securities and Exchange Commission (SEC) is to protect investors and maintain the integrity of the securities market," it was rewritten by SEC Commissioner Chris Cox to read:

"The mission of the U.S. Securities and Exchange Commission is to protect investors, maintain fair, orderly, and efficient markets, and facilitate capital formation."

And so, in two short years, both honesty and integrity were forever eliminated as the stated mission of the governing body of the United States stock market.

In January of 2000, there were 13,300 companies listed on the Over the Counter Exchanges. As of October, 2006, there were 2,700 left standing…and the number keeps falling. Every day that passes that we don't address the problems facing our financial markets, the potential fallout becomes worse. Even now we face serious consequences, and unchecked, our country, and by extension the entire world, is facing a potential economic meltdown.

After years of effort by stock market reform advocates and disenfranchised investors, recent events have given hope that rampant problems in our financial system might come under closer scrutiny. On March 26th, Dave Patch, founder of *www.investigatethesec.com* and an early advocate for stock market reform, met with David Kotz, the inspector general of the SEC, and an unnamed official from the General Accounting Office.

Among the information on numerous companies that Patch provided to Inspector General Kotz was information excerpted from this as-yet-unreleased book and accompanying interviews about negligence committed by individuals within the SEC in dealing with the CMKM Diamonds case. Although Patch acknowledged that company insiders and their cohorts defrauded the shareholders, the inspector general is looking at charges that individuals within the SEC violated regulations and failed to properly protect CMKX shareholders. This author is supplying evidence to the Inspector General Kotz showing that the SEC knew about the existence of fraud in CMKX at least as early as May of 2004, and yet allowed the company to dump hundreds of billions of shares of stock before finally delisting CMKX in October of 2005. While the Saskatchewan Financial Services Commission first halted trading in the company on October 26, 2004, CMKX continued to trade in the U.S. for another full year.

Possible actions include an audit into the SEC's overall regulatory practices, or investigations into specific allegations of wrongdoing in various companies, including CMKX. While Kotz specifically cited naked short selling in his comments after the meeting, his office will most likely address the broader issue of systemic SEC regulatory failures.

Stock counterfeiting, either in the form of naked short selling or fails to deliver, is a very real and damaging problem, but as this story illustrates, it is only a small part of a much larger issue. The central issue here is that our entire system is in danger of reducing the American Dream into nothing more than an illusion dangled like the promise of diamonds in front of middle class America. As long as the game is rigged in favor of the ultra-wealthy and the ultra-connected, then that dream will forever be just out of reach of the vast majority of our citizens. Unless we overcome the culture of greed that permeates our political policies and our financial institutions, government "for the people, by the people" will soon become, like integrity and honesty in the SEC's Mission Statement, nothing more than a footnote in the history books.

For updates and additional information about the ongoing saga of CMKM Diamonds, Inc., go to www.thenakedtruthbook.com

For additional information about corruption and reform efforts in our financial markets, go to www.faulkingtruth.com

Author's Note

The story of CMKM Diamonds was in many ways a life-changing experience for me. After almost four years of chronicling the pandemic corruption in our financial markets, and two years of trying to confirm or refute rumors, uncover the truths, and expose the lies in the CMKX story, I feel that in some ways I have become a part of the CMKX family. I am not a shareholder, although I have often thought that I wouldn't mind picking up a million shares just so I could make it official, just to feel the rush of "owning a million shares of a diamond mining company." Even without being an official shareholder, I have bonded, argued, laughed, cried, hurt, and hoped along with thousands of those who are the real subjects of this story. In short, they have begun to feel like family to me. Finishing this project has filled me with a sense of relief (Thank God it's finally over!), but also left me with a feeling of sadness. Like thousands of others who either by design, predestination, or merely by accident found themselves absorbed, and yes, obsessed with the story of CMKX, I have forged friendships along the way, and became a part of something larger than me. To steal a line from an email I recently received from Janie, one of my CMKX family members, "There are certain days I feel very lucky to be a part of it all....and other days that I feel cursed."

Along the way, I found myself sharing information with the FBI, IRS, and DOJ, and working to convince them to take advantage of the wealth of evidence that Bill Frizzell and Kevin West have accumulated. I was fortunate to interview legendary figures who were (and some say still are) a part of American history. I looked on as the person who introduced me to the story in the beginning became the central character of that same story two years later. I even found myself pulled into the story itself while doing my weekly radio shows on *CFRN.net* (and later on *TogiNet.com*), and writing for *The Faulking Truth* website. I listened in amazement as my former co-host on *The Faulking Truth Show* and avowed Urban devotee spent an entire hour bashing me and called me a "spineless jelly eunuch" on her final radio show. On another show that originally aired on September 29, 2006, after confirming the criminal investigation targeting CMKX, I used extremely poor judgment in referring to the investigation as a "sting." The comment was of course immediately interpreted as confirmation that CMKX had been conceived from the start as a way to trap the corrupt brokers, bad guys, etc. and clean up the entire market under the skilled guidance of Urban Casavant, Bob Maheu, and Roger Glenn. To this day, after dozens of explanations and clarifications, and after admitting that calling it a "sting" was the worst choice of words that I had made in my entire life, there are still those who believe I confirmed the biggest rumor of all time involving CMKX.

While writing the book I became the CEO and president of TogiEntertainment, Inc., the company that evolved from this book and my background in entertainment and writing. I forged what I hope is a lifelong relationship with The Owners Group, Inc., a company born out of a desire to help others avoid the pitfalls of a corrupt market. Other writers' careers were launched as a result, and I have developed close relationships with them and with my new co-workers. Most recently, we launched *TogiNet.com*, an internet radio network that has in turn helped to raise the profile of numerous national issues, including financial fraud and voting fraud, and given a voice to numerous up and coming talk show hosts, indie musicians, and artists.

Life is an adventure. You never know what seemingly ordinary event might change the direction of your own life forever, for better or worse, and alter your perceptions of the world around you...and the infinitely larger world that exists inside of you. Don't be surprised if the next journey that you embark upon leads you down unexpected paths to a destination that is nothing like you originally envisioned. In the meantime, just strap yourself firmly into the roller coaster of life...and sit back and enjoy the ride.

APPENDICES

Appendix A: Degrees of Separation

The players involved with CMKM Diamonds, Inc. can be tied to one another, as well as dozens of familiar faces connected to other scams or questionable companies. In a "six degrees of separation" scenario, it is possible to link this group to a vast majority of the scams on the OTC Bulletin Board and Pink Sheets Stock Exchanges. It would take hundreds, or even thousands of pages to list all of the connections between the CMKX players and players in other OTC and pink sheet companies.

This example illustrates how the world of penny stock fraud is interconnected:

NanoSignal Corp. (formerly MicroSignal), was largely financed by Gary Walters and John Edwards, with Rupert Perrin on the company's board of directors. Mike King of Princeton Research represented NanoSignal, and Richard Taulli was connected to the company through BBX Equity. Brian Dvorak issued an opinion letter for a group of shareholders releasing 25 million shares of a company called Exxcode that were exchanged for free-trading NanoSignal shares, just as he would for CMKX.

And Gary Walters, John Edwards, Rupert Perrin, Brian Dvorak, Mike King, and Richard Taulli were all connected to CMKX.

In January of 2004, NanoSignal announced a deal with Energy Ventures Organization to buy fuel cell generator units. Scott Ervin was the CEO of NanoSignal at the time, but would later be replaced by Walters, who was subsequently replaced by Perrin. Mike King of Princeton Research represented Energy Ventures. The CEO of Energy Ventures was John Bonaventura...who together with Gary Walters ran a company called Ramoil Management Ltd. In 2001, Ramoil was charged by the SEC in a stock fraud case that cost investors over $30 million.

Six months later, Bonaventura, who was a Nevada county assemblyman and county commissioner, lobbied heavily for Gary Walters and BBX Equity Group to win the property rights to develop a 5,000 unit condominium project dubbed "Flags of All Nations." Bonaventura even went so far as to trash Las Vegas kingpin Steve Walters, saying that Walters was only interested in the property in order to secure the water rights for his other resorts. In press releases touting Gary Walters and BBX Equity, no mention was made of Bonaventura's connections to Gary Walters or to NanoSignal.

Also, BBX Equity proposed a new stock exchange called the International Nevada Stock Exchange, or NVSE, which would be the hub of the Flag of All Nations project. The project manager of the proposed Flag of All Nations project was none other than Scott Ervin, who had also run an unsuccessful campaign for the Nevada State Legislature in 2004. Ervin was also at one time or another CEO of 20/20 Networks (TWNK), Micro Bio Medical Waste (MBWS) and Sienna Broadcasting (owned by Golf Entertainment). Rupert Perrin was on the board of directors of Micro Bio Medical Waste.

Other connections between the involved players included Steve Onoue, who was connected to Ervin as an officer/director of 20/20 Networks, and who with John Bonaventura had signed consulting agreements with NanoSignal. Onoue was also on the board of directors of Crown Partners, Inc., whose president was John Bonaventura…and of which Rupert Perrin was a stockholder.

And don't forget that Gary Walters was charged with 36 counts of theft and fraud, and the presiding judge was Joseph Bonaventure, who is the uncle of John Bonaventura…who is connected to Walters through Ramoil Management, the "Flag of all Nations" project in Vegas and the deal between NanoSignal and Energy Ventures.

In this single example, the nine major players are linked to ten companies in varying configurations, without even taking into account their connections to dozens of other players and scams. It is just one example that can be repeated dozens of times involving nearly every player in the CMKX scam. Las Vegas Division FBI Agent Ryan Randall wasn't exaggerating when he said "I believe that if we can bring down this group that it will eliminate 80% of the fraud in the state of Nevada."

Appendix B: The Players

There were dozens of players either directly or peripherally involved in the CMKX saga (even more if the message board gurus are included). Below is a partial list of the primary and secondary players and companies they were associated with:

Primary

Urban Casavant	CEO CMKX
John Edwards	Elusive Venture Capitalist: stock manipulator: con man
David DeSormeau	Chief Financial Officer CMKX
Rendal Williams	CEO USCA/ President CEO Barrington Foods
John Edgar Dhonau	CEO Nevada Minerals; Minera Nevada, S.A.
James & Jeannie Kenny	CMKI Cons. (issued billions of shares): Pt Time Mgmt.
Michael Williams	Conspirator with Urban to defraud shareholders; con man
Neil Levine	CPA hired by Edwards
Ginger Gutierrez	Sec/Treas Part Time Management
Roger Glenn	Attorney for USCA and CMKM Diamonds
Brian Dvorak	PA Holdings; Attorney for CMKM Diamonds
Donald Stoecklein	Attorney for CMKM Diamonds

Secondary

John T. Moran III	Attorney for CMKM Diamonds
Shawn Hackman	Convicted Fraud Felon / Ed Dhonau Associate
Rick Walker	ETGMF/TSX Ventures/ KPG
Emerson Koch	Pres. 101047025 Saskatchewan Ltd., held CMKX claims
Mike King	BBX Equity Group / Princeton Research
Chris Jensen	BBX Equity Group/Set up CMKX; Edwards' front man
Robert Maheu	BOD CMKX
Ian McIntyre	President CMKI
John Jarvis	Involved in acquisition and sale of CMKI
Samuel Singal	Early president of CMKI
Sherwood Cook	Attorney for John and Diana Lee Edwards
Melvin O'Neil	IR for CMKX
Helen Bagley	Transfer Agent 1st Global Stock Transfer
Michael Mitchell	Possible alter-ego of John Edwards
Ron Casavant	CEO CIM and Urban's brother
Don Yarter	Partner of Chris Jensen
Vincent LoCostro	CMKX shareholder, tied to PCBM

Gary Walters	BBX Equity Group
Richard Taulli	Juina Mining
David E. Coffey	CPA / Auditor
Rupert Perrin	Geologist BOD CMKI
Diana Lee Flaherty	Wife of John Edwards; found guilty of stock scams
William Hazeltine	SGGM president
Jay McFadden	GEMM executive
John Lee	Resident agent of Edwards' First Colony Merchant
Dan Lee	CFO for the Mirage in Vegas
Thomas Cook	CMKI attorney
John S. Woodward	Attorney/signatory for USCA
Wesley Casavant	Urban's son
Anthony Demint	Securities Law Inst., subsidiary of Stoecklein Law Group
Kevin Ryan	Global Intelligence partner / CEO Crystalix
Mark Hutchinson	Geologist

Appendix C: Companies with Association to CMKX Players

101047025 Saskatchewan Ltd.
1st Global
2dobiz Com Incices Inc
2themax Com Inc
ABDU
Absolute Glass Prot. Inc
Access Network Corp
Advantage Capital Development Corp
Afv Solutions/Inc
AGAP Serene
Albert Finch & Associates
Alberta Resource Consortium
AMDI International Inc
AMDI Petroleum Inc
American Career Centers Inc
American Water Star Inc
Ameritrade
Anchor
Anita Cohen
Anthony Rick
Anthony Rick acct 2
Aruma Mining Inc
Aurora Corp
Auxer Group Inc
Bali Nevada Corp Default
Bankhaus Suisse Alliance Corp
Bargain Products Inc
Bazarro Gears
BBX Equity Group
Beeston Enterprises Ltd
Berama Giorgio
Blencathia Acquisition Corp
Blini Hut Inc
British Columbia Mining Syndicate
Broadleaf Capital Trust
Bucktv Com Inc
Bullion River Gold Corp
Business Trans.n Serv Inc
Business Works,

Cal-Bay International Inc
Can Cal Resources Ltd
Canadian Diamond Fields Inc
Canadian Tundra Resources
Capstone Int'l Corp]
Caredecision Corp
Casavant Golf Co.,
Casavant Int'l Mining Corp
Casavant Racing Corp
Cash 4 Homes 247
CMKXtreme
Codatek Corp
Coffee Pacifica Inc
Communications Vue Management,
Consistorium Patruum
Curcuma Holdings Inc
Datascension Inc
Dead Man's Hand
Del la Norte Trading
Desert Stock Transfer
Diretvuer
Docket Reporting Services
Dogs International
Dolphin Knowledge
Doyle Trust
Dynasty Corporation of Nevada
Dynasty Int'l Corp
Dynasty Organization, Inc.
EBAIT
E-COM Inc
E-Connect
Ehomeone Com Inc
Elan First Merchant
Eleta Brunelle
Elite Flight Solutions, inc,
Enhanced Leasing International, LLC
Entertainment Direct TV Inc.
Eton Prop. Anthony/Ormstead

Eton Properties
Eupa Int'l Corp/NV
Euro Technology Outfitters
Eurosoft Corp
Exxcode
Eye Cash Networks
Fastraxx
Faza Gee Industrial
Feasibility Mining Services
Feasibility Studies International
Firestone Diamonds in UK
First Colony Merchant
First Nat'l Power Corp
Flexxtech Corp
Full Time Management

Futula Alloys Inc.
Futula Alloys Inc. (Vegas)
Gateway Int'l Holdings Inc
Genesis Capital Corp of Nevada
Giorgio Metals
Glass Container Corp
Global Network Inc
Globalwide Investment Co
GM Steel Trust
Goldstate Corp
Gourmet Gifts Inc
GS Energy CORP
Guardian Security Trust
Haley Corporate Consulting Inc
Hiaget Gears
Holmes Biopharma Inc
Holmes Herbs Inc
Horizon Prime
Huntion Trading
IB 2000.com
Immediatek Inc
Incubus Acquisitions (blank ck co.)
Inde Enterprises
Industrichem Trust
Inov8mobile Trust
Inseq Corp
instaCare Corp

Intergold Corp
Interlock Serv Inc
International Fuel Technology Inc
International Peace Foundation
International Success Builders Inc
Internet Acquisition Group Inc
Internet Culinary Corp
Intrac Inc
Investor Group of Las Vegas inc,
Issg/Inc
ITC trust
Jagged Peak/Inc
Jasmine Tree Farms (L)
Javelin Pharmaceuticals/Inc
John Di Properties
JT Trust
Juina Mining
Jules Englehardt Inc
Jules Englehardt Inc. Trust
Jules Englehardt Trust
Kart Trust
Kdgsports Com inc
Kenroy Comm Corp
Kolba Meadmakers
Lajolla Leathers
Lexington Resources Inc
Loan &Development Corp
Mantica Trust
Matrix Solars, LLC Default
McCarthy Grenache Inc
McClendon Transportation Trust
MCM Trust
Merchant Resources
Millennia Automated Products Inc
Millennium Plastics Corp
Millennium Software Inc
Minera Nevada, S.A
Mineral West Associates
Moderngroove Entert Inc
Moncom Enterprises (L)
Moodys Corp/DE
Moving Bytes Inc

Muller Media Inc
Navitone Tech Inc
Network Installation Corp
Nevada Corp HQ,
NoAngel Glass (Langley)
Nothing Corp
Oles Books
Oretech
Oretech Trust
PA Holdings
Pacific Industrial Corp
Patruum Services
PBS Holding/Inc
Pennaco Energy Inc
Petrol Oil & Gas Inc
Phoenix Metal U.S.A., LTD
Phoenix Metals U.S.A. II, INC.
Platinum Group Metals, Inc.
Pony Express USA Inc
Primary Business Systems Inc
Prime Equipment Inc
Prime Holdings & Investments Inc
Princeton Research
Project Group Inc
PTI Trust
Quapple Toffee (Langley)
Red Bluff Corp
Reginella Tackle Inc.
Relesden Constru
Rhino Enterprises Group Inc
Robert F. & Diana L. Flaherty, Inc.
Royal Phoenix
Rubicon Financial Inc
Sandias Azucara
Saskatchewan Min. Developments
Seaena Group International
SFH Holding II
SFH Holdings I inc
Shareholder Relations USA
Silver Fox Capital,
Silver St. Vending Crp
Silver Stream Corp

Siteworks,
SL Int'l Investments Inc
Source One Inc/NV
Stevenson Mgt. Grp
Suerlan Gezebos
Suisse Alliance Corp
Tagami Holdings, Inc
Tell A Tale Inc
Terax Energy Inc
Tobian Trading
Tourpro Golf Inc
Transport Limited
Trezac International Corp
Tundra Resources Inc
Twin Faces East Entertainment Corp
Ubrandit Com
Ukraine Bus. Cp
Vanity Enterprises Inc
Vegas Equity Int'll Corp
Vidmar Limited Trust
Viford Trading Trust
Viva International Inc
Wakefield Services Corporation
Web St Journal
Web Street Journal
Wesco Finance Corp
Western Sky Inc
Wireless Xcessories Inc
World Wide Web Inc
Yankee Dynamo Steel
Yfc 355 Corp
Your Domain Com

Appendix D: Edwards Companies and Assigns

Company Name	Shares Issued
ABDU	1,000,000,000
AGAP Serene	6,659,000,000
Alberta Resource Consortium	12,000,000,000
Albert Finch and Associates	8,000,000,000
Aruma Mining Inc	2,070,000,000
Barrington Foods Trust	200,000,000
Bazarro Gears	1,070,000,000
Berama Giorgio	3,756,168,000
British Columbia Mining Syndicate	8,000,000,000
Broadleaf Capital Trust	200,000,000
Canadian Tundra Resources	2,300,000,000
Chen Trust	1,100,000,000
Anita Cohen	4,000,000,000
Consistorium Patruum	7,140,000,000
Dela norte Trading Langley	4,391,500,000
Del la Norte Trading (Vegas)	400,000,000
Docket Reporting Services	8,000,000,000
Doyle Trust	4,400,000,000
Elan First Merchant (Langley)	2,183,009,571
Elan First Merchant (Vegas)	1,080,000,000
Eleta Brunelle (Langley)	1,972,084,000
Eleta Brunelle (Langley)	140,056,000
Jules Englehardt Trust	4,760,000,000
Eton Properties	30,958,346,596
Fastraxx	200,000,000
Faza Gee Industrial	4,346,465,996
Feasibility Studies International	714,000,000
Feasibility Mining Services	6,000,000,000
First Colony Merchant	20,000,000
Futula Alloys Inc.	1,500,000,000
Futula Alloys Inc. (Vegas)	240,000,000
Giorgio Metals	2,070,000,000
GM Steel Trust	23,850,000,000
Guardian Security Trust	200,000,000
Hiaget Gears	1,500,000,000
Huntion Trading	2,331,033,600
Inde Enterprises (Vegas)	327,000,000
Inde Enterprises (Langley)	1,220,000,000
Industrichem Trust	200,000,000

Inov8mobile Trust	200,000,000
ITC trust	200,000,000
Jasmine Tree Farms (Langley)	1,070,000,000
John Di Properties	6,940,000,000
Jt Trust	1,500,000,000
Juina Mining Trust	200,000,000
Jules Englehardt	4,760,000,000
Jules Englehardt Inc	1,600,000,000
Jules Englehardt Inc. Trust	465,500,000
Kart Trust	3,000,000,000
Jeannie Kinney	8,000,000,000
Kolba Meadmakers (Langley)	870,000,000
Kolba Meadmakers (Vegas)	80,000,000
Lajolla Leathers	870,000,000
Loan and Development Corporation	1,657,142,857
Lajolla Leathers (Vegas)	80,000,000
Mantica Trust	200,000,000
McClendon Transportation Trust	200,000,000
MCM Trust	1,500,000,000
Mineral West Associates	12,000,000,000
Moncom Enterprises (Langley)	9,704,382,283
NoAngel Glass (Langley)	950,000,000
Oles Books	1,070,000,000
Ortech Trust	200,000,000
Patruum Services	6,000,000,000
PTI Trust	27,715,067,030
Quapple Toffee (Langley)	950,000,000
Reginella Tackle Inc.	950,000,000
Anthony Rick	6,000,000
Anthony Rick acct 2	1,600,000,000
Eton Properties Anthony / Ormstead	400,000,000
Frank Ormstead	6,000,000
Sandias Azucara	500,000,000
Saskatchewan Mineral Developments	8,000,000,000
Shareholder Relations USA	7,295,250,000
Suerlan Gezebos	1,070,000,000
Tobian Trading (Langley)	8,166,394,407
Tobian Trading (Vegas)	160,000,000
Vidmar Limited Trust	3,500,000,000
Viford Trading (Langley)	5,252,112,308
Viford Trading Trust (Vegas)	134,900,000
Wakefield Services Corporation	16,262,858

Totals for Edwards Companies and Assigns:

289,537,675,506

Appendix E: Edwards Trading Accounts

AGAP Serene Services, Inc. (1)
AGAP Serene Services, Inc. (2)
American Seaways Trust
Barrington Foods Trust
Broadleaf Capital Trust
De La Norte Trading
Debra Ann Edwards
Delaware Charter John Edwards Roth
Eton Properties Corp.
Fastraxx
Faza Gee
First Colony Merchant Trust
GM Steel Trust (1)
GM Steel Trust (2)
Guardian Security Trust
Hiaget Gears
Huntion Trading
Industrichern Trust
Inov8mogile Trust
ITC Trust
Jasmine Trading Trust
Julna Mining Trust
Jules T. Engelhardt, Inc.
Mantica Trust
McClendon Transportation Trust
Microsignal Trust
Moncom enterprises LTD Trust
Oretech Trust
Patruum Services SA
PTI Trust
Saskatchewan Mineral Development Trust
Shareholder Relations USA, Inc.
Shareholders USA, Inc.
Tobian Trading
Vidmar Trading Trust
Viford Trading

Appendix F: The Anatomy of a Rumor" or "I'll Take the Kool-Aid"

by Mark Faulk, June 17, 2006
www.faulkingtruth.com

ru·mor   P Pronunciation Key ('ru mər)

> n. A piece of unverified information of uncertain origin usually spread by word of mouth.
> Unverified information received from another; hearsay.

> tr.v. ru·mored, ru·mor·ing, ru·mors
> To spread or tell by rumor.

rumor

> n. gossip (usually a mixture of truth and untruth) passed around by word of mouth [syn: rumour, hearsay]

Yesterday, I did my weekly radio show on *cfrn.net*. All in all, it seemed to be a rather low key show, probably more subdued than my shows with Debi Kiontke, who wasn't with us yesterday. In fact, I was certain that the most controversial thing I did was a tongue-in-cheek segment where I wrote "BULL" in big letters across a picture of CNBC's Jim Cramer and threw it on the floor. Boy was I wrong.

Within minutes, the emails began to come in, my phone began to ring, and the accusations began to fly. I was accused of "taking cheap shots at shareholders of CMKX, putting them down and regarding them as uneducated and not understanding of what is going on," and of not knowing the difference between illegal naked short selling and legitimate short selling.

Then, someone emailed me a two-hour section of after the show discussion from one of the chat rooms. While a couple of people defended me in the room, others were...how should I put this? Not so kind. I was accused of calling the CMKX shareholders "Kool-Aid drinkers," saying that they were "stupid," referring to them as "sheep," and being generally condescending. One poster offered to send me a year's supply of Kool-Aid, and then added "Jonestown grape...That's poisonous, isn't it?" Another one called me a "faulking jerk" (yeah, haven't heard THAT one before), and yet another said "well mark probably snorts his refreshment" (okay, that one's kind of funny...not true, but funny). Even someone named Ines emailed me, describing herself as "the owner of the room that has 500 people revolving in it an any time" got into the act, and in fact seemed to delight in stirring things up even further. And then there was the stupid guy who said "I WOULD ROTHER READ THE CAT IN THE HAT THE HIS STUPID BOOK!!!" And yes, I called that idiot stupid, and you can quote me on that.

But the one that hurt the most? Someone really took the low road, and trashed me using the "Name Game Song": "MARK MARK FO FARK BANNANA NANA DOE DARK." Ouch.

Okay, let's be clear about this: the vast, vast, vast majority of the 50,000 plus CMKX shareholders are intelligent, kind, caring people who just want to do the right thing. I have spoken with many of them, and believe that they are wonderful people. However, it's obvious that an isolated few among them are spreading unfounded rumors and distorting the truth. It only serves to divert the focus from the real issue, which is the wholesale fleecing of innocent shareholders by insiders enabled by a corrupt financial system.

I'll just pull a few of the better quotes from that chat, leaving off the names to protect the innocent, and so the offenders won't be offended....again.

(2:02 PM) Paltalk: This is a G rated voice room intended for a General Audience including minors. Offensive language is not permitted. To speak, hold the ctrl key down.

(2:02 PM) Poster 1: forget about this guy book. we can tell how his attitude is toward CMKX. This guy is a poor loser. IMO

(2:02 PM) Poster 2: I HATE KOOL AID I DRINK COUNTRY TIME LEMONADE

(2:03 PM) Poster 3: MARK AGAIN, KNOWS WERE LISTENING, HE MAY KNOW MORE THAN WHAT HE IS SAYINGM HE MAY ALREADY HAVE THE END TO THE BOOK, AND I HONESTLY AM NOT OFFENDED BY THE KOOL-AID COMMENT I DO DRINK KOOL-AID AND ALWAYS WILL, ROTFLMAO

(2:03 PM) Poster 4: I'll drink Limonade flavored Koolade. Lol

(2:04 PM) Poster 5: SO THIS GUY BETTER PAY ATTENTION TO HOW HE REFERST TO US.

(2:05 PM) Poster 5: IF IT IS STAGED,, FOR SURE NOBODY CALLED HIM AND TOLD HIM TO CALL US STUPID, OR COOLAID DRINKERS FOR BELIEVING IN VALUE

(2:05 PM) Poster 5: THAT WAS HIS PERSONAL CHOICE TO PUT US DOWN

(2:06 PM) Poster 5: THERE IS NO PLACE IN THE STING TO CALL US STUPID.. FOR BELIEVING IN ANY VALUE.

(2:08 PM) Poster 5: YOU WANT TO CALL US STUPID,, ? WELL KIND OF MAKES ME FEEL YOU DONT NEED MY MONEY

(2:08 PM) Poster 11: I must have listened to someone else this morning. I don't remember him saying any of this, at least not enough to upset me.

(2:09 PM) Poster 6: You are right. What is Kool Aid anyway?

(2:09 PM) Poster 7: I do like Tang, do they sell Tang?

(2:10 PM) Poster 3: AGAIN I ASKED WHAT DID MARK SAY BESIDES THE KOOLAID COMMENT AND NO1 ANSWERED

(2:11 PM) Poster 3: MARK SAID WERE STUPID INES?

(2:11 PM) Poster 8: When did he call anyone stupid? I didn't hear that?

(2:11 PM) Poster 9: Did he call us stupid?

(2:11 PM) Poster 3: MARK SAID WERE STUPID INES?

(2:11 PM) Poster 8: When did he call anyone stupid? I didn't hear that?

(2:11 PM) Poster 10: he didn't say that

(2:11 PM) Poster 12: WHO CALLED WHO STUPID?

(2:11 PM) Poster 9: Did he call us stupid?

(2:11 PM) Poster 13: Mark needs to come in here and prepare to answer questions for his remarks

(2:12 PM) Poster 14: I hear people calling others koolaid drinkers all the time on this board, but it hurts when someone else does it. Lmao

(2:12 PM) Poster 15: CONDESCENDING?

(2:13 PM) Poster 13: perhaps he could have used different words to describe the investors who have been damaged

(2:13 PM) Poster 13: koolaid drinkers was definitely unkind

(2:14 PM) Poster 5: ITS NOT UP TO HIM TO BE CONDESCENDING TO US

(2:14 PM) Poster 16: koolaid drinker is a title that came OUTof the ROOMS

(2:14 PM) Poster 16: sheep is another word that came out of the ROMS

(2:13 PM) Poster 13: perhaps he could have used different words to describe the investors who have been damaged

(2:14 PM) Poster 17: those people can if you bought cmkx..you drank their hool aid>that label is SO OVERUSED and MEANINGLESS...

(2:14 PM) Poster 13: ah okay, was that the reference in context only?

(2:15 PM) Poster 16: right we know that

(2:15 PM) Poster 17: sheep...kool aid...bla bla bla...

(2:15 PM) Poster 17: whatever..

(2:15 PM) Poster 18: Book sellers and writers couldn't care less about whether their info offends, exhorts or is indifferent. The want the money. I agree with genxer (believe i did last time she mentioned her opinion a while back). I think he planned on getting some controversy going and therefore get his name out a bit more. It seems to be backfiring

(2:15 PM) Poster 19: then don't say it comes from a chat room

(2:15 PM) Poster 13: not what I meant, how did he reference it in the interview today?

(2:15 PM) Poster 18: as referenced by the 'new' screen names defending him in here and asking when he called anyone stupid

(2:16 PM) Poster 3: AND GEN (NOT TO ATTACK YOU) I'VE HEARD YOU THREATEN PEOPLE ON HERE IF THEY PICKETT OR WRITE LETTERS THAT WAS MORE OFFENDIDNG TO ME THAN WHAT MARK SAID, BUT I DONT CARE!! BECAUSE I UNDERSTAND HOW PEOPLE CAN GET FRUSTRATED OR SAY THINGS AND MAY NOT HAVE MALICE IN THIER HEARTS

(2:16 PM) Poster 20: I have listened to the interview twice. I think everything is being taken out of context

(2:19 PM) Poster 21: TELL HIM WHERE GOING TO BUY COOL AID WHEN THIS IS OVER WITH!!!!!

(2:20 PM) Poster 6: I say we all chip in and buy Mark Faulk a years supply of Kool Aid when CMKX money does materialize.

(2:20 PM) Poster 6: What's the worst flavor of Kool Aid?

(2:20 PM) Poster 21: IM GOING TO OWN COOL AID COMPANY SOON

(2:25 PM) Poster 6: Jonestown grape....that's poisonous isn't it?

(2:29 PM) Poster 14: nobody works for free. He has done alot to fight nss and we should be grateful

(2:32 PM) Poster 22: WHAT THE HECK IS GOING ON? WHY IS EVERYONE UPSET? WHAT HAS HAPPENED?????????????????????? UPDATE?????

(2:42 PM) Poster 23: Mr. Faulk: I am a cmkx shareholder and I HATE koolaide. Actually you have offended many of us who have previously pre-ordered The Faulking Truth book. I and many other shareholders have acquired much due diligence of this co. and many others associated with it.

(2:43 PM) Poster 23: The participants also. I really don't feel I have to write you a book of the last 2 1/2 years I have experienced with other dedicated shareholders of cmkx.

(2:43 PM) Poster 23: If you really cared about us, you would come to our Paltalk room and clear the air with over 500 cmkx shareholders. If you don't know how to get in, ask CFRN. The password is capital letters PAYDAY. Signed A. H/

(2:47 PM) Poster 3: EXACTLY, THATS WHY I ASKED THE QUESTION, I WANTED TO BE CLEAR THATS WHAT HE SAID

(2:52 PM) Poster 3: I WOULD LOVE FOR HIM TO COME IN HERE ALSO TO CLEAR THE AIR..I DONT THINK HE MEANT THINGS THE WAY THEY WERE TAKEN, BUT HE PROPBABLY ALREADY COMES IN HERE IF I WREER WRITTING A BOOK I WOULD

(2:54 PM) Poster 12: MARK MARK FO FARK BANNANA NANA DOE DARK

(3:02 PM) Poster 8: Mark Faulk and Bud Burrell are the 2 biggest pioneers in the naked shorting battle. In December you were all mad at Burrell when he had to present BOTH sides of the issue in the radio interview. That is a requirement for them IMO.

(3:04 PM) Poster 21: THE PR IS THAT MR. FAULK IS A FAULKING JERK!!!

(3:05 PM) Poster 24:...pls...the pioneers are J.Cline, and Dave Patch, they've done more for our cause than u can imagine....

(3:06 PM) Poster 24: bud burrell called me 4 yrs ago for info....pls, burrell & faulk mean nothing to our cause

(3:10 PM) Poster 21: I WOULD ROTHER READ THE CAT IN THE HAT THE HIS STUPID BOOK!!!

(4:39 PM) Poster 19: well here is the recap of today

(4:39 PM) Poster 19: mark faulk called us kool aid drinkers

(4:39 PM) Poster 25: what????????????

(4:39 PM) Poster 25: wow

(4:39 PM) Poster 25: mark did?

(4:39 PM) Poster 19: that was worth 3 hours of discussion. Was most enteraninment we had in weeks.

(4:39 PM) poster 27: lol... he must come in this room

(4:40 PM) Poster 25: well mark probably snorts his refreshment

(4:40 PM) Poster 19: thank you happy

(4:40 PM) Poster 25: I'll take the koolaid

Begrudgingly, I forced myself to listen to the show again this morning, just in case I really had slipped into an unconscious trance at some point and began unknowingly spewing expletives like Linda Blair in The Exorcist. Well guess what? Not only did I not say the things that I was accused of in the way that was implied, I DIDN'T SAY THEM AT ALL. The word "stupid" is nowhere in the hour and a half show, nor is the word "sheep." "Kool-Aid" was never mentioned, and as far as I know, no one on the show was even drinking Kool-Aid. (Disclaimer: This is in no way intended to be a negative commentary about Kool-Aid. Growing up in a family of eight trying to subsist on a teacher's salary, Kool-Aid was the only luxury we could afford. I love Kool-Aid.)

And that, fellow Kool-Aid drinkers, is the Faulking Truth.

Appendix G: A Brief History of Accadacca:
"Checks Are in the Mail!"

*"Only two things are infinite, the universe and human stupidity, and
I'm not sure about the former."*
~Attributed to Albert Einstein

Of all the so-called CMKX gurus, `Accadacca` was perhaps the most outrageous and gained the most notoriety. Despite one failed prediction after another, he has continued to frequent message boards and chatrooms for over three years, despised by some shareholders and treated with adulation by others. `BrainDamage`, a co-founder and early administrator of Proboards66, recalled `Accadacca`'s short posting history on that message board:

> *By Tuesday, March 22nd, 2005, `Accadacca` had been registered on ProBoards32 (later renamed to ProBoards66, or as the Kool-Aid drinkers preferred to call us, "the 666 board") for almost two months...and so far he'd managed to keep a pretty low profile.*
>
> *In mid-March of 2005, 100-150 members were active on 32 at any given time throughout the day. Most of us still more-or-less believed in our CMKX investment, thinking there was a legitimate company there to DD. So, those who referred to UC as a scammer were still banned as bashers because, well, how could they know for sure?*
>
> *On March 22nd, 2005, `Acca` posted that a "structured settlement" of some kind involving CitiGroup and CMKX was imminent. Then, on Saturday, he posted:*
>
> > `Subject: CitiGroup to Buy us out next week!!`
> > `Just got off the phone, very credible source!! Next`
> > `week EOM....`
>
> *Perhaps the single most outrageous post in `Acca`'s entire history, across all the boards, came on March 23rd. Another member asked him:*
>
> > `And what are you putting on the line if you are wrong?`
> > `So, We will know by Thursday evening right?`
>
> *and this was his reply:*
>
> > `Swear on my Mothers Grave By thursday!!!`

After a "private message" exchange with `BrainDamage` where `Accadacca` claimed everything he posted was true (ending with "TAKE THIS TO THE

BANK!!!!!!!!!!!!!!!!!!"), Acca set a self-imposed deadline of the following Friday for the official announcement of the CitiGroup buyout:

"I am sick of people questioning me, this is the real DEAL, you will all see if it doesn't happen I will never post again PERIOD!!!!!!"

BrainDamage replied:

"I know..."

Nothing happened by Friday, and BrainDamage banned Accadacca the following day. Unfortunately, Accadacca has continued to post and comment on other message boards and chatrooms, where his unbelievable predictions are repeated to thousands of CMKX shareholders. While a complete compilation of his posts and chatroom messages would fill a book in and of itself, here are a few selected highlights (or lowlights, as the case may be) from the guru who most CMKX shareholders now refer to as AccaCrappa:

9/14/2004: Urban will buy us out of CMKX for .005, Dividend us into CIM at 4 for 1 & then "Roll up IPO CIM" and after a 1 Trillion dollar valuation CIM will IPO price at $25 pps for October IPO. We get Wealthy and Urban becomes the wealthiest Man ...aka..."The Neuromancer" the worlds first Trillionair.

3/17/2005: I do not lie

3/22/2005: The Volume Weighted Average Price Today for CMKX was .1875. VWAP is used mainly In PENSION PLANS! This coincides with my tax free settlement I posted Earlier!! jmo.

3/23/2005: Swear on my Mothers Grave By thursday!!!

3/26/2005: CitiGroup to Buy us out next week!!! Just got off the phone, very credible source!! Next week EOM....

3/26/2005: I don't BS!!

3/26/2005: My brother-in-law works for CG NUFF SAID!!! I DONT BS, REPEAT I DONT BS!!

3/27/2005: My claim is actually substantiated as you will all see, I know there are doubters, but everything I said will come to fruition this coming week!!
I am sick of people questioning me, this is the real DEAL, you will all see if it dosent happen I will never post again PERIOD!!!!!!!

384

3/28/2005: Listen, any news of this caliber, I can't hold to myself, you people don't even know the extent of the bashers that surface on this board!! All I can say is SHARE THE WEALTH!! God Bless, And Take Care!!!

3/29/2005: OK, WANT AN EXACT TIME FOR PR? SERIOUS! 9:25 AM Thursday (eastern) Mar 31 Guaranteed!!!!!

3/29/2005: No Illegal Insider trading here, all good. No Pump, c'mon people just tired, what I say I say from the Heart take it what i'ts for!!! I am so done with this board!!!!
Trust me I don't get PAID TO WRITE THESE POSTS!!!! EOM

3/30/2005: How much??????? .20-.37 My Info as of now!

3/30/2005: ONE LAST TIME AND I MEAN IT, I HAVE NOTHING TO HIDE AND PR WILL HIT BEFORE THE BELL THURSDAY, LONG AND STRONG 1000000% GET IT?

3/31/2005: The "Deal" is Oh so Imminent, you people haven't a clue!

4/1/2005: Buyout Imminent!! Just confirmed, All will be stated Monday! in an official PR! And Don't Get sucked into the $25 lawyer fee!, won't be necessary! EOM!

4/1/2005: They are just Dotting the I's And crossing the T's. Done Deal!!

4/3/2005: There won't be a court case! EOM!

4/22/2005: No Hearing! No Hearing! Get It!!! eom!

5/22/2005: Listen please, No Hearing!!!! Will Never Happen!!

5/27/2005: I GUARANTEE IT!!!!!!!!!!!!!!!!!!! MARK THIS POST!!!!!!!!!

8/25/2005: My Boldest Statement To Date!!!: IT IS OVER, PARTY TIME! NIMHO, FACT!!!? I Congratulate All Who Kept The Faith!? Do Not Waver, Be Strong, Matter Of Hours Now!!!!?Willy's Room, Thumbs Way Up!!!

11/19/2005: CMKX Share Holders: In The Past, The SEC Would Just Shrug This Off, But Not This Time!!!! Approaching 4 Trillion Counterfeit Shares. Fact!, Fact!, Fact!!! END OF DISCUSSION!!!!!!!!!!!!!!! God Bless!! Gotta Go!!!!

12/22/2005: ADP Clearing Now Reporting Cash Payout, Have A Nice Day.

12/22/2005: At Present, It Is No longer "If" But "When." In Addition, As Of 12/23 Accadacca Will No Longer Be Posting Or Speaking, For he Has Retired! Merry Christmas And God Bless!!

12/29/2005: You Must Ask Yourself Why One Individual Would Be So Dilligent Over The Past Year Faithfully Holding Shareholders Together Through At Times Of Great Turmoil And Emotional Grief!! The Reason Is For You To Answer!! Every CMKX Shareholder Has WON!!!! Period! Gotta Go!! EOM!

1/19/2006: The Time Is Now! The Secret Is No Longer A Secret! The Funds Are Ready To Leave The Trust!!!

4/3/2006: 90% Monday, 100 % This Week, I Have Stated That In My Conversations With Many Of You! Take Care!

5/9/2006: I Know I Have Won, The Two Years Of Hell Will Be Vindicated!!! I Do Know That As Fact!!! Nothing You Say Will Deter This!?

5/21/2006: I Love It When The Low Life Scumbags Come Crawling When I Post, Gives Me A Warm Fuzzy Feeling All Over, It Really Does!!! LOL, Good Night!!!!!!?

5/23/2006: Can't Imagine Money news not coming this week, (notice lower case on the latter words)?

9/7/2006: Money In Hand No Later Than 10-31-06.

12/13/2006: Dec 22. Although Money Will Not Be In Hand, This Will Clearly Outline For You That Payment Is Imminent. This Is Not A Rumor, This Is A Phone Call I Received Shortly Ago, From A Company Official.

12/15/2006: 7 Days To "Closure!"

12/21/2006: My Stance Is More Positive Than Ever That This Holding Will Change Your Life Forever, Financially Speaking! I Look Forward To Saturday!! ~Acca.

1/4/2007: You (CMKX Shareholder) Are About To Embark On Something So Monumental, It Will Be Extremely Hard   To Grasp!! These Are

Very Exciting Times!!!!!!!!!! The Present Disorganized Law Suit Group Will Not Be An Obstacle. For Their Efforts Will All Be For Naught!! ~Acca?

1/5/2007:   I Would Like To Add That I Do Not Add IMO To Any Of My Posts! This Is Done At The Discretionary Of The Owner Of The Board!

1/5/2007:   I Would Like To State This: I Am Here And Always Have Been Here For The Shareholder First And Foremost!!! I Am Not Here To Divide, Yet To Unite!

1/8/2007:   I Know For A **ACCA FACT** That An Individual That Has Preferred Shares (In Cert Form) Will Be Payed In Cash For Those Shares This Coming Friday! I Will Not Field Questions About This Thread! This Is Very, Very Exciting! I Have Confirmed This!!

1/17/2007:   Paid Pumper???? Keep Grasping And Try To Garner A Handle Of The Situation, Which You Never Will! To All True Longs, Thank You For Weathering The Storm!!! This Is My Last Post Ever On RB! ~Acca!?

1/17/2007:   This Is My Final Farewell

2/8/2007:   NEXT WEEK, End Of This Ongoing Saga!!!!! The Statement Will Be Cut And Dry!

2/23/2007:   Way North Of .17,, If You Are Lucky Enough To Hold Cim You Have No Future "How Well Off Will I Be Theory Worries"!!!!! Take That To The Bank!

2/26/2007:   Look Forward To A 6 Digit Control Number In Aproxymately 2 Weeks.

3/1/2007:   Near Future, Will Be A Life Changing Experience! A "Settlement" Will Be Forthcoming

3/12/2007:   I'll Tell Ya What INSANE Is, People Who Actually This Is All Smoke And Mirrors, Now Thats INSANE! Remember A Buck 50 Will Get Ya A Cool 300k. Now that Could Be Considered INSANE? BTW How Are You? ~Acca Is Out!

3/28/2007:   Roger Glenn And Myself Are On The "Right" Side, And That JE Is As Crooked As They Come! Nevwest Securities Is Just A Needle In A Haystack!

3/29/2007: No More Fluff!!! You Are Within Days Of Closure!

5/11/2007: You Just Have To Dissect The "Old" And "New" PR'S (Updates?) As Far As Being Labeled A Compensated Liar, I Take Great Offence To That Accusation. The End Result Will Be, Veni Vidi Vici! ~Acca

5/12/2007: BH, I Expect Notification Early June And Payment Soon After. EOM.

6/1/2007: That The Mark Faulk's, John Martin's And Bill Frizzel's Of This World Are Spinning My Updates As They Have Done With Every Update Or "Unofficial" Press Release Of The Past." It Is A TWO WAY STREET! May The Best "Camp" Win!! ~Acca

6/12/2007: I Want To Make It Very Clear That I Am Not Hear To "Toy" With Peoples Emotions, That Is Not My Intent. No Matter What I Say Or Type There Will Be People To Denounce It And Go To Any Length To Twist It!

6/12/2007: I Promise To Each And Everyone Of You That The ROI Will Be Historic! You Will Be Ecstatic At The Offer For Your Loyalty And Patience! Be Prepared To Be Very, Very Wealthy!!!!!!

6/23/2007: Remember, There Are No COINCIDES', CONGRATULATIONS! ~Acca?

7/11/2007: I Do Understand That It Is Extremely Hard To Grasp The Impending Financial Windfall That Will Eventually Be Upon You, Having Said That, No Matter The Negativity Surrounding Your Investment Be Assured That A Few Hundred Dollar Investment On Your Part Will Financially Secure Yourself For The Future And Your Friends And Family!! And Please Remember The Majority that Bash Me And This Post Are Also Shareholders. ~Acca

7/12/2007: The Tyler Group Are Bringing A Knife To A Nevada Gunfight!! Bad, Bad Idea!

7/16/2007: restripe2007, Payday, Guaranteed! EOM!!!!!!?

7/31/2007: Many, Many Thanks Go Out To Each And Everyone OF You For Enduring An Excruciating Past Few Years! I Have, To (Under Extreme Scrutiny At Times) The Best Of My Ability Tried To Keep The SH Base Together And Not Divide It!
I Have Pushed The "Envelope" As Far As I Can And I Know When It Is Time To Step Down, And That Time Is Now! Regardless Of

What You Read Or Hear I Have Devoted Three Years Of My Life For The Subsequent Pot Of Gold At The End Of The Rainbow!

THE CHECKS ARE IN THE MAIL! See You At A Party Very Soon! ~Acca

1/17/08:   To The Tyler Texas Group:
Although You Are Guilty Of "Extortion," Let It Be Known Here That You Made Your Bed And You Will Ultimately "Lie" In It! Kevin West Is No More Than A Small Time Criminal, Bill Frizzell Is No More Than An Ambulance Chasin' Low Life, Turned Extortionist, Karma Is A Bad Motherf___er, Enjoy Your New Found Wealth While You Can!!!! Game On! ~Acca

Appendix H: A Dvorak 1000 to 1 Opinion Letter

DVORAK & ASSOCIATES, LTD.
Attorneys and Counselors at Law

136 Arbor Way
Henderson, Nevada 89074

P.O. Box 230656
Las Vegas, Nevada 89123
702.768.2960
(Fax) 702. 920.8732
bdvorak@cox.net

December 18, 2003

Board of Directors
Casavant Mining Kimberlite International, Inc.
1481 West Warm Springs, Suite 135
Las Vegas, NV 89014

Re: **Issuance Of Stock Neglected To Be Issued At The Time Of Purchase, September 17, 2001, To Eric Reid Of The Current Number Of 4 Billion (4,000,000,000) Shares Of Casavant Mining Kimberlite International, Inc., (hereinafter the "Company") Stock Pursuant To, And In Compliance With, Rule 144k.**

Sirs:

I am an attorney licensed to practice law in the State of Nevada. I have been asked to render an opinion as to the problem that has arisen in the case of one of your investors, Mr. Eric Reid, who purchased 4 million shares of Company stock on or about September 17, 2001.

You have advised me in your December 18, 2003 letter that Mr. Reid purchased these shares in the original company in 2001 and you have supplied me with a signed Subscription Agreement showing the purchase. You have further advised me that the Board of Directors of the Company have now acknowledged the mistake of not issuing those shares at that time and it is the wish of the Directors to issue those shares now subject to the 100 to 1 forward split the Company has undergone since the original purchase date.

You have further advised me that Mr. Reid invested in the initial company prior to it going public through a merger with Cybermark and a name change to Casavant Mining Kimberlite International, Inc., and that the company is still engaged in the same business as it was originally when Mr. Reid purchased shares in the company on September 17, 2001.

There are three issues which must be addressed. Should Mr. Reid receive his stock now for his purchase 2 years ago? How many shares should be issued to him and, Should those shares be issued without a restrictive legend?

002203

Should Mr. Reid Receive His Stock?

Mr. Reid rightfully purchased 4 Million shares of the Company over two years ago as indicated by the Subscription Agreement. You have also acknowledged this mistake in your correspondence to me requesting that this wrong situation be corrected.

Since the company has a subscription agreement and the Board of Directors are in concurrence that the shares were not issued in error, it is clear that he should receive the stock he purchased even though it is over two years late. The 4 million shares that Mr. Reid bought <u>must</u> be issued to him at this time **as if they were issued properly** on September 17, 2001, and your company records should reflect the correction and ratification of your actions correcting this mistake.

How Many Shares?

Mr. Reid's purchase of the 4 million shares is also subject to the 100 to 1 forward split that the company has gone though as if he had possession of those shares at the time of the split or dividend. In reality, the company has been holding these shares in what amounts to a Constructive Trust, and they were subject to all actions relating to them. Therefore, the actual number of shares which should be issued by your Transfer Agent to Mr. Reid is <u>4 Billion shares</u>.

Should The Shares Be Issued Without A Restrictive Legend?

We need to look at Rule 144 to see if the shares may be issued without a restrictive legend.

The requirements under the appropriate 144 Rule (issue 2 years or more) is as follows:

K. Termination of certain restrictions on sales of restricted securities by persons other than affiliates. The requirements of paragraphs (c), (e), (f) and (h) of this rule shall not apply to restricted securities sold for the account of a person who is not an affiliate of the issuer at the time of the sale and has not been an affiliate during the preceding three months, provided a period of at least two years has elapsed since the later of the date the securities were acquired from the issuer or from an affiliate of the issuer.

Since Mr. Reid was not an affiliate at the time of purchase of the shares and has not been an affiliate during the last three month and more than two years have passed since the purchase

002204

of the shares, Mr. Reid should be issued 4 Billion shares without restrictive legend, as fully paid and non-assessable.

Conclusion

Therefore, it is our conclusion and opinion that Mr. Reid should be issued 4 Million shares which should be subject to the 100 to 1 forward split and that pursuant to Rule 144k, he should receive from your Transfer Agent, 4 Billion shares which are fully paid and non-assessable.

Please feel free to forward this letter to your Transfer Agent to support your request.

Respectfully,

Brian Dvorak, Esq.

002205

393

Appendix I: A Glenn Opinion Letter to Release Shares

Edwards & Angell LLP

750 Lexington Avenue   New York, NY 10022   212.308.4411   fax 212.308.4844

September 29, 2004

VIA FACSIMILE

Helen Bagley, President
1st Global Stock Transfer, LLC
7341 W. Charleston Blvd., Suite 130
Las Vegas, Nevada 89117

      Re: New Issuance of 55,500,000,000 Shares of
            CMKM Diamonds, Inc. Common Stock

Dear Ms. Bagley:

      We have acted as counsel to CMKM Diamonds, Inc. (the "Company") in connection with its issuance of 55,500,000,000 shares of common stock (the "Shares"), par value $0.0001 per share, to the persons listed below (the "Shareholders") in the amounts opposite their respective names:

Vince Mazzei	16,000,000,000
Marty Johnson	6,000,000,000
Viacomb Holdings	12,000,000,000
Dale Casavant	4,000,000,000
Max Casavant	4,000,000,000
Rick Walker	1,000,000,000
Bill Dwyer	10,000,000,000
Arnold Gutka	1,000,000,000
Graeme & Vaughn Langman	300,000,000
Andy Petryshen	1,000,000,000
Mike Wiwchar	100,000,000
Brian Wiwchar	100,000,000
	55,500,000,000

      Half of the Shares were fully paid for in 2001, but certificates evidencing the same were never issued. The remainder of the Shares were issued later as part of a 2 for 1 stock dividend but, as with the originally issued shares, certificates evidencing the Shares were never issued.

      In connection with rendering the opinions expressed herein, we have relied upon opinions dated September 8, 2004 of Dvorak & Associates, Ltd. as to due authorization of the Shares and

007237

other matters of Nevada law, and as to the fact that the half of the Shares that were originally issued were fully paid for more than two years ago. We have also relied upon the Company's representation that none of the Shareholders is an affiliate of the Company or has been an affiliate at any time during the preceding 90 days. We have examined such certificates, certified copies of organizational and governance documents, certificates of good standing, certifications of factual matters, company resolutions and other records, pertinent documents and instruments, and have investigated such other matters of law and fact, as we have deemed necessary for the purpose of rendering the opinions set forth herein. We have assumed that (i) all signatures are genuine, (ii) all documents submitted to us as originals are authentic, (iii) all documents submitted to us as copies conform with the originals of those documents, (iv) all documents examined by us are accurate and complete, (v) all public records and documents have been properly filed and indexed and are complete and accurate, and (vi) all laws, ordinances and regulations have been duly and validly issued.

Based upon the foregoing, and subject to the limitations, qualifications and exceptions set forth herein, we are of the opinion that the Shares may be issued to the Shareholders in the amounts set forth opposite each Shareholder's name above, and that the certificates evidencing the Shares need bear no restrictive legend.

We are members of the Bar of the State of New York, and we express no opinion as to matters governed by the laws of any other jurisdiction except the registration requirements of the Securities Act of 1933, as amended.

We render no opinion on matters except as specifically stated. The opinions expressed in this letter are given solely to the addressee of this letter in connection with the issuance of the Shares by the Company and may not be relied upon, in whole or in part, by any other person or by any person for any other purpose without our prior written consent, which may be withheld, with or without a reason, in our sole discretion.

The opinions expressed in this letter are rendered as of the date hereof. We do not express any opinion as to the circumstances or events that may occur subsequent to such date, and we undertake no obligation to update or revise this letter or the opinions expressed herein.

Very truly yours,

Edwards & Angell, LLP

EDWARDS & ANGELL, LLP

cc. Urban Casavant

Appendix J: Timeline for CMKX Events
by Ric

In the Beginning:

- CMKM Diamonds was incorporated in Delaware in 1998 as Cyber Mark International Corporation.

- In April 2002, Cyber Mark changed its corporate domicile to Nevada.

- On November 25, 2002, Cyber Mark agreed to acquire certain mineral claims held by five companies owned by the family of Urban Casavant (Casavant) in exchange for $2 million and almost 3 billion shares of Cyber Mark restricted common stock with registration rights.

- Prior to his resignation on November 25, 2002, Cyber Mark's sole director appointed Casavant sole director, president, and chief executive officer.

- On November 26, 2002, Casavant appointed his wife, Carolyn Casavant, as vice president of claims, his son, Wesley Casavant, age twenty-two, to the position of corporate treasurer, and his daughter, Cindy Casavant, to the position of corporate secretary.

- On December 3, 2002, the company changed its corporate name to Casavant Mining Kimberlite International.

- In February 2004, it changed its name to CMKM Diamonds.

- In the most recent information it has provided to the public through a periodic filing, a Form 10-QSB for the quarter ending September 30, 2002, CMKM Diamonds reported total assets of $344.00, all in cash, and total liabilities of $1,672.00.

- Casavant currently is the president, chief executive officer, and co-chair of CMKM Diamonds' two-person board of directors.

- Casavant and his wife have signatory authority on CMKM Diamonds's bank accounts.

- CMKM Diamonds has failed to file annual reports for its fiscal years ended December 31, 2002, 2003, and 2004.

- On March 31, 2003, the company filed a request for an extension of time to file its annual report for the year ended December 31, 2002, because it had not yet completed its financial statements.

- Despite having not filed an annual report for 2002, CMKM Diamonds erroneously represented in this filing that it had filed all required reports for the preceding twelve months.

- On July 22, 2003, CMKM Diamonds filed a Form 15, signed by Casavant, pursuant to Exchange Act Rule 12g-4, in which it certified that it had approximately 300 shareholders of record as of that date.

397

- IM appears on several of JE's trust documents provided to NevWest as part of the new account documentation. During relevant times to the complaint, IM was the former President, director and shareholder of CMKM, and IM also acted as the Registered Agent on behalf of CMKM.

Before the hearing:
- John Edwards opened 32 accounts at NevWest and sold more than 250 billion shares of a sub-penny stock, which generated total sales proceeds of over $53 million. NASD alleged that NevWest earned commission revenue on the sales totaling $2.5 million -- 36 percent of the firm's total revenues during the relevant period.
- CMKM opened 100 bank accounts of which 64 million dollars passed through at Silver State Bank.
- 703 billion O/S.
- Authorized Shares increased from less than 1 billion to 800 billion.
- Outstanding Shares increased from less than 1 billion to 779 billion.
- 600 billion in dilution in the year 2004.
- 407 billion in Cede and Co. as of March 2005.
- Ameritrade holds 180 billion shares of CMKX for its clients.
- Was told we would be pleasantly surprised by O/S and made to believe it was under 400 billion. Melvin on the air denies that the O/S is over 400 Billion after TA fiasco.
- CMKX Transfer Agent gagged per direction of the UC.
- UC gave shares in a deal but issued himself those shares just prior to announcement.
- 16.5 billion shares buyback and the o/s never decreased and after the PR the o/s doubled.
- Refuses to give investors basic information on company.
- Refuses to give share structure.
- CMKX trading unregistered shares in SASK, trading halted there.
- SASK inquiry into CMKX valuations ignored.
- CMKX partner USCA under investigation by the SASK.
- No revenue stream from company operations.
- Repeated claims of being close to reporting when in fact no attempt had been made.
- Claims in Canada for mineral rights, made to believe 100's of holes drilled. but only 15.
- claimed buybacks yet O/S raised after each claim.

- Goldak would not sign off on the PR of the TDEM survey because the PR was misleading.
- UC buys a 3.5 million dollar property, motor-home, hummer, boat, likes to gamble, likes to race funny cars while shareholders value decreases.
- UC at race track almost every weekend.
- Spent investors' money to sponsor motorcycle and drag racing.
- Advertises stock instead of company, Got CMKX?
- Voids in records.
- UC says he doesn't know how to run a public company.
- UC blames others for mismanagement.
- SEC investigation and temporary halt.
- Lied on form 15 more then 100% off (claimed under 300, had 689).
- Lied on SEC documents about the Address and tried to cover it up.

During the Hearing:
- Judge ruled that NS is not going to be admitted into evidence because company did not claim it was a factor in not filing.
- She asked SEC if they think CMKX has NS and the SEC said no.
- When asked by the SEC, TA stated there was no record of CMKX management inquiring into the number of shareholders in July 2003.
- RG was paid $250,000 and one page report was presented.
- Urban shows up with his own personal lawyer.
- Urban invokes his 5th Amendment right to not answer any/all questions asked by the SEC attorneys (12 minutes of "I take the 5th").
- Maheu testifies he was not aware of the problems the new accountant and attorney were having in receiving documentation from Urban to get filings completed.
- Maheu can't answer question on companies operations.
- We find out Urban runs CMKX from his house, not the company PR'd new offices in Las Vegas.
- Maheu paid $40,000 a month. Has been paid for 2 months pay even though he has been there 4 months and Judge makes joke about the amount he is paid.
- Accountants: all quit after frustration in not being able to do their jobs. Current accountant, Neil Levine, resigns on May 9th one day before the hearing.
- Rendal Williams (CEO of UCAD & 50/50 partner with CMKX) has a "failing memory" when questioned on the stand, he apparently is distancing himself from CMKX/Urban Casavant.

- Dhonau met UC at the slot machines.
- Carolyn Casavant wrote checks against the company account although she is not an officer of the company, explanation given to the court "that's what wive's do."
- Current financial status, over $30 million in debt.
- Judge says this is a filing issue.
- Has till 29th of June for rebuttals and decision will be by July 15th.

After the Hearing:
- Two .011 micro size diamonds.
- Only 15 holes drilled, nothing found in any except in one hole see above.
- Drilling report says to give it up people.
- Company issued PR that 100's of anomalies found from goldak fly over yet 8K states 16 from goldak fly over & some of them may not be worth drilling.
- Refuses to give investors basic information on company.
- Refuses to give share structure.
- Auditor files 10-A letter for possible illegal activities with CMKXtreme, deals, and loans to officers. It was illegal that the company did not keep records.
- Bill issues a Shareholder Derivative Letter.
- UC can't afford to sponsor Arends car anymore.
- Frizzell working on proving NS.
- Revoked by the SEC.
- UC refuses to let the shareholders know whats going on or give any reassurances.

After the Appeal was Dropped/Cert Pull:
- Entourage deal for 45 million shares to be distributed to bonafide shareholders.
- Cert Pull was announced before you can get your Entourage distribution.
- 8-K states due to lack of funds that they have defaulted on claims (United Carina, 101047025 Saskatchewan Ltd. ("1010"), and American Shaft).
- 8-K states Maheu resigns and UC will resign due to health reasons after distribution.
- Task Force formed with Maheu, Stoecklien, and Frizzell.

- 1st Corp. Update - As CMKM is effectively a non-operational company holding only the Entourage shares and intangible assets.
- 2nd Corp. Update - The Task Force was formed solely for the purpose of establishing a Distribution Plan and supervising the distribution of the Entourage shares and other assets of CMKM, if any. The Task Force will not be conducting any due diligence to determine the validity of any other potential assets of CMKM other than those stated above.
- And - The Task Force has been apprised of the significant rumors pertaining to the receipt of funds and erroneous agreements reached with brokerage firms short in CMKM's stock. Other than the funds received from Casavant to pay for certain of the costs associated with the Task Force's operations, there have been no funds received from brokers/ dealers or any other sources.
- Stoecklien no longer represents CMKX.
- We find out that CIM lost it zinc claims and as of now is in Default in Nevada.
- Lawsuit against UC, CMKM, and CMKXtreme for unpaid bills.

After the Cert Pull:
- Stoecklien and the TF recommends and interplead.
- Stoecklien and Maheu resign the Task Force and no longer has any involvement in CMKM.
- Was understanding that a PR was to be released in a week which never happened.
- Bill Frizzell no longer represents shareholders and doesn't no anything more then us.
- TF is dissolved.
- 18 months after the last update from UC he issues a PR stating the company's intent to file an interplead and hire a new CEO.
- Kevin West is named interim CEO.
- NevWest was charge for Money Laundering with John Edwards as the client funneling shares through numerous companies.
- Company still refuses to communicate with shareholders.
- UC refuses to testify at his own civil trial taking the 5th yet again.
- After phone calls to Moran the Company was forced to issue a PR in Dec. '06. Company wants shareholders to stop calling Moran's office.
- The Company met with their corporate attorney, John T. Moran III of the Moran Law Firm, to discuss the status of interpleader to be filed with the Federal Court as discussed in the PR of 8-28-06. The Company was informed that the pleadings are almost complete, however, Attorney

Moran was made aware of and discovered additional Company information that dictated further investigation and due diligence that needed to be performed by all of the attorneys involved before the document can be completed.

- Kevin West, interim CEO seems to be nothing more than an IR person to answer phone calls.
- Company promises to write a PR once a month to keep shareholders informed of interplead.
- Kevin claims Interplead is treading on new grounds and that is for the delay.
- In telephone calls, Kevin tells each shareholder that called there is no settlement, that the Interplead is all that is happening at the moment.
- Interplead has been postponed again. And it looks like it is to the magic statue of limitation date.
- Gene Hurd files a lawsuit in federal court before the 2 year statute of limitation date against CMKM Diamonds, Inc., Urban Casavant, Robert Maheu, David DeSormeau, Rupert Perrin, Carolyn Casavant, Wesley, Casavant, Cindy Casavant, and 50 roes and 50 does.
- Bill Frizzell issues a second Shareholder Derivative Letter.
- Bill Frizzell files suit against DeSormeau, Edwards and 50 Does and 50 Roe Corporations.

Urban Retires and Turns Over the Company to Kevin West:
- Kevin learned the truth about Urban and has been talking to Bill Frizzell on what to do.
- Kevin takes over CMKM as Urban Casavant issues a PR of his resignation.
- Kevin receives several boxes of information from an attorney in Canada about CMKM which leads to a lawsuit against Urban Casavant.
- Kevin West Hires Frizzell Law Firm.
- The Frizzell Law firm has hired Las Vegas attorney George Cromer as local counsel to file these first two lawsuits on behalf of the Company. Los Angeles attorney, Al Hodges, will be assisting the legal team as it proceeds.
- Bill Frizzell files suit against DeSormeau, Edwards and 50 Does and 50 Roe Corporations.
- Kevin west announces that they are moving the corporation from Nevada to Texas and converts out of Nevada.
- The company instructs 1st Global to stop further transfer or issuance of CMKM Diamonds, Inc. stock effective immediately.

402

- The Company has instructed the law offices of Moran and Associates to cease any and all legal work on behalf of CMKM Diamonds until further notice.

- The As of March 29th 2007, the Company had 3 pending lawsuits, a Wells Notice from the SEC that was supposed to have been answered by March 9, 2007 (of which current management was totally unaware, until an official at the SEC contacted them on 4-10-07), and ongoing investigations by at least four government agencies. In addition there is documentation showing the forfeiture of all claims and mineral rights, no corporate records for the past 4 1/2 years of business and taxes that have never been filed. The only tangible asset is a 45 million share certificate of Entourage Mining stock.

- Company only has $558.00 left out of approximately $250 million from the sell of CMKM shares.

- A lawsuit was filed naming Urban Casavant, The UAJC 2005 irrevocable trust, Mike Williams, DeShawn L. Wayne, Brian Dvorak, James Kinney, Ginger Gutierrez, P.A. holdings, Bucko LLC, 20 does and 20 roes.

- Susanne Trimbath has agreed to help the Company in our efforts to determine "fails to deliver" in our stock.

- CMKM Attorney David Koch files a Temporary Restraining Order against several trust and properties related to those involved with CMKM.

- CMKM Diamonds, Inc. has engaged the accounting firm of Henry & Peters, P.C. with a certified fraud examiner.

- On April 7, 2008, the SEC charges 11 individuals and 3 companies with fraud in the CKM Diamonds case.

Appendix K: Part Time Management Incorporation

This document refers to the formation of Part Time Management by Urban Casavant noted on page 300 of the book.

ANNUAL LIST OF OFFICERS, DIRECTORS AND AGENTS OF   FILE NUMBER

PART Time MANAGEMENT INC

The Corporation's duly appointed resident agent in the
State of Nevada upon whom process can be served is:

*DAvid DeSoRMeAu
1603 MowbRAy Ct.
HeNdeRSoN NV 89014*

| FOR OFFICE USE ONLY |
| FILED (DATE) |
| *01-02* |
| FILED # *C 8143-01* |
| MAR 2 9 2001 |
| IN THE OFFICE OF
DEAN HELLER, SECRETARY OF STATE |

☐ IF THE ABOVE INFORMATION IS INCORRECT, PLEASE CHECK THIS BOX AND A CHANGE OF RESIDENT AGENT/ADDRESS FORM WILL BE SENT.

PLEASE READ INSTRUCTIONS BEFORE COMPLETING AND RETURNING THIS FORM.
1. Include the names and addresses, either residence or business, for all officers and directors. A President, Secretary, Treasurer and all Directors must be named. There must be at least one director. Last year's information may have been preprinted. If you need to make changes, cross out the incorrect information and insert the new information above it. An officer must sign the form. FORM WILL BE RETURNED IF UNSIGNED.
2. If there are additional directors, attach a list of them to this form.
3. Return the completed form with the $85.00 filing fee. A $15 penalty must be added for failure to file this form by the deadline. An annual list received more than 90 days before its due date shall be deemed an amended list for the previous year.
4. Make your check payable to the Secretary of State. Your canceled check will constitute a certificate to transact business per NRS 78.155. If you need the below attachment file stamped, enclose a self-addressed stamped envelope. To receive a certified copy, enclose a copy of this completed form, an additional $10.00 and appropriate instructions.
5. Return the completed form to: Secretary of State, 101 North Carson Street, Suite #3, Carson City, NV 89701-4786. (775) 684-5708.

FILING FEE: $85.00   PENALTY: $15.00

| NAME *URBAN CASAVANT* | TITLE(S) **PRESIDENT** |
| P.O. BOX   STREET ADDRESS *1603 Mowbray Ct*   CITY *Henderson*   ST. *NV*   ZIP *89014* |

| NAME *URBAN CASAVANT* | TITLE(S) **SECRETARY** |
| P.O. BOX   STREET ADDRESS *1603 Mowbray Ct*   CITY *Henderson*   ST. *NV*   ZIP *89014* |

| NAME *URBAN CASAVANT* | TITLE(S) **TREASURER** |
| P.O. BOX   STREET ADDRESS *1603 Mowbray Ct*   CITY *Henderson*   ST. *NV*   ZIP *89014* |

| NAME *URBAN CASAVANT* | TITLE(S) **DIRECTOR** |
| P.O. BOX   STREET ADDRESS *1603 Mowbray Ct*   CITY *Henderson*   ST. *NV*   ZIP *89014* |

| NAME | TITLE(S) **DIRECTOR** |
| P.O. BOX   STREET ADDRESS   CITY   ST.   ZIP |

I hereby certify this annual list.

X Signature of Officer *Urban C___*   Date *3/29/01*

PART Time MANAGEMENT INC

The Corporation's duly appointed resident agent in the
State of Nevada upon whom process can be served is:

David DeSormeau
1603 Mowbray Ct.
Henderson NV 89014

┌─ FOR OFFICE USE ONLY ─
│ FILED (DATE)
│
│ 01-02
│
│ FILED # C 8143-01
│
│ MAR 2 9 2001
│
│ IN THE OFFICE OF
│ DEAN HELLER SECRETARY OF STATE

☐ IF THE ABOVE INFORMATION IS INCORRECT, PLEASE CHECK THIS BOX AND A CHANGE OF
RESIDENT AGENT/ADDRESS FORM WILL BE SENT.

PLEASE READ INSTRUCTIONS BEFORE COMPLETING AND RETURNING THIS FORM.

1. Include the names and addresses, either residence or business, for all officers and directors. A President, Secretary, Treasurer and all Directors must be named. There must be at least one director. Last year's information may have been preprinted. If you need to make changes, cross out the incorrect information and insert the new information above it. An officer must sign the form. FORM WILL BE RETURNED IF UNSIGNED.

2. If there are additional directors, attach a list of them to this form.

3. Return the completed form with the $85.00 filing fee. A $15 penalty must be added for failure to file this form by the deadline. An annual list received more than 60 days before its due date shall be deemed an amended list for the previous year.

4. Make your check payable to the Secretary of State. Your canceled check will constitute a certificate to transact business per NRS 78.155. If you need the below attachment file stamped, enclose a self-addressed stamped envelope. To receive a certified copy, enclose a copy of this completed form, an additional $10.00 and appropriate instructions.

5. Return the completed form to: Secretary of State, 101 North Carson Street, Suite #3, Carson City, NV 89701-4786. (775) 684-5708.

FILING FEE: $85.00   PENALTY: $15.00

NAME		TITLE(S)			
URBAN CASAVANT		PRESIDENT			
P.O. BOX	STREET ADDRESS 1603 Mowbray Ct	CITY Henderson	NV	89014
NAME		TITLE(S)			
URBAN CASAVANT		SECRETARY			
P.O. BOX	STREET ADDRESS 1603 Mowbray Ct	CITY Henderson	NV	ZIP 89014
NAME		TITLE(S)			
URBAN CASAVANT		TREASURER			
P.O. BOX	STREET ADDRESS 1603 Mowbray Ct	CITY Henderson	NV	ZIP 89014
NAME		TITLE(S)			
URBAN CASAVANT		DIRECTOR			
P.O. BOX	STREET ADDRESS 1603 Mowbray Ct	CITY Henderson	NV	ZIP 89014
NAME		TITLE(S)			
		DIRECTOR			
P.O. BOX	STREET ADDRESS	CITY	ST.	ZIP

I hereby certify this annual list.

X Signature of Officer _Urban Ca___   Date 3/28/01

406

INDEX